Vanguardia

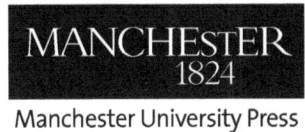

Manchester University Press

Vanguardia

Socially engaged art and theory

Marc James Léger

Manchester University Press

The right of Marc James Léger to be identified as the author of this work has been asserted by him in accordance with the Copyright, Designs and Patents Act 1988.

Published by Manchester University Press
Altrincham Street, Manchester M1 7JA

www.manchesteruniversitypress.co.uk

British Library Cataloguing-in-Publication Data
A catalogue record for this book is available from the British Library

ISBN 978 1 5261 3489 9 hardback

First published 2019

The publisher has no responsibility for the persistence or accuracy of URLs for any external or third-party internet websites referred to in this book, and does not guarantee that any content on such websites is, or will remain, accurate or appropriate.

Typeset in 10.5 on 12.5 pt Bembo Std Regular by
Servis Filmsetting Ltd, Stockport, Cheshire
Printed by Lightning Source

Contents

Acknowledgements   *page* vi

Introduction: a thousand contradictions   1
1   Alter-globalisation, revolutionary movement and the state mode of
     production   27
2   A brief history of Occupy Wall Street   45
3   Vanguardia   68
4   Psychoprotest: dérives of the Quebec Maple Spring   113
5   The unrealised extravagance of the avant garde: Test Dept and the
     subsumption of labour   134
6   No strawman for the revolution   147
7   Beyond socially enraged art   164
8   The only game in town   179

Notes   214
Index   242

Acknowledgements

The chapters of this book cover a range of social, political and intellectual phenomena that have affected and informed cultural production since the early 2000s. In particular, the advent of social practice or socially engaged art encapsulates the sense that postmodern theory and culture wars were not adequate responses to the crises of global capitalism. As cultural research on the left, this book does not present the various reasons why, to cite Clement Greenberg's famous claim in 'Avant-Garde and Kitsch,' socialism is the best means to keep modernist culture moving, but rather, in neoliberal times, the ways in which contemporary culture is able or not to sustain the vision of a world beyond capitalism. This book is dedicated to the comradely encouragement of those people who have helped me make a small contribution to this end.

My deepest gratitude goes to Cayley Sorochan for her cheerful companionship and support over the years. During the Quebec student strike, Cayley and I formed the Badiou-Žižek book bloc, a unit of two in a sea of red militancy. My affections also extend to my dearest friend, Rosika Desnoyers, with whom I have had the pleasure to discuss my ideas and research. Thanks are due to the many people who have been involved in one way or another with the original publication of the texts in this book, in particular Claude Lacroix, Oliver Ressler, Vicky Chainey-Gagnon, Jennifer Gradecki, Karen van Meenen, Gregory Sholette, Deborah Fisher, Benjamin Fraser, Alexei Monroe, Imanol Galfaroso, Sean Sayers, Jorinde Seijdel and Sven Lütticken. Special thanks go to Emma Brennan and Manchester University Press for their support of this publication. A word of appreciation also goes to the artists and designers who generously contributed their visual works to this project: Bruce Barber, Gregory Sholette, Oliver Ressler, Petra Gerschner, John Jordan/The Clandestine Insurgent Rebel Clown Army, Occupy Together, David Shankbone/Occupy Wall Street Creative Commons Project, Jeremy Deller, Phil Collins, Designers United, Brian Layng, Adam Turl, Guy Debord, G.U.L.F., Janez Janša, Janez Janša, Janez Janša, Winnie Wong, sub Rosa,

Institute for Applied Autonomy, École de la Montagne Rouge, Critical Art Ensemble, Brett Turnbull/Test Dept, Strike Debt Bay Area/Sandy Sanders, PublixTheatreCaravan, Not An Alternative, Thierry Geoffroy, Isaac Julien, Oree Originol, Shepard Fairey/Amplifier and Jonas Staal/Artist Organisations International.

The following credits the original place of publication for those texts that are reproduced in whole in this volume. A shorter version of 'Alter-globalisation, revolutionary movement and the state mode of production' is published in the catalogue *A World Where Many Worlds Fit/Un monde dans lequel plusieurs mondes s'inscrivent* (Lennoxville: Foreman Art Gallery/Bishop's University, 2010). A short version of 'A brief history of Occupy Wall Street' was published as 'Leftist Notes on Occupy Wall Street' in the online catalogue for the 2012 exhibition *Capital Offense: The End(s) of Capitalism*. The chapter 'Vanguardia' is comprised of previously published book reviews: 'Art and Activism in Parallax,' a book review of Gerald Raunig's *Art and Revolution: Transversal Activism in the Long Twentieth Century* (2007) and BAVO's *Cultural Activism Today: The Art of Over-Identification* (2007) was published in *Art Journal* 68:3 (Fall 2009): 108–11; 'Revenge of the Surplus,' a review of Gregory Sholette's *Dark Matter: Art and Politics in the Age of Enterprise Culture* (2011) was published in *Monthly Review* 63:8 (January 2012): 58–63; the review of Gregory Sholette and Oliver Ressler, eds. *It's the Political Economy, Stupid: The Global Financial Crisis in Art and Theory* (2013) was published in *Afterimage* 40:6 (May/June 2013): 37–8; 'Avant-Garde vs. Collaborative Art,' a review of Grant H. Kester's *The One and the Many: Contemporary Collaborative Art in a Global Context* (2011) was published in *Afterimage* 39:6 (May/June 2012): 38–9; the review of Critical Art Ensemble, *Disturbances* (2012), was published in *C Magazine* #117 (2013): 56–7; the review of Nato Thompson's *Seeing Power: Art and Activism in the 21st Century* (2015) was published in *Afterimage* 43:4 (Jan/Feb 2016): 40–1; the review of Yates McKee's *Strike Art: Contemporary Art and the Post-Occupy Condition* (2015) was published online at *Marx and Philosophy Review of Books* (17 April 2016), as were the reviews of Mikkel Bolt Rasmussen's *Crisis to Insurrection: Notes on the Ongoing Collapse* (2015) (27 November 2015) and Rebecca Gordon-Nesbitt's *To Defend the Revolution Is to Defend Culture* (2015) (17 March 2016). 'Psychoprotest: dérives of the Quebec Maple Spring' was co-written by myself and Cayley Sorochan and published in Benjamin Fraser, ed. *Marxism and Urban Culture* (Lanham: Lexington Books, 2014), 89–111. 'The unrealised extravagance of the avant garde: Test Dept and the subsumption of labour' is a review of Graham Cunnington, Angus Farquhar and Paul Jamrozy, *Test Dept: Total State Machine* (Bristol: PC Press, 2015) that was originally published as 'Maximalism on a Scale You Rarely See' in the electronic journal *PDF* 2 (2015). 'No strawman for the revolution' was originally published in the *International Journal of Žižek Studies* 10:3 (2016): 1–27, and

'Beyond socially enraged art' was published online in *Open! Platform for Art, Culture & the Public Domain* (27 October 2015). A few lines are also drawn from my article, 'Democracy Without Guarantees,' published in *esse: arts + opinions* 92 (Winter 2018): 11–13.

Introduction:
a thousand contradictions

What can culture contribute to radical political practice in the age of global markets, neoliberal austerity, neo-imperial militarism and environmental end times? Advocates of socially engaged art and art activism want to do something to change the world and not passively contemplate all of life's contradictions. The keyword and the modus operandi of social change today is not the political party but the activist network, the ad hoc involvement of participants around a pressing social problem, who later recombine around other issues. Everything else in the world of museums, biennials, art fairs and auction houses seems to amount to little more than institutional and economic power affirming the status quo. But project work and activism is difficult to sustain without some kind of institutional support, least of all financial resources. A sign of the times is a June 2017 proposal by a New York state congresswoman to provide $10,000 of student loan forgiveness to cultural workers who provide social services to children, adolescents and seniors. Another is a graduate programme in social practice art at a university in Indiana that teaches courses in 'social entrepreneurship.' If the neo-avant gardes were sublated by the culture industry, social aesthetics are embedded in neoliberalism's precarisation of life and labour. This process of recuperation is most evident in relational aesthetics, with its transformation of the relations between people into relations between people as art things. It is less obvious, however, in the case of art actions that are organised by leftist activists who know all too well what they are up against. The challenge for socially engaged art, as it vies with other kinds of art practice, is to be able to engage not only with social contexts but to challenge capitalist social relations. From a Marxist perspective, what, we might ask, is the class function of socially engaged art in today's global neoliberal regimes? The political imaginary of progressive academics and art institutions responds positively to new art practices that propose ameliorative solutions to local problems and empowerment for minority constituencies, especially as such practices correspond to the non-ideological, horizontalist and participatory ethos of social movements. Moving away from big ideo-logical struggles towards micropolitical social change, art activism threatens to supplement rather than challenge neoliberal governance. The neoliberal project emerged in the 1970s as a business-led effort to reorganise power around the interests of capital and at the expense of labour and the vestiges of the welfare state. While the rhetoric of neoliberalism promotes free markets and free trade, the corporate state subsidises capital and supports monopoly power.[1] Just as neoliberal government policy destroys social programmes and social safety nets by orienting these towards market calculation, and just as it undermines unionised work through privatisation, outsourcing, offshoring and flexibilisation, it calls on virtuous citizens and groups to fill in the cracks that it otherwise pushes more and more people into. In the context of the real subsumption of labour in advanced post-Fordist economies, the field of culture is today a paradoxical component of this system of lived domination. Whether one wishes to accelerate this process or slow it down, it seems inescapable.

Vanguardia makes the case for a renewed avant-garde praxis in the fields of both art and politics. In the relative absence of an organised, effective and democratically-based left, the task of the avant garde is to elucidate the con-temporary workings of capital and to support the existing forms of progressive cultural and political expression, however weak and disoriented they may be. Vanguardism is work in leftist militancy. It is neither high theory, produced by the 'traditional' intellectual in their so-called ivory tower, nor is it simply 'organic' grassroots pragmatism, defined solely by fieldwork with people who are otherwise too busy with projects to question the broader effectiveness of their work. Socially engaged art and theory is autonomous in the sense that it is not always immediately useful, yet it constitutes engaged praxis by providing concepts and works with which to makes sense of our predicament.

Written between the years 2010 and 2018, the texts assembled in this book are militant cultural research undertaken after the recent 'communist turn,' which is informed by such eventful broadsides as Alain Badiou's *The Return of History* and Slavoj Žižek's *The Year of Dreaming Dangerously*.[2] The substance of such so-called 'post-Marxism,' and indeed, of the intellectual influence of Žižek and Badiou, is privileged in these pages over liberal-left, micropolitical, schizo-anarchist, identitarian and countercultural trends in con-temporary art and politics. Addressing the political and cultural movements that coalesced around anti-globalisation protest and the 'movements of the squares' in Greece, Spain, Egypt, Brazil and the United States, *Vanguardia* detracts from a moribund 'end of ideology' postmodernism and relates the new contestatory forms of engaged culture to what Peter Bürger refers to as the unrealised extravagance of the avant garde.[3] The work of Žižek and Badiou in particular is singular in its rethinking of the main categories of the political left, especially as work that has been produced after post-structuralism became the dominant trend in progressive academia. This work allows contemporary theory and practice to remain connected with the radical past while at the same time challenging the more deterministic aspects of today's new materialisms and theoretical immanentism. My political outlook is nevertheless committed to a left ecumenism. It is clear that in terms of most major struggles we are comrades, despite our myriad differences and social contexts. While the goal for us must be to increase our ranks, rather than fight one another, we must do so as leftists. The stakes of this book are therefore defined by the potential for a renewed vanguard militancy in both art and politics.

The ideology of the avant garde

The countercultural spleen of the nineteenth-century bohemian avant garde has now become an integral aspect of today's administration of cultural markets and creative industries. In my essay titled 'Welcome to the Cultural Goodwill Revolution,' published in *Brave New Avant Garde*, I argued that what Pierre Bourdieu had defined as the dispositions, or class *habitus*, of the French petty bourgeoisie in the 1970s has today become the dominant class habitus.[4] The function of autonomous art and aesthetic disinterestedness, as defined by bourgeois ideology, shifts with the petty-bourgeois disposition to that of allodoxia, which is based on the anxious consumption of culture as a mark of distinction, which is then transposed to worry about class mobility and the obsession with lifestyling. For Bourdieu, the petty-bourgeois habitus emphasises the anti-hierarchical, anti-authority and anti-bourgeois motifs of the counterculture, with an emphasis on the euphemisation of avant-garde seriousness, psychological therapy, an imperative of sexual relation, the taste for the new, new media, the fun ethic and distance from market forces.[5] I combined Bourdieu's Marxist sociology of class dispositions with Bürger's historicised model of the development of the bourgeois ideology of aesthetic autonomy and added to it a new phase that might help us think about the class function of contemporary culture.[6] In the shift from the international bourgeois phase, or modernism, to today's global petty-bourgeois era, the function of art changes from the portrayal of individual self-understanding to that of social integration, much like the kind of subjectivity that is produced for a Reality TV show or an Instagram page. The mode of art production shifts from individual studio work to networked participation in projects, or from culture industry to creative industry; the mode of consumption changes from an individual and alienated critical reception to that of post-enlightenment enjoyment; and the status of the work shifts from autonomous avant-garde work to a vacillation between art as market value and biopolitical activism.

The hegemonic status of the petty-bourgeois habitus among university-trained cadres underscores the 'allodoxic' evasion of class identifications and

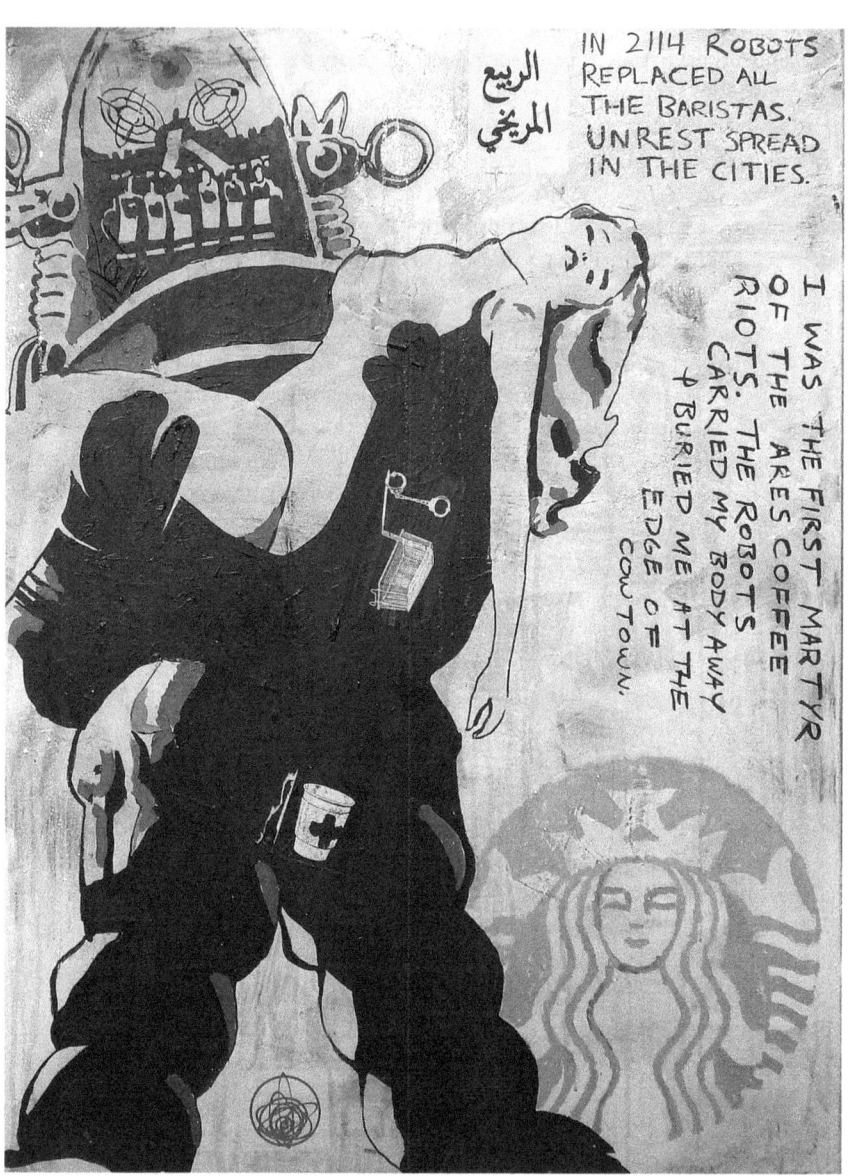

Adam Turl, *Ares Coffee Riot (Red Mars)*, 2016. Acrylic, coffee, sharpie meteorite dust, glitter stickers, photocopies and wheatpaste on canvas, 121.92 x 91.44 cm. *Red Mars* is part of the *13 Baristas* project, a series of works about a group of fictional coffee shop workers and artists living in a socially precarious not-too-distant future. Courtesy of Adam Turl.

emphasises instead a 'middle' and 'non-ideological' position vis-à-vis the means and forces of production. Today's global petty-bourgeois class compositions are not only comprised of redundant, proto-proletarian 'dark matter,' as Gregory Sholette argues, but also include the rank and file of those individuals who have gallery, museum and university jobs, not to mention all of those people in fields like advertising and software development, which Richard Florida refers to as the creative class.[7] From a cultural point of view, class struggle is difficult to fathom when unemployed graduates with low-wage jobs share more or less the same culture as middle and upper-class professionals.[8]

A simple schematic model can help to elucidate some of the standard political orientations of progressive art practice. My goal with this chart is to make some use of class analysis that would allow contemporary art theory to interact with class analysis and radical politics. The left section of the chart represents the category of *anti-art*, which is concerned primarily with the heteronomy of social content and seeks to dissolve art into life, escaping the protocols of aesthetic discourse through various kinds of immanentism and also through an 'exodus' from the cultural authority and conservatism of art institutions. On the right is *anti-art art*, which describes the various efforts to defend aesthetic theory as a critical discourse and as a means to secure the historically defined and hard-won field of autonomy. Whereas academic cultural production is for the most part no longer concerned with modernist aesthetic reduction and partakes of contemporary art's condition as art in the expanded field, it is also concerned to philosophically salvage and reproduce the separation of art from other categories of experience. We could consider tactical media interventions and transversal aesthetics as examples of the former and participatory relational aesthetics as well as various forms of the politics of representation, new institutionalism and neo-conceptualism as examples of the latter. As John Roberts puts it in *Revolutionary Time and the Avant-Garde*, one seeks to escape aesthetics into politics and the other to escape politics into aesthetics.[9] A dialectical *anti-anti-art* would be avant-garde in the sense of maintaining a relation to both art and politics, effecting less a distribution of the sensible, as Jacques Rancière has it, than a communism of the senses in which living labour frees itself materially and ideologically from the forms of exploitation that structure today's biocapitalist creative industries.[10] Only the avant-garde model radicalises the theory of autonomy as part of revolutionary class struggle.

In the introduction to my 2015 book on film, *Drive in Cinema*, I remarked that this schema corresponds neatly enough to Gene Ray's distinction between critically affirmative art, avant-garde practices and nomadic practices.[11] While all three models respond to the capitalist art system and its tendency to treat art as an ahistorical category, only the latter two, Ray argues, are committed to anti-capitalism. The makers of *critically affirmative art* are invested in the reproduction of the art system. While such artists may break certain cultural

ANTI-ART	ANTI-ANTI-ART	ANTI-ART ART
Negation	Negation of the negation	Affirmation
Anarchism	Socialism	Capitalism
Petty bourgeoisie	Proletariat	Bourgeoisie
Counterculture	Revolutionary art	Academic art
Transgression	Dialectics	Formalism
Atheism	Atheism as belief	Belief
Bohemian avant garde	Historical avant garde	Neo-avant garde
Collapse base/super	Dialectics of base/super	Separate base/super
Nomadic	*Avant-garde*	*Critically affirmative*
Discourse of the Hysteric	*Discourse of the Analyst*	*Discourse of the University*

conventions, they are indulged by the status quo as symbols of its relative free-dom. The art departments of the neoliberal university now advertise artistic rebellion as a conventional attitude. The *avant gardes*, in contrast, seek to radi-calise culture so as to bring about political change. The avant gardes, according to Ray, seek to overcome aesthetic autonomy insofar as it proscribes giving equal importance to politics. The avant-garde model is a renewable vector, he argues, and necessary to anti-capitalist practices. Lastly, the model of *nomadic practices* is wary of both of these strategies and so more consciously refuses to invest in autonomy and the institutions of art. The purpose of this third model is to operate in undefined border zones and trigger catalytic processes within social as well as state formations. Such anti-systemic struggles cut transversally across sites, situations and events, taking advantage of the art system and looking for openings and connections on the terrain of struggle. For Ray, only nomadic practices, along with avant-garde breakouts, have the potential to function as anti-capitalist forces.

In today's post-Fordist societies, artists are increasingly blackmailed into forms of self-exploitation. There is no solution to the contradictions of pro-gressive art in its affective, networked and activist forms insofar as these are part of neoliberal biocapitalism. The ethical turn, as Rancière calls it, with its post-traumatic witnessing of twentieth-century fiascos becomes insidious inso-far as revolutionary politics disappears into consensus politics, with its cautious, self-censoring pragmatism. Embodiment, empowerment, sexual politics, victim politics, multiculturalism – all of these are today part of the ambient milieu of the neoliberal creative city and the hegemony of a global petty bourgeoisie for which the revolutionary left is either a matter of nostalgia or nightmare. In this context, socially engaged art tends towards a culturalisation of politics rather than a politicisation of culture. Žižek argues that when we are blackmailed by neoliberal capitalism we should resist acting out in anger and should instead ask what kind of society makes this kind of blackmail possible.[12] In other words, what possibilities have not been recognised by socially engaged artists in a situation that calls for more democratic participation, social networking and free labour, along with more socially responsible capitalism? Why has the working class not constituted itself into a revolutionary subject? Some answers, Žižek proposes, can be found in unconscious libidinal mechanisms. In terms of ideological fantasy, reality cannot be seen in the same way by both the ruling capitalist class and the working masses, whether we define the latter as a blue-collar proletariat or a no-collar precariat. Class struggle is therefore concerned with the form and not only the content of reality. The form of thought, in terms of Hegelian abso-lute knowing, relates to a class consciousness that is historically contingent and that allows the class subject to understand his or her place in society from the perspective of imaginary capture and fantasy. For real change to occur, a change must take place in the objective conditions of one's existence. However, the predominant perspectives on power fail to divest themselves from their fantas-matic attachment to subjection and therefore their own ontological form of thought. While revolutionary theory 'lays bare' the 'contents' of domination, the 'form' of the existing relations of production and social relations within everyday life obscures the basis of exploitation. Psychoanalysis, however, does not consider the function of ideology at the level of objective conditions, but at the level of subjectivity. Even Karl Marx addressed the 'metaphysical subtleties and theological niceties' of the commodity.

In *Brave New Avant Garde* I made a case for what I refer to as *sinthomeopathic practices* – projects that rely on contradictory forms of identification with the symptoms and institutions of art under contemporary capitalism. The works by Andrea Fraser, Komar & Melamid, Janez Janša, Janez Janša, Janez Janša, Jakob Boeskov, Neue Slowenische Kunst and the Yes Men that I described sometimes seem to lack a progressive stance but not a progressive aim. As a way to develop this theory I referred to the work of the Dutch collective BAVO, whose texts *Cultural Activism Today: The Art of Over-Identification* and 'The Spectre of the Avant-Garde,' criticise today's NGO-style practices as a new form of official art.[13] The avant-garde tactics of some artists differ from the more pedagogical and collaborative methods of 'NGO artists,' even if the two can potentially overlap, as I argued was the case with Komar & Melamid's *Asian Elephant Project*. In order to develop the notion of an art sinthome, I drew on Žižek's hypothesis that the deepest identifications that hold a com-munity together are not the official written laws, but the identification with the transgression or suspension of the law itself as an obscene secret code. I argued in this sense that part of what structures the logic of the field of com-munity, relational and dialogical art, the official (progressive) art of our time, is an identification with the prohibition of avant-garde radicality.[14]

What I emphasised in my comparison of collaborative community art and avant-garde strategies of subversive affirmation is the importance of the notion

of the Lacanian split law in contrast to the Foucauldian view that law produces its self-sustaining forms of transgression. I made use of Jacques Lacan's
Discourse of the Analyst as a way to model avant-garde fantasy away from
questions of knowledge, and closer to the problems of belief and ideological
enjoyment, which provide new methods and concepts with which to understand cultural production in the context of biopolitical creative industries and
networked activism. As it happens, Ray's distinction between critically affirmative, nomadic and avant-garde practices corresponds not only to Bourdieu's
breakdown of bourgeois disinterestedness, petty-bourgeois allodoxia and
working-class necessity, but also to Lacan's schema of the 'four discourses,'
which Lacan developed during his seminars XVI–XVIII from 1968 to 1972.
Nomadic practices correspond to Lacan's Discourse of the Hysteric (anti-art),
the avant garde brings into effect a Discourse of the Analyst (anti-anti-art), and
critical art reflects the milieu of the Discourse of the University (anti-art art).
What was left out of Ray's schema as well as my own in earlier texts is the
category of art as such, which Lacan's four discourses provides a solution to as
an 'extra-class' enigma. An unreconstructed approach to art *qua* art runs the
risks associated with naive forms of romantic and neo-aristocratic pretentious-
ness. Such a Discourse of the Master, however, subtends the 'titles of nobility'
and 'marks of infamy' that Bourdieu associated with the aesthetic disposition.
Perhaps more than ever before, the category of art now has the superannuated
characteristics of exemplariness, sovereign will, absolutism, aristocracy and
heredity.

To better appreciate how Lacan's theory can inform the theory of the
avant garde, it is necessary to outline the basic structure of the four discourses.
Lacan's 'discourse theory' is his means to account for the ways in which language makes the social link operative. Because we are dealing with structures
of the unconscious, it is necessary to understand that the subject is typically and
in some ways necessarily unaware of the structures of discourse. Lacan's four
different mathemes offer variable placements for four elements that refer to
subjectivity in terms of the unconscious structured like a language. The symbol
$ refers to the split subject or subject of the unconscious. The symbol 'a' refers
to Lacan's concept of the *objet petit a*, otherwise referred to as the object-cause
of desire. The *objet a* also stands for the unconscious or the bar of difference
that makes all social meaning unstable. S1 stands for the master signifier, the
pure or phallic signifier that is a signifier without a signified. S2 refers to the
chain of signifiers or knowledge. In each case the top left quadrant refers to
the space of the agent of a communication or a command. The top right
refers to the Other or addressee. What concerns Lacan is that the structure of
communication always in some way fails or is incomplete. This impossibility is
explained through recourse to the bottom level of these formulas. The bottom
left quadrant refers to the hidden symptom of the agent. It is the function of

$\dfrac{a \quad\quad \$}{S_2 \quad\quad S_1}$	$\dfrac{S_2 \quad\quad a}{S_1 \quad\quad \$}$	$\dfrac{S_1 \quad\quad S_2}{\$ \quad\quad a}$	$\dfrac{\$ \quad\quad S_1}{a \quad\quad S_2}$
analyst	university	master	hysteric
anti-anti-art	anti-art art	art *qua* art	anti-art
avant-garde	critically affirmative art	autonomous art	nomadic practices

truth that the agent is unaware of. The bottom right refers to the product of the communication, its surplus *jouissance* and the function of loss.

In the Discourse of the Master, the master signifier addresses knowledge – the know-how of the slave – and produces desire as a function of loss. While the Master appears absolute in his or her authority, he is unaware of what conditions his existence as the castrated father. In the Discourse of the Analyst, desire occupies the place of the analyst who compels transference from the analysand. This discourse results in the symptom as the master signifier and is underwritten by psychoanalysis as the system of knowledge. The Discourse of the Hysteric finds the split subject in the position of an agent who addresses the master signifier and seeks knowledge of his or her condition as a function of loss. Lastly, the Discourse of the University finds that the system of knowledge is in the role of agent and that this knowledge is addressed to a desire that produces the subject. The Discourse of the University is underwritten by the master signifier, which makes the Discourse of the University one of the most vehement of discourses since it is unaware of the question of power. In a lecture delivered in 1972 Lacan added to his schema a matheme for the Discourse of the Capitalist, whose structure explains the conundrum of anti-capitalist movements today. In this discourse, the split subject is the agent who addresses knowledge and produces his or her own desire as loss. Like the University, the Capitalist is underwritten by the master signifier and so is equally unaware of relations of domination.[15]

In today's world of social networks, cybernetic surveillance and security regimes, as well as in the context of the rise to hegemonic status of the petty-bourgeois habitus, it appears that what is most readily available and encouraged are practices that correspond to the discourses of the activist Hysteric and the academic University. In comparison, the art Master seems to belong to an earlier, bourgeois epoch, with its corresponding utopian and scientific socialist party Analysts. The correspondence of art *qua* art with the status of the Master finds its most uncanny appearance in a shrewd text by Dave Beech, whose purpose it is to identify art's exceptionalism in classical, neoclassical as well as Marxist economic theory.[16] From the perspective of radical art theory, Beech's work seems somewhat apropos since Marx not only defined art as unproductive labour, he also considered art to be superstructural, and so the traditions of Western Marxism and the Frankfurt School that address culture from the perspective of political struggle against capitalism cannot be opposed to the study of capital or of economics as a specialised field. In some ways, Beech could have saved himself a great deal of trouble by starting with Bourdieu's field theory of art, which explains the class determinations of the art world's ideological self-conception as the 'economic world turned upside down,' even if today, and for various reasons, it seems increasingly less the case that artists can be defined as 'the dominated sector' of the 'dominant class.' Beech's point, nevertheless, is that this self-perception is not only falsely ideological but also material, since the value of artworks does not conform to the labour theory of value, as argued in classical, neoclassical and Marxist traditions. For example, the journalist who argued that the sale in 2017 of a rare copy of Marx's *Das Kapital* for $40,000 US undermines Marx's theory of capital simply does not understand the economic relevance of the price of rare objects – or for that matter of any object or commodity – to the corresponding concept of value, measured in socially necessary labour time. What becomes interesting for us, then – if we agree to ignore for the time being all of the questions having to do with reification, commodification, culture industry, spectacle, the subsumption of labour and post-Fordist immaterial labour – is the way in which art's ostensible separation from economic determination corresponds to the Discourse of the Master, in which the art Master addresses the know-how of the economist while at the same time being unaware of his hidden symptom: the artist-theorist finds himself at a loss insofar as he becomes his slave's slave.

No wonder then that artists like Jeff Koons and Damien Hirst, whose work is based on speculation, have almost no impact on the University Discourse or on the hearts and minds of the Hysteric multitude. Nor, for example, are we convinced that Jean-Michel Basquiat deserves as much recognition as Pablo Picasso just because certain art collectors are driving up the prices of his work at auction. The flipside to this, from the perspective of a Marxist critique of exploitation, are the kinds of precarious jobs that one finds in today's hyper-connected world of 'bio-economic totalitarianism,' to borrow of phrase from Franco Berardi.[17] For example, in March 2007 the Art Gallery of Ontario posted an employment opportunity that provides a detailed picture of the new model of the creative employee. The museum required that its candidate for the position of community arts facilitator have experience in the 'design and delivery of workshops, projects, special events and other experiences that encourage people to explore local identities as well as institutional collections.' The projects were to evolve with community members working in schools, community centres, public spaces and community festivals. The prospective employee was to facilitate the creation of 'legacy projects' that 'reflect issues of concern and that propose mechanisms for sustainable creative engagement at the local level.' The facilitator was to develop content and delivery of web-based initiatives, mediating the presentation of collections with public constituencies. The facilitator was expected to demonstrate experience working collaboratively with other artists as well as diverse communities, to have a degree in fine art or art history with two years of experience working as an artist/facilitator 'within a variety of community-based situations,' to have experience developing curricula, experience working in museums and/or other cultural institutions. She or he was also to have technical proficiency in digital photography and video production as well as skills in image manipulation and video editing. The clincher is that the position was part-time and temporary.[18]

But the AGO is something of a conservative institution. Another job posting, this time by the Media Co-op, a cross-Canada grassroots independent media organisation, was announced in April of 2014. This was an employment opportunity for a Publisher, someone, they said, who should be an energetic person, able to work independently, who would spread out across the country with the rest of the editorial collective and find the best in radical media for the Media Co-op's flagship magazine *The Dominion*. The publisher would oversee the 'administration and overall direction of the co-op, serve as financial co-ordinator (working closely with the bookkeeper) and carry out various design and editorial tasks.' They would be expected to work with the membership co-ordinator on fundraising and grant writing, should be bilingual, highly organised, with knowledge of desktop publishing software (InDesign and Photoshop, Open Office, Drupal), web-publishing and social media. Experience working in social justice and community-based movements was required, as well as experience working with budgets, financial forecasting, non-profit administration and journalism. The job, however, was minimum wage and only ten hours per week. Further, it was a virtual position – the prospective employee was to have their own computer equipment, Internet connection and preferably live in Montreal. And the Media Co-op is all about equity, the ad said, giving an unintended picture of equal opportunity exploitation: 'People from marginalized communities, including women, Indigenous people, visible minorities, people with disabilities, deaf people, gay men, lesbians, bisexuals, two-spirited people, transgendered and transsexual people, and working-class people are especially encouraged to apply.' According to Gene Ray, the ideolgoical command from the creative industries sector is 'enjoy your precarity!' Autonomy, creativity and even criticality become hip libidinal investments that allow us to misperceive the real potential for resistance and the extent to which strategic social transformation is blocked by the violence of capitalist reproduction.[19]

Avant-garde art continues to be in conflict with the value form as well as capitalist relations. The ideology of vanguardism, I argue, is not easily dispensed with. One could say the same thing about Marxist cultural theory.

In terms of evaluating art that takes a progressive stance but lacks aesthetic interest, Marx in his day gave us the concept of *tendenzkunst*, or politically correct art. The notion that art is superstructural and therefore dialectically separable from the social system from which it emerges is derived mostly from Marx's 1859 Preface to the *Contribution to the Critique of Political Economy*, in which he asserts that the art of the ancient Greeks can continue to have artistic value even if it is the product of a slave-owning society and pre-capitalist mode of production. One finds similar contradictions between the economic base and the ideological superstructure in Stalinist cultural policy. Despite the strictures of Zhdanovist Socialist Realism, Stalinism nevertheless allowed artists and intellectuals to study and appreciate what was progressive in previous eras, providing that such histories were understood in terms of class analysis. This was consistent with Marx's argument that art need not offer solutions to capitalism nor even take a correct political stance in order to be considered realist.[20] Along these lines, the Hungarian theorist Georg Lukács gave the example of the writer Honoré de Balzac.[21] Although Balzac did not support the most progressive social forces in his day, he was nevertheless an exceptional realist. Despite his conservative social attitude, he perceived the changing reality around him better than most other authors. The problem of class reductionism came to a head in the Soviet Union during the Lyssenko debates concerning whether or not hybrid wheats constituted a form of 'bourgeois science,' which, because it was the product of the West, should be rejected. More recently, debates among autonomist theorists like Raniero Panzieri and Mario Tronti, including more contemporary scholars like Antonio Negri and Félix Guattari, have sought to determine whether post-Fordist capitalist modes of production can be recuperated for communist purposes. Certainly, the so-called 'formalism' of Badiou's truth procedures of art, science, politics and love causes many to seek a more 'grounded' approach informed by political economy or some other kind of materialism. There are nevertheless two principles that are useful here. One is that there is no 'axiomorphic' correspondence between artworks and the people who make them. The other is that there is no absolute homology between the level of the superstructure, which includes ideas, philosophy, law, religion and culture, and the economic base, which in Marxian analysis includes the mode of production, the social relations of production and the technical means of production.

The well-known lesson from Marxist theory is that works of art have a relative autonomy from the social circumstances in which they are embedded. This includes the ideology of art as such. Without this relative autonomy the social space would be thoroughly saturated and neither artworks nor any other kind of social mediation would have the ability to affect social change. Contradictions and meaningful change could therefore be located only at the level of so-called 'material' processes. One possible limitation of Marxist theory for socially engaged art is that it does not provide practical instructions for cultural practice. The benefit of Marxism is that it addresses the problem of bourgeois humanist ideology as an invariable norm. The aesthetic, as Roberts argues, undergoes change as a historical category. The 'end of art,' understood in Hegelian terms as an ontology of conceptualisation, explains art's emancipation from mimesis and from artisanal skill into generalised social technique.[22] Roberts' theory of 'post-art' makes the case for socially engaged art as a model of contemporary avant-garde art. In this regard, however, it is not enough for artists to be anti-art anti-capitalists. Culture needs to be revolutionised against the autonomy principle of bourgeois ideology, but this does not automatically imply that art must be instrumentalised and directly linked to such expedients as contribution to GDP, philanthropic reform, job creation, regional development, and other such expedients within a neoliberal risk society.[23] For Roberts, art is a non-identitary, adisciplinary, prefigurative and emancipatory force. Art's condition as an always unfinished site of struggle is a reflexive and experimental project that does not abolish itself as art and that is based in theoretical investments, defined in its 'suspensive' form as irreducible to the heteronomy of non-art and as a dialectically and historically open research programme. The avant garde is therefore hardly a matter of nostalgia. As Roberts puts it:

> This obsession with that which is no longer as that which can be no longer ... is regularly called upon by art history and cultural theory to discipline what is held to be the unobtainable and hubristic claims of art on the extra-artistic real. This is why the most assiduous writing on the avant-garde since the 1980s has insisted on the avant-garde as an open-temporal experience rather than a failed event.[24]

If the avant garde is a failed concept, this is in part due to the perception that communism is an outmoded ideology and so we need to be able to address the status of communism in contemporary culture. The level of class struggle within radical art theory relates very specifically to what Badiou has referred to as the 'communist hypothesis.' The communist hypothesis, he says, is a 'space of possible failures' that invites us to revisit its histories and think of new possibilities in new circumstances in which 'we are now forbidden to fail.'[25] There is no reason for us to retain the earlier forms of the artistic avant gardes and political vanguards. However, there is every reason to reinvent these for ourselves today.

My claim is that it is as difficult today to conceive of a communist Master-Analyst as it is to for us to approach art as either avant-garde or autonomous. The question of allodoxia applies equally to politics insofar as leftists have to a great extent abandoned the political party in favour of social protest movements and micropolitical collectives. In the US, the 2016 Bernie Sanders election campaign provided some indication of what social energies could be mobilised with a semi-socialist programme. After Sanders was betrayed by his own party, the vestiges of his campaign failed to materialise through the Green Party, while some momentum was later directed into the #movementforbernie headed by the Seattle socialist Kashma Sawant, and more recently, through a sizeable membership increase in the Democratic Socialists of America, which includes high-profile members like Cornel West, Barbara Ehrenreich and Medea Benjamin. With the hegemony of the petty-bourgeois habitus, however, the effects of allodoxia are radically transformed. It is no longer the case that anxiety about class status causes people to pretentiously identify with formal culture, but rather that there is no longer the perception of a need or an incentive to do so. The very terms of cultural authority, including political authority, are now conditioned by transformations to the relations and modes of production, with prosumer, precarious and flex workers feeling more empowered by YouTube and Facebook than by elected officials or a visit to the museum. There is at the same time what Žižek refers to as the weakening of symbolic efficiency. The value of art is not simply relative, but it is nevertheless sustained by the interpassivity of belief. We believe in the social value of art because the institutions of art believe for us. As institutions become both more communicational and decentralised through education as well as through neoliberalisation, their class function changes accordingly. The status of culture and politics in today's petty-bourgeois hegemony corresponds to a new social imaginary of networked self-organisation that connects infrastructural platforms with communities of interest. The result is a de-aestheticisation and depoliticisation of practices and meanings.

All tomorrow's parties

If there is a stereotype of the militant avant-garde artist and vanguard communist party, there is also a stereotype of the spontaneous, non-representative, rhizomatic, molecular, horizontalist, leaderless and activist multitude. According to Žižek, the activist model is the deepest of today's illusions and the most difficult to renounce.[26] If art and politics were grounded immediately in political economy, as activists and autonomist theorists propose, we would likely have gotten rid of capitalism a long time ago. The question then is how to change people's attitudes and ideas rather than compromise with the predominant democratic ideology.

Among some of the keywords that are routinely used in the socially engaged art world and that carry a great deal of significance as ideology, we find an emphasis on such concepts as undecidability, ambiguity, permeability, decentralisation, nomadism, performativity, dialogue, non-mastery, affect, etc. These terms correspond indirectly to what Badiou, in his lecture 'Does the Notion of Activist Art Still Have Meaning?,' argues about the possibility of a militant art today.[27] 'In a militant art,' he says, 'the place of ideology is the place of the contradiction and of the dubious results of the struggle. And so we have, in some sense, an art of the dubious struggle as opposed to an art of the glorious victory.'[28] 'Militant art,' Badiou argues, 'is an art of what has not yet been completely decided. It's an art of the situation, and not an art of the state of the situation. And so militant art cannot be the image of something which exists, but must be the pure existence of what is becoming.'[29] Militant art would seem therefore to correspond to these keywords of contemporary society. However, Badiou adds,

> Today there is no common ideology and we must observe that democracy is the clear example of a weak ideology, and not a strong ideology. It is too consensual; it is too much in complete equivocation between the reactionary camp and the revolutionary camp, between progressives and conservatives, and so on. In fact, everybody is a democrat today. But when everybody is a democrat, we can see that the ideology is certainly weak.[30]

Vanguard art is therefore what Badiou would consider to be an art that is in a concrete relationship with local political experiences and that creates a common space based on the existence of a strong ideology and strong organisations.

If we are to in some way challenge the activist model as a fantasy of integration with biocapitalism, we require what Badiou proposes as the fidelity to the truth procedures of a universal, generic event and the organisation of life around new master signifiers. The ability to change people's attitudes is the characteristic of what Žižek calls a Master. Žižek makes use of the psychoanalytic concept of transference to suggest that the analysand's identification with the analyst is similar to the identification with the Master as 'the subject supposed to know.' The purpose of analysis, however, is not subjection to the Master as the path to liberation, but rather the traversal of the fantasy in a move beyond identification. Communism, Žižek argues, cannot be based on the pragmatic ameliorism of today's social movements. A Master is therefore needed as a figure of transference. In this regard, Žižek claims, 'we should shamelessly reassert the idea of "vanguard," when one part of a progressive movement assumes leadership and mobilises other parts' and should therefore 'reject the ideology of "anarchic horizontalism".'[31] The actions of vanguards, who are always a minority and never a mass subject, contribute to 'a higher revolutionary unity.'[32]

Although Žižek and Badiou reject anarchist horizontalism as an adequate organisational form and theoretical outlook, they are not indifferent to the efforts of social movements. Regardless, what they say about social movements provides us with useful concepts with which to assess what is and is not a vanguard. In an essay titled 'Answers Without Questions,' Žižek credits the Occupy Wall Street protests with having opened up the space for a new political content and a new political subjectivity.[33] Notwithstanding the movement's rejection of political representation, Žižek wonders how many of the 99% would be willing to accept the protesters as their voice. All who protest claim the right to employment and to affordable housing, health care, education, and so on. The political establishment is denounced as corrupt and so there is no one to whom one can adequately address one's demands. Intellectuals and artists cannot operationalise these demands and with the fall of communism, he says, 'they forever forfeited their role as a vanguard which understands the laws of history and can guide the innocents along its path.'[34] The problem for Žižek is that 'the people' do not know either. The ignorance of the former is not equal to the ignorance of the latter, however, and it is only the people who can have the answers, if only they knew the questions. Žižek says that the OWS protests are answers to questions that we do not know and so we as intellectuals should not provide clear answers but should propose the questions to which they are answers. For our purposes, the question is not only whether socially engaged art is a symptom of the political economy of global capitalism, but beyond this, what is an adequate, progressive contemporary avant-garde art and vanguard politics? What kinds of practices allow a new model of the avant garde hypothesis to be deployed?

What is apparent in today's biocapitalist security regimes is that we are all to a lesser or greater degree in the proletarian position of the excluded. The forms of oppression based on gender, race and sexuality are ideological components of the class struggle and means through which capitalist hegemony now functions. It could be that just as Marxists once looked to peasants and students, the revolution this time will call on all of those who have been mobilised by identity issues to take up the class struggle and reassert the communist hypothesis. In this they could join all of those self-organised and socially critical artists who have already recognised art's ideological construction. The quest for revolutionary unity, however, has its readymade objections, either as part of the liberal-democratic objection to 'totalitarianism' and revolutionary violence, or as part of anarchist objections to constituted forms of state power. In his 1993 text *Spectres of Marx*, Jacques Derrida addressed the political consensus that the fall of Soviet communism represents the end to any viable political alternatives to free-market capitalism.[35] The book came as a response to the 1990 declaration by George H.W. Bush of a New World Order to be led unilaterally by the United States, with as its first missions the invasion of Iraq and the NATO bombing of ex-Yugoslavia. Francis Fukuyama, then deputy director of the State Department policy planning staff, responded to the disintegration of political regimes in Eastern Europe with the Alexandre Kojève doctrine of the 'end of history.' Fukuyama celebrated technology as the solution to the limitless accumulation of wealth and satisfaction of human desires, noting that economic modernisation and cultural homogenisation would replace all traditional forms with centralised planning. This process was to be facilitated by global markets and the spread of consumer culture, a teleological evolution directed by capitalist social relations.[36]

Somewhat less sanguine, Derrida criticised 'end of history' teleology for its premature embrace of actually-existing democracy. He listed in *Spectres of Marx* the ten most pressing problems of the New World Order, which, in his words, make the 'euphoria of liberal-democratic capitalism resemble the blindest and most delirious of hallucinations.'[37] These are: structural unemployment, homelessness and deportations, economic war, the inability to control the contradictions of the free market, foreign debt, the arms industry and trade, nuclear proliferation, interethnic wars, the mafia and drug cartels, and finally, the present state of international law.[38] Derrida's book was a slight departure from the kind of post-Marxism that was championed by postmodern theorists, including Derrida himself. In his ironic revision of Hegel and Marx, he refuted the possibility of an end to new ideological formations, writing:

> At a time when a new world disorder is attempting to install its … neo-liberalism, no disavowal has managed to rid itself of all of Marx's ghosts. Hegemony still organizes the repression and thus the confirmation of a haunting … [This] spectre is the future, it is always to come, it represents itself only as that which is to come or come back.[39]

As long as capitalism is the dominant horizon of our thinking and mode of production, it is bound to give rise to a return of the repressed: the meaning of Marx today. This is particularly significant since the problems that Derrida enumerates have only deepened. Not only has offshoring by transnational corporations exacerbated unemployment and starvation wages, but geopolitical standoffs continue unflaggingly, with NATO presently engaged in a new Cold War with Russia and China – a phenomenon that even Henry Kissinger denounces as reckless. Drone strikes, kill lists, torture, extraordinary rendition and indefinite detention characterise today's distorted constitutional law, supported and sanctioned by all major western governments. Foreign debt has shaken both the US economy as well as the Eurozone, where now even the IMF has conceded to Greece that its austerity policies are inoperative. Nuclear proliferation continues unabated as the White House declared in September 2014 that the US would spend more than $1 trillion over the next decade to upgrade its nuclear weapons capability, and this as the US and its willing executioners are operating in more than 120 countries and deeply involved in military conflicts in more that six regions of the globe, from Afghanistan, Iraq and Syria, to Yemen, Jordan, the Gulf monarchies, Egypt, Libya, Somalia, Niger, Chad, Congo, Liberia, Korea, Ukraine, Armenia, Georgia, and across the Pacific. Meanwhile, on the domestic front, the Donald Trump administration passed a bill to cut $1 trillion from Medicare, Medicaid and Social Security over the next decade. This war on the working class represents the overall global trend, in which ten percent of the world's population controls ninety percent of global wealth, one percent controls fifty percent of global wealth, and fifty percent of the world's population owns less than nothing. Not mentioned by Derrida is the ecological crisis, in relation to which economic wars over the control of energy sources have led to spiralling CO_2 emissions that are now beyond the 400 parts per million 'safe path' for global surface temperatures and are expected to climb to 550 ppm in this century.

Little wonder then that following the 2008 banking crisis, which cost the US government $22 trillion (and which has mostly padded the pocketbooks of the wealthy), and after the $4.4 trillion spent by the US on wars since 9/11, sales of books by Marx increased 100 percent from 1990.[40] Marxist theory continues to be relevant in these neoliberal times. Private property regimes and neoliberal free trade are oriented towards innovation through competition, with a focus on new technologies and new organisational forms that seek to deliver more efficient labour processes for the sake of higher profits.[41] Competition, however, leads to declining rates of profit. Innovation becomes an impetus to the kinds of monopoly control that destroy innovation, as seen for instance in the energy sector. The quest for superior military power, with its now unparalleled surveillance capacities, has directed innovation in the quest for global economic advantage. Innovation, however, as David Harvey argues, is also destructive of value and capital itself, relying on the perpetual reorganisation of labour and the destabilisation of social relations through chronic job insecurity, deskilling and reskilling.[42] Displacing labour, he argues further, tends in the long run towards internal contradictions to capitalism that can be counteracted through various forms of creative destruction: increasing exploitation, increasing unemployment and precarity, reducing production costs, encouraging foreign trade in order to lower production costs, product innovation, automation, the devaluation of capital, the absorption of capital through the production of physical infrastructures, and lastly, monopolisation, as in the Walmart and Amazon phenomena. According to István Mészáros, the contradictions of capitalism, to which even capitalists must submit, represents the necessity of the renewal of Marxist concepts. Although Marx could not have foreseen how capitalism would renew itself through Keynesianism, monetarism and financialisation, he did predict how at every historical stage capitalism would be pitted against the interests of workers.[43]

Today's global political and economic crises call on leftists to renew the communist project that animates the critique of political economy of Marxists like Harvey. In the words of Bruno Bosteels in his contribution to *The Idea of Communism*, this is 'communism as a common horizon for thinking and acting in the twenty-first century.'[44] On average, Bosteels says, 'the left' serves mainstream journalism as the mirror image of the extreme right, both of them to be rejected as political curiosities. What concerns Bosteels is the strife between leftism and ultra-leftism, the latter referring to those groups that reject parliamentary politics, unions and party discipline – variously described as 'petty-bourgeois revolutionism,''adventurism,' 'pure communism' and 'massism' – and for whom the vacillation between exuberant fanaticism and melancholy dejection replaces the patient work of party organisation.[45] The first line of contradiction to be mediated, he argues, is the simplistic one, perpetuated by today's anarchist left as well as the post-1968 *nouveaux philosophes*, which would pit the masses en bloc against the state. As the *Communist Manifesto* teaches, 'the people' are themselves split into competing classes. Such anti-dialectical, generic anti-capitalism, a target of Marx and Engels, supplements the defence of liberal democracy, with its humanitarian interventions and promotion of popular resistance.[46]

Perhaps the most optimistic theoretical approach to ultra-left communism is that put forward by Italian workerist and post-operaist Marxists, whose most well-known protagonists are Michael Hardt and Antonio Negri. Hardt and Negri contend that the new forms of immaterial symbolic production in the contemporary post-Fordist digital economy – the stage of advanced capitalism that has moved from industrial wage labour to a service and creative economy – represent a novel kind of biopolitical production, the most advanced form of capitalist social relations, which, despite their updated mechanisms of exploitation and control, provide labour with new means of self-valorisation. For Hardt and Negri, contemporary digital capitalism contains in *statu nascendi* the potential for communism. As Hardt puts it in his essay 'The Common in Communism,' the current composition of capital and class demonstrates the importance of the commons and the 'affirmation of open and autonomous biopolitical production, the self-governed continuous creation of new humanity.'[47] For Hardt, the more that capitalism comes to rely on the biopolitical commons, the closer we get to communism. Does this, however, not imply a certain teleology and faith in historical necessity that is comparable in some ways with the Soviet hubris that the transition to communist society had been achieved sometime in the 1950s? While it is true that Marx and Engels addressed the radical potential of capitalism's productive powers, it would be nothing but fatalistic to think that capitalism's latest round of self-revolutionising will be emancipatory.

In 'Communism as Commitment, Imagination, and Politics,' Étienne Balibar makes the useful observation that Badiou's and Žižek's instigation of the debate on the 'new communism' compels us to ask: who are the communists, what are we communists thinking of and what are we doing and/or fighting for?[48] All communists, Balibar says, have been idealists dreaming of another world and not post-humans in a fully rationalised order. This means that the communist's commitment is autonomous and not fully part of the existing state of affairs.[49] Communism is not premised on an objective description of the reality we already know, but on an overcoming of the contradictions of existing material conditions. The idea of communism and the idea of the avant garde are master signifiers through which subjects are constituted negatively and collectively as those who wish to radically change the complex of social relations. Because it is based on solidarity and universality, the class struggle that is implicit in the idea of communism is therefore both more intense *and* more disinterested, Balibar says, than any imagined community such as the nation or other form of organic community. The communist 'we' is fundamentally emancipatory and therefore different from the substantive 'we' of nation, identity group and ethnic community.

In terms of how to achieve this ideal, communists have diverse interpretations that are based on different understandings of the crises of capitalism.[50] Reflection requires the supplement of political projection or anticipation, however, with the future conceived, in Žižek's terms, as an ontological rupture in the present.[51] On this, Balibar remarks that Badiou's and Žižek's views are opposed to those of Hardt and Negri, who consider that many of Marx's presuppositions are no longer tenable. Whereas Hardt and Negri focus on the economic base, Žižek focuses on materialist dialectics and ideology critique, understood in relation to the Lacanian approach to the virtuality of the split subject and the *objet petit a*. Change from above, directed by a revolutionary force, is reconceived in Žižek's analysis as the presence of the Real in the space of ideology and less a matter of the organicity of the productive forces.[52] In contrast to the tendency to think in terms of networks and assemblages, Žižek emphasises ontological incompleteness and the impossible character of reality itself. His theoretical challenge is to break with transcendental idealism without regressing to naive materialism. In Lacanian terms, the Real is not simply a Void that precedes the Symbolic, and which symbolic regimes attempt to control, but is rather a negativity at the core of subjectivity and the symbolic order as such.[53]

Communism seems impossible today. What is the *juste milieu*, Balibar asks, between Žižek's notion of revolutionary 'divine violence,' defined against the neoliberal impasse, and Hardt and Negri's emphasis on labour processes? What is it, he asks, that self-avowed communists are fighting for? The state of the 'post-traumatic' left, as I call it, accounts in some ways for the paradoxical popularity of Antonio Gramsci's theory of hegemony, or domination through consent, among postmodern and post-political activists.[54] Are today's hegemony contests – identity struggles that seek to give voice to what is repressed by the dominant consensus and that question the dominant hegemony – not a kind of Clintonian wink? 'I smoked the Gramscian notion of hegemonic contestation but I didn't inhale the noxious communist orthodoxy.' Chantal

Mouffe, for example, argues that the idea of the avant garde must be abandoned in favour of the multiplicity of social movements who oppose all programmes of 'total social mobilization.'[55] Ernesto Laclau and Mouffe's notion of radical democracy combines difference with contingency.[56] It does not, as Žižek argues, combine contingency with struggle. Žižek's argument, in contrast, is that the empty place of power is always barred or uncannily fetishised rather than only temporarily hegemonised.

The specific terms that Laclau and Mouffe bring into play in their theory of radical democracy are *contingency* (as a necessary correlate of the universal), *equivalence* (of the forms of struggle based on race, class, gender and sexuality) and *antagonism* (as all of the latter vie for the space of power). It is the structuralist overlap of contingency and equivalence, derived from Saussure, that Žižek rejects with the concept of displaced and vanishing mediation: the place of overlap of genus and species, the particular element in the series that stands for all of the others. For Žižek, the emphasis on difference mostly avoids the problem of struggle, especially as the function of capitalism as the concrete universal is precisely to transform problems of economic inequality into problems of diversity and the recognition of multicultural differences.[57]

In his well-known essay, 'Class Struggle or Postmodernism? Yes Please!,' Žižek refuses the blackmail of the current predicament – defend liberal capitalism or else support totalitarianism – without renouncing class struggle as a universal project.[58] The problem with class struggle, however, is that it does not exist without the remainder of an excluded third element. Today the contradiction of labour and capital is sustained not so much by the exclusion of a 'foreign element,' but by the exclusion of the idea and the actuality of leftist vanguards. In *The Courage of Hopelessness*, Žižek argues against decentralised collaborative networks and calls on leftists to organise forms of power that are external to the commons and that can regulate its functioning.[59] Dreaming of alternatives prevents us from thinking through to the end the limits of our condition. Such wishful thinking leads us to waste time and effort on pseudo-conflicts such as yes or no on Brexit, voting for the military or for Erdogan in Turkey, favouring Putin or right-wing nationalists in the Ukraine, hedonism versus Muslim rights in France, or Assad versus Daesh in Syria. Such pseudo-conflicts, as between Clinton and Trump in the US, or LePen and Macron in France, prevent the appearance of the true conflicts, in relation to which we would see emerge new leftist organisations that would replace populist rage against global capitalism with articulated programmes that would allow for the building of a new society that can function at the level of world government. Only such programmes, after the failures of state socialism, are according to him worthy of the name communism.

There is an ontological-epistemological gap, however, that remains untouched in the background of political programmes and choices, a

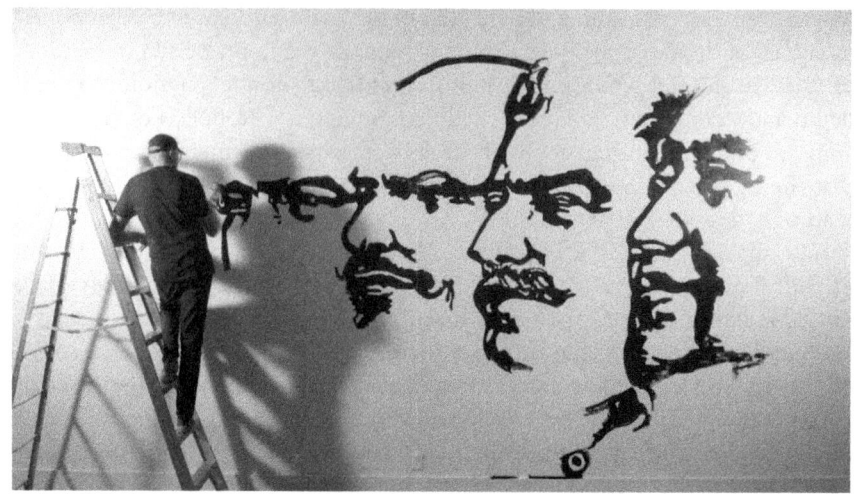

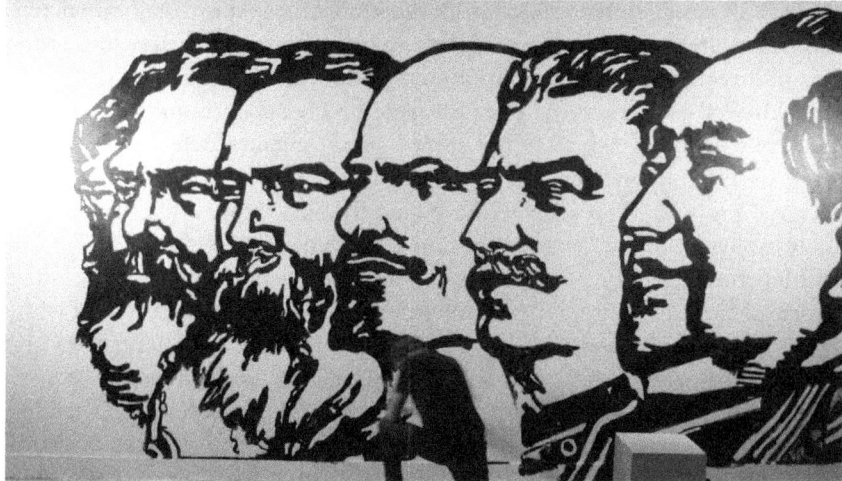

pre-transcendent mediation that transposes the failure of knowledge into the structure of the subject before and after political interpellation. Such a 'spectral entity' as the Lacanian *objet a* mediates the fantasy of the subject in ideology, and indeed, of the subject of difference. The subject of 'castration,' to put it in Freudian terms, displaces facile readings of Hegelian Marxism, according to which a premature synthesis presumes a positive starting point. In some ways artistic avant gardes, especially in current circumstances, are more easily able to embody the Hegelian modalities of negation that define the mediations of split subject and *objet a* than are political vanguards. This perhaps explains why political practices and not only labour practices are increasingly informed by the artistic mode of critique. In the age of the withering of symbolic efficiency,

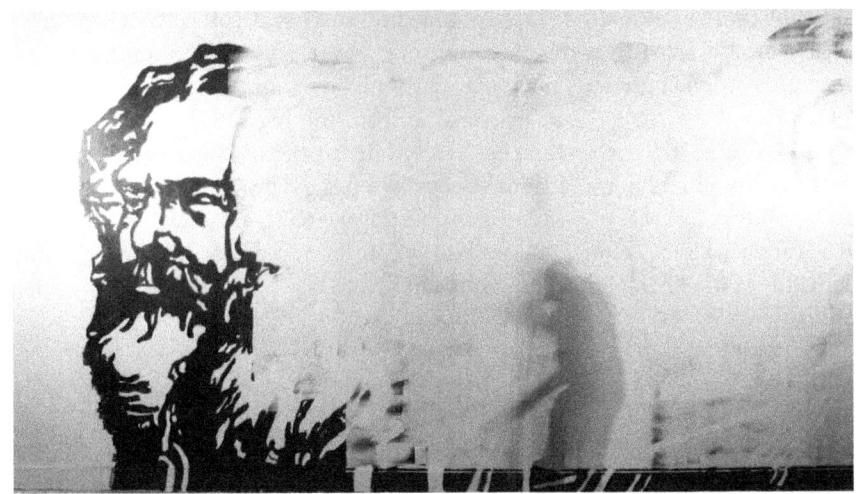

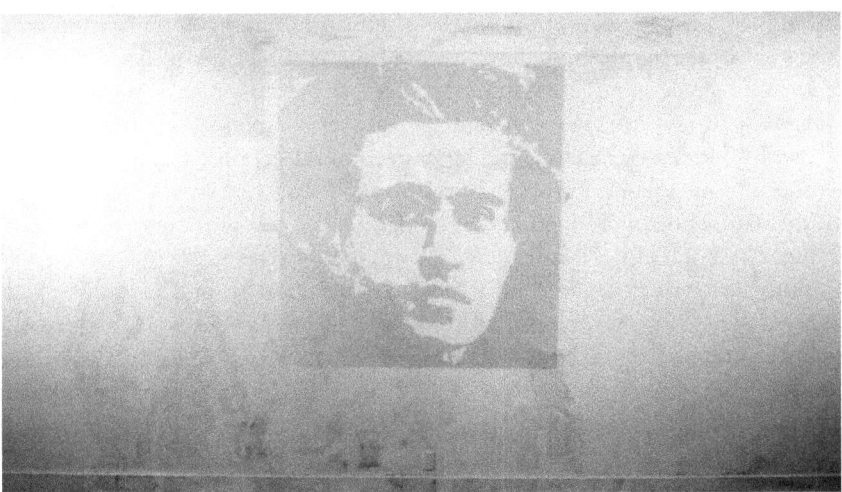

Bruce Barber, [Performance] of *Spectres of Marx* for video documentation,
2015. The ten-minute time-lapse video documentation is displayed continuously
for the duration of the exhibition alongside its end result. Presented by
the Global Art Affairs Foundation in conjunction with the Venice Biennale.
Courtesy of Bruce Barber.

it is not so much that 'God is dead' and there is no big Other who knows, but
rather that 'God is unconscious,' which implies that something is nevertheless
registered in the space of the big Other, in the 'quantum oscillations' of the
'God–systems' of art and politics. The real vanguards were never those who,
as Badiou says, proposed the glorious victory, but those who organised the
struggle and who made provisions for their eventual disappearance, their

self-sublation. They have always been aware of what Žižek refers to as symbolic castration: the 'loss of something one never possessed.'[60] Insofar as the symbolic order conditions *jouissance*, the only way for the subject to enjoy is to conceal the fact of (non-)possession from the big Other. It is therefore symptomatic that today's vanguards rarely refer to themselves as such, leading to the many different expressions of socially engaged art and end-of-ideology post-politics. I refer to such engaged artistic practices and social movements as a 'vanguardia' of cultural and political expression, more or less aware of the demands of neoliberal biocapitalism for means to reproduce the existing social order.

Vanguardia

The essays that comprise this book were written largely in the context of discussions on socially engaged art, art activism and social movement politics, and not in the context of discussions on the avant garde and revolutionary politics. Regardless, it is my purpose here to sound the possibilities for the rethinking of an avant-garde programme in relation to today's anti-capitalist social forces. I begin with a consideration of anti-globalisation protest and Occupy Wall Street. In both cases I address the limitations of decentralised antagonism and workerist post-politics. I propose in relation to Henri Lefevre's 1970s writings on the state mode of production that biopolitical protest is not merely opposed to the state but is also a feature of its self-revolutionising.

With respect to the shift away from the postmodern end of history and towards the resurgence of emancipatory leftist praxis, the chapter 'Vanguardia' examines the growing body of engaged literature on social practice art. Through reviews of books by Gerald Raunig, BAVO, Gregory Sholette, Oliver Ressler, Grant Kester, Critical Art Ensemble, Nato Thompson, Yates McKee, Mikkel Bolt Rasmussen and Rebecca Gordon-Nesbitt, I explore various strands of contemporary leftist culture. Today's globalisation obliges us to understand culture in relation to capital circulation, a process of emptying out and de-substantialisation that post-structuralist cultural studies tend to avoid. I am concerned therefore with theories of radical culture that address the totality of the world system.

Emancipatory struggle has to start somewhere. In the context of Montreal, where I live, one important event allowed me to consider the prospects for revolutionary culture today. The chapter 'Psychoprotest: dérives of the Quebec Maple Spring,' co-authored with Cayley Sorochan, describes our participation in the student strike demonstrations of 2012 in terms of Lettrist and Situationist theories of psychogeography, the dérive and broader critical frameworks. The article was written with the understanding that real cultural transformation can occur only when there is coordination among militant intellectuals, artists and the working masses. Insofar as the revolt of the masses is typically appropriated by dominant forces, emancipatory movements are caught between civil society and the coercive machinery of the state. Against a pure leftist reason, only a dialectical rethinking of class and political organisation can go beyond polemics. The seeds of such radical collective organisation were evident in the Maple Spring where the combative syndicalism of the student groups allowed for the combination of both political programme and democratic radicalisation over an extended period of time.

Another book review, this time of *Test Dept: Total State Machine* (2015), examines the theoretical issues that are raised in this eclectic retrospective of one of most activist of British industrial music groups. From the South London of Thatcherite England and the context of the struggles of the early 1980s – the Miners' Strike, the Poll Tax strike and the Polish Solidarity movement – Test Dept developed an original approach to music performance and materials based on the Stakhanovite model of the industrial worker. The eclipse of industrial work at the moment of the group's emergence allows us to ask questions about contemporary social practice art in the context of contemporary post-Fordism. In contrast to what was still imaginable to early Test Dept, today's state of precarity and shift from class politics to nomadic anarchism bring into view some of the effects of the postmodern theory of the 1980s that were otherwise occluded in Test Dept's Bolshevik classicism.

'No strawman for the revolution' addresses new possibilities for thinking about avant-garde art and vanguard politics through a review of recent debates between Žižek and McKenzie Wark, and further, through an examination of the limits of cultural revolution as we have known it since the late 1960s. The impasse of Occupy Wall Street and similar protest movements has led Žižek to shift from a view of the party in terms of the Lacanian Discourse of the Analyst towards reflections on the Discourse of the Master. The consequent critiques of Žižek that are examined are shown to have evaded his ideas and fail to adequately address his Hegelian-Lacanian approach to dialectical materialism. On the other hand, one finds that Žižek's renewal of radical politics is challenging others on the progressive left to do the same. The following chapter, 'Beyond socially enraged art,' proposes that the task of cultural revolution is to redefine today's political struggle in class terms. Through Badiou's study of the Chinese Cultural Revolution as well as Régis Debray's analysis of guerrilla struggle in Cuba, I address the effort to unite socially engaged artists at the January 2015 symposium of Artist Organisations International.

A concluding chapter, 'The only game in town,' poses the now acute problem of class struggle in relation to identity politics. Contemporary political campaigns like Black Lives Matter and MeToo transform the experience of victimisation directly into demands for accountability, a process that tends to reproduce the political and structural frameworks within which structural violence takes place. Against 'victim politics,' I argue for a democracy without guarantees that rejects various solutions to the rise of the political right: masochistic self-culpabilisation, appeals to civil society, scapegoating and nihilistic destruction. I explore Marxist literature for concepts with which to break with the postmodern pluralism that prevents the emergence of a radical left universalism.

If biocapitalist protest typifies the strategy of leftist cultural work in an age of post-enlightenment enjoyment, how can we possibly confront the limitations of micropolitical, identitarian and horizontalist post-politics? One might begin by understanding how it is that politics does not determine every aspect of human existence, which includes questions of art, culture and social values. My argument in these pages is that the rejection of vanguardism is a major symptom of today's neoliberal hegemony that must be dissolved.[61] *Vanguardia* reads such symptoms like so many bumps on the head, some of them produced by police batons, but most of them bits of data in a biometric matrix to which we are every day contributing as the product of the general intellect. It is a challenge for us in these times to reflect on what aspects of cultural and political praxis have not worked and what progressive political practices on the left will be able to win the day.

1

Alter-globalisation, revolutionary movement and the state mode of production

What happens to art when it is put in the service of oppositional political practices? Does the politicisation of art destroy its autonomy status and consequently weaken its potential resistance to the forces of capitalist exchange? The premise of avant-garde praxis is that it is class struggle that mediates the relation between reflexive and experimental autonomy and the heteronomy of everyday life. There is no sense then of thinking of the sociality we are familiar with as the arbiter of avant-garde values. If the avant garde does anything, it breaks with the established circuits of the art world, along with its usual methods of art description, evaluation and consecration. The exhibition *A World Where Many Worlds Fit*, a presentation of anti-globalisation protest artworks curated by the Austrian artist Oliver Ressler, provided an opportunity to reflect on the stakes of contemporary anti-capitalist art, especially as the latter coalesced around the anti-globalisation movement. First shown in the context of the 2008 Taipei Biennial and in 2010 at the Foreman Art Gallery of Bishop's University in Lenoxville, Quebec, the exhibition was dedicated to artistic practices that are in solidarity with the social movements that mobilised against the summits of the world's leading institutions of neoliberal globalisation – the WTO, the World Bank, the IMF, the G8 (G7) and G20.[1]

The artists included in *A World Where Many Worlds Fit* were Zanny Begg, Christopher Delaurenti, Noel Douglas, Etcétera, Petra Gerschner, John Jordan, Oliver Ressler, RTMark, Allan Sekula, Gregory Sholette, Nuria Vila + Marcelo Expósito and Dmitri Vilensky. The Quebec version of the exhibition also involved the Montreal collective ATSA (Action Terroriste Socialement Acceptable). The most prominent piece was created by Zanny Begg: a wall painting timeline that depicts the anti-globalisation movement, from the WTO protests in Seattle in 1999 up to 2008. Embedded in this work is hers and Ressler's video, *This Is What Democracy Looks Like!*, which includes interviews with activists and intellectuals who participated in the 2001 World Economic Forum in Salzburg, Austria. RTMark presented pink, blue, black and purple mirrors like those that had been used as direct intervention tools during the 2001 G8 summit protests in Genoa. ATSA presented black baby strollers from the 2001 Summit of the Americas in Québec City. Graphic material by Noel Douglas, including banners, posters, t-shirts, books and magazines, showcases the English artist's contributions to various protests, including the 2003 demonstrations against the Iraq War. A mixed media installation by John Jordan documents the actions of the Clandestine Insurgent Rebel Clown Army during the 2005 G8 summit in Gleneagles, complete with the map that was used by activists to plan their operations. A video by Nuria Vila + Marcelo Expósito documents the protest activity of Spanish pink bloc activists and a video by Chto Delat member Dmitry Vilensky commiserates with the Russian demonstrators who were corralled into the Kirov Stadium so as to be prevented from disrupting the 2006 G8 summit in Saint Petersburg. Photographs by Allan Sekula and Petra Gerschner illuminate the 1999 Seattle demonstrations against the WTO and the 2007 G8 summit in Heiligendamm. For those who wish to look back nostalgically on the Seattle protest, Gregory Sholette produced a collectible action figurine that is based on a newspaper photograph of a protester wanted by the police.

There is a reluctance among contemporary socially engaged artists like those involved in this exhibition to refer to themselves or to their work as avant-garde. There are no doubt various reasons for this but one of them

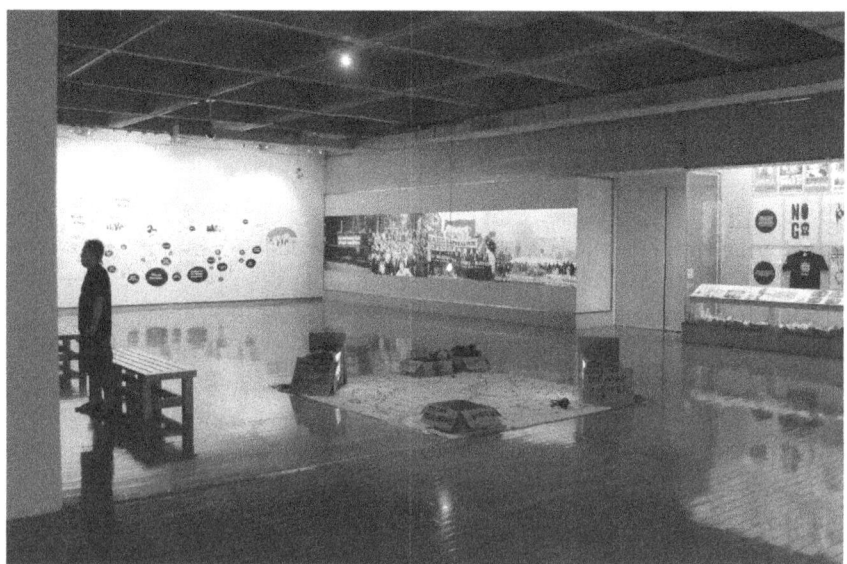

Oliver Ressler, *A World Where Many Worlds Fit*. A section on the counter-globalization movement curated by Oliver Ressler, Taipei Biennial, 2008. Courtesy of Oliver Ressler.

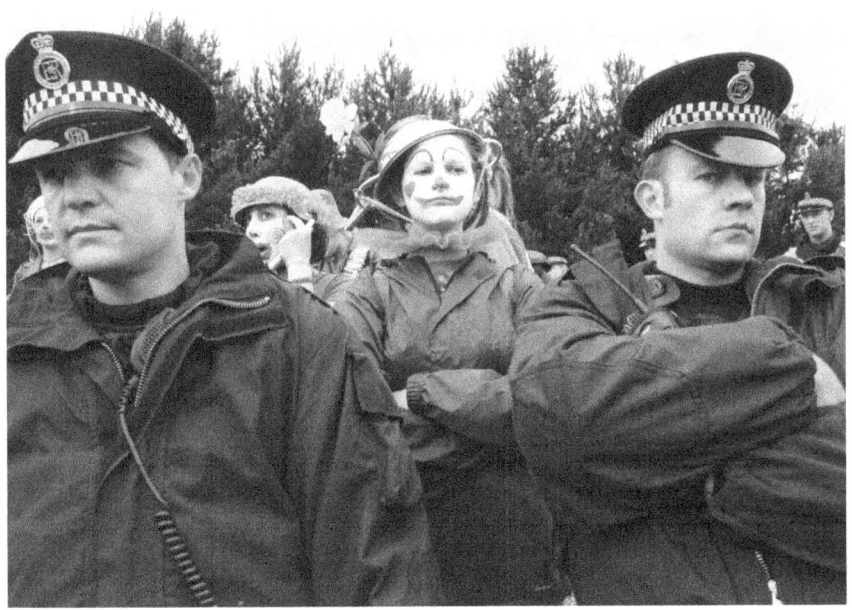

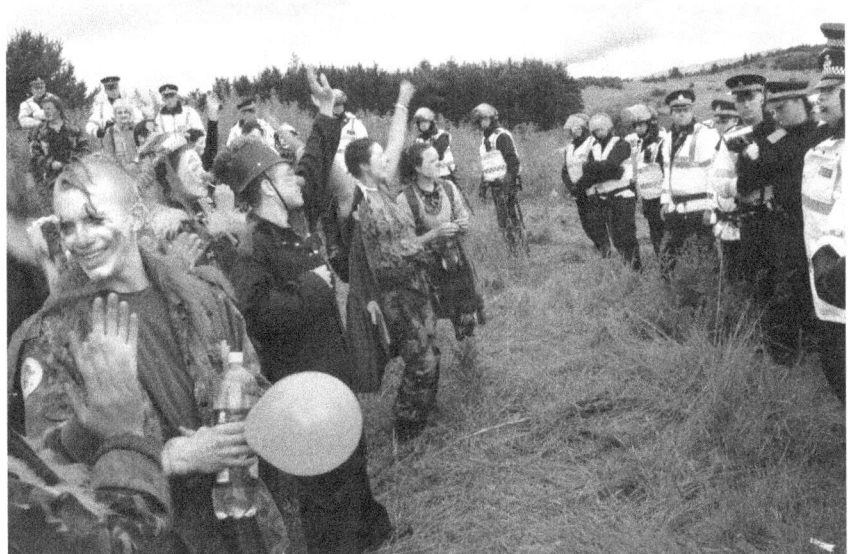

Police encircle the *Clandestine Insurgent Rebel Clown Army* during the days of action against the G8, Gleneagles, Scotland, July 2005. Shown as part of John Jordan's installation in *A World Where Many Worlds Fit*, 2008–10. Photos by Ian Teh. Courtesy of John Jordan.

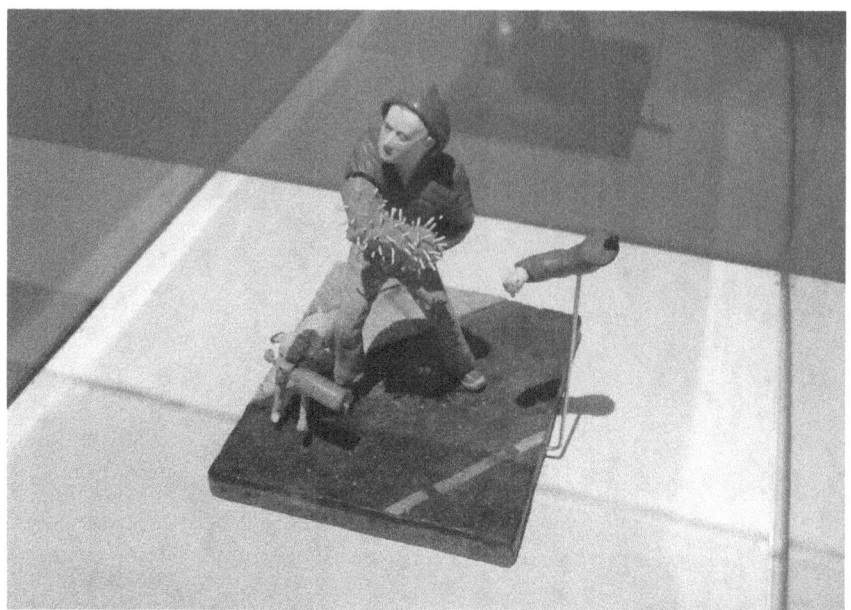

Gregory Sholette, *WTO Action Collectible*, 2002–13. Action figure shown in
A World Where Many Worlds Fit, 2008–10. The action figure comes with a
poster that refers to the police tactic of labelling unarmed protesters as violence-
prone, as was the case in Seattle in 1999. The figure comes with a removable
action arm useful for deflecting tear gas and a mascot carrying a Molotov
Cocktail, a reference to militant political protest in the United States.
Courtesy of Gregory Sholette.

relates very specifically to the history of Marxism-Leninism and the corruption of communist parties and party artists as Leninism transmogrified into
Stalinism. The art world equivalent to this narrative can be found in Nicos
Hadjinicolaou's account of the ideology of avant-gardism, which begins with
the early utopian phase of socialism. The Saint-Simonians considered artists
to be the de facto avant garde of society. Their mission was to propagate
the most advanced ideas of the day. This phase is followed by the tendency
to consider only certain advanced artistic practices as avant gardes within
the restricted field of art, those that lead the way forward in a sucession
of art movements. According to Hadjinicolaou, who otherwise dismissed
avant-gardism as middle-class ideology, the notion of an artistic avant garde
comes about at around the same time as the Bolshevik Revolution. From that
moment, left-wing tendencies of artistic avant-gardism that reject apoliticism
in art, as well as the quest for novelty in the service of nationalism, opt for
the adherence either to a political vanguard or to an artistically as well as
politically revolutionary tendency.[2] Referring to this process more generally

as 'modernism,' Raymond Williams rejected the postmodern ideology that presumed that the avant-garde movements' anti-bourgeois stance died as they gradually achieved 'comfortable integration' in transclass and transnational capitalism.[3] The exceptions in contemporary praxis, according to Williams, are radical anti-bourgeois artistic movements that are both cultural and political. The notion of political radicalism shifts, however, in the case of contemporary practices where politics no longer relates exclusively to class struggle and is rather conceived as everyday and micropolitical. One can now be political by riding a bicycle or going vegan.[4]

In the absence of any radical socialist tendencies among new social movements, the prospects for anti-capitalist articulation by contemporary engaged artists seem delimited by more pragmatic kinds of 'biopractice' like relational aesthetics, community art and ameliorative activist art. Mikkel Bolt Rasmussen applauds micro-utopian relational aesthetics for leading the way beyond the postmodern critique of representation but finds that the corresponding forms of socially engaged art, interventionist art and tactical media have otherwise neglected the avant gardes' historical-philosophical orientation. The best candidates for an avant garde today, he surmises, are those practices that focus on activist networks in the context of anti-globalisation and which organise new creative protest strategies along with extra-artistic social movement actors.[5] While the works in *A World Where Many Worlds Fit* would seem to reject what Rasmussen refers to as a reformist and post-revolutionary 'art of modest proposals,' they do not fit the model of a typical leftist avant garde, as Hadjinicolaou understood it, in either its mode of political organisation or in its avoidance of a singularly artistic notion of supersession. The task of art theory, then, with regard to such practices, is to engage in the struggles that animate the movement.

In his statement for the exhibition, Ressler emphasises the links between the 'movement of the movements' and the workerist themes of non-hierarchical, autonomous organisation and the collective intelligence of the multitude.[6] Despite the plurality of left-wing organisations that assembled in Seattle and at later summit protests – anarchists, social democrats, union locals, civil society organisations, NGOs, church groups, anti-poverty groups, environmentalists, Marxist-Leninists, Trotskyists – it would appear that anarchist and horizontalist politics best characterise the anti- and alter-globalisation protest movements of the late 1990s and first decade of the 2000s. The key text of the movement was Michael Hardt and Antonio Negri's *Empire*, a work that takes an autonomist Marxist approach to the communist emphasis on the most advanced mode of production, level of technology and new class compositions. *Empire* brought international attention to the EuroMayDay movement, inaugurating in Europe and North America a new language with which to define struggles around cognitive and creative labour, and set in motion a series of concepts

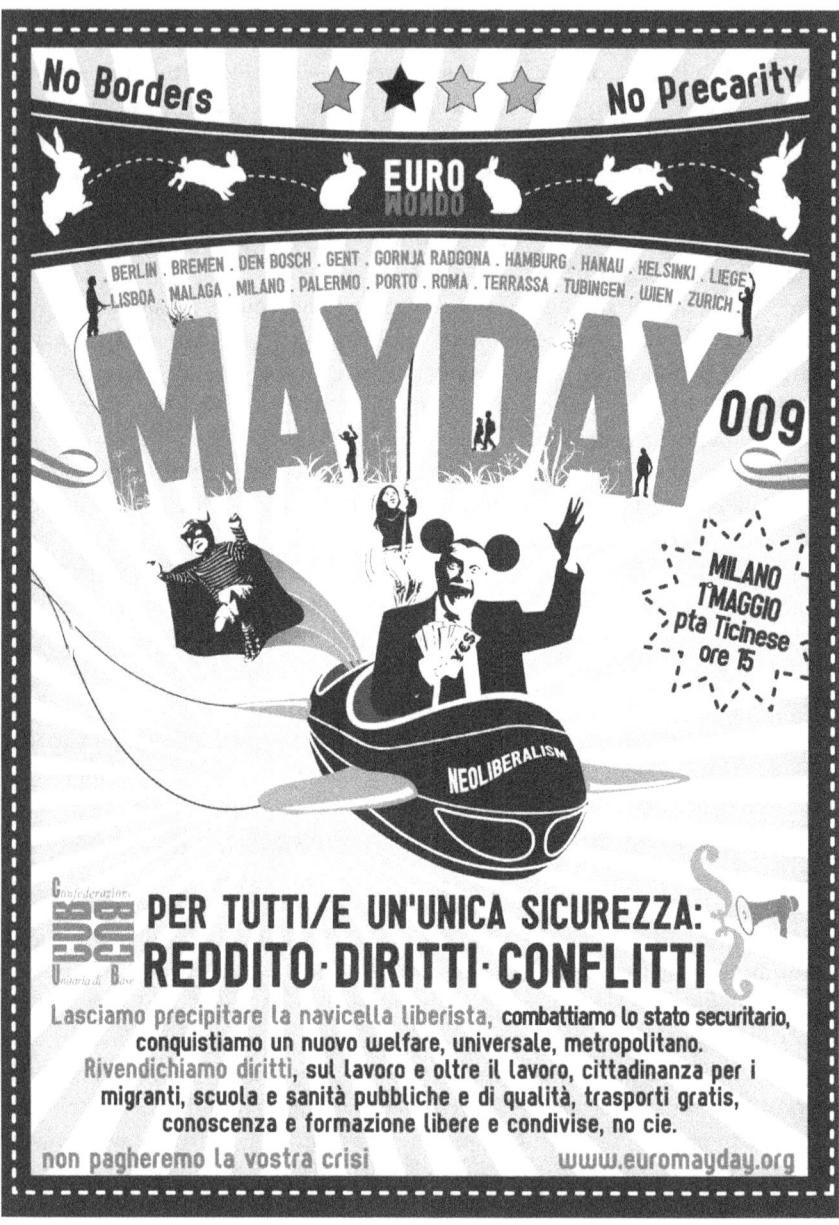

EuroMayDay poster, 2009. May Day actions established in Milan in 2001 became EuroMayDay in 2004 and spread throughout Europe, bringing together the unemployed, students and squatters, the precarious and people of all backgrounds to fight neoliberal policies. Formerly available at www.euromayday.org.

like the new political subjectivity of the multitude, cooperating humanity, constituent activity, mass intellectuality, the social factory, immaterial labour, affective labour and nomadic production.[7] Inspired by workerist theories, alter-globalisation activists argue that post-Fordist modes of production bring with them a new mode of thinking that obliges us to reconsider some of the core concepts of Marxism and the analysis of industrial labour. Today, instead of an organised revolutionary proletariat, an undefined, decentred multitude of struggles responds to capitalist directives through a counter-power that is limitless, non-hierarchical and nomadic.

Needless to say, post-Fordist globalisation has facilitated flows of production that lead to new forms of interdependence and cooperation, but it has also helped to create, especially in developed countries, new conditions of exploitation and self-precarisation. Isabell Lorey argues that under conditions of neoliberal governmentality, self-precarisation appears to cultural workers as a choice, a normalised 'economisation of life' associated with liberal ideals of individual autonomy, lifestyle choice and even deviance or freedom from institutions. Such imaginary self-relating and self-discipline masks the fact that the mass precarisation of labour is 'forced on people who fall out of normal labour conditions.'[8] In the age of post-Fordist capitalism, and with an increasingly educated population, control is managed through the productivity of sociality itself. The point of contention here is whether it is the productivity of the immaterial worker that is valorised in excess of capital, or whether this now fetishised nomadic labour of directly participatory energies functions as the very engine of economic transformation. Does the eclipse of the welfare state and the commodification of social relations not then come to operate as the biocapitalist basis of political activism? Some have argued that the theories of post-Fordist or 'immaterial' cultural production that are associated with the work of Paolo Virno, Maurizio Lazzarato and others, effectuate a certain depoliticisation, in particular, as communicative semio-capitalism is taken to be social cooperation as such, and as it sometimes presumes the obsolescence of the Marxist approach to the value theory of labour.[9]

Although Marx long ago described the forms of social cooperation that are a feature of the capitalist mode of production and capital accumulation, the autonomist theory that inspires today's movement of the movements asks us to take the advanced stages of post-Fordist capitalism as already communistic, a virtual communism in which immaterial work prefigures a world of equality and freedom from toil. There are different ways in which the autonomist approach both departs from and remains within the perspective of Marxism. The workerist concept of general intellect, for instance, is in some ways more totalising than what Marx envisioned since it is tautological, conflating the capitalist mode of production with capitalism's self-negating limit, thereby avoiding the question of political praxis that was central to *The Communist Manifesto*.

Regardless, today's class compositions are taken to embody the emergence of the multitude as the excess of the social relations of production. As the multitude recognises nothing in itself that is more than itself, its signifier collapses into its signified. The movement thus comes to favour communal and biopolitical self-relating. In the form of networked decentralisation, the movement tends to avoid the task of universalising leftist ideology and instead organises people around the critique of existing institutions. Autonomist Marxism and activist post-politics therefore tend to deny the contradictoriness of this self-relating by arguing against universality. It proposes instead an exodus from the universal towards new assemblages comprised of 'dividuals' and singularities.[10]

From a Marxist point of view, contemporary capitalism not only provokes resistance, it also requires participation and cooperation. We can therefore understand the kinds of competition that characterise contemporary social relations as cooperation in reverse. Cooperation and networked sociality become capitalist competition by other means. In *Capital*, Marx argued that capitalist productivity leads to the self-valorisation of capital. Efficiency in labour requires that large numbers of people work jointly in order to engender a revolution in the means of production. As classical political economists understood, the cooperation of wage-labourers finds its externality in competition between capitalists. To think that autonomous workers and activists can cooperate among themselves without there being a reciprocal effect at the level of capitalist production is to ignore the self-revolutionising power of capital to overcome resistance as well as ideological competition. If it was once possible for factory workers to recognise that their cooperation is 'a plan drawn up by the capitalist,' this is perhaps less apparent to today's networked entrepreneur or immaterial worker-activist.[11] As Luc Boltanski and Eve Chiapello argue in *The New Spirit of Capitalism*, the shift to post-Fordist forms of organisation that emphasise initiative, teamwork, egalitarianism and networked participation, represents a shift away from the hierarchical and administrative forms of managerial capitalism.[12] Along with this, the communist state planning of the Cold War period appears conservative in contrast to today's decentralised production.[13] The rights and benefits that might accrue for workers in post-Fordist societies are expropriated by the ruling class of plutocrats as the left depoliticises the historical processes that led to the new economy and contemplates the end of ideology.

Why have new social movements renounced the strategies and political theories of the so-called old left? The following statement by the Peruvian peasant leader Hugo Blanco is emblematic of the 'postmodern' features of today's fragmented left:

> One thing Trotsky said that has been vindicated is that if the working class doesn't take power from the bureaucracy, the bureaucracy will be displaced by

capitalism. This is what has happened. Today the principal directors of the Soviet Communist Party are the big neoliberals in Russia. Trotsky said that either the working class will triumph, or the bourgeoisie will, that the bureaucracy is not a social class and has no historical future. Unfortunately, its power was not broken by the working class, so it was broken by the bourgeoisie. But now that there is no Stalinism, why do I have to be a Trotskyist? I don't feel the same imperative. Of course, there are things I have learned from Marx, things I have learned from Lenin, things I have learned from Trotsky – and from other revolutionaries, from Rosa Luxemburg, from Gramsci, from Che Guevara. But now I do not feel it is logical to form a Trotskyist party. The youth who organized the conference yesterday – they want answers to the questions of *today*. We don't have to resuscitate old debates from the last century. It is enough to still believe that another world is possible. I am old, and if I can teach something about Marx, Lenin and Trotsky and so on, this is something I can contribute. I still believe in standing up and struggling and not pleading with the government, so in a sense I am still a Trotskyist. But I don't feel the need to say, 'Listen everybody, this Trotskyism is the answer!' And when I speak of the *indigenas* of the Amazon as the vanguard, I do not mean it in the Marxist-Leninist sense, that others should copy their methods. And when I speak to indigenous peoples, I speak of 'collectivism,' not 'communism.'[14]

Blanco's statement, however well-adjusted it is to local struggles, not to mention *A World Where Many Worlds Fit*, defines the false choice between collectivism and class struggle. Aside from the question of what form communism can have today, the point is not, as Blanco argues, that we have to choose between communism and collectivism, especially since the forms of left solidarity in Latin America remain pressured by global capitalism, but that the option of communism is simply no longer desired by most leftists. Moreover, collectivism is less a choice and increasingly a necessity for survival. Postmodern leftists can replay the usual denunciations of bourgeois individualism but what post-Fordism demands is not individualism, it is absolute determinism, now defined in various ways as deterritorialisation, flexibilisation, connectivity, and so on. The option is not simply between conformity and individuality either. In today's post-political context, there is an ideological injunction against the choice of the vanguard party and its avant-garde cultural projects. The very prohibition on the prohibition, the fact that we more often than not cannot even talk about this as an issue, makes it so that all we can do is present these options without taking the risk of choosing the wrong strategy. Much of today's activist citizenship thus has the features of what Slavoj Žižek calls an empty gesture. As he puts it: 'the system is compelled to allow for possibilities of choices which must never actually take place, since their occurrence would cause the system to disintegrate, and the function of the unwritten rules is precisely to prevent the actualisation of these choices formally allowed by the system.'[15] If the slogan of the Situationist International and the *enragés* of May 68 was 'Beyond Washington and Moscow,' one should now simply ask whether it is possible to go beyond the current global neoliberal hegemony. What then is the status of the political in a world that proscribes the organisational structures that have historically advanced the class struggle? This is a different matter from advocating collectivism and local solidarity infrastructures.

Against post-political orthodoxies, it becomes necessary to consider that the series of struggles associated with new social movements and the postmodern critique of meta-narratives challenge our ability to think in terms of the needed revolutionary change. The tendencies and practices that emphasise difference, dispersal, decentredness and fluidity mitigate the view that revolution is a total, inexhaustible phenomenon. Analysis of the totality of the social space is replaced with the partiality of contingent struggles, with libertarian practices and with thinking that is conjunctural and indeterminate. Instead of a leftist metapolitics, we are asked to confront the various problems of class exploitation, global warming, agribusiness, immigration and militarism as issues that can be treated separately. The current renewal of leftist solidarity since the rise of the anti-globalisation movement therefore also causes us to question the potential of grassroots, decentred, networked and non-hierarchical movements to challenge political institutions. Postmodern academics, meanwhile, continue to put their hopes in the various forms of anti-humanism. What the market economy model of academic critical and cultural production leads us to is therefore not only the problem of choice, but the very question: what is a revolutionary subject?

We have come to believe that the working class is no longer *the* revolutionary subject, who, as a result of the internal contradictions of capitalism, will lead the way to communism and the eventual withering of the state. Today's world of institutionalised cultural activism is anxious to demonstrate affinity with 'all of the above' struggles, and so has a tendency to foresake political ideology and replace it with a free-floating subject in a state of becoming, a cipher of undecidability overdetermined by the networked flows that are regulated by the rhythms of capitalist production and digital information. Instead of working through the challenges that are posed by a universal political project, we turn to questions of bodily affect, transculturalism, hybridity and performativity. The problem, I would argue, is that emancipation begins to function as a by-product of the dominant social order. If the movement of the movements has any momentum, it is in its potential to rethink postmodern pieties and reclaim the space of critical praxis, which in part must work to occupy the universities, publishing companies, newspapers, web services and various other instruments of the general intellect. To pretend that we can win the struggle in the streets is to ignore the broad layers of petty-bourgeois workers who form capitalism's reserve army. Despite the organised power of corporate and state capital, it is this global 'classless class' for which 'there is no ideological relation' that has become the de facto hegemonic class in developed countries; and it is this class that has shaped the lifestyle and identity concerns of the vast majority of activists. The fact that the global petty bourgeoisie has failed to serve the interests of the world's excluded does not prevent its culture from shaping most of the alternative and independent spaces that we would otherwise look to for political renewal.

The ideological success of the anti-globalisation movement and horizontal-ist activism resulted in the renewal of debate among left factions. For example, Alex Callinicos, International Secretary of the Socialist Workers Party in Britain, debated with Antonio Negri on the subject of 'working class or mul-titude' during the 2003 European Social Forum in Paris. Callinicos and auton-omist theorist John Holloway addressed divergences between workerism and revolutionary socialism at the Marxism 2008 festival. As well, the conference 'On the Idea of Communism,' which was held at the Birkbeck Institute in March 2009, brought together some of the leading theorists of the movement to work through past disputes and put concepts like multitude and commons to the test.[16] Of course none of these discussions make any sense outside of the practical activity of the political movements themselves, whether they are organised as networked and autonomous, as trade unions, NGOs, or as traditional political parties.

Despite the long tradition of revolutionary thought and experience that we have to draw upon, the movement currently tends towards horizontalist anar-chism, in part due to the success of academic post-structuralism and the failure of democratic labour parties to challenge the neoliberal status quo. The issue of the day, then, has to do with organisation. The title of Begg and Ressler's film, *What Would It Mean to Win?* (2008), one of the works in the exhibition, asks us to think about not only the neoliberal world order that we are up against, but how we wish to organise and according to what principles. Its title revisits the slogan of the 1999 Seattle WTO protests, 'we are winning,' and is also the title of the free newspaper that was handed out at the G8 summit protests in Heiligendamm in June 2007. For this issue of the journal *Turbulence*, fourteen groups and individuals were asked to answer the question 'what would it mean to win?'[17] The cover of this issue shows the busy, swarming activity of bees. In *Capital*, Marx famously contrasted the planned (theoretical) activity of the architect to the unconscious (practical) activity of bees. Does this magazine cover and the movement's desire for collective, bee-like militancy not belie a connection to the avant-garde imagery of revolutionary communism? Brian Holmes suggests instead that today's precarious generation takes the globalisa-tion process itself as the only vanguard.[18] As such, the bee and swarm metaphor reflects the Deleuzian presuppositions of schizo-capitalism. On the one hand, we have the conjunction of singularity and multiplicity, which stand as the

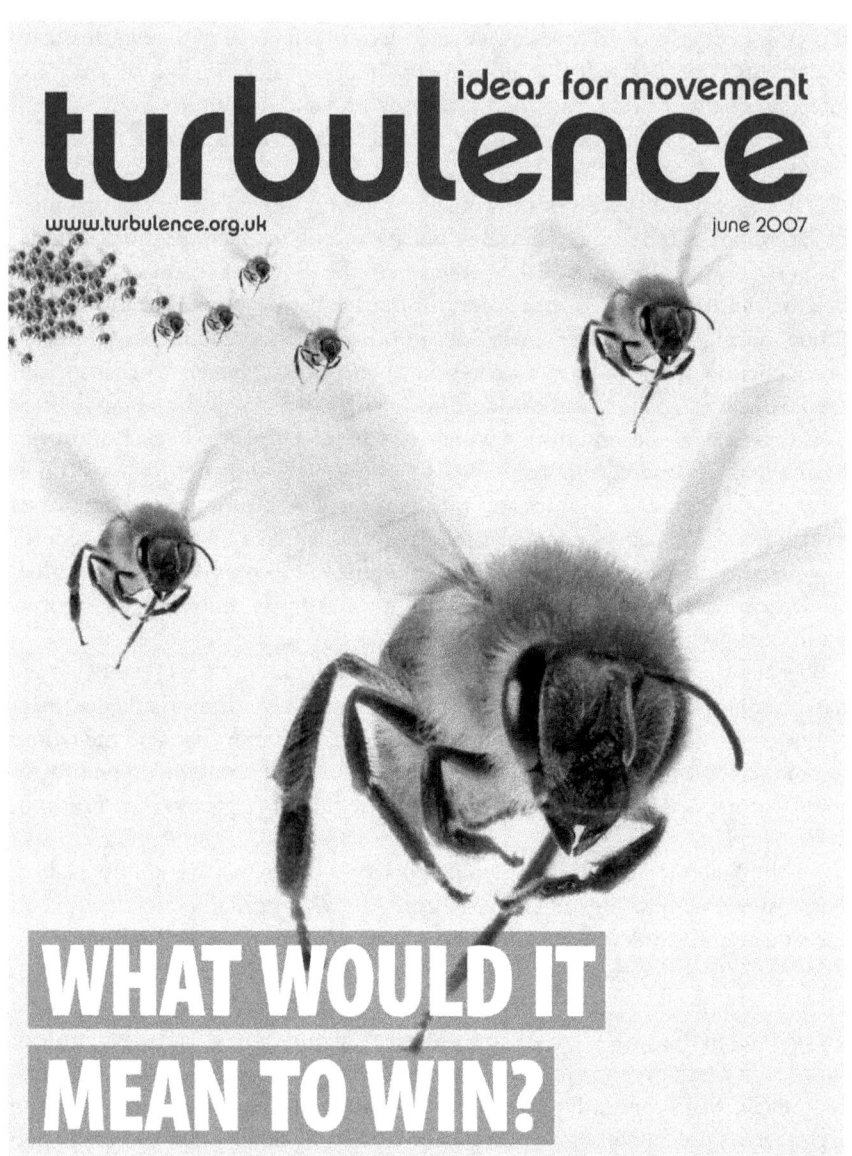

Cover of the June 2007 issue of the magazine *Turbulence*, issue 1, *What Would It Mean to Win?*, a free newspaper distributed at the blockades and alternative summits that mobilised against the G8 summit in Heiligendamm. Design by Brian Layng. Courtesy of Rodrigo Nunes and David Harvie. www.turbulence.org.uk.

root concepts for the autonomist notion of the multitude. For Hegel, the singular does not relate to the concrete so much as to the determinations of the concept of the infinite in its historical temporalisation. In the *Grundrisse*, Marx warned against the inability to think of historical forms as anything other than 'the latest form of historical development,' and with regard to 'the previous one as steps leading up to itself,' a hubris that made the contemporary era unable to criticise itself. The present, like the value form, leads a tautological, antediluvian existence.[19] For this reason, Alain Badiou argues that multiplicity is not available as a consistent delimitation but as a process of 'limitless self-differentiation,' a condition for thought's freedom from determination and calculation. The multiple is therefore to be distinguished from vitalism. Here, neutral multiples substitute for pure multiples, undermining the 'undecidability' and 'difference' theses of contemporary post-structuralism and replacing them with 'paradoxical multi-dimensional configurations.' The undecidable is rather an 'errant excess' that undermines the opposition between virtual and actual. According to Badiou, 'Deleuze has no way of *thinking* singularity other than by classifying the different ways in which singularity is not ontologically singular.'[20] In our case, in order to deploy the intuition of the virtual, one is obliged to deploy an analogy: the movement = bees. But a universal politics should have a greater idea of itself than the mere embrace of globalisation processes. In Marxian terms, the planned activity of the architect, in contrast to the busyness of swarming worker bees, offers the political alternative of a universal programme.

The editors of *Turbulence* argue that while they believe it is not possible to represent a movement as complex as ours, it is possible and indeed necessary to move beyond the Leninist politics of 1917 and the anarchism of 1936, and to carry on with investigations of contemporary political realities. The variety of progressive movements in the last decades – in Brazil, Bolivia, Argentina, Chiapas and Venezuela especially, and everywhere solidarity movements have resisted and offered alternatives to neoliberal free-market policies – indicates that people are experimenting with alternatives within and outside of representative democracy. However, the editors of *Turbulence*, some of whom are featured in the Begg and Ressler film, hold a number of convictions that place restrictions on a revolutionary left movement.[21] While most agree with the need for more self-management, more ownership and worker control of the means of production, more action on global warming and production that takes the local and the ethical into consideration, today's post-politics avoids acting and thinking at the level of state bureaucracy and electoral politics. The other question that arises is how to unite the left.

A World Where Many Worlds Fit provides another occasion to ask the questions that function as chapter headings in the Begg and Ressler film: What would it mean to win? Who are we? What is our power? It might be instructive here to consider a strange occurrence that accompanied the G20 protests in Pittsburgh in September 2009. On this occasion, Barack Obama criticised the protesters with the suggestion that 'focusing on concrete, local, immediate issues that have an impact on people's lives is what really makes a difference and ... having protests about abstractions [like] global capitalism ... is not really going to make a difference.'[22] Obama's critique of decentralised grassroots progressivism echoes the ideological presuppositions of those same activists who focus on the concrete issues that affect people's lives while putting off bigger, macropolitical and ideological issues. Despite the growing proletarianisation of the world's population, we hold to the now orthodox idea that there is no privileged agent of social change that can become conscious of its historical mission. To take one example, John Jordan, a participant in *A World Where Many Worlds Fit*, and who is well-known for instigating the affinity groups Reclaim the Streets and the Laboratory of Insurrectionary Imagination, writes in *The Guardian* that autonomous peasant movements like those in Argentina are freed from ideologies, 'liberated from abstract dreams of a pending revolution and futile dreams of taking power and running governments.'[23]

Is the control of state power a desirable goal on the left today? This issue represents one of the major rifts on the left. Most would agree with Franco Berardi that the post 9/11 and post-Genoa summit years witnessed the entrenchment of economic austerity, surveillance, police repression and global warfare, as capitalism responded ever more violently to any challenge to its hegemony.[24] In *Change the World Without Taking Power*, Holloway argues that the exercise of anti-power can help people reclaim human capacities and energies that are repressed by capitalism.[25] Arguing that there is no outside to capitalism, Holloway and other autonomist thinkers look for moments of subversion within capitalism, which includes subversion of the categories of Marxian analysis. Revolutionary socialists, in contrast, argue that the desertion and evasion of power leaves it in the hands of forces that are undemocratic and unaccountable, and thus the long march through the institutions remains a necessary task. According to Callinicos, anti-capitalism is not merely a problem of organisation, but a matter of political struggle. He writes:

> [Democracy] requires a political struggle within the new forms of workers' power to win the majority to the recognition that, unless the capitalist state is dismantled, sooner or later it will use its coercive power to crush the mass movement. This is the supreme function of a mass revolutionary party: not to seize power for itself, but to win the argument that the new democracy should storm the last strongholds of capitalist power ... Revolution *has* to be about seizing power, because otherwise the capitalist state will survive to become a launching pad for counter-revolution.[26]

Callinicos' defence of revolutionary struggle challenges one of the central tenets of the anti-globalisation movement. The main worry in this regard is that the means of such struggle would be violent and subject to centralised control. According to Žižek, the critique of capitalism implicates the left in the universality of that contradiction. He writes: 'What, today, prevents the radical questioning of capitalism itself is precisely *the belief in the democratic form of the struggle against capitalism.*'[27] In other words, the intervention against capitalism should be political and not essentially economic. In this sense, Žižek argues that autonomist Marxists are too orthodox when they assume that emancipation is on the side of materialist immanentism. When capitalism proves to be the engine of revolutionary social change, he argues, Marxism responds with the view that only a communist party apparatus can maintain modernisation and prevent social disintegration. The example of socialist Venezuela is instructive. Whereas the civil liberties of anti-democratic right-wing media were curbed, poverty was nearly halved in the first six years of the Bolivarian experience.[28]

The relaunching of the macropolitical left in the 2000s led to a reconsideration of concepts of popular democracy, radical organising and revolutionary theory. Distinctions were drawn between the generation of 1968 and the generation of 1989 that grew up with the first war against Iraq and the New World Order that came on the heels of neoconservatism. How much political

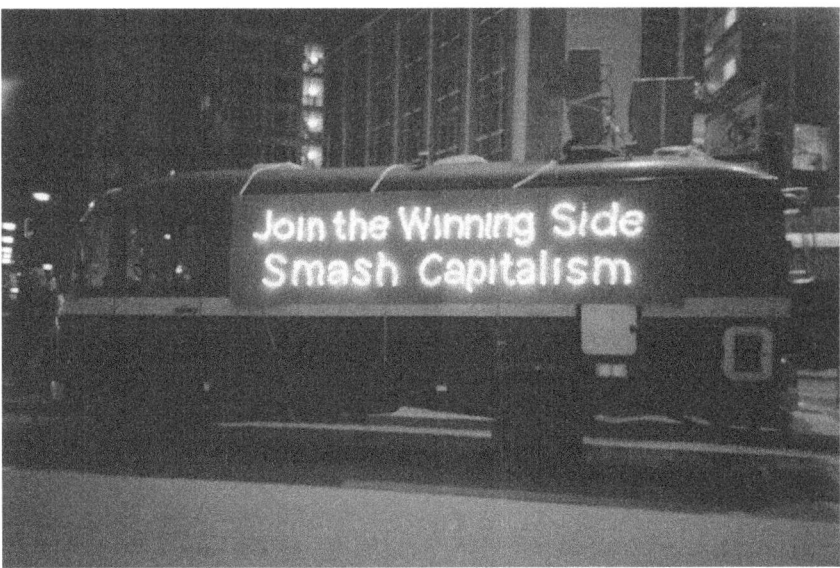

Petra Gerschner, from the slide series *History Is a Work in Process*, 2007–9, shown in *A World Where Many Worlds Fit*, 2008–10. Gerschner was part of the group that created the slogan and the van light-installation that was used at the G8 summit in Heiligendamm, 2007. Courtesy of Petra Gerschner.

energy was channelled towards the fields of 'difference' and 'becoming,' and in the selective elimination of distinctions between the personal and the political, the private and the public, work and play? What have today's artists, activists and intellectuals contributed to the politics of universal emancipation?

In response to the view that we have entered the stage of a truly global era of production, or world system, we should perhaps recall Henri Lefebvre's concept of the state mode of production.[29] For Lefebvre, Stalinism inaugurated a new, fully technocratic state, one that also happens to characterise contemporary neoliberal governance. If we seek to fully confront the meaning of globalisation, and indeed, anti- and alter-globalisation, we should be prepared to consider the ways in which the culturalist intellectual forces that have dominated postmodernist theory disallow what Marx foresaw as the withering of the state as a Hegelian overcoming of contradictions.

The European 'movement of the movements' has an uncanny resemblance to the Hegelian concept of the state as a 'system of systems.'[30] In the second volume of his four-part series *De L'État* – a forgotten precursor to his more familiar writings on the social production of space and the planetary system of late capitalist production – Lefebvre argues that the state form has a logical and practical coherence that goes beyond individuals and specific classes, a coherence that approaches the neoliberal idea of the free market and the Marxist notion of productive activity. The twentieth-century state introduced a shift from the logic of social progress to that of economic growth, overseeing and producing a global surplus based on finance, taxation, loans and militarism. Violence becomes an irrationality that is inherent to the contemporary state in all its theatricality and monumentality, a process that is mystified by the spectacle of elections and political parties, by culture and politics, the environment and population control; in short, by all manner of institutionalised knowledge and criticism. This process, Lefebvre argues, is far more total than those who talk about molecular revolution care to acknowledge. From this rationalisation of knowledge, the Hegelian 'Spirit' passes to the justification of the real. The state overcomes its own contradictions through its conquest of nature and all of human endeavours. It appropriates needs, works and classes; it sweeps in its path all of history, religion, the family, the nation, politics, art and philosophy. An ominous catastrophism marks its limit and its negation: revolution.

Around the same time as his 1970s writings on the state, Lefebvre proposed that any radical break with the state mode of production, what we might otherwise refer to as neoliberal globalisation, involves the thought of Hegel, Marx and Nietzsche.[31] The world is now Hegelian, he argues; knowledge is linked to power and the constraints of global markets. In its political reason, the state subordinates civil society and seeks to establish the parameters of civilisation as we know it. The 'historico-philosophical' mission of the avant garde or of modernism is therefore embodied, as Holmes argues, in the objectivity of bourgeois power, its institutions, its legal, intellectual and financial apparatuses, bureaucracies, its transnational corporations and its orientation to economic growth. Yet this same universe is fully Marxist in people's relation to state planning and the capitalist control of production. For Lefebvre, and contrary to the experience of state socialism, Marxism is not a system, if only because capital is not a system. The question put to us is not whether Marxist political economy adequately describes the current post-Fordist regimes but rather how do the concepts of forces of production, relations of production and ideological superstructures illuminate contemporary contradictions. Human self-creation implies the sense of history, which Marx defined as the proletariat's overcoming of bourgeois ideology through revolutionary class struggle. New social relations and social conflicts prevent the stability of the state mode of production. Violence, whether it is pursued by the state that defends class interests or by the collective power of workers, does not bring about the world we want to see but a world we cannot know in advance. From here Lefebvre passes to Nietzsche, the prophet of despair who viewed history as a series of barbarisms. If God is dead then so is liberal humanism and so is Marx's species being. The struggle of wills is without necessity, rationality or justification. In a world without civilisation, pathology gives rise to nihilism and a cruelty that rejects all forms of transcendent knowledge. Those who are fit to survive in this maelstrom of destruction must renounce what is human in themselves.

Marx famously sought to complete the Hegelian division of social being with the concept of productive activity and with this he announced the critique of the state in its political idealism. Could his rupture with Hegel not also represent the 'movement of the movements' as the product of revolutionary disalienation and a new form of work? If the networked immaterial worker is also a prosumer, someone who produces content as much as he or she consumes information, is the protester not also a feature of the biopolitical state, with its security apparatus and newly militarised police forces? The artists who have participated in the anti-globalisation protests in Seattle, Genoa, Quebec City, Prague, Gleneagles, Buenos Aires, Saint Petersburg, Heiligendamm and elsewhere have created works that correspond to the new assemblages of the protest factory. These works are indeed in excess of democratic idealism and the pluralistic forms of cultural citizenship. They are some of the most advanced forms of precarious art work we have today. The state's cruelty towards protesters and anti-capitalist organising proves, Lefebvre argues, that the state is a living entity that harbours within itself a will to fight to the death. Our shocked reaction to the violence of the state confronts us with what Žižek has identified as the psychoanalytic truth of Hegel, the sickness unto death that underscores the Freudian concept of drive, the *passage à l'acte* against which the state appears as both an obstacle and a condition of possibility. Whatever vanguard political organisations we have or do not have today, they are the complement to the avant-garde artists who are its moving shadow. The utopian socialism that gave us the concept of the avant garde has been eclipsed by the utopia of the state mode of production on a global scale. If the working class is not to become a new subject, Lefebvre argues, then the avant garde will do so through the deployment of a pure act of creation with universal dimensions: the totality of what is possible and the refusal of alienation.

2

A brief history of Occupy Wall Street

The bourgeoisie, wherever it has got the upper hand, has put an end to all feudal, patriar-chal, idyllic relations. It has pitilessly torn asunder the motley feudal ties that bound man to his 'natural superiors' and has left remaining no other nexus between man and man than naked self-interest, than callous 'cash payment.'
– Karl Marx and Friedrich Engels, *The Communist Manifesto*

The Occupy Wall Street demonstrations began September 17, 2011. According to *Adbusters*, the magazine that is credited with having sparked the Occupy event, 5,000 people assembled in the financial district of Lower Manhattan on this day, held a people's assembly and set up an encampment in Zuccotti Park on Liberty Street.[1] Modelled on the assemblies of the Spanish *indignados*, a people's assembly was to be held at 3 p.m. at One Chase Manhattan Plaza and was to continue, *Adbusters* declared, 'until our one demand is agreed upon by all.'[2] Before this, in the July issue, *Adbusters* printed a double-page poster that became the initial call to occupy Wall Street. Almost immediately, activists began to organise general assemblies in New York City in anticipation of the occupations. A video was also put out by the hacktivist group Anonymous and was viewed by as many as 100,000 people before YouTube removed it from circulation. It was hoped that as many as 20,000 people would show up on the 17th and the Department of Homeland Security went so far as to warn banks of potential mayhem. The National Lawyers' Guild was prepared to aid pro-testers with legal advice and a telephone support system was established. The revolutionary organisation of the masses in Tahrir Square and the *acampadas* of Spain provided the model for a leaderless, nonviolent movement that like the revolts of the Arab Spring could pose a challenge to Wall Street bankers, Senators, Congressmen, wealthy campaign donors, lobbyists, overpaid CEOs and Forbes 500 billionaires, by simply setting up tents, peaceful barricades and kitchens, and by organising people's assemblies that could focus on popular political demands. Echoing an articled by the Nobel Prize-winning economist

Occupy Wall Street poster (2011) created by #occupytogether, an independent group of activists working to help people get involved in the Occupy movement.

Joseph Stiglitz, *Adbusters* declared that the 99% will no longer tolerate the greed and corruption of the 1%.[3] Anticipating the 2012 US presidential election, *Adbusters* proposed the possible demand of 'One citizen. One dollar. One vote.'

From the outset, Occupy Wall Street would seem to be concerned primarily with radical left politics. However, writing for the *Adbusters Blog*, Nathan Schneider cited Alexa O'Brien, founder of the US Days of Rage, who argued that OWS has no distinct ideological platform, something, she added, that is typical of the Internet generation. What is going to save us, she argued, is more of a process than an ideology. Schneider, for his part, recognised in OWS something of *Adbusters'* anti-consumer culture jamming aesthetic: 'What's drawing people to Wall Street on Saturday sometimes seems to be an aesthetic more than anything, a longing to see Wall Street full of the people whose concerns its operations have been blind to, and who are ready to get their due. But it's an aesthetic with teeth.'[4] Indeed, OWS is a cultural as well as a political movement. Its political orientation, however, is wary of recuperation by any one specific political tradition, as well as by the established trade unions and political parties. The overall concern of the movement is with the loss of the commons and the creation of autonomous spaces where people can relate to each other as non-consumers. The encampments and their various forms signal a rage that needs no other justification than the perspective of organised resistance that it brings into view.

In an earlier historical conjuncture, the commons was referred to in a more general sense as 'everyday life' within modernity. In our own times, modernity reads more specifically as globalisation. For all of the changes in automation and information technologies, the features of modernity in late capitalism remain largely the same. Everyday life is alienated and social interactions are lived according to the rhythms of commodity exchange.[5] Regardless, the everyday offers the possibility of something that is not reducible to bureaucratically controlled existence. OWS is the everyday life of our moment, pre-packaged by *Adbusters* yet indicating a lived experience that not only can keep up with everything that is wrong with Wall Street, but can act as an immanent critique of everything else. Lefebvre's theory of everyday life exposed the specialised ways of understanding society and called for an interdisciplinarity of investigation. All of this was so that the everyday could be politicised and made the basis of a permanent revolution.

In these terms, it is possible to think of the OWS movement as a critique of everyday life under global capitalism. As Jodi Dean argues, the movement's disruption of public space asserts a contradiction that 'opens up cuts through democracy as the real of class antagonism.'[6] Dean argues in a Žižekian manner that the Occupy movement disrupts the capitalist fantasy that denies the antagonism on which it is built, the division, she says, 'between those who have to sell their labor power to survive and those who do not, between those who not only have no choice but to sell their labor power but nonetheless cannot … and those who command, steer, and gamble upon the resources, fortunes, and futures of the rest of us.'[7] It is fair to say and to reflect on the fact that OWS was and is an unfinished project. The observations I make in the following are a tribute to those who undertake the immense task of disalienating our everyday lives from the malevolent planning of our servitude and suffering.

Class war?

At a voter rally with Republican presidential candidate Mitt Romney on October 4, 2011, Romney said about OWS: 'I think it's dangerous – this class warfare.'[8] Another candidate, Herman Cain, said to an audience of supporters: 'Don't blame Wall Street, don't blame the big banks; if you don't have a job and you're not rich, blame yourself! It's not a person's fault because they succeed; it is a person's fault if they failed. And this is why I don't understand these demonstrations and what it is that they're looking for.'[9] There is of course a difference between the ways that capitalists and communists understand class inequality. Whereas for the former, class is an index of two different kinds of people, winners and losers, for the latter class is a permanent contradiction within the matrix of a society based on the capitalist mode of production.

According to Marx's analysis of capital, the falling rates of profit that are due to capitalist competition and monopoly would gradually lead to the weakening and destruction of capitalism as a social system. For the most part it is this vision that sustained the communism of the Third and Fourth International. In the postwar period and by the mid-1970s, according to Nicos Poulantzas, a so-called 'third way' capitalism was characterised by the augmentation of banking services, commerce and bureaucracy. The growth of unproductive services was related politically to the refutation of Marx's labour theory of value.[10] Throughout the twentieth century, the growth of an intermediary petty-bourgeois class gradually led to the replacement of class struggle with class polarisation, a process in which the new intermediary class and its political offshoots – new social movements – transformed the modes of class reproduction. Regardless, social hierarchy and the divisions of labour continue to exist. As Leon Trotsky anticipated in the 1920s, in contrast to the bourgeoisie, 'the proletariat will [gradually] free itself from its class characteristics and thus cease to be a proletariat.'[11] However, throughout the twentieth century proletarianisation has been accompanied by the development of a 'middle' petty-bourgeois class phenomenon that mediates global capitalist hegemony.

Despite the vast economic inequality that is the focus of OWS, there is a simultaneous transformation of class outlook that cannot be attributed to any successful socialist experiment but that can be attributed to the effects of late capitalism on a global scale. OWS and similar protest movements give a clear indication that there are significant factions of the educated petty bourgeoisie that understand their political and ideological class position as that of workers. The simple reason for this is that the cadres of the new service class know that they do not belong to the bourgeoisie, nor do they identify with its corporate ideology. This is why the former New York City mayor Michael Bloomberg, one of the fifteen wealthiest individuals in the world, could claim that the Occupy protesters were interfering with people's livelihoods on Wall Street. On October 1, after the arrest of 700 protesters, Bloomberg stated:

> The protesters are protesting people who make $40,000 to $50,000 a year and are struggling to make ends meet. That's the bottom line. Those are people that work on Wall Street or in the finance sector … We need the banks, if the banks don't go out and make loans we will not come out of our economy problems, we will not have jobs. And so anything we can do to responsibly help the banks do that, encouraging them to do that, is what we need. I think we spend too much time worrying about how we got into problems as to how we go forward.[12]

Bloomberg forgot to add that these same financial service providers, even if they themselves are being exploited, are nevertheless engaged in class war.

The theme of class war, surprisingly, was given a great deal of lip service in 2011 in the form of the conservative red baiting of the Obama administration. The use of the phrase peaked for a short while after billionaire businessman Warren Buffett wrote his August 14 article for the *New York Times*.[13] In this piece, Buffett warned that too much poverty is not good for the economy but that legislators in Washington nevertheless feel compelled to protect million-aires and billionaires, who pay very little income tax on earnings compared to the working majority. Lower tax rates for the rich have over the last three decades resulted directly in lower job creation. Buffett warned that in its subservience to moneyed interests, Congress had shown itself unable to deal with basic fiscal problems. On September 19, Obama announced that he would work to bring forward what he called the 'Buffett tax,' a tax hike on those who earn more than $1 million per year. Almost as soon as he made this announcement, Paul Ryan, the chairman of the House of Representatives budget committee, reported to Fox News: 'Class warfare may make for good politics, but it makes for rotten economics.'[14] It punishes those people who create jobs, he argued. 'We don't need a system that seeks to prey on people's fears, envy and anxiety. We need a system that creates jobs and innovation and removes these barriers for entrepreneurs to go out and rehire people.'[15] The proposal for the Buffett tax was to be made to the special joint Congressional super committee, which was stacked with Republicans who want to impose deep cuts to social services at all costs. As Republican speaker John Boehner said, 'Tax increases are not a viable option for the joint committee.'[16] In a later speech Obama stated: 'This is not class warfare – it's math. The money is going to have to come from someplace.'[17]

The Buffett tax was presented by the Obama administration as one way to offset the $3 trillion that the government claimed it would cut from the deficit over the next ten years. While $1 trillion could have been saved by ending the war in Afghanistan, both parties preferred to watch Americans fight amongst themselves to see who would shoulder the debt burden – the working majority or the power elite. Given that the US economy was then in recession, placing the burden on the poor would play into prejudicial stereotypes of the unemployed as being undeserving, of university students being too lazy to get real jobs, of immigrants stealing badly needed jobs, and of environmental and other protections being job killers. A report in *The Economist* at the time blew a hole in the media story by explaining that the Buffett tax was an electoral public relations ploy. 'Mr Obama *is* a class warrior,' the report states. 'The trouble is he's on the wrong side.'[18] United States government fiscal and monetary policies serve Wall Street giants and its Federal Reserve creates money to bail out large companies that benefit from loopholes and subsidies. The Buffett Rule that was part of the American Jobs Act was designed to make Obama seem like he was concerned with economic fairness in anticipation of the 2012 elections. According to Patrick Martin, the Rule was nothing more than a suggestion to the Congressional committee, where it had no chance of being implemented. Even if implemented, the Buffett tax would have done almost nothing to shift the burden off of the middle and working classes. Corporations that are sitting on billions of dollars in profits and who nevertheless fire employees are clearly involved in class war. Martin mentions that in the three decades since the 1980s, the income gap between the top one percent and the bottom forty percent has tripled. In 2007, the wealthiest ten percent controlled more than two thirds of the total national wealth in the US.[19] Regardless, Republicans complain of class warfare. Just what is the class project in the United States and how can a radical redistribution of wealth be combined with a political project that would tackle the problems of capitalism?

Class polarisation

The background to the OWS slogan 'We are the 99%' consists of countless studies that have analysed and verified the growth of income gaps worldwide. One particular reference for the slogan is Joseph Stiglitz's article 'Of the 1%, by the 1%, for the 1%,' which was published in the May 2011 issue of *Vanity Fair*. A former chief economist with the World Bank, Stiglitz anticipated the connection between the Arab Spring and the American Autumn: 'Americans have been watching protests against oppressive regimes that concentrated massive wealth in the hands of an elite few. Yet in our own democracy, 1 percent of the people take nearly a quarter of the nation's income – an inequality even the wealthy will come to regret.'[20]

Stiglitz added that the top one percent control forty percent of the wealth. Where did their money come from? Since the 1970s, the working class has seen its income fall by twelve percent and go directly to those at the top. All of this is justified according to 'marginal-productivity theory,' which holds that higher incomes at the top are linked to greater productivity. Despite the overwhelming evidence that this theory is unfounded, those who bring the global economy to ruin are rewarded. Stiglitz argued that because of growing inequality, the US economy would continue to worsen. He argued that whereas talent and effort should be guided towards infrastructure, education, public health and technology, it is too often driven towards finance and speculation. In a bad economy the wealthy are reluctant to invest. Their efforts to break unions are supported by the governments that they help bring to power and the poor are forced to borrow beyond their means. Meanwhile, the corporatisation of the commons destroys health, the environment, labour rights and efforts at world peace. Stiglitz exhorted his readers to imagine a government that would instead provide economic security for workers:

> In recent weeks we have watched people taking to the streets by the millions to protest political, economic, and social conditions in the oppressive societies they inhabit. Governments have been toppled in Egypt and Tunisia. Protests have erupted in Lybia, Yemen and Bahrain. The ruling families elsewhere in the region look nervously from their air-conditioned penthouses – will they be next? They are right to worry … As we gaze out at the popular fervor in the streets, one question to ask ourselves is this: When will it come to America?[21]

There are other ways to explain how and why we have arrived at such high levels of inequality. The noted economist and geographer David Harvey wrote in 2009 that the neoliberal class project has been fairly successful insofar as its goal has been the restoration of class power.[22] The ruling elites decided in the mid-1970s that the burden of the financial crisis at that time was going to be weathered by the working population and not the capitalist class. The US government's pro-Wall Street attitude following the 2008 bailouts indicated that it was repeating the same doctrine that was established in the 1970s, allowing for greater seamlessness between government and big business. Because labour organisation was perceived to be a limit to capital accumulation, it was deemed that it could be controlled through increased immigration, technological transformation and offshoring. Workers have not seen any real gains for the past fifty years, Harvey says, yet they have not risen in revolt. By the 1990s, the collapse of the Soviet Union and the entry of China into the global economy added two billion workers into the world economy. The resulting wage repression led to household debt, which grew from an average of $40,000 in 1980 to $130,000 in 2009. Financial institutions supported working-class debt, allowing sub-prime mortgages to spawn a new market in financial services. Growing this debt in turn boosted construction and stabilised the entire economy, that is, until the housing market crashed.

What could have been done instead? The problem with the inflation of asset values, Harvey says, is absorption. How is surplus to be reinvested when less is going into real production and more is going into financial speculation? Bailing out banks does little to help the economy and contributes mainly to greater class inequality. Harvey argues that rather than bail out the system again and again, we need to rethink the cosy relationship between government and financial institutions. He anticipated Stiglitz when he wrote: 'The only thing they would care about is if we rose up in revolt. And until we rise up in revolt they are going to redesign the system according to their own class interests.'[23] Harvey proposes that the banking system could serve people by socialising the surplus. Sustainable development first means realising that it will not be possible in the future to sustain two percent and three percent rates of accumulation. Our demand, according to Harvey, should be to insist on popular control of production and distribution through the building of schools, hospitals, clean energy, working cities and neighbourhoods, housing and social infrastructure, and through the disentangling of government from financial interests and big corporations. The system of exploitation is breaking down and unless people take control of government, he argues, the ruling classes will turn to more oppressive forms to legitimate their class war.

Analyses and statistics overwhelmingly point to the need to junk the neoliberal project of class consolidation. In developed nations real wages have not increased significantly since the 1970s. The US economy is today more unequal than any other in the advanced industrialised economies. This is not a negligible accident of the free market. According to James Laxer, the neoliberal flexibilisation of labour, the suppression of wages and the creation of a precarious work force directly benefits capitalists. Whereas corporations used to take their employees into account, neoliberal economists argue that job security is bad for the economy. Younger, better educated contract employees are pitted against aging and permanent employees. Starting in the late 1970s, high unemployment accompanied the transition to a deregulated, globalised economy, destroying the cooperation between capital and labour.[24]

The result of neoliberalisation policies since the 1970s has not been a healthier economy but wealth concentration at the top. In unequal societies with less union control and fewer social programmes, people have to work more to make ends meet, their standard of living goes down and corporate investment declines at the same time. Such economies, in which tax cuts are presented as a panacea, are in the end less competitive and less innovative. The resulting social insecurity undermines political democracy and social wellbeing, leading to health problems, reduced life expectancy, higher infant mortality and less equity altogether. Governments that attempt to improve this situation by raising tax revenues are threatened by corporations, their high-paid CEOs, think tanks and lobbies. Consequently, neoliberal governments do the bidding of the wealthy, focusing on Wall Street money managers' goal of debt reduction. Obama's promise to tax the wealthy and close tax loopholes for corporations was cover for his overall bipartisan deficit reduction strategy, which adversely affected working people. After the 2008 financial crisis, and after the average American family lost one quarter of its wealth, Obama and the Democats reassured Wall Street that nothing would change.[25]

The 2000s on the whole were terrible years for most people who quite rightly began to question the need for troops stationed in Iraq, Afghanistan, Libya, Yemen and Somalia. But foreign misadventures only reflect a similar brutality on the domestic front, with cuts to social spending, education, environmental protection, transportation and housing. Ratings agencies call for greater cuts, even in times of recession. The only conclusion that can be drawn is that today's neoliberal governments have no reasonable economic policy, let alone any vision of society that corresponds in any way to social prosperity. The greater volatility in the economy not only reflects class inequality, but racial inequality is compounded as blacks and hispanics are hardest hit by recessionary unemployment. Racial inequality in the US was higher in 2012 than it had been in the previous twenty-five years. In this context, more borrowing leads to more bankruptcies, and more insecurity and poverty leads to more crime, policing and incarceration. In cities like Detroit the poverty rate is roughly forty percent. Meanwhile people like Treasury Secretary Timothy Geithner claimed that the government must go ahead and destroy social programmes. Enter stage left: the movement known as #occupywallstreet. The first item of order for the movement was not to decide on specific demands, but to create the seeds of a political alternative to the two major parties and the neoliberal consensus.

We are the 99%

At the very start of the OWS protests, the scholar and activist David Graeber helped to give the movement a media presence and established that the 5,000 who first came to Wall Street were not there to riot, as Michael Bloomberg had let on to the media, but to alert people to the fact that the political system, as he put it, 'is not even trying to propose solutions to our problems.'[26] On September 19, on the news show *Democracy Now*, Graeber stated:

I think that for the last 30 years we've seen a political battle being waged by the super-rich against everyone else, and this is the latest move in the shadow dance, which is completely dysfunctional economically and politically. I mean, it's the reason why young people have just abandoned any thought of appealing to politicians. We all know what's going to happen. The tax proposals are a sort of mock populist gesture, which everyone knows will be shot down. What will actually happen would be more cuts to social services. The very fact that the rhetoric is about debt, which is really a non-issue, is itself the problem ... The crisis now in Europe is an example of the same thing. The austerity regimes that are being imposed now on Europe and on America are remarkably similar to what happened – you know, what used to be called the Third World debt crisis. First you declare a financial debt – a financial crisis. You bring in these people who are supposedly neutral technocrats, who are in fact enforcing this extreme neoliberal ideology. You bypass all democratic accountability and impose things that no one [would] ever possibly have agreed to. It's the same thing. And one reason it's happening to us now is that there was really successful mobilization around the world against those policies. In a lot of ways, the global justice movement was successful. The IMF was kicked out of East Asia. It was kicked out of Latin America. And now it's come home to us.[27]

But the IMF is not the only thing that came home. On Saturday September 17, 2011, people arrived in New York City's financial district with banners, cardboard signs, sleeping bags, Guy Fawkes masks, tents and mattresses. Their plan was to march around the bronze *Charging Bull* statue in the financial district but police deterred them. The protests then moved to Zuccotti Park, which was renamed Liberty Square. The news media reported on the first day that no one demand had been determined, setting up the expectation that a singular demand was soon to follow.[28] Fittingly, those who created this expectation gave some of the first media reports. Kalle Lasn, the co-founder of *Adbusters*, told CNN:

> There's a feeling that we need a revolution in the way that our economy is run, the way that Washington is run ... What we are hoping for is to have a very large number of people turn up in Lower Manhattan and start walking toward Wall Street peacefully, signs in hand. If we have peaceful assemblies and debates about what our demands to President Obama should be, then bit by bit we can create a situation that will rival what happened in Egypt.[29]

With respect to the one demand, Lasn told reporters: 'The demand could be some stupid lefty thing like "overthrow capitalism." We're hoping it's something specific and doable, like asking Obama to set up a committee to look into the fall of U.S. banking. Nothing extreme about that.'[30] Micah White, the former senior editor of *Adbusters*, said for his part: 'We're trying to follow the model set up by the Egyptian activists to have an encampment and hold a people's assembly. This is how it's done – you pick a symbolic place, set up camp, and hold a people's assembly and decide what your demands are.'[31]

White called on Obama to come to Wall Street to talk to the demonstrators. Obama never did but the encampment received emails, tweets and phoned-in food donations from around the world. Cell phones were omnipresent, as were digital cameras and several websites were soon created.[32] Given the fact that the form of the assemblies and the assertion of the right to assemble and organise took precedence over the delivery of one or even many demands, the mainstream media very early on sought to discredit the occupation by suggesting that the people who were assembled did not know what they wanted. On September 30 a statement titled 'First Official Release from Occupy Wall Street: Declaration of the Occupation of New York City' was posted online. It established a declaration of demands, principles of solidarity and documentation on how to form direct democracy occupation groups. Around one week after the encampments were organised the protests began to attract global attention and received the support of prominent activists and intellectuals.

Making class inequality a mainstream media topic would not have been possible without the determination of those who camped out, set up committees and resisted the various efforts at police intimidation. On Monday, September 26, a message from Noam Chomsky was read aloud to the assembly. It stated: 'The courageous and honorable protests underway on Wall Street should serve to bring this calamity [of concentrated wealth] to public attention, and to lead to dedicated efforts to overcome it and set society on a more healthy course.'[33] The same day, documentary filmmaker Michael Moore visited OWS and told the crowd: 'Whatever you do, don't despair because this is the hard part. You are in the hard part right now. But, everyone will remember, three months from now, six months from now, that you came down to this Plaza, and you started this movement.'[34] Later in the day, on the Keith Olbermann television show, Moore made the point that had the Tea Parties held such assemblies the mainstream news would have given them top coverage. He promised the 'kleptocracy' in Washington and on Wall Street that the movement would grow. 'They're holding two trillion dollars of cash in their bank accounts,' he said. 'They've never done this before. Never held on to that much money. They've taken that money out of circulation, and they know the other shoe's gonna drop.'[35]

In anticipation of a union solidarity event on Wednesday, September 28, statements of solidarity were put out by the Transport Workers Union Local 100, by the American Federation of Labor and Congress of Industrial Organizations, Moveon.org, the Coalition for the Homeless, the Alliance for Quality Education, the Service Employees International Union, the Teamsters and the United Federation of Teachers. The fact that many of these unions are backers of the Obama administration made their politics somewhat antithetical

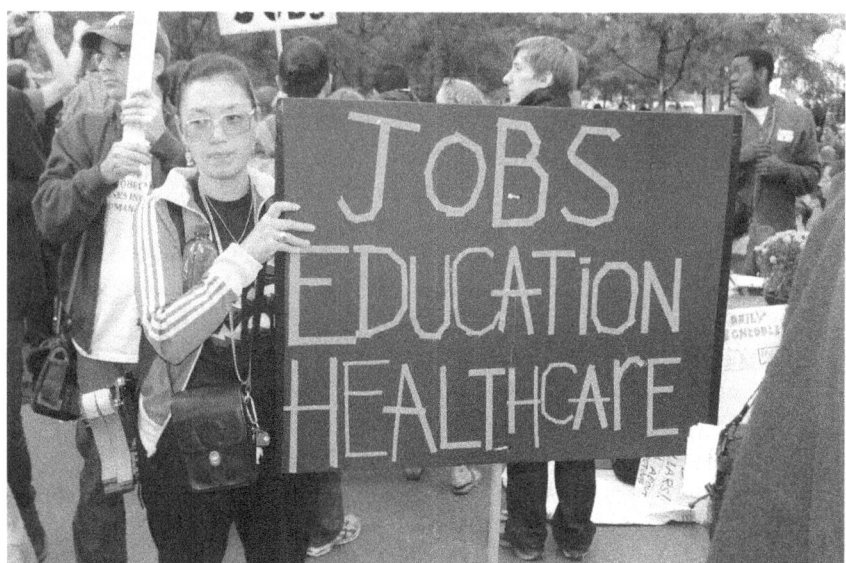

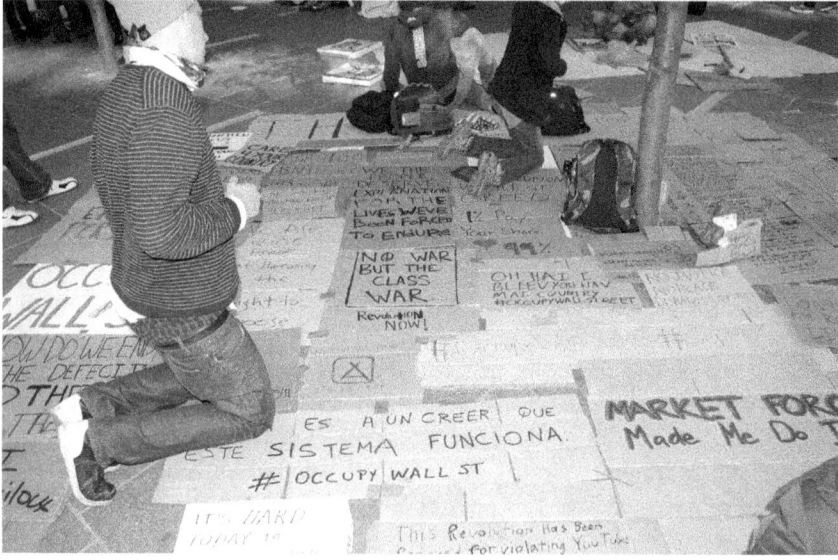

to the 'no politics' and 'no leadership' ethos of OWS. On the day of the actual event, Moore spoke again, this time on the news show *Democracy Now*. He noted that it was highly ironic that one hundred of the protesters had been arrested while not a single banker or CEO from Wall Street had so far been held responsible.[36] Moore was joined by Cornel West, who also visited the OWS encampment and spoke to the general assembly through the people's mic:

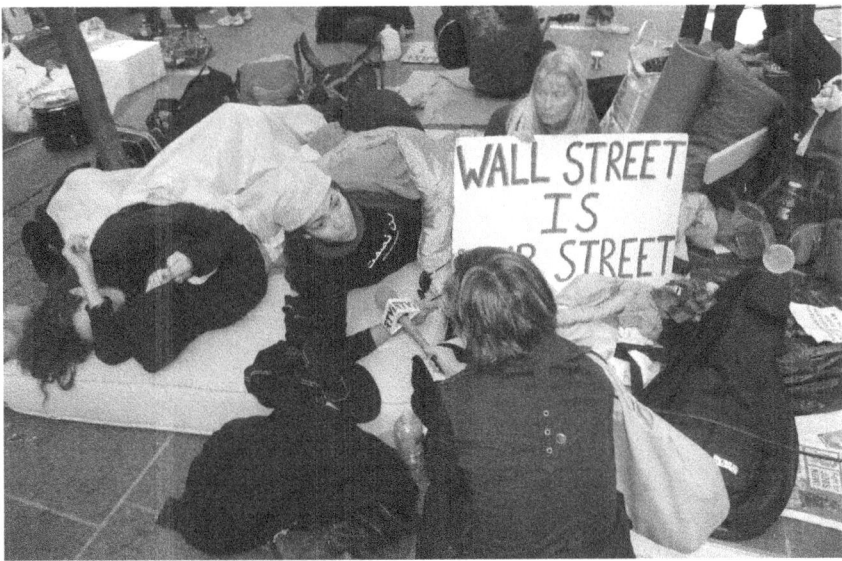

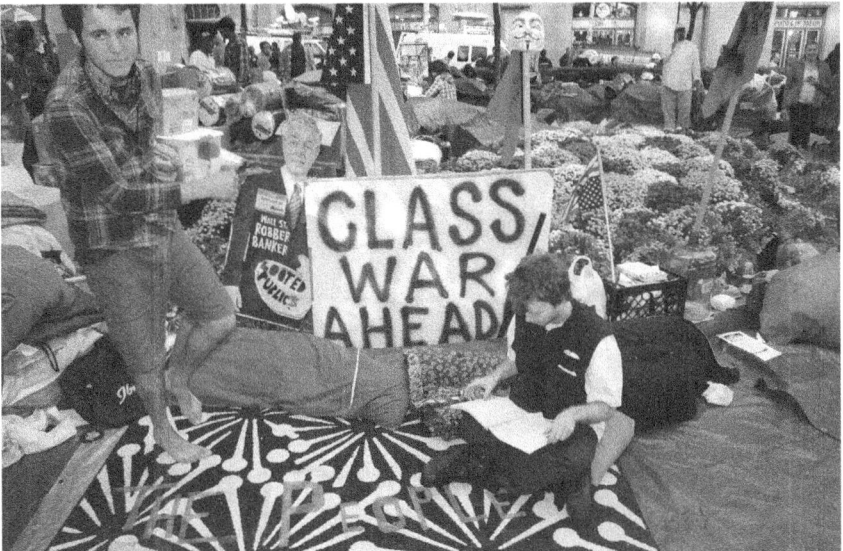

Occupy Wall Street, September 17 to October 6, 2011. Images courtesy of David Shankbone and the Occupy Wall Street Creative Commons Project.

we will send a message that this is the U.S. Fall – responding to the Arab Spring, and it's going to hit Chicago and Los Angeles and Phoenix, Arizona, and A-Town itself, moving on to Detroit. We going to hit Appalachia, we going to hit the reservations with our red brothers and sisters and Martin Luther King Jr. will smile from the grave and say, we moving step by step for what he called a revolution.[37]

The following weekend, as many as 700 OWS protesters were arrested while on the Brooklyn Bridge. The arrests were supported by mayor Bloomberg, a man whose personal assets are valued at over $19 billion. Fifty percent of the income that is generated in the city of New York goes to the top one percent, approximately 35,000 wealthy households. By the week of October 3, support protests had been anticipated for the cities of Los Angeles, Boston, Austin, San Francisco, Chicago, Hartford, Seattle, Washington D.C., Detroit, Portland, Philadelphia, San Diego, Norfolk, Nashville, Ithaca, Las Vegas, New Orleans, Dallas, Houston, St Louis, Minneapolis, San Antonio, Anchorage, New Orleans and Santa Fe. A video that was put out by Anonymous on October 1 declared the spread of the movement as a 'wave of resistance' that had sprung up in over thirty US cities and that was part of a global movement. By October 15, the New York demonstrations were joined by more than 1,300 cities in more than 27 countries.

During the week of October 3 a number of Democrats began to voice their support for the OWS protests, sentimentalising people's 'frustration' rather than acknowledging their grievances and their complete disapproval of the party.[38] The demonstrators were of course aware that the Democrats had helped to facilitate cuts is social services, delivered health care to insurance companies, helped to roll back union rights, wages and pensions, and increased unemployment. Obama's statement on October 6 that he 'feels the pain' and the 'frustration' of the 'folks' he had 'seen on TV' was a refusal to acknowledge OWS as a political movement.[39] Giving a speech at OWS on October 5, activist journalist Naomi Klein asserted the immensity of what the movement represents and called for solidarity, stating:

> We have picked a fight with the most powerful economic and political forces on the planet … Always be aware that there will be a temptation to shift to smaller targets – like, say, the person sitting next to you at this meeting. After all, that is a battle that is easier to win. Don't give in to the temptation … Let's treat this beautiful moment as if it is the most important thing in the world.[40]

A few days later, on October 9, Slavoj Žižek gave a speech in support of the movement, reversing Moore's assessment that protest is the difficult part, and warning:

> Don't fall in love with yourselves. We have a nice time here. But remember, carnivals come cheap. What matters is the day after, when we will have to return to normal time. Will there be any changes then? … We know that people often desire something but do not really want it. Don't be afraid to really want what you desire.[41]

After the weekend of October 8, news media reported on the dangers of cooptation. The movement had been clearly aware of this from the start and the significance of OWS for the left is that it provided a rallying point for all those who are oppressed by the existing social system. This is not to say that the usual tensions between different left tendencies were not present, but that there had been an effort to avoid giving precedence to any one ideological viewpoint. Regardless, the horizontalism and decentralisation that character-ised the movement also had its problems.

In a short essay, Mark Read questioned the effectiveness of consensus deci-sion-making for large gatherings, where it tends to yield pernicious hierarchies and favours those who feel comfortable arguing indefinitely for their point of view.[42] According to Barbara Adams, some felt like the main actors while other felt like supporters.[43] The consequence of factional scuffles was that the assemblies were supplemented by the spatialisation of separate sensibilities.[44] Read broke the movement down into three groups: the poetic types who were looking for one demand; the technocratic policy types who wanted to put forward many demands; and those who want a 'permanent revolution' that could ultimately reform the system and who argued that no specific demands should be put forward.

For others still, the constituent power of the 99% was not categorically progressive, in particular, as it eradicates class consciousness. Aidan Rowe, for example, argued that the 'Occupy X' movement's aversion to politics, especially Leninist parties, was not only tactical but ideological, a 'post-leftist anti-organisationalism' that considers the distinction between left and right to be irrelevant after the fall of Soviet communism.[45] Rowe considered this to be an effect of the success of the media and of neoliberal governance to drive pol-itics out of all public discussions on social and economic issues. This he argued is definitional of liberal capitalist consensus, which leaves technical problems in the hands of experts. Post-politics on the left allows for inclusiveness but also for mutually contradictory ideas, for reactionary ideas and for progressive ones, to be treated with the same seriousness. While people ignore ideas that have already been formulated in leftist criticism, what then comes to the fore are reformist ideas. The call for the stabilisation of the banking system, for example, and thus for the stabilisation of capitalism, is a case in point. As Rowe put it:

> The problem is capitalism, not regulatory failure, or corporate greed or a lack of economic patriotism, and the inadequacies of these analyses need to be exposed rather than uncritically welcomed … The theory of this anti-politics, so far as I can gather, is this: no two people experience oppression in the same way, and thus any attempt to unite people under a political programme inevitably ends up erasing some people's perspectives.[46]

Rowe argued that the constituent power of the 99% is not inherently radical, in particular as it ignores the processes of capitalist domination and eradicates class consciousness. This, he said, represents a victory for neoliberalism. The working class, he concluded, is not a group of people, but a social relation between people that is derived from the organisation of labour. Oppression is therefore not directly produced by Wall Street but in the workplaces that are being restructured, as well as in the courts, prisons and militaries.

The fact that the movement did not have a clear political message was both a strength and a weakness. Its amorphousness left it open to cooptation by different forces, including the Democratic Party, the unions and the media. The unity of the movement grew, however, with various attempts to shut it down. As it grew internationally, with occupations in Europe, Canada, Asia, Australia and New Zealand, Africa and South America, the slogan 'We are the 99%' that was proposed by Graeber gave the movement a popular character that both confirmed and challenged the mandates of representative institutions. For sociologist Immanuel Wallerstein, the OWS movement passed through three crucial stages: the initial demonstrations, the publicity and police repression, and the legitimation by academics and media. The next step, he said, would be the danger of counter-demonstrations and dissolution.[47] The movement seemed poised to do two things: first, encourage the short-term minimisation of austerity, and second, change the way that large segments of American society think about the crises of capitalism. With regard to the latter, he argued, it had already succeeded. In New York City polls from late October, two thirds of voters supported the protesters' criticism of the banks and eighty-seven percent supported their right to demonstrate and remain in Liberty Square. These reports contradicted mainstream media news coverage of the detrimental effects of the encampments on local businesses. Polls by the *New York Times* and CBS also indicated that as of October 25, as many as forty-three percent of Americans agreed with the basic aims of OWS and only twenty-five percent disagreed – with the remaining thirty percent unsure. Polls also showed, however, that eighty-nine percent of Americans distrust their government, a situation in which it is difficult not only to gauge political opinion but also to build a radical political movement.[48]

Politicising OWS

The dangers of counter-demonstrations and dissolution, as Wallerstein has it, are not only external threats; they are a feature of the movement's own internal contradictions. More to the point, they are part of the contradictions of contemporary biocapitalism. Rowe's argument that the post-political character of today's university-educated multitude works against the possibility of OWS becoming a genuine leftist opposition was echoed by Patrick Martin, who stated:

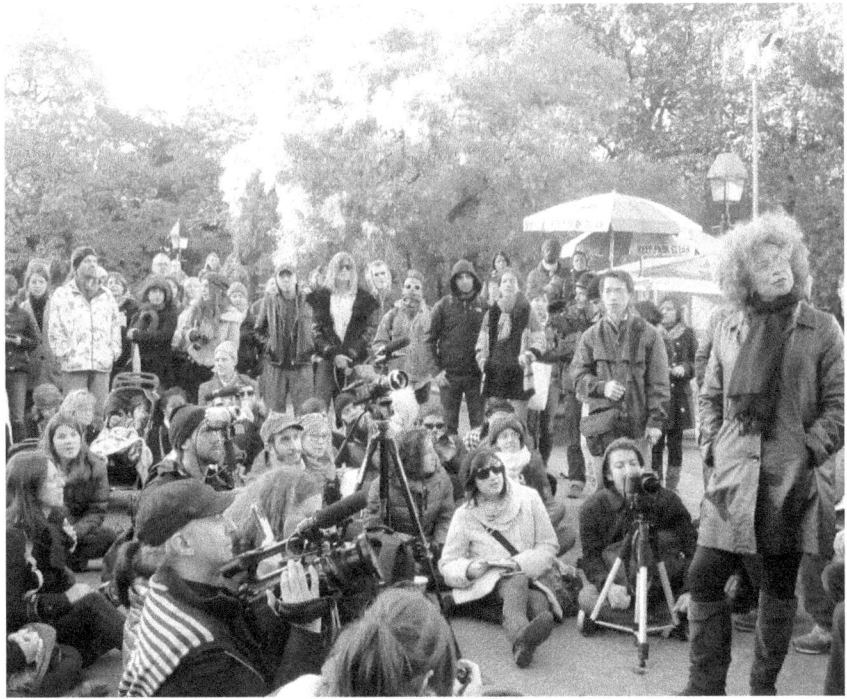

Angela Davis at Occupy Wall Street, October 30, 2011. Image courtesy of
Winnie Wong at Seismologik.

> The centrality of class cuts across the efforts of the middle class 'left' organizations
> that have for decades promoted various forms of identity politics, focusing on
> race, gender and sexual orientation, as a means of blocking the development
> of an independent political movement of the working class and bolstering the
> parties of the bourgeois political establishment … The growth of understanding
> of the international character of the struggle of the working class is the political
> hallmark of 2011.[49]

Martin says that this macropolitical class conflict is more deeply rooted in the
US than anywhere else. Of course there are far greater threats to the dissipation
of the Occupy movement than the internal dissensus represented by culture
wars and identity politics, even if this issue emerged in various instances
around the encampments.[50]

To my knowledge, the most direct statement on the relevance of difference politics to OWS was not so much Rufus Wainwright's performance
of Madonna's 'Material Girl,' but a speech by Angela Davis, who spoke on
October 30 at Washington Square Park in New York City. In response to
some questions from those assembled, Davis stated:

We have to learn to be together in a complex unity; in a unity that does not erase our differences; in a unity that allows those whose voices have been historically marginalized to speak out on behalf of the entire community. I am sure that as the days and months go by we all learn more about this process than we know now. It is important that this movement expresses the will of the majority from the outset. But that majority must be respected in terms of all the differences within it … We have to become fluent in each other's stories … It is important to insist on the involvement of people of color, of women, of people with marginalized sexualities, of immigrants, and especially undocumented immigrants. Everyone has to be willing to listen to their voices. Those who have traditionally exercised privilege have to become conscious of the way that privilege can continue to be marginalizing. So this is work we must all do.[51]

To be sure, there were many reports of violence and discrimination in the camps and these have to be judged according to the degree of seriousness. Davis' culpabilisation of privilege, however, ignores many things, least of all the political limits of difference politics as it relates to macropolitical change. Not only may difference politics actually reinforce the role and identity of the privileged, but it may also undermine many of the strengths of the kind of revolutionary politics that Davis once endorsed. Davis is now perhaps all too knowingly post-structuralist in her politics. Difference politics, in contrast to emancipatory politics, and especially when it is thought of in terms of identity, attempts to find a unified field of emergence and a unified theory between reality and psyche. Efforts to localise the antagonisms of social difference become a means to have politics without paying the price for politics. Culture wars in particular become a means to not only redress but also disavow the logic of political antagonism.[52]

What is truly traumatic, psychically speaking, other than the experience of discrimination, is that the Real of this experience cannot be properly symbolised. Academic micropolitics, while sometimes aimed at conservatives who fear liberals who wish to interfere with their perceived values and ways of life, can just as easily and just as often be used as a mark of distinction and a set of entitlements against working-class people, the 'lower classes' who are blamed for upholding chauvinism and forms of religious or cultural intolerance. Rather than aiming at collective demands, a hermeneutics of suspicion is applied to the narcissism of small differences. Another difficulty is that micropolitics cannot occupy the instruments of power, including the police and the military, and instead become a feature of the obscene underside of the Law, creating unofficial exclusions within minority enclaves. As for placing women and blacks in positions of power, the politics of people like Barack Obama and Hillary Clinton should be proof enough of the limits of liberal inclusion. Formal inclusion is a democratic veneer to the formal 'equality' of wage relations and the universality of capital. For liberals this would seem to be precisely the kind of ameliorist progress that justifies a system that guarantees the poverty of the majority. But capitalism cuts across ethnicity and gender and defines these struggles as aspects of the social reproduction of capitalism. Class struggle becomes a culture war between enlightened liberals and those they would seek to exclude from their world of economic and social privilege, an inclusiveness that is built on structural impossibility. This impossibility was defined by Oskar Negt and Alexander Kluge in relation to the students' protest activities of the 1960s, which were premised on the disintegration of the bourgeois public sphere and on petty-bourgeois conversion strategies. The latter involved calls to transform your individuality and your lifestyle, a rebranding of the self that was consistent with the new public spheres of capitalist production.[53]

According to Žižek, the relation that is proposed by post-colonial academia in the era of global capitalism is one of 'auto-colonisation.' Multiculturalism, he argues,

> is a racism which empties its own position of all positive content (the multiculturalist is not a direct racist, he doesn't oppose to the Other the *particular* values of his own culture), but nonetheless retains this position as the privileged *empty point of universality* from which one is able to appreciate (and depreciate) properly other particular cultures – the multiculturalist's respect for the Other's specificity is the very form of asserting one's own superiority.[54]

The universal therefore appears as its exception, the point at which the universal is suspended and seems to disintegrate. This is one reason why formal inclusion misses the point: the problem is integration itself as a condition of impossibility. Civil society, Žižek argues, gives rise to a class of people who are excluded from the benefits of civil society: the homeless, the unemployed, undocumented immigrants, prisoners, detainees or individuals placed on government kill lists, etc. The exclusion of such groups from society is structural not only to conservative values, but to progressive liberal politics as well – the struggle for gay and lesbian rights, the rights of ethnic minorities, feminists, ecologists – insofar as the establishment of 'chains of equivalence' between the different, 'complex' forms of oppression actively represses the centrality of economic struggle. The elitism of this politics is to often conceive so-called 'normal' people as being caught in their narrow ethnic or sexual confines. The result is a populism that is sustained by a 'false transparency,' Žižek says, that paves the way for global capitalist modernisation. The strategic response to this is not to assert that there is 'no war but the class war,' nor is it to defend nationalism or one's right to one's identity; it is rather to identify the ways in which culture wars are shaped by class struggle. One should therefore reject the liberal centre's opposition between post-ideological tolerance and particularist fundamentalism, and instead underscore the link between universality and the groups that are excluded from rights and privileges.

A more promising direction in recent political philosophy has been to assert the commons and political solidarity. Neither relativism nor absolutism are the correct answer to the impossible Real that mobilises and dissolves social conflicts. Freedom lies in the choice of how one wishes to be determined, as opposed to freedom from any determinations. The wager of Marxism, Žižek says, is that class struggle is the 'ultimate referent and horizon of meaning of all other struggles,' an overdetermination that 'allows us to account for the "inconsistent" plurality of ways in which other antagonisms can be articulated into "chains of equivalences".'[55] Interpellations on the basis of identity or ability do not have any direct correlation with a specific politics. Body-based politics should therefore be discarded. If OWS causes postmodern academia to take notice that a class politics can still be waged then let us hope that the movement will be resolute in its substitution of identity agendas, including nationalism, with an international solidarity of struggles. As Ken Knabb argues, the slogan 'We are the 99%' is not precise class analysis, but it is good enough as it puts the focus on economic institutions.[56]

Beyond questions of identity, another dimension of difference politics is the anarcho-Deleuzianism that has become immensely popular among activists in the 2000s. One proponent of such autonomist Marxism is Franco Berardi, who wrote along with Geert Lovink in mid-October that OWS is a consequence of the growing precarity of labour.[57] Our collective intelligence, they say, is submitted to processes of exchange that benefit the wealthy. Our life becomes their money. Our enemies are not human beings, they suggest, they are machines, an automated process of predatory power, or FINAZISM. The solution they propose is to awaken from the software that captures our labour and take to the streets where the erotic social body breaks its chains. Nevermind the sustainability of the movement, they argue, everything is transient and besides, we are here to stay.

Autonomist intellectuals Michael Hardt and Antonio Negri also put out the statement that OWS gives voice to 'indignation against corporate greed and economic inequality.'[58] The issue for them is the extent to which the movement will understand itself as a constituent power and whether or not it will mistakenly appeal to the established representational political system. 'This protest movement could, and perhaps must,' they write, 'transform itself into a genuine, democratic constituent process.'[59] The banks, the political parties and the financial industries do not represent the multitudes of Tahrir Square, Wisconsin, Syntagma Square and the Israeli encampments. The multitude is characterised by the new democratic practices it is experimenting with: the general assemblies, the participatory decision-making, the social networking and the leaderless horizontal structures. They conclude with the hypothesis that these shifts make the existing forms of democracy obsolete.

While the schizo-anarchism of Berardi, Hardt and Negri and others does not accept the capitalism that exists, it also does not propose the classic Marxist overcoming of the contradictions through the agency of the proletariat as the 'gravedigger' of capitalism. Because of this, it does not believe that the proletariat has to take possession of the representative institutions of state power. In relation to this phenomenon, Žižek argues that the dogma of today's petty-bourgeois left has the features of a 'humorous superego' that bombards those in power with impossible demands – for example, the demand for constant resistance, for continuous subjective deterritorialisation, and for rebuilding every known institution from the ground up. This superego agency then mocks us for failing to meet these demands.[60] This nomadic indeterminacy is paradoxically consistent with the technological and labour determinism that anarchists associate with communicative semio-capitalism. The productive aspect of this superego is that it constantly compels us to enjoy life, to give way on libidinal impulses, to go out into the streets, to stop working and stop shopping. The excessive, traumatic character of this limitless set of injunctions is that one has always to move beyond one's comfort zone. It turns politics, Žižek argues, into a 'weird and twisted ethical duty.'[61] In the case of OWS, one is asked to camp out for weeks and months but no one has any idea of what this burdensome duty is oriented towards. One is expected to listen to

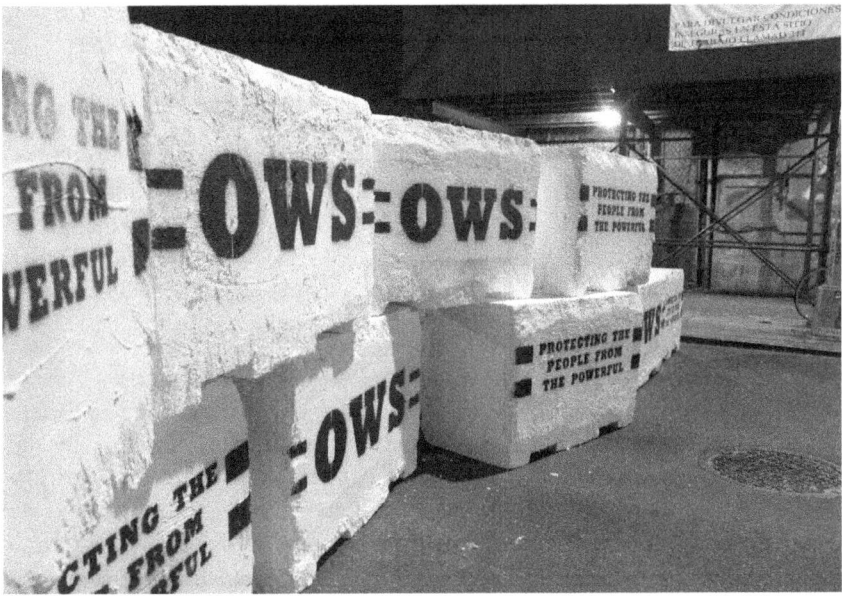

Not An Alternative, *Occupy Police Blocks*, 2012. NAA created OWS protest tools like the polystyrene blocks that mimic the design of NYPD police cinder blocks. Courtesy of Not An Alternative.

endless deliberations, but one cannot rely on established channels, experts and leaders. The new forms of playful organisation are consequently thought to be in themselves better forms, even if these have also been tested and proven inadequate. What matters in such political movements is therefore not the end of capitalist exploitation but the formation of new subjectivities.

Žižek argues that liberal-democratic state politics and anarchist micropolitics exist in a relation of interpassive and mutual interdependency. In the end, he gives more or less the same advice that Harvey had for us, which is that we should not bombard those in power with infinite demands but rather with strategically well-selected, precise and finite demands that authorities cannot absorb as easily as they can the countercultural attitude. However, almost contradicting himself in light of the potential opened up by OWS, Žižek stated on October 26, at a lecture in New York City: 'We should maintain this openness [of no demands] in all its ominous directions. We don't need dialogue with those in power. We need a critical dialogue with ourselves. We need time to think … The system is in crisis, the important thing is precisely that a vacuum is open.'[62]

In a later interview with *Harper's* magazine, Žižek then brought these two points together. To the question 'So what should the protesters be asking for?' he replied:

> Just two things. On the one hand, at this point more important than asking is to think, to organize, to lay down the foundations for some kind of a network so that this will not just be some kind of magic explosion that disappears. And point two, the way to start to think about doing something is to select some very specific issues … which in a way are very realistic. One of the strategies for doing something concrete is to pick very carefully issues for which you fight, and then you try to organize a popular movement – which has two features. First, they are realistic; but at the same time, they have dramatic points which are extremely penetrated by ideology. So things that are possible but that are unacceptable within the ideological frame – like universal healthcare – this is, I think, maybe the thing to do at this point, apart from laying the foundations, getting ready.[63]

The years 2012 to 2018 in the United States have been characterised by ever more brutal exploitation. The banking system was not reformed and former US Attorney General Eric Holder left his government post, where he did nothing to criminally prosecute any of the bankers involved in the mortgage crisis, and went back to work in the private sector for a law firm that serves Wall Street clients. The Pentagon stymied the revelations of torture during the Iraq war. Obama extended the Patriot Act. Although Edward Snowden exposed the extent of National Security Agency surveillance, he was obliged to join the growing ranks of persecuted whistleblowers. The militarisation of the police continued unabated despite pressure from Black Lives Matter to end police repression. A 2015 US Department of Defense report titled 'The National Military Strategy of the Unites States of America' identified Russia and China as targets for military action, despite the fact that these are major nuclear powers. Under Donald Trump, this policy has been extended as the so-called 'war on terror' has been replaced by a new 'great-power politics' version of the Cold War, combined with anti-immigrant chauvinism in domestic policy and corporate tax cuts. Three American billionaires now control more wealth than the bottom half of the US population. In these circumstances, small realistic demands become less and less realistic, even if their smallness provides an indication of the enormity of the challenge.

Strategic issues are important but they are not a substitute for a comprehensive political project. In this regard, OWS remains an important event in its sweeping demands for social change. According to Yates McKee, OWS – together with offshoots like Strike Debt, Occupy Museums and the Gulf Labor Coalition, to name only a few – represents a renewal of the avant garde as 'self-conscious left-wing cultural work.'[64] Its ideological orientation and methods of distributed leadership are only some of the means that engaged art practices can contribute to the class struggle against global capitalism. To speak of a post-Occupy condition is therefore not only to be mindful of the event of OWS but of the event of communism, of which OWS is a vanguard manifestation.

3

Vanguardia

In his critique of institutions and the desire of radicalised artists and theorists to work outside the limits of established disciplinary structures, Brian Holmes argues that discourse-based context art and institutional critique have undergone a significant phase change, a shift towards extradisciplinary, transversal assemblages that link actors from the art world to projects oriented towards political contestation.[1] The world in which networked art activists operate today is characterised as 'cognitive capitalism,' a new global situation in which affect and creativity, immaterial and communicative labour are key components of the biopolitical engineering of subjectivity, a voluntary machinic enslavement within a bureaucratically regulated process of continuous evaluation that is increasingly geared towards the requirements of a service economy. The new forms of art activism, associated with new social movements, autonomous collectives and alternative media are certainly shaped by this new class composition. However, they also bear a striking resemblance to avant-garde predecessors. Renato Poggioli once referred to the avant garde as an 'anti-tradition tradition,' something that could easily be said about today's biopolitical activism, which typically refuses identification as an avant garde.[2] In its willingness to break with the past, today's anti-avant garde avant garde dispenses with notions of totality, universal reason and dialectical negation, and favours instead the spectral event as an alternative path of becoming. As background to this paradigm shift, however, there is a long tradition of radical engagement with art and politics on the part of various strands of revolutionary theory, all of which had some notion of consciousness of the totality. In his book on the concept of totality, Martin Jay argues that 'Western Marxism has been open and experimental in a way that is not compatible with anything in [the last] century except perhaps aesthetic modernism, which also exploded in a whirl of movements and counter-movements.'[3] The most significant problem for an intellectual avant garde, he adds, has been the problem of political representation – representing those who could not represent themselves. How does one talk about an avant garde that refuses representation?

Today's phase change does not relate to a break with a previous artistic tendency or style as much as it does to a previous politico-philosophical tradition, namely, Hegelian Marxism and its various permutations in Frankfurt School Freudo-Marxism, existentialism and structuralism. As far as today's activists are concerned, and in particular those who are inspired by the work-erist concept of the multitude, the problem of avant-garde representation and leadership is cancelled by the critique of both party-based and state-oriented politics, by constituted forms of power, and by the current modes of and relations of post-Fordist production. According to Maurizio Lazzarato, struc-tural changes to the labour market, introduced primarily by the post-Fordist state apparatus, have today transformed the artist into a 'worker,' a hybrid of employer and employee, and thus into 'human capital' that contributes to a new cultural market. Lazzarato argues that neoliberalism signals not only a shift towards privatisation, but a change in the mode of governing behaviour among individuals in a context of inequality and competition.[4] In traditional terms, competition takes place among manufacturers of goods. In a prosumer environment, however, in which affect and sociality are incorporated into the logic of accumulation and surplus value extraction, the critique of avant-gardism among the new cadres of activists has an unusual character. In order to challenge the status quo, one has to compete with oneself as an avant garde.

Although the idea that today's workers no longer automatically form a blue-collar proletariat might seem to be the result of new information tech-nologies and public management, the shift towards a precarious cognitariat also has a twentieth-century prehistory, analysed brilliantly by Siegfried Kracauer in the 1920s and by C. Wright Mills in the 1950s.[5] The world of the new 'middle' classes that they described now defines the class situation of the majority of today's creative workers who are otherwise in the same situation as traditional labour insofar as they do not control the means of production and cannot live from the labour of their own autonomous efforts. According to the US census of 2005, among the two million people who consider themselves to be career artists, more than ninety-eight percent of them do not live from selling their artwork and so must find other means to secure an income.[6] Because of their education and lifestyle ambitions, however, the no-collar salaried masses come to identify with capital rather than as labour. If the social relations of production have been largely the same throughout the twentieth century, the ideology of revolution that once accompanied them seems to have vanished.

One level of difficulty here is that the managerial creative class, those fortunate enough to occupy positions of curatorial, editorial and educational power amongst the broad progressive class of cultural service workers, adopt almost universally the global petty-bourgeois model of protest politics, as opposed to what is considered the tired revolutionary models of organisation. They are, as Tiqqun says apropos of the 'Young Girl,' fiendishly biopolitical.[7] One example of this is the theoretical stance of Jen Delos Reyes in her short piece for the Blade of Grass website, 'What Are We Trying to Get Ahead of? Leaving the Idea of the Avant-Garde Behind.' Delos Reyes proposes that artists should avoid the avant-garde model of transgressive innovation, a statement that was echoed on the Blade of Grass website by Stephen Pritchard, who says: 'I'm down with dropping ideologies.'[8] One presumes that Pritchard wants to get on with making more socially pragmatic art and dissolve art into useful life projects, working collaboratively with communities in struggle. Delos Reyes concludes with the Buckminster Fuller statement that 'artists are now extraordinarily important to human society' and asks: 'so, what is there to get ahead of?'

Considering that artists are increasingly integrated in the new service economy, Delos Reyes avoids the question of capitalist social relations, which are now facilitated by technology and social media. She sidesteps the political reading of avant-garde contestation and ignores Peter Bürger's well-known diagnosis that the neo-avant gardes were integrated into the culture industries. The networked aspects of contemporary creative industries facilitate the institutional demobilisation of the oppositional energies of social practice art. As Lane Relyea argues, the shift away from ideological struggles towards micropolitics and local forms of agency has developed alongside the transition to the post-Fordist economy, with its networked model of mass customisation and platforms. The mass model of political ideology is here replaced with improvised subjectivity and do-it-yourself action-oriented autonomy, and with projects that allow art activists to engage flexibly in projects while at the same time avoiding traditionally defined institutional, bureaucratic and state levels of mediation.[9] Neoliberal governments and corporations are increasingly interested in culture's contribution to the economy and at the same time encourage artists to fill in the gaps created by the degradation of social safety nets, to become virtuous community builders after the institutions of the welfare state have been dismantled and the initiatives for social justice transferred to private and unaccountable agencies. This is the context in which it is possible to talk about the socially engaged artist as a kind of unofficial official artist, subsumed by the machinations of the information and service economy. The integration of useful activist art and the shift away from radical ideology towards soft forms of bio-empowerment is nevertheless a forced choice that is presented by activists to others and even themselves as an end of history.

The point that Delos Reyes makes is both wrong and correct. Yes, we are in a relatively new phase of social practice art, but no, this biopolitical stage of activism, protest, multiculturalism and lifestyle is not beyond capitalism – and so there is indeed something to get ahead of. The question, as Eric Cazdyn and Imre Szeman put it, is what comes after globalisation, a stage in which all cultural production is seemingly operationalised by exchange.[10] As Gene Ray writes, 'there are at this point just two irreconcilable options: either to be enlisted in culture's affirmative function ... or to press forward with the revolutionary process.'[11] What, in this context, is an adequate model of radical cultural practice and what are its theoretical premises? The following reviews the recent writings of several prominent art theorists in the field of socially engaged art: Gerald Raunig, BAVO, Gregory Sholette, Oliver Ressler, Grant Kester, Critical Art Ensemble, Nato Thompson, Yates McKee, Mikkel Bolt Rasmussen and Rebecca Gordon-Nesbitt. Each offers a highly sophisticated leftist analysis of the current mediation of art and politics.

Transversal concatenations

One of the most challenging models of contemporary radical practice is that put forward by Gerald Raunig in *Art and Revolution: Transversal Activism in the Long Twentieth Century*.[12] First published in 2005, the book opens with a comparison of two modern figures who have written about art and revolution: the German composer Richard Wagner and the Bolshevik critic Anatoly Lunacharsky. These very different personages, one a 'leftist right-winger' and the other a 'right-wing leftist,' allow Raunig to introduce the theme of his book: the temporary and partial *concatenation* of art machines and revolutionary machines, and its schizo-anarchist focus, the place of the state in modernist approaches to revolutionary cultural praxis and how to overcome it by betraying all efforts to become a disciplined, centralised, hierarchical and structured form of representative power. Without belabouring the specifics of these two writers' social circumstances and ideas about art, we could say that one, following an anarchist line of descent, considered revolution to be in the service of art, an aristocratic view that mixed radical democratic aims with the restoration of class power, while the other, following Marxist-Leninist tenets, considered art and cultural policy, with some remnants of bourgeois ideology wrenched from pure formalism, to be in the service of a new society, agitating the masses in the direction of revolutionary change.

Raunig's book intervenes in this shorthand representation of modernist radicalism by addressing the two in terms of content and container. What Wagner and Lunacharsky have in common is a totalising view of the masses and history, a political and philosophical common ground that could be transposed onto most of the twentieth-century avant gardes. Whether or not one agrees with his critique of dialectical materialism will largely determine how one responds to Raunig's transvaluation of tradition. His critique removes art from its Marxist-Hegelian understanding and in turn hypostatises terms like art, state and life in order to propose a deterritorialisation where Wagner and Lunacharsky can figure within a transhistorical pattern of art practice and politics, liberated into a series of concatenations that overlap into zones of emergence that neither follow a teleological development nor are thought to be permanent.

Addressing Gustave Courbet's participation in the Paris Commune, Raunig develops the concept of a *sequential* practice, wherein the artist abandons his practice as an artist and so defies the idea of a dialectical synthesis of art and life – presumably *the* defining ambition of twentieth-century avant-garde practice – in order to participate as a political activist in the 1871 Commune, which Raunig defines as a 'war machine' that experimented with constituent power through the development of nonrepresentational practices like collectives, assemblies and barricades. Raunig unearths an unknown Courbet who, during his time as Commune functionary, sought to eliminate state subsidies to the École des Beaux-Arts and who, contrary to the popular view, actually tried to save the Vendôme Column from destruction. Raunig associates the actual demolition, which Courbet participated in and was later held accountable for, with the constituted power of the National Guard. Courbet's role as protector of culture is presented as an example of 'resisting transversalisation' that was made possible by the autonomisation of art in the nineteenth century. In this case, art's political particularism oscillates in a sequential relation with revolutionary universalism wherein no systematic overlapping of revolutionary machine and art machine is possible.

The concepts of *hierarchy*, *juxtaposition* and *negative concatenation* are then deployed in order to define the relation between art and revolution in Soviet Proletkult, the Situationists and Viennese Actionism. Raunig offers an insightful reading of Walter Benjamin's essay 'The Author as Producer' in the context of its 1934 presentation to the Paris Institute for the Study of Fascism, an official organ of the Comintern. Benjamin's focus on changing the conditions of artistic production is linked by Raunig to his critique of writers associated with *Die Aktion*, a journal of the leftist bourgeois intelligentsia that, minimally, could be credited for its distance from tendency art and from militarism. Since Benjamin could not directly criticise the content-based stance of those who were revolutionary in attitude but not in production, *Aktion* writers could at least be taken to task for neglecting the relation of form to an idealised content. This leads Raunig to consider counter-examples, from the Soviet writer Sergei Tretyakov to Bertolt Brecht, Sergei Eisenstein and the Situationist International, as agents who rejected the framework of representing the proletarian revolution. These artists refused to supply the bourgeois apparatuses of theatre and cinema, and instead engaged in forms of collective authorship that could be associated with what Gilles Deleuze and Félix Guattari might refer to as a 'mechanical-intellectual-social assemblage.' Such mass intellectuality

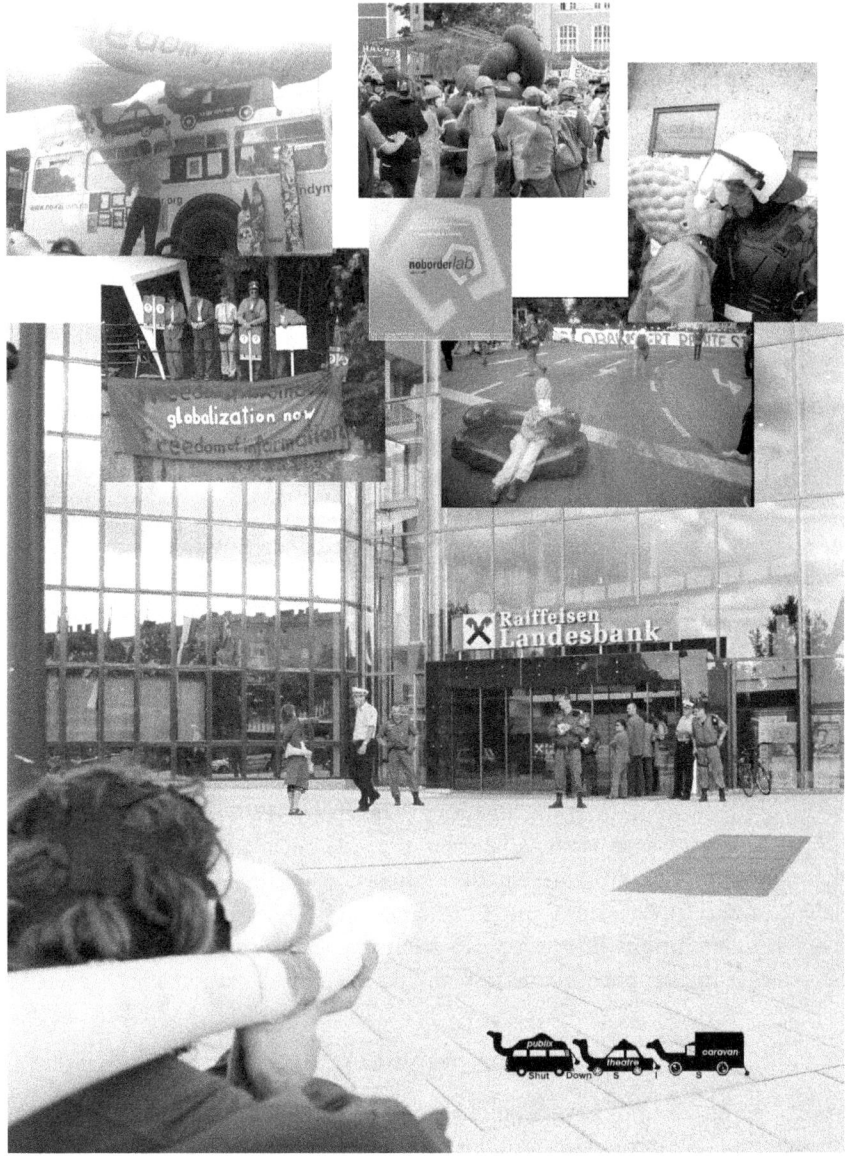

PublixTheatreCaravan, 2001–3. Courtesy of Gini Mueller.

is open to different concatenations in different contexts and to subcultural and micropolitical practices of subversion against structuralisation. Comparing Soviet experiments in theatre with the notion of the situation and the Viennese Actionists' weak form of collectivity, Raunig demonstrates how changing the production apparatus can lead to specialised forms of organisation that leave out the possibility of molecular radicalisation. The Situationists fare the best, in his estimation, for having successfully mixed cultural criticism, and for having devised the situation as being unexploitable as art, with anti-party revolutionary practice in political agitation supplemented with revolutionary theory and texts.

Raunig's view that the dialectical synthesis of art and life has the unfortunate effect of cancelling out difference is tested in relation to the transversal and transnational constellations of contemporary activists associated with counter-globalisation and anti-racism. The successes and failures of the experimental Austrian theatre groups VolxTheatre Favoriten and PublixTheatreCaravan are presented in terms of Michel Foucault's idea of *parrhesia*, a form of critical speech that comes with the risk of persecution. In contrast to Foucault's examples, the activists involved in the Volx performance and agitation do not speak as individuals but collectively and through the relative autonomy of art and politics. The protest work of the PublixTheatreCaravan is deployed to explore the feature of overlap in the micropolitical *transversal concatenations* of art machines and revolutionary machines. With these examples Raunig links a self-critical, micropolitical network of nomadic flights that offers, in its practice, a form of social and institutional criticism. In the context of the rise of right-wing conservatism in Austria, and more specifically, the 2001 G8 summit in Genoa, the threat that a ragtag caravan of thirty or more performance artists and media activists represents to the state, as marked by undue persecution and criminalisation, is taken by Raunig as an example of how competition against the violence of the state becomes itself a war machine that defies the logic of representation. Finally, against the homogenising tendency of anti-globalisation and anti-war protest, Raunig gives examples of specific interventions in concrete locations by small groups of activists who circumvent media spectacularisation and police criminalisation.

Yes revolution

On the same grounds of artistic challenge to the neoliberal ideology of free markets and state repression, but written in this case from a Žižekian perspective, is a small collection of essays put together by the Dutch collective BAVO (Gideon Boie and Matthias Pauwels). Titled *Cultural Activism Today: The Art of Over-Identification*, the book includes essays by Alexei Monroe, Benda Hofmeyr, Dieter Lesage and Boris Groys.[13] First presented in the context of a 2006 symposium, the essays explore the work of Neue Slowenische Kunst, Laibach, Atelier van Lieshout, Rem Koolhaas, Michael Moore and Christoph Schlingensief. With the exception of Groys, who offers a defence of critical autonomy and museums in light of the terrorism of mainstream media representation, these authors present contrasting versions of over-identification as an ethical strategy that confronts the desire of the Lacanian big Other, or what appears as the fundamental fantasy of one's own desire.

If we were to compare BAVO's project with Raunig's, the Deleuzian 'anti-Oedipal' politics of the latter might come across as more Oedipal than expected. Unlike micropolitical exodus and transversality, over-identification operates through the risky traversal of the Lacanian 'Law,' exposing the unwritten social codes that double both the official and the obscene identifications of the Law through post-ideological *jouissance*. Such post-enlightenment enjoyment involves dispersal into digital, viral and communicational networks. What is at stake, then, is what Žižek refers to as the paradox of truth: the obedience to Law as a symbolic prohibition that accepts the excess of identification as a consequence of the path to social progress. The revolutionary act, supplemented by cultural devices as the mediated form of subjective destitution, seeks to overcome this mediation and its logic of transgression. More concretely, this implies according a place to the state as a factor in the movement towards a higher stage of international law, a global political federation that is able to counter the destructive action that free markets impose on working conditions and the public interest.[14] Over-identification is presented by BAVO as a form of cultural activism and defined as a strategy of over-identification with the worst features of late capitalism. This contrasts directly with the idealistic styles of 'NGO art' and 'embedded cultural activisms' that propose constructive solutions to the problems created by neoliberal globalisation – precisely what is demanded of the field of art as an adjunct to representative democracy.

In the introduction and the first chapter of the book, 'Always Choose the Worst Option: Artistic Resistance and the Strategy of Over-Identification,' BAVO defines the 'blackmail of constructive critique' as the symptom of the impossibility of real critique. The paradox is the fact that politically correct tendency art, diplomatic cultural consultancy designed to engage local actors in social empowerment, is viewed primarily from the place of neoliberalism. If art's circulation as another failed attempt to change society functions mostly as a means to reproduce the economy of art, these authors argue, it is because criticism is either not wanted or impossible within existing conditions. Neoliberalism accommodates the activist and engaged art sectors as palliatives but only inasmuch as they do not radically politicise the contexts in which they operate. BAVO suggests that artists should work to expose the demand to offer practical solutions to social problems as symptomatic, a 'pragmatic blinding'

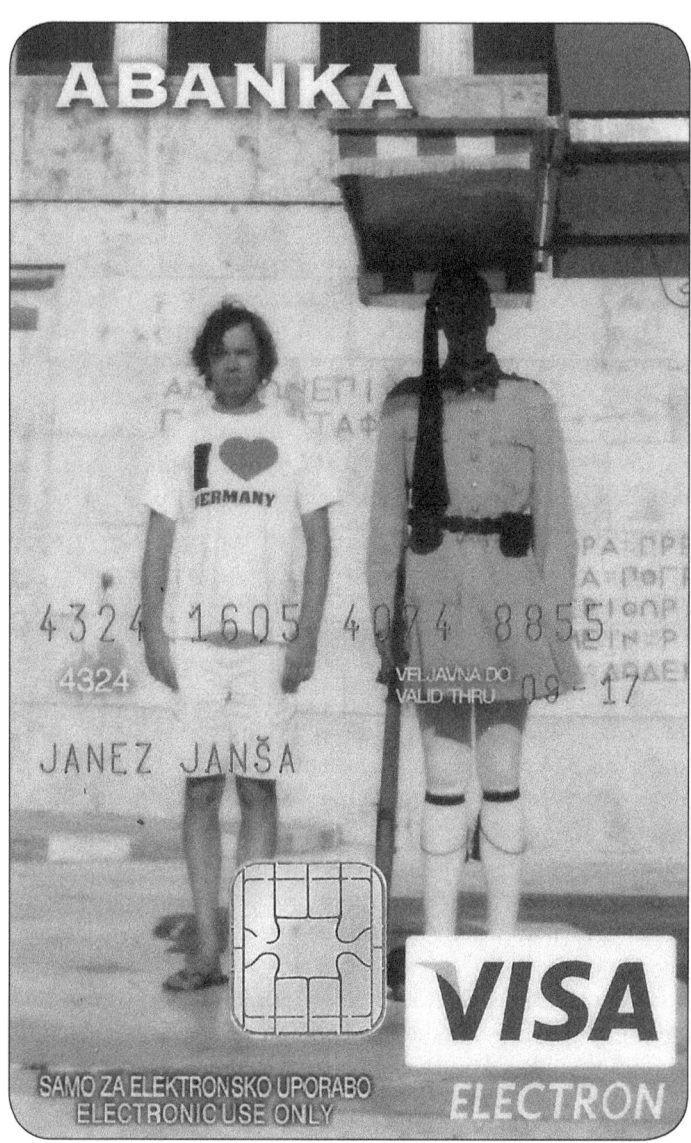

Janez Janša, Janez Janša, Janez Janša, *I Love Germany –
Greece / part of CREDITS* series, 2013. Print on plastic, 8.5 x
5.4 cm. Courtesy of Janez Janša. The artists in this collective
changed their names to the name of the leader of the Slovene
National Party and former Prime Minister. They often display
official documents like passports and identity papers as part
of their work. In the case of *I Love Germany – Greece*, they
operationalize 'I heart' t-shirts in the context of the crises
of the Eurozone.

to the deep, systematic nature of inequality. This demand should be refused as a sign of the impotence and unwillingness of the ruling order to do what it can and must do to impose pragmatic solutions. And how might one do this, BAVO asks. By giving a big Yes! to capitalism.

One example of the art of over-identification is the work of the Yes Men. In their performances the Yes Men ruthlessly apply neoliberal, free-market ideology more unscrupulously than neoliberals typically do in order to make it more ideologically consistent and to relieve people of the burden of having to believe in the system, which most neoliberals themselves only do cynically. The impact of the Yes Men's work is limited, however, inasmuch as they rely on strategies of cathartic desublimation. What they do most successfully, nevertheless, is create situations in which it becomes difficult to make excuses for the dominant order insofar as a political system's repressed ideals are identified and taken seriously.

One could respond to BAVO's strategy of over-identification with the classic Marxian criticism that what is missing in its aesthetico-political project is the actuality of mass revolutionary organisations that could lead the capitalist democracies to a better world situation. On this score, Raunig mentions the Bolivarian constitutional process that transformed Venezuelan politics. What we encounter in the disjuncture between over-identification and transversal concatenations might be productively understood in terms of what Žižek defines as a 'parallax gap,' an impossible short-circuit of the levels of art and politics as two shifting perspectives that can never meet. Despite their proximity, no synthesis is possible.[15]

Tactical media interventions

Another publication that seeks to influence today's post-institutional phase change through a reconfiguring of the relationship between art and politics is Gregory Sholette's 2011 *Dark Matter: Art and Politics in the Age of Enterprise Culture*.[16] Following his co-edited catalogue for the exhibition *The Interventionists* (2004–5) and his co-edited anthology *Collectivism After Modernism* (2007), Sholette has authored yet another important theoretical intervention in the field of critical art practice. Known also for his work in the art collectives Political Art Documentation/Distribution (PAD/D) and REPOhistory, Sholette provides an experienced view of cultural subversion from below. His book is interesting not only for its sympathetic treatment of a wide array of practices, but in particular for the way that it makes sense of them with the concept of dark matter.

The overall argument of *Dark Matter* is that 'a shadowy social productivity' haunts the world of high art. Like the dark matter that structures the universe, the dark matter of the art world is everywhere yet invisible. The many excluded practices and failed artists who keep the world of galleries, collections and magazines operating are now threatening this pyramidal system as their dark energy slowly becomes more visible. *Dark Matter* thus presents itself as a 'lumpenography' of this invisible mass of makeshift, amateur, informal, unofficial, autonomous, activist, non-institutional and self-organised practices. While engaged art practice is a minefield of con-tending leftist tendencies, the core concept of dark matter is that these are increasingly gaining visibility and momentum as they make common cause within and against neoliberal enterprise culture. The book's main argument is that art critics, art historians, arts administrators, collectors and dealers have little interest in creative dark matter. There is no question that the art world is not only made up of what is known about art, but involves a complex division of labour that works to keep a multi-billion-dollar industry operating for the benefit of a minority of high-profile artists and investors. This system keeps the vast majority of professionally trained artists in a state of subservience and underdevelopment.

The first and most general question that is asked by Sholette is what would happen if this superfluous majority went on permanent strike and gave up on the art system's means of legitimation. This question is only one of many in the book that bring to mind Pierre Bourdieu's analysis of the field of cultural production. Whereas Bourdieu understood that art's challenge to the usual capitalist motivations makes the cultural economy an inverted version of the political economy, Sholette suspends this understanding by challenging the assumption that today's high art actually operates in this way. Rather, con-temporary high art is thoroughly connected, he says, to what Julian Stallabrass calls 'Art Incorporated' and does not hide its profit motivations. It is only those dark practices at the margins that still hold on to the former task of challenging commercial goals and capitalist ideology. This does not altogether make things easier for Sholette's argument, however, as he still needs at some point to return the world of creative dark matter to the broader social space. While he is clearly appreciative of the labour theory of value, he overlooks the Marxist notion that most forms culture are unproductive and dependent in complex ways on profits collected elsewhere in the proletarianised global marketplace. This helps to explain why it is that so much cultural production and investment takes place in the global North.

Dark matter appears to reiterate the tropes of what Peter Bürger defined in his *Theory of the Avant-Garde* as the bohemian avant garde – those artists whose transgressions of the norms of bourgeois culture and society are actually required for institutions to reproduce and renew themselves. As Žižek's work has sought to explain, an ideological identification exerts the greatest pressure on us when we fool ourselves into believing we are not fully identical to it. The crisis in the arts should therefore not be thought to directly reflect the crisis in global capital, though the connections between these spheres do indeed need to be drawn. Much to his credit, Sholette does not propose a new aesthetic model nor does he consider dark matter to conform to a particular genre category. Those who make art, he writes, can define it on their own terms. The book, instead, sets out to articulate the politics of dark matter.

Sholette reiterates Marx's view that labour processes generate their own immanent, resistant forces, and that neoliberal capitalism looks for ways to harness this excess productivity. He contrasts the working situation that confronted PAD/D in the late 1970s and early 1980s to that of the networked productivity that affects the work of a contemporary collective like Paper Rad. The desire for collective, cultural autonomy, Sholette says, is overshadowed by surplus productivity. Social networking sites, file sharing, open-source programs, role-playing games, and so on, exude qualities that are anathema to serious art and also to serious criticism. While critics try to keep up with ambiguous art collectives and media activists, everything solid melts into air, especially within a risk society in which precariousness and indeterminacy are the material living conditions of so many cultural phantoms, incapable of much more than occasional upheavals.

In this context, Sholette believes that the best model for the activist, which he contrasts to the committed radical, is that offered by Michel de Certeau in his 1984 book *The Practice of Everyday Life*, and in particular the distinction that the literary theorist made between tactics and strategies. Sholette cites Geert Lovink's view that proponents of tactical media abhor ideology. Tacticians are 'patently anti-ideological,' Sholette says, and resist anything having to do with organised politics. The new social forces, he says, place the absence of ideology at the very centre of their own narrativisation. Sholette's avoidance of the logic of vanguard contestation, however, and with it of dialectical negation, prevents him from making distinctions between counterculture and radicalism. He considers that revolutionary politics offer little more than means of cultural visibility. This leads him to argue that today's surplus artists look to capitalism – as opposed to socialism – to preserve whatever culture we have left. This 'conservative' impulse is supplemented by what otherwise amounts to aesthetic anarchism, an anything goes strategy that undermines modernist attempts to separate art from commerce and political propaganda.

Sholette thus finds himself in the paradoxical position of regretting that art institutions exist at all, resentful of the pleasures of art in its consumer context. All cultural authority, he says, now acts in a manner that is typical of the alienated vanguard modernist artist of the twentieth century. Here I would only slightly disagree and say that much cultural administration today is modelled instead on the attitudes of the nineteenth-century Baudelairean bohemian, like David Brooks' 'bourgeois bohemians' and Richard Florida's 'creative class,' who reject class identifications and favour 'anti-authority' lifestyles and attitudes that ostensibly challenge the normative practices of the boring bourgeoisie. The maintenance of the fiction of art, the function of the *numerus clausus* as Bourdieu defined it, is today the prerogative of an executant petty bourgeoisie, the professional managerial class whose public management and creative industry policies are the subject of countless studies. We might then reasonably ask: How many neoliberal cultural policy makers and arts administrators are today promoting the rehabilitation of the Fourth or the creation of a Fifth International? Sholette's stance therefore makes a constructive omission of the potential of cultural authority to present an effective critique of enterprise culture, since the conditions in which we work are 'emphatically non–dialectical.'

The most utopian dimension of dark matter is that it not only distinguishes between the aesthetic and the political economy, but also on occasion collapses them, assuming that both operate without ideological remainder. The fundamental problem, I would argue, is whether dark matter's model of redistribution is destined to reproduce the cultural economy that we already have, the product of a thoroughly administered creative industry. Whereas Sholette might hope that the incorporation of PAD/D and Paper Rad into the bowels of art institutions will act as corrupting agents, this redundant surplus productivity might turn out to be just that. On the other hand, and more optimistically, it might actually be generative of alternative use values.

As part of this narrative, Sholette provides details concerning the contents of the PAD/D archive, which was included in the Museum of Modern Art's collection in the late 1980s and after the group folded. He describes this period as the political context in which the political right not only took control of the history of the radical left, but also began to appropriate its protest strategies. PAD/D members and activities challenged sexism, racism, ecological damage and all forms of oppression. Their work lasted for roughly ten years and ended just around the time when the intellectual legacy of the new left had come to a close. This was the context in which neoliberal structural adjustment had wiped away much of what was left of New York City's welfare economy and created a 'global citadel culture,' with its attendant demand for 'fresh artistic products,' the fruit of a new entrepreneurial bohemia. Once the threat to institutional authority had passed, the museum went on to archive and document the art of post-1960s radical groups.

The terrain in which PAD/D and REPOhistory operated, in short, is understood as counter to the culture industry. In particular, we are concerned here with the context of critical art practice in the 1980s and 1990s, of the culture wars of this period and the efforts of interventionists and site-specific artists to provide an alternative view of time and place. Various projects by REPOhistory, such as Queer Spaces and Civil Disturbances, worked with public strategies of address to reclaim suppressed histories and access to urban space. These projects were set against the ruinous conditions of economic privatisation and deregulation. Such interventions in public spaces contrasted with the dominant postmodernism and instead examined the lives of the disenfranchised and superfluous: the homeless, immigrants, radicals, trade unionists, sexual and racial minorities. From the artist as ethnographer to the anti-globalisation activist, the 1990s gave rise to a model of cultural democratisation that was not built on class consciousness but on the re-appropriation of signs, generating what Sholette calls an 'outlaw archive,' the dark matter of social production as it exists within social consciousness.

Further to this, the work of Temporary Services and many other contemporary interventionist collectives are referred to in the context of gift-giving economies and new social practices of generosity. The familiar bugbear – that the avant gardes sought to dissolve the distinction between art and life – is used, in these cases, to breath legitimacy into culture jamming and Situationist *détournement*. Rather than prefiguring a world of administration, the avant gardes are mentioned here as avatars of non-hierarchical fun. Much of this 'playbour' is archived and disseminated through the electronic commons of the Internet, with its websites, videos, blogs and social networking platforms. What this commons requires of people is essentially participation and self-expression, a deregulated aesthetic that finds ways to give value to surplus time. Such 'counter-institutionality,' 'networked resentment,' 'ignorance effects' and creative free for alls provide a space of imagination for those wounded by the deterritorialisations of global capitalism.

On the question of glut, overproduction, redundancy, and on the topic of precarity, *Dark Matter* includes an interesting critique of the work of Olav Velthius and his description of the contemporary art world as a messy field of social antagonisms. The basis of aesthetic judgement for Velthius is the global art market and he considers that artistic value is nothing more than a series of language games. The figure of Velthius allows Sholette to distinguish his theory of enterprise culture, which is based on the problem of an inherent asymmetry between the chosen few and the precarious many, arguing for a homology between the workings of economic and cultural capital. Sholette does not address the question of the ontological specificity of culture in any way and so we are not surprised that art cannot be the object of mere appreciation. This leads him to a very useful and interesting discussion of various historical efforts to organise artists into workers' unions as an alternative to the market model – or rather as an alternative market model. If the restless flexibility of artists makes them the model workers of enterprise culture, there is no reason why artists should not develop a class consciousness that makes them aware of the demands that are imposed on them to constantly produce just-in-time entertainments for a disciplinary regime that is unable to organise their productivity on anything other than an economic basis.

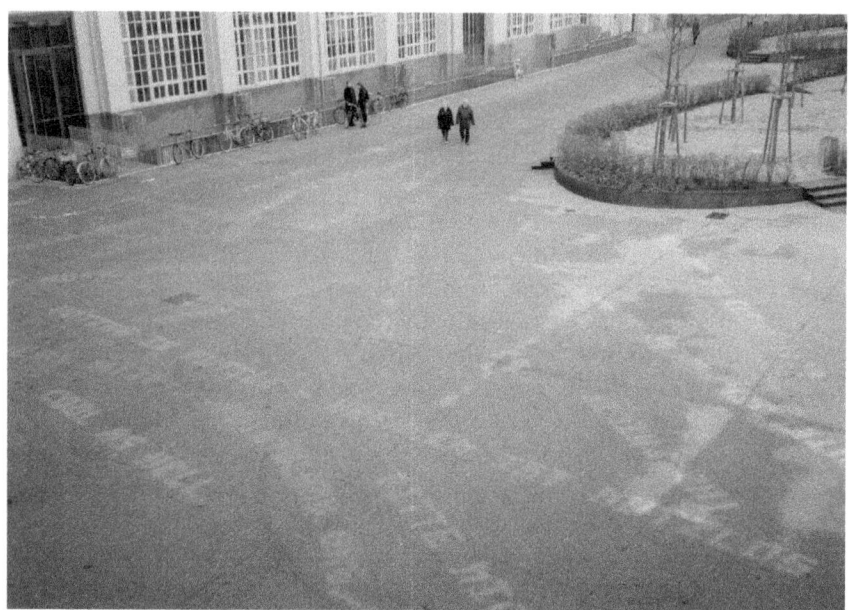

Institute for Applied Autonomy, *GraffitiWriter*, 1998 ongoing. GraffitiWriter is a tele-operated field programmable robot that employs spray cans to write linear text messages on the ground and can be deployed in highly controlled spaces from a remote location. GraffitiWriter is part of the IAA's Contestational Robotics and a form of resistance activity. Potential targets are US federal buildings and shopping malls. Courtesy of IAA.

What happens then to those who refuse to make art on demand and who instead choose to challenge the disciplinary forces of neoliberalism? How does one understand the interpassive relations that confront art activists when they are brought into the disciplinary orbit of ideological and repressive state apparatuses? The case of Critical Art Ensemble member Steve Kurtz and his collaborator Robert Ferrell is addressed in the context of a detailed discussion of tactical media. At its best, contemporary tactical media practitioners, such as Electronic Disturbance Theater, Reclaim the Streets and subRosa, believe that art should be oriented towards social and political dissent. Although today's activist tactics may not involve the same forms of political resistance that we associate with the old and new lefts, Sholette insists that we see in them more than just a failure to return to strategic thinking. The fact that the FBI and the Department of Justice considered CAE's genetically engineered food experiments to be potentially dangerous gives credence to the social, cultural and political potentials of tactical media.

Dark Matter captures with aplomb the tenor of a generation that possesses abundant academic qualifications but few expectations and even less desire

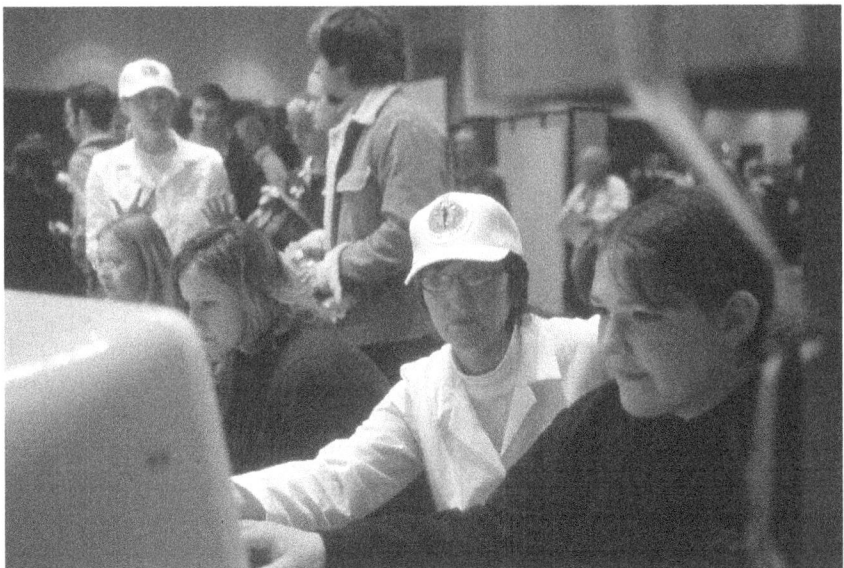

subRosa, *Biopower Unlimited!*, 2002. A team of consultants performs an intervention into the Bowling Green State University campus Art and Tech Fair. Participants fill out an online biopower questionnaire enabling them to compare how they allocate their labour power and leisure time. The consultants then analyse the results and give advice on possible life changes. Courtesy of subRosa. See cyberfeminism.net.

for rewards that are consonant with corporate culture and neoliberal administration. Sholette wonders how it would be possible, on the shores of a new collective imagination, for these dispersed practices to be mobilised into a new revolutionary politics. A chapter on mockstitutions provides examples of this imaginary of organisation: 'ersatz institutions,' 'bureaus' and 'bogus corporations' like those of the Yes Men, the Center for Tactical Magic, Neue Slowenische Kunst, Infernal Noise Brigade, the Carbon Defense League and the Institute for Applied Autonomy. By wearing the masks of authority, the kinds of second-order social reality that these artists' groups generate allow for temporary interventions. Their forms of radicalism amount to fractured resistance, to be sure, but who knows what lies on the other side of enterprise culture.

The inversion of normal expectations, which Sholette says includes those of traditional socialism and communism, is based on a rejection of nineteenth and twentieth-century leftist movements. He states with equanimity that political agency is no longer found on picket lines and barricades. This is not an entirely accurate picture of the events witnessed in 2011 in Tunisia, Egypt, Yemen, Syria, Bahrain, Morocco, Greece, Spain and the

UK. Social movements around the world that seek to wrest themselves from tyranny and economic austerity have in fact returned to those 'familiar old places' of struggle. In the US, in the years after Occupy Wall Street, it seems that the movement is increasingly becoming aware of the need for more effective and sustainable institutions. Rather than signal the demise of collective resistance, these protest events speak to the virtuality of the past and of possible futures.

Post-Marxist aesthetics

Sholette's notion of dark matter practices is further explored in *It's the Political Economy, Stupid*, an exhibition curated by Sholette with Oliver Ressler and first presented in Vienna in 2011.[17] The first version of this exhibition included works by four artists and artist groups that examined the ways in which art can represent and resist the colonisation of everyday life by deregulated capitalism. Following the global financial economic crisis of 2008 and occurring at the same time as the social rebellions of the Arab Spring, the urban encampments of Southern Europe and the Occupy Wall Street movement, the exhibition travelled to New York, Thessaloniki, Pori and Limassol, and along the way incorporated the work of eleven more artists and art groups. The catalogue of the exhibition functions both as a record of the exhibition, incorporating three essays that provide descriptions and images of the artworks, and as a snappy theoretical toolkit, with essays by a small but representative collection of artists and theorists on the left.

It's the Political Economy, Stupid is also the title of an essay by Slavoj Žižek that was published in 2009 and that is reprinted at the beginning of the book. The artist-editor-curators refer to this essay as an exercise in backtalk and a useful reference point for art that seeks to disable capitalist 'econospeak.' The assertion made in the introduction is that economic determinism 'has become an inescapable visage within the realm of the cultural superstructure … making it impossible to avoid previously ignored processes of value forma-tion.'[18] Political economy is thus presented as the first line of defence against narratives that reinforce economic austerity and military imperialism. The book avoids orthodoxy, however. Following Žižek's essay, Liz Park challenges Marxist universalism with Chantal Mouffe's agonistic pluralism, a postmodern difference politics that is echoed later in the book by Julia Bryan-Wilson. A short piece by the anarchist figurehead of Occupy Wall Street, David Graeber, chides Marxism as a joyless dedication to ballistic missile systems, and a reprint of an essay by Judith Butler also questions ideology as her work emphasises the simultaneous creation and disturbance of public space through the agency of vulnerable bodies coming together to make demands.

While this exhibition and catalogue correspond to the events mentioned

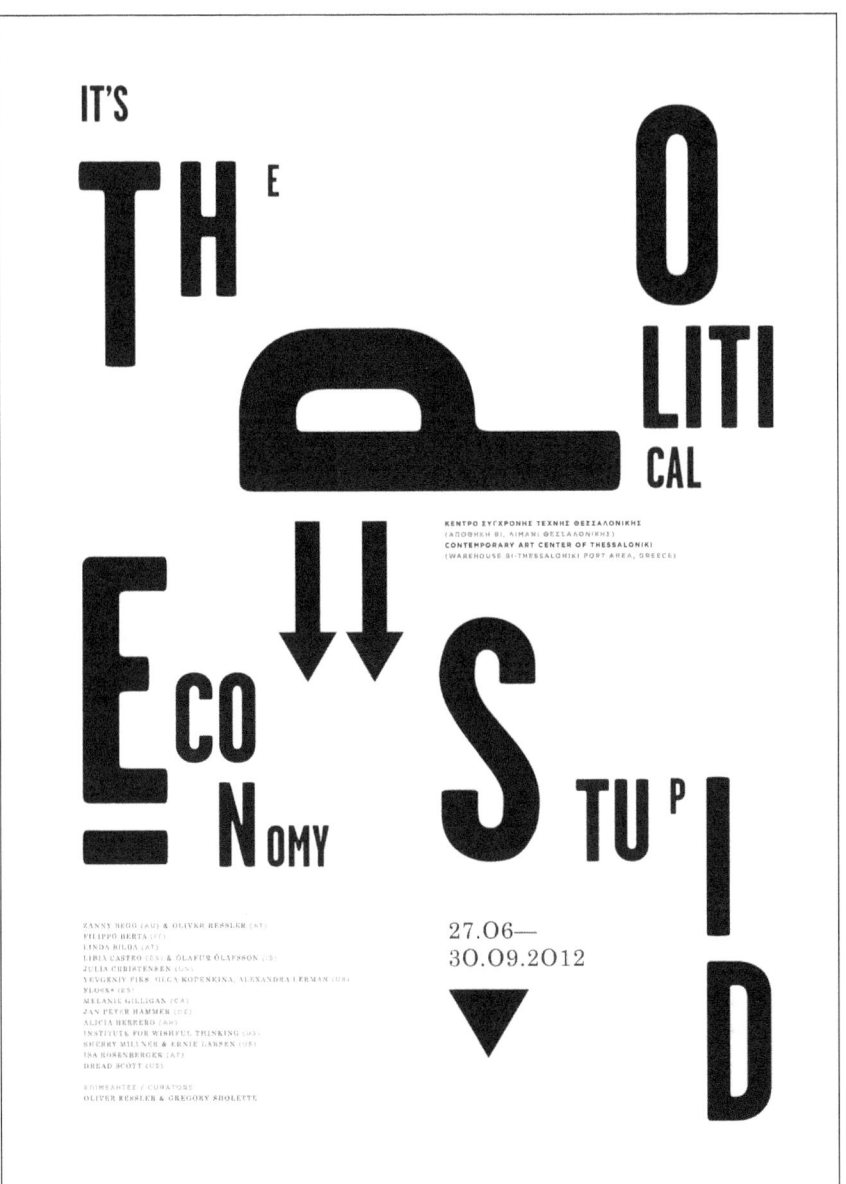

Poster for the exhibition *It's the Political Economy, Stupid* at the Contemporary Art Center of Thessaloniki, Greece, 2012. Design by Designers United. Courtesy of Oliver Ressler.

above, its more general frame of reference is the anti-globalisation politics that emerged in the years after the defeat of Soviet communism and the hegemonic rise of neoliberal governance. In this respect it makes sense as a follow-up to and perhaps even a theoretical sharpening of Ressler's concerns in *A World Where Many Worlds Fit*. The claim made by the curators that this is the first exhibition since the 1920s and 1930s to look at art that directly addresses issues of economics is perhaps overstated. I am aware of at least one such exhibition, *Capital Offense: The End(s) of Capitalism*, a 2012 project curated by Jennifer Gradecki and Renée Fox.

The contradiction that is taken by this project to its impossible aporetic climax is the fact that, as contributor Kerstin Stakemeier states plainly, all commodity production under capitalism, including art production, is subsumed by capitalist relations. The question of social reproduction presents both an ideological and an organisational challenge to anarchist and difference politics. The foregrounding of Žižek's essay is perhaps the clearest admission of this fact. Žižek argues that although the politics of the commons – the environment, biogenetics and intellectual property – pose a series of endemic social problems, capitalism seeks to manage all of these with the usual mechanisms. In this sense, it does not really matter, as John Roberts assumes in his piece, that we need to shift from blue-collar struggles for wages to struggles for a living wage within a context of sustainability. The overarching contradiction of capitalism, one that capitalism is not able to solve, is the increasing immiseration of excluded populations. As Žižek argues, the liberal politics of inclusion that focus on the protection of minorities loses from sight the proletarian position – the capitalist reduction of subjectivity to a 'part of no part.'

In light of the above, Roberts' essay on 'The Political Economisation of Art' is perhaps the most pertinent contribution to the book and considers in detail 'what is to be done' by artists in the context of the 'assimilation of art theory and practice into the categories of labor and production.'[19] 'What changes to art and labor,' he asks, 'have brought about this theoretical expansion of art into the categories of political economy?'[20] The overall state of capitalist decadence, he argues, has caused contemporary artists to examine their place within existing labour conditions. What is significant for Roberts is that exhibitions such as this one display a keen sense that we are beyond both modernism and postmodernism and that the stakes of writing on art and politics are far higher than the art world typically recognises. The strength of this book, therefore, is that it helps to bring the dark matter of the activist art world to a new level of class consciousness.

According to Roberts, the devalorisation of capital will lead either to radicalisation or to a cleansing of the system through imperialist war. The recent western misadventures in Iraq, Afghanistan, Pakistan, Yemen, Libya and Syria, the constant threats made to Iran, North Korea, Venezuela, China and Russia, and the re-colonisation of Africa, all tell us something about our actual political prospects. While *It's the Political Economy, Stupid* offers analyses with a bit of everything for everyone on the left, it leaves out the role that the state can and does play in social movements and in cultural production. The main concern of the state is that contemporary art should contribute to its GDP version of the political economy. Certainly, from a neoliberal point of view, it is an open question whether art should be based on realism rather than dissimilitude, collaborative activity rather than authored works. What is certain is that for those who seek to make common cause with social movements, the zeitgeist now favours social practice art.

Collaborative art versus avant-gardism

A significant contribution to the discussion on social practice art is Grant Kester's *The One and the Many: Contemporary Collaborative Art in a Global Context*.[21] The title of this 2011 book references Spinoza's theological reconciliation of the individual and the collective as part of an elaborate cautionary tale on the pitfalls of aesthetic autonomy. In his previous title, *Conversation Pieces* (2004), Kester put forward one of the most elaborate rationales for engaged community art to date, to which he gave the name 'dialogical aesthetics.' He did so by suggesting that community art represents a paradigm shift away from the non-discursive tactics of avant-garde contestation. Such avant-garde methods, he argued, separate artists from their audiences by construing the latter as non-discursive raw material that needs to be radicalised. While the better part of *Conversation Pieces* is dedicated to descriptions of dialogical art practices, Kester's subsequent book focuses much more on the theoretical claims of the first to draw a far more rigid line in the sand between community art and the avant garde.

Kester is a seasoned art critic with a long track record of insightful writing on the shift from public art and identity politics in the 1980s and 1990s to the phenomenon of community art in the 1990s and 2000s. The type of site-specific collaborative work that he champions unfolds, he says, through an extended interaction with local communities. Like many proponents of the new tendencies, he has worked to anchor his criticism in both social and political history as well as the history of aesthetics. In the first of three dense chapters he takes aim at the criticism of Nicolas Bourriaud and Claire Bishop, two authors whose ideas rely on what Kester considers to be an outmoded modernism. It is not so much that the boundaries between the avant garde and community art cannot be determined, he says, but rather that the mainstream of art has not fully understood the social and political implications of the new practices, which 'complicate conventional notions of aesthetic autonomy.'[22]

   While rigorously argued, Kester's polemic is also intensely prescriptive. For the sake of new artist groups like Park Fiction, Ala Plastica and Dialogue, so much critical theory must fall to the wayside: Barthes, Derrida, de Certeau, Lyotard, Kristeva, Blanchot, Badiou, Deleuze and Guattari, Agamben, Nancy, Lenivas, Rancière – anyone associated with the post-May 68 generation of postmodern pessimism and who guards against premature totalisations. In this Kester shows signs of courageously going beyond 'end of history' and 'end of meta-narratives' discourse, but he is cautious to not return to the tropes of the militant past. All avant-gardism and post-structuralism, he argues, forecloses the possibility of social interaction and real political engagement. If these strains remain legitimate in any way, they are at best limited.

   The second chapter looks at the discourse of development and compares the work of Dialogue in India and Huit Facettes in Senegal with that of Superflex in Tanzania and Brazil. He distinguishes his model of co-labouring from the possessive model of subjectivity that he finds implicit in the schizo-anarchist themes of Hardt and Negri. Social practice may be less about political solidarity on the left – defined as a 'chaste revolutionary desire' – than it is about winning hearts and minds for reformist practices of negotiation.[23] In his thinking Kester is far more beholden to academic post-structuralism than he otherwise lets on. He mentions Žižek, but this is strictly in order to disarm Bishop's approach from the insights of Ernesto Laclau and Chantal Mouffe. Otherwise, the Lacanian implications for social and subject formation are unexamined. And as if Kester's readers will be none the wiser, we are offered mostly postmodern, implicitly Foucauldian, understandings of critical theory.

   A book cover endorsement by Amelia Jones describes Kester's work as 'loosely Marxian.' This is tested in comparisons between the agitational work of Santiago Sierra and the documentary photography of Jacob Riis. Kester also contrasts the community work of Park Fiction and Project Row Houses with the over-identification strategies of the Yes Men. He delves into the contradictions of reform, suggesting that revolutionary practices offer only agonistic uses of the aesthetic. His contribution to theory therefore champions the pragmatism of incremental social change, negotiated with willing and sometimes resistant participants. In this sense Kester's work dwells in the gaps between aesthetics and politics. My sense is that the privileged site of Kester's discourse is not strictly out there in the activist social world but also in the universities and institutions that champion such progressive pragmatism. Today's universities and art institutions are not ivory towers and they are now certainly under pressure to prove the usefulness of knowledge and of culture to the new technocratic order. Ideology, however, and according to Žižek, cannot be explained pragmatically. Kester, a consummate pedagogue, shows us ideology at work by comparing different kinds of art.

Serious trouble

In the first of his 'two lectures' from 1976, Michel Foucault developed what he called a 'non-economic model of power' for which the strange efficacy of 'dispersed and discontinuous offensives' that 'lack systematic principles of coordination' might very well be able to counteract traditional morality and hierarchy.[24] The trouble for Foucault with many such offensives is that their resistance presupposes the power that generates their desire. Already, the post-modern scene had determined that disturbance is part of the game of power. In response to the dead ends of postmodern nihilism, a few art critics set out in the 1990s to provide some 'reconstructed' theories of engaged art. Among them Miwon Kwon argued in *One Place After Another* that because the Critical Art Ensemble overestimates the complicity of artists with capitalist institutions they are 'prematurely defeatist.'[25] In *Conversation Pieces*, Kester thought that because the critical insights that are generated by CAE are produced within their own core group rather than through a process of open-ended exchange with a given audience, they are 'prone to negation.'[26] In their own terms, CAE stated in the book *Digital Resistance* that they are neither interested in what they consider to be the 'liberal idea' of community, nor advocating nihilistic gestures: 'CAE still insists that productively challenging institutions will [occur] through forcing changes in the semiotic regime on an institutional basis while leaving the material infrastructure intact for reinscription.'[27]

Not unlike Kester, one of the major institutions that CAE has clearly had its sights on is the modernist edifice of art production. In this regard, *Disturbances*, an overview of the group's twenty-five year trajectory, is a kind of users' manual for how to not participate in the art world's unwitting function of providing cover for global capital's quest to impose authoritarian plutocracy.[28] In their own words, as they say, 'Institutes, *Kunsthalles*, and major festivals function as corporate alibis for good cultural citizenship, and too often function within the frame of research and development of cultural products in the service of profit and empire.'[29] The question then is how to effectively make use of cultural activity in order to subvert the beneficience of disciplinary agencies. CEA's basic word of order on this count is their *détourned* Malcolm X slogan 'by any media necessary.'

The first medium that is described in the book is the collective. Although not presented as a chronology of their work, but rather in terms of loosely orchestrated themes, the book nevertheless opens with a brief account of the formation of the group, which was established from the start as a critique of individual expression. The 'aggregate intelligence' of the ensemble was developed in the early years and then replaced by a 'collective' and 'organic model' where interdependency overcomes individualism but still allows members to exercise their best skills. Their panoply of means, overall, far surpasses the average multitasking artist's repertoire of experimentation and includes video, live multimedia production, lecture, performance, activist campaign, road trip, installation, theory, poetry, eco-intervention, provocation, hoax, agitprop, website, newspaper insert, workshop and amateur public lab. A

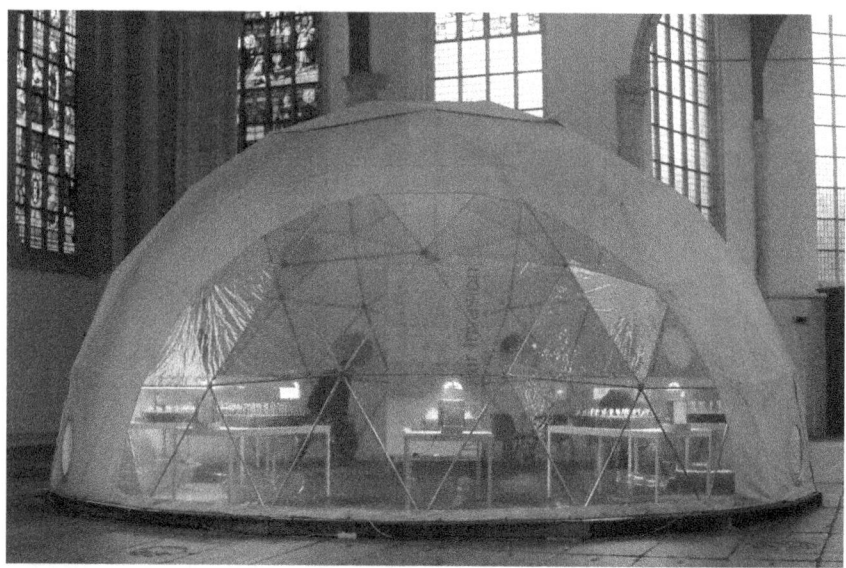

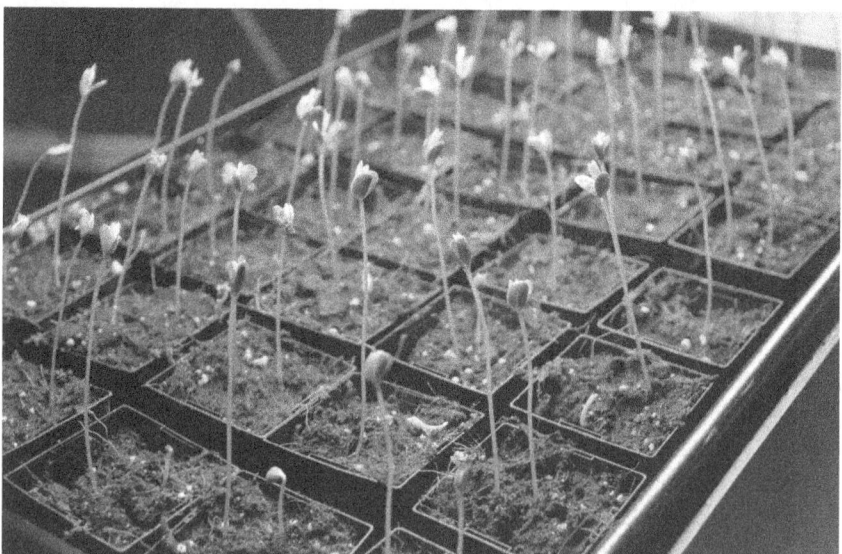

Critical Art Ensemble, *Molecular Invasion*, Installation View, 2002, World Information Organization, Amsterdam manifestation. Courtesy of Critical Art Ensemble.

lengthy series of projects is presented along with supporting texts as well as a generous display of visual documentation, including handouts, invitations, newspaper coverage, posters and book covers. The reader is invited to join CAE in their merry-making adventures down the rabbit hole of contestation. In this respect, Brian Holmes is quite right to state in his introduction that the book is a 'memory palace for the latest generation of political interventionists,' the rising generation of 'people on the ground' who are disillusioned not only with the territorial state machine but with archaic social forms promulgated by the 'vanguard' of the technocratic class.[30]

Disturbances gives the reader the feeling of catching up with and even getting inside the group, which after all is said and done remains a mirage, a kind of collective phantom or Robin Hood myth. One project that stands out is *Molecular Invasion*, a 2002 intervention and public experiment that reverse engineers Monsanto's Roundup Ready herbicide and makes the results of this experiment available to farmers who might want to protect their crops from nearby polluting GMO farms. *Molecular Invasion* is a participatory science-theatre project in which CAE, Beatriz da Costa and Claire Pentecost reverse-engineer genetically modified canola, corn and soy plants through the use of nontoxic chemical disrupters. This theatre of live public experimenta-tion attempts to transform artificial biological traits of adaptability into ones of susceptibility and to establish a model for contestational biology. *Molecular Invasion* caused Monsanto lawyers to threaten CAE with litigation and the group believes that the publication of their findings in an essay on 'fuzzy biological sabotage' was one of the main reasons that the US Department of Justice decided to indict CAE member Steve Kurtz on counts of mail fraud.

To give some credence to Kester's critique of the patronising attitudes of vanguards, it has to be said that CAE consider themselves to be always disrupting 'norms,' especially those that they consider to be deserving of deconstruction. While CAE are more than able to decipher the dominant structures of capitalism, they neglect or resist providing a class analysis of today's symbolic regimes, though more recent works like *A Public Misery Message*, presented at documenta 13 in 2012, address questions of economic inequality. CAE demonstrate a keen appreciation of the split law that regulates both official discourses and the 'obscene' aspects that are mediated by today's post-ideological institutions.

Social aesthetics

Anyone who has been involved in or has researched activist art in the last two decades is likely to be familiar with the work of Nato Thompson. As a curator at MASS MoCA, he co-edited with Gregory Sholette the cata-logue for the groundbreaking exhibition *The Interventionists: Art in the Social*

Sphere (2004–5), and as the former chief curator of Creative Time, he edited the massive anthology *Living as Form: Socially Engaged Art from 1991–2011.*[31] Whereas these previous books presented short essays by Thompson, *Seeing Power: Art and Activism in the 21st Century* provides readers with a better appreciation of the thoughts of one of the most well-known and whimsical of activist curators. *Seeing Power* is a detailed argument on the issues defining activist art today.[32] With no endnotes, no bibliography and no image captions, the book is a pleasant, user-friendly experience that discusses the work of leading socially engaged artists, including REPOhistory, W.A.G.E. (Working Artists and the Greater Economy), Thomas Hirschhorn, Tania Bruguera, Paul Chan, WochenKlausur, Yomango, William Pope L., Rick Lowe, Laurie Jo Reynolds, Center for Land Use Interpretation and Trevor Paglen.

From the start, Thompson tells us that *Seeing Power* is not a typical book about art and politics, but rather a combination of philosophy and practice, with observations based on twenty years of immersion in the activist milieu and the art world. The productive tension between contemporary art and Thompson's approach to a distinctly American grassroots version of anarchist politics is the distinguishing feature of this undertaking. It is clear from the outset that the purpose of conjoining activism with art is to bring about radical social change. The capitalist system is throughout the text an ominous force affecting all social institutions and in particular that of cultural production. Whereas from the title of the book one might have expected a Foucauldian lens through which to 'see power,' it is Antonio Gramsci's notion of hegemonic contestation that is first evoked as a way to define the practices of everyday life and the alternative spaces that animate the book.

One of the main points of Bürger's *Theory of the Avant-Garde* is that the postwar neo-avant gardes failed to sublate art and life in a revolutionary manner so that consequently this overcoming of contradictions was effected by what Max Horkheimer and Theodor Adorno defined as the culture industry. *Seeing Power* makes a similar assessment of the difficulties that have confronted the kinds of activist art that emerged in the mid-to-late 1990s. Referred to variously as tactical medial, socially engaged art, social practice art and Thompson's own 'social aesthetics,' such tendencies have had to confront the problems of commodification and recuperation that have affected avant-garde movements since the nineteenth century. Thompson is consistent throughout the book in approaching artistic production and consumption in terms of the cultural contradictions of capitalism. This for him, however, is a condition that cannot be escaped. What concerns him instead is capitalism's 'ecstatic devotion' to cultural production, its endless diversification of needs and its overwhelming ability to absorb anything that reacts against it.

Despite his professed anti-capitalism, Thomspon ignores the processes by which revolutionary impulses were abandoned in the postwar period along

with class politics. What replaces these in his description of events are countercultural movements, cultural trends and people organised around identity
issues. All of these intermingle with the culture industries in such a way that
resistance becomes more difficult. However, for Thompson, this condition
of near-total cooptation also allows us to see power with greater clarity.
The packaging and reselling of signifiers of resistance indicates a paradoxical
embrace and recognition of alternatives. He therefore situates his thinking as a
post-politics for which, in terms of today's common sense, 'there is no outside'
to capitalism: TINO. As he notes, the replacement of the term culture industry
with the more positive 'creative industries' only serves to indicate the extent to
which culture and capital are increasingly intertwined. Thompson's assertion
that the artists he discusses operate self-consciously at the intersection of art
and politics steers the question of politics in an ultimately pragmatic direction.
Seeing Power is less concerned with a productivist revolutionary art and is
more interested in art that reacts to the excesses of capitalism. Within these
parameters, Thompson's writing flows effortlessly between, for example, radical collectives like the Situationists, Superflex and Critical Art Ensemble, and
social movements around alter-globalisation such as the *indignados*, Occupy
Wall Street and Black Lives Matter.

Whereas the critical task for activist artists, Thompson says, is to create more
effective and affective forms of activism, one is left with the difficulty that arises
when critical cultural theory has abandoned the concept of totality in favour
of a more 'realistic' capitulation to immanentism, attempting to transform the
system from within – through spatial occupations, nonhierarchical organising
and anti-branding – rather than from without, through cultural revolution,
radical political parties and ideology critique. A key intellectual reference
point for his book is Bourdieu. One gets a sense of Bourdieu's influence as
Thompson addresses the suspicion that activists tend to show towards socially
engaged artworks that are ambiguous and elusive rather than straightforward
and didactic. It so happens that the dichotomy that is used to structure this
argument corresponds in Bourdieu's analysis to the class dispositions (*habitus*)
of the bourgeoisie and working class. Of course, as a result of more widespread
cultural education, the traditional social circumstances of class distinction are
no longer adequate. Nevertheless, the outer shell remains, and so this dynamic
between artists' ostensible preference for the ambiguous and activists' supposed
preference for the didactic has to be addressed. Giving the example of Jeremy
Deller's Iraq War project, *It Is What It Is* (2009), in which a bombed vehicle
was toured across the US as an incitement to public discussion, Thompson
emphasises artistic intention and the use of didactic means to reach a more
complex level of ambiguity where viewers have to decide for themselves
the meaning of a work. When the intentions of an artist are not legible, the
gap between the artist and the audience may widen, but this at least allows

```
It is What it is: Conversations about Iraq
        A project by Jeremy Deller
   Presented by Creative Time and the New Museum
```

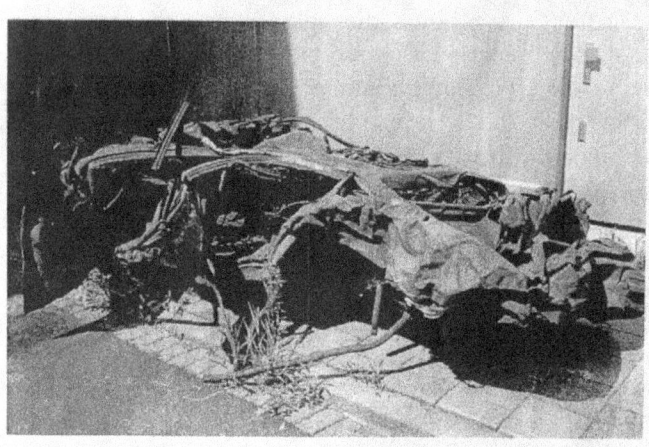

```
This exploded car is part of a traveling project
about the ongoing situation in Iraq. The RV and
car will travel from New York City to Los
Angeles stopping in cities across the United
States offering an opportunity to discuss Iraq
itself. On hand to answer questions are Jonathan
Harvey, a reservist in the military who recently
served in Iraq, as well as Esam Pasha, an Iraqi
artist who sought asylum in the United States in
2005. Feel free to ask them questions or look at
materials from Baghdad on the tables.


     More information and updates on the road at:
          www.conversationsaboutiraq.org
```

Jeremy Deller, *It Is What It Is*, 2009. Flyer given to members of the US public
during the touring of a car destroyed in the war in Iraq.
Courtesy of Jeremy Deller.

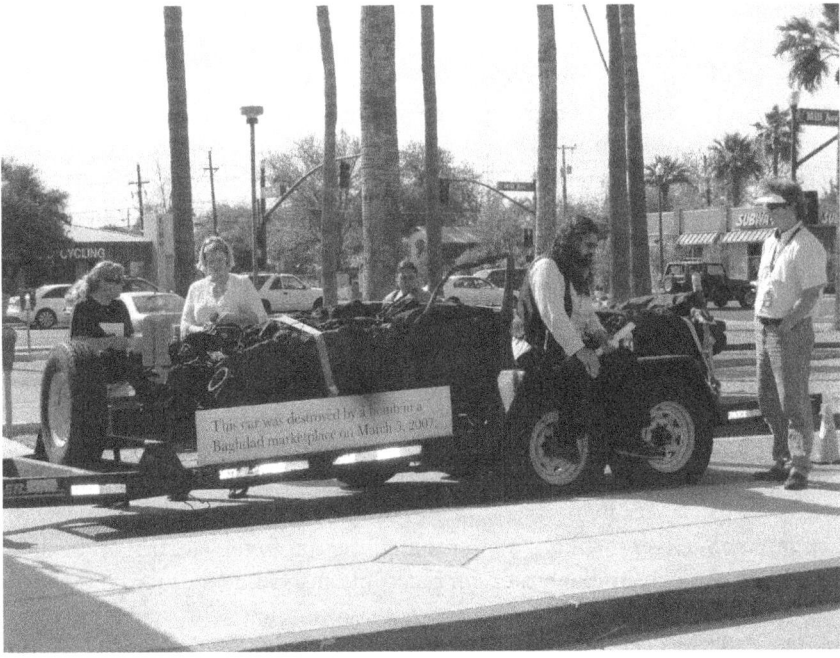

the work to escape singular interpretations. Thompson's insight is that in an unambiguous world of exchange relations and media manipulation, an atmosphere of 'visual suspicion' has been created in which people become paranoid and mistrustful.

While he could have made productive use of Žižek's discussion of the weakening of symbolic efficiency and the interpassivity of belief, Thompson opts for a somewhat more naive theory of paranoia regarding the ambiguous gesture. This comes into play in another chapter where Bourdieu's influence is present through the use of concepts like cultural and social capital. Unlike Bourdieu, however, who developed these ideas as means to go beyond vulgar materialism, Thompson is more deterministic in his emphasis on how the predominance of exchange relations and the fact of cooptation make social capital the object of paranoid critique. Here too, however, there is a saving grace for living as capitalist form. When one's authentic street cred and radical merits are offered up to bigger institutions and subsumed by capitalism, when social networking and the accumulation of social capital become necessary for survival in a world with more demands and fewer job opportunities, we might, he suggests, ease up on denunciations of careerism and selling out. Since the logic of neoliberalism is to set people against one another, Thompson argues that politically minded people should work to build trust and social cohesion rather than satisfy themselves with outings and purges. The activist artist who can build social capital and better navigate more fields and infrastructures has a better chance of effecting change.

The notion of infrastructure is the central concept of *Seeing Power*. The organisational capacity of activists to develop sustainable alternative spaces, or 'infrastructures of resonance,' marks what he refers to as a shift from temporary tactical actions to long-term strategic structures that can also act as 'transversal' sites of becoming. In this sense, groups like Gulf Labor are picking up where people organised around Art Workers' Coalition left off in the late 1960s. If the world is full of complicated bureaucracies and interconnected infrastructures that shape our lives, then these spaces can be occupied, reclaimed or created from the ground up in such a way that their impact can accommodate new forms of collective intersubjectivity. New infrastructures like the *Journal of Aesthetics and Protest* or 16 Beaver give themselves the power to legitimate practices and lend activist artists the kind of recognition they may not otherwise receive in the mainstream media and major art institutions. Thompson's personal experiences living in a student co-op in Berkeley and working with Temporary Services in Chicago offer some insight into the fact that art institutions need not be run like businesses but could instead be far more integrated with everyday life and with the need for communion with others through mutual networks. He writes: 'This ability to read a phenomenon based on the infrastructures of resonance around it is what I refer to as seeing power.'[33] Such infrastructures benefit the ambiguous artistic gesture by couching it in a world of discovery and connection rather than the underlying neoliberal economy. Thompson's experience as a high-level curator here allows for some understanding of the failings of what he refers to as the 'nonprofit industrial complex,' with its increasingly conservative values and financial pressures. New infrastructures might therefore legitimate activist practices while at the same time providing added social capital for its users.

Although we all need to make money to survive, there is no need, Thompson says, to abandon our radical ambitions. It is never altogether clear in *Seeing Power* to what extent cultural capital is ever anything more than a cipher for social relations under capitalism. Such is the consequence of theoretical immanentism. Because of this limitation on the subject of ideological reflection one cannot consider *Seeing Power* to be a work with much bearing on radical art theory. As Thompson says humorously: 'If the art world were a car, we have handed over the transmission, engine, body, and tires so we can work on the windshield wipers.'[34] But what about the other side of this equation – the one that makes an activist anti-capitalist? Thompson's book avoids the opportunity to more rigorously critique capitalism. This might seem an unfair assessment given the fact that capitalist cooptation is mentioned at every turn. However, instead of a radical ideology critique, or even a better understanding of political economy, Thompson's default intellectual horizon seems to be social constructionist discourse theory. Of course he himself can hardly be blamed for the current intellectual climate and no one to my knowledge has found an adequate solution to capitalism. Thompson nevertheless broaches the issue when he writes: 'This contradiction between [cultural] content and capital is part and parcel of the very fiber of contemporary art.'[35] In this sentence he is very close to identifying capital as form. Had he followed up on this insight he might have further considered ways beyond the loop of power and resistance. But then, had he done so, his book would have also been about revolution and dialectics.

Creative direct action

Activist scholar Yates McKee's *Strike Art: Contemporary Art and the Post-Occupy Condition*, a book dedicated to art that is embedded in direct action and social movement activism before, during and after Occupy Wall Street, is one possible answer to the limitations of Thompson's *Seeing Power*.[36] From the outset, McKee considers 'the relation of art to the practice of radical politics.' In his famous 1936 essay on the work of art in the age of mechanical reproduction, Benjamin concluded that the task of engaged artists was not to aestheticise politics, as Leni Riefenstahl had been doing for the Nazi regime, but to politicise aesthetics, for instance in the manner of the Dada artist John Heartfield. Closer to us today, Žižek has suggested that it might be time to turn around Benjamin's longstanding injunction and reverse it. *Strike Art* would seem to tilt in this direction, sharing the tools of contemporary aesthetics with movements for social change. Žižek is mentioned in the book in particular with regard to the speech he gave at OWS, where he warned young protesters to not fall in love with themselves and with the spectacle of the encampment, that the hard work of real social change comes the day after the moment of carnivalesque upheaval. McKee's book, you could say, dwells on this Žižek meme. In Lacanian terms, *Strike Art* understands that Occupy is not a unified, coherent movement, but it also understands that the 'situational apperception' that conditions its 'ego ideal' is that of an unacceptable neoliberalism.

Like the group Strike Debt (~~Debt~~), *Strike Art* uses a Derridean deconstructive register to place the word Art under erasure. This refers to the strike as a tactic of worker revolt as well as its use by other kinds of action such as the student strike, the art strike and the climate strike. It also alludes obliquely to Marxist dialectics when McKee suggests that the groups that emerged in the context of Occupy are 'engaged in a simultaneous negation and affirmation of art itself.'[37] McKee refers to this as a renewal of the ambition of the avant garde to sublate art into life, or in terms that are more specific to him, as the 'dynamic articulation' of art and direct action. While such an assertion might elsewhere lead to an extensive philosophical and theoretical exposé, McKee's book is short on art theory and long on examples of art activism, which he narrates in his introduction and four chapters as someone who has been directly involved in and is passionate about the movements that are discussed.

Because he is both committed to what he narrates but also nuanced in his criticisms, McKee's book is one of the most coherent presentations of the new kinds of activist art that have emerged alongside the development of social media and by and large after the rise of the alter-globalisation left in the late 1990s. McKee, however, would seem to think that Occupy has a special status in this regard and refers to it as an 'event,' citing in this instance the work of Alain Badiou. Although Badiou welcomes such movements as Occupy, he is also critical of the horizontalist massism that is presupposed by much anarchist political theory and the writing on multitudes. The ideas of communist thinkers like Badiou and Žižek are therefore referenced as touchstones of contemporary political theory on the left rather than engaged in their critical specificity. This is McKee's modus operandi on the whole, however. For example, although he identifies his writing and activism with the 'new anarchism,' he does not delve much further into anarchist theory.

On the level of art theory, McKee makes only a few modest claims. He is not concerned to determine the aesthetic criteria of art made in the context of social movements, as might for example someone like Bishop. By the same token, he is not trying to invent a new category of aesthetic practice, as with for instance Bourriaud's 'relational aesthetics' or Kester's 'dialogical aesthetics.' He argues instead that many different strategies and tactics could come in handy in the process of cultural contestation. A stronger claim is that the imaginaries of social movements like Occupy take us beyond contemporary art and beyond the control of art institutions like museums and academies. Autonomous movements and activist groups do not entirely dispense with art and its institutions, but 'leverage' these according to the needs of the moment. For McKee, art has lost the superstructural autonomy ascribed to it by thinkers like Adorno and is now thoroughly embedded in capitalist exchange relations. This concession to biopower, which one finds in theories of immanentism is what, according to McKee, defines the vanguardism of Occupy as 'creative direct action.' The sublation of art therefore implies that Occupy has superseded the parameters of social practice and socially engaged art, which he identifies with the moment when participants at the 2011 Creative Time Summit decided to leave the conference and join the people agitating in Zuccotti Park. This moment, he says, 'represents the end of socially engaged art' and its dissolution into 'an expanded field of "social engagement"' that repurposes art as a form of 'collective creativity.'[38]

Unlike some of the avant gardes of the past, Occupy's critique of capitalism is not articulated as an attack on bourgeois ideology. Rather, the operative term here is the commons, which acts as an ontological placeholder for the shift away from social democratic Keynesianism, unionism and welfare state reform, and from the representational politics and state control of communist parties. McKee is therefore keenly aware of the contradictions of OWS. While the concept of the 99% cannot incarnate the plurality of identities, its non-compliance with neoliberalism allows for 'cross-sectorial alliances.' However, affinity among different groups does not necessarily solve the problem of collective precarity. McKee mentions in this regard a question posed by Raunig, who wonders what it means to strike when the idea of the working day has been relegated to the Fordist past. Another contradiction that McKee rightly acknowledges, this time in relation to Sandy Relief, is the fact that such new autonomous biopolitical infrastructures are attempting to fill the void created by a negligent state apparatus. Such emergency relief groups are poorly compensated and in some cases may have less expertise than public infrastructures that have already proven to be effective. Assuming that the neoliberalisation of everything continues as planned, we could imagine the eventual need for Occupy Mail, Occupy Firefighters, Hospital Relief, Police Relief, and so on.

McKee is at his best when he describes the many facets of Occupy and its proliferation of experiments in self-organisation, from assemblies to slogans, embodied technologies and popular kitchens, practices of commoning knowledge and resources that lead to new subjective and affective assemblages against the undemocratic forms of state and capitalist control. He is cognisant of radical precedents to Occupy and dedicates many pages to political groups such as the Situationists, Black Mask, the Motherfuckers, the Diggers, the Black Panthers, Art Workers' Coalition, Reclaim the Streets and Direct Action Network, but also to the 'social aesthetics' of people like Krzysztof Wodiczko, Allan Sekula and Martha Rosler, and 'art' groups like ACT UP, REPOhistory, Critical Art Ensemble, Temporary Services, Yes Men, 16 Beaver, W.A.G.E., MTL and Not An Alternative. When he comes to the subject of Occupy Wall Street he does not spend much time describing the occupation itself but focuses on the 'aesthetico-political antinomies' that would come to structure Occupy, from its 'psychogeographical dramaturgy' to the site-specific aspects of the encampment, its 'formal' properties, its new performative signals, as well as its new lexicon of class warfare of the 99%. The result is the construction of a 'biopolitical assemblage' that involves 'embodied assembly' and 'technical mediation.' These forms had a durable structure and after the eviction would move to other sites of struggle and what Stephen Duncombe refers to as 'ethical spectacles.' Among those described in the book are Duarte Square, Occupy Faith and Occupy Arts, as well as Occupy Museums, Occupy Homes, Arts and Labor, May Day, Strike Debt, Rolling Jubilee and Gulf Ultra Luxury Faction (G.U.L.F.).

The book concludes by proposing a critique of Occupy based on what Marxists would have at one time identified as problems of uneven development,

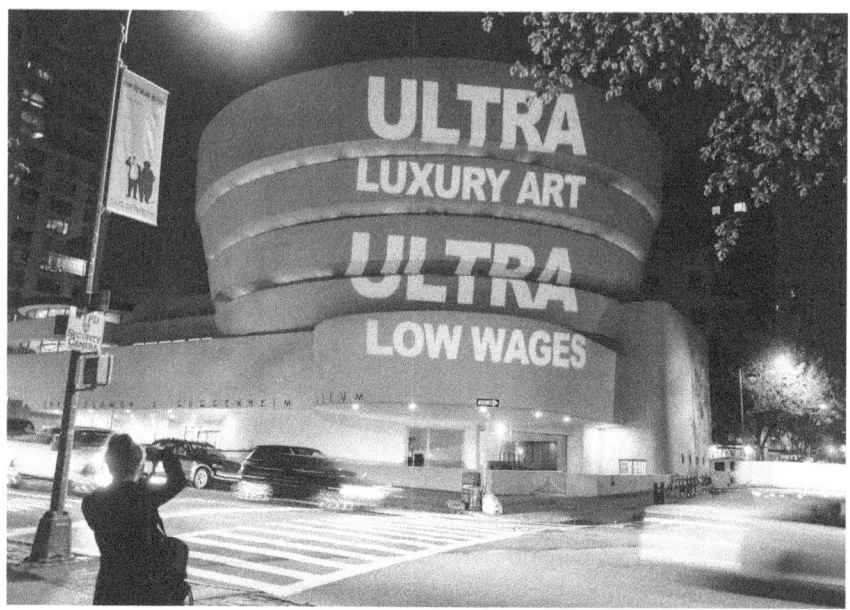

Gulf Ultra Luxury Faction (G.U.L.F.) action by the Illuminator on the façade of the Guggenheim Museum, April 27, 2016, after news that the Guggenheim Board of Trustees would no longer negotiate with the Gulf Labor Coalition (GLC) the labour conditions of the workers building its new museum in Abu Dabi. Courtesy of Gregory Sholette and G.U.L.F.

described by McKee as the 'universal culpability' of the life and death issues surrounding global warming and struggles by racially marginal communities against systemic state and police violence. In both cases, whether we are talking about the 'survivalist communisation' of groups like the Common Ground Collective, Hands Up Don't Shoot, Black Lives Matter and Direct Action Front for Palestine, or the 'eco-socialist planning' of groups like Survivor Village, Climate Action Camps, Liberate Tate, Art Not Oil, 350.org and Flood Wall Street, such 'ecologies of Occupy' represent the proliferation of biopolitical infrastructures that are concerned with social reproduction. 'Strike art' is therefore, according to McKee, art that is embedded in the 'living fabric of collective political struggle' and as such challenges the complacency of the contemporary art system.[39] This 'post-Occupy condition,' he argues, upends existing institutions. While such efforts may not be successful in terms of revolutionary goals, McKee says, they could be scaled up to build collective power, and, one might assume, lead to some kind of commonist transition.

When that day comes, weather permitting, people will be relatively free from alienated labour and will be able to determine for themselves, as well as with and for others, what forms of art they wish to pursue. In his concluding note, to come back to Žižek, McKee refers to this collective liberation of art as not an ideal image of harmonious identity but as an activity without end. A further enigma, about not 'falling in love' with ourselves, has to do with the difference that Žižek and Badiou have noted between the genuine event of falling in love and arranged marriages. Badiou refers to love as the immanence of a construction that is without the romantic illusion of unity and that is simultaneously a struggle against separation. Love therefore has something to tell us about the new relations that are being forged in today's radical art and politics. On the other hand, Badiou argues that there is no politics of love since politics is concerned with enemies. In love, he says, there are no enemies. Too bad then for the 1%. But then Marx also teaches that the contradictions of capital cannot be ascribed solely to the greed of the wealthy.

Revolution time again

The phenomenon of leftist political engagement through culture has grown exponentially since around the time of the Seattle protests of 1999. This came along with a complex rethinking of the limits of post-structuralist social constructionism in academia and a further development of leftist macropolitics that has influenced both theoretical work and the forms of organised resistance. In contrast to those who might think that the 'communist turn' in cultural theory is merely an academic pastiche or outmoded revivalism, Mikkel Bolt Rasmussen's *Crisis to Insurrection: Notes on the Ongoing Collapse* is a welcome intervention and a staid rejoinder to the kinds of post-politics that are popular in these neoliberal times.[40] Rasmussen's book examines the current potential of Marx's arguments in the *Communist Manifesto*, the *Grundrisse* and *Capital*. It maintains Marx's approach to the labour theory of value as well as his 'Critique of the Gotha Programme' in order to describe not only the failures of Soviet modernism but the limits to the wave of protests from 2011 and 2012. It is also an indication of the adisciplinarity of radical thought that this book should be written by an art historian and without recourse to descriptions of contemporary art. Whereas Rasmussen is known mostly for his writings on the Scandinavian section of the Situationist International, this slender volume is a fascinating and detailed exploration of what the Situationist line might look like in the current world situation.

Crisis to Insurrection first addresses the financial fiasco of 2008 and the sources of this in the protracted advancement of neoliberal economic policy since the 1970s. Concomitant with this decades-long process is the decline of class politics and the transformation of the idea of revolution. These two questions, divided neatly into an investigation of the current capitalist order and the global class composition of labour, leads to an analysis of the worldwide protests of 2011 and an assessment of their limits. To think beyond the recent round of resistance, Rasmussen offers a critique of various theoretical options, namely the multitudes idea and workerist politics of Hardt and Negri, the Leninist vanguardism of Žižek and the democratic socialism of the *Kilburn Manifesto*.

From the start of the book, it is not altogether clear what it is that Rasmussen has to add to Marxist politics other than to underscore the standard position that the current crises – financial, geopolitical, environmental – are an expression of the inherent contradictions of capitalism, the limits of accumulation and the exploitation of workers in the process of social reproduction. As neoliberal policy is used to justify structural transformation in the western economies through outsourcing, new technologies, credit and unemployment, both the working class and economists are pushed into ideological confusion, looking to neo-Keynesianism, protectionism and nationalism as possible alternatives. What then is to be done in the absence of a clear political programme as a point of departure? From the cover of the book, with its image of Lenin, constructivist design and faux-Cyrillic font, one might expect that Rasmussen is proposing a party politics of some sort. But as we discover, the situation is according to him more desperate today than it was in 1917. This is not altogether a problem since the ruined state of labour politics might be an unexpected benefit for a truly revolutionary vision of society beyond wage labour, capital and property relations. As he puts it, the loss of a revolutionary perspective is the starting point of his book. What is clear then is that the crisis and the responses that we have seen in Greece, Portugal, Iceland, Egypt, Bahrain, Tunisia, South Africa, Bangladesh, China, Chile, Bolivia, Brazil, the UK and the US, indicate, as he puts it, that thirty years of one-sided class war is over. All of these are not local crises but symptomatic of the contradictions of global capitalism. The avant-garde project, he argues, still holds. The question is learning from what it is that has not worked.

Rasmussen's discussion of the conditions of capital and labour in the last several decades will be familiar to readers of critical left literature. His text is short on cited references and as such does not engage in the kinds of complicated arguments one can otherwise find in writings on political economy. It is nevertheless thoroughgoing and convincing in its synoptic range, making connections between experiences on different continents. One slight omission is the discussion of socialist state experiments in Latin America. Another is the singular focus on the working class and the neglect of the class effects of polarisation. This 'middle' class phenomenon was once the cornerstone of analyses of the 'post-industrial' society and although Boltanski and Chiapello's research is addressed, the analysis of the 'cultural logic of late capitalism' is otherwise kept to a minimum. This is unfortunate since as a cultural theorist Rasmussen could have addressed the overall shift from postmodernism, as Fredric Jameson defined it, to the more recent wave of capitalist globalisation and the hype about creative global cities and alternative modernities. In addition to Boltanski and Chiapello's discussion of management discourses, Rasmussen addresses Lazzarato's work on debt, Mike Davis' work on slums, Giorgio Agamben's idea of bare life, as well as the recent focus on the Anthropocene. He asserts that both Leninism and Keynesianism are no longer adequate strategies for the left, a view that is presented as axiomatic rather than proven through argumentation. Regardless, we have with this the basic elements of Fukuyama's thesis on the end of history and the view that there are no alternatives to the global regime of capitalist democracy. Indeed, whereas the war on the working class persists, the revolutionary imaginary suffers from a lack of praxis. Badiou's notion of fidelity to the idea of communism is aluded to but with the caveat that such commitment is nowhere to be seen. The revolution, he writes, 'is just not on the agenda.'[41] If it exists anywhere it is more in the way that we labour than at the level of class consciousness. In terms of ideology, it is neoliberalism that has triumphed, with social democratic parties and third world dictatorships jettisoning everything having to do with equality, universality, political freedom, the rule of law and a free press.

The main problem with the disappearance of the working class as the agent of historical change is the lack of coordination among the various waves of protest and resistance to neoliberalism. Although he takes great care to not flatten out the differences between events in different parts of the world, Rasmussen is at times unclear concerning the extent to which the events in Libya, Syria and Ukraine qualify as anything more than civil wars and foreign incursions. Such conflicts are not only reactions to neoliberal hegemony but also, despite the potential for change, the direct result of imperialist machinations. Rasmussen makes better use of his critiques of the occupation movements in Southern Europe and the United States. The indignation of the protesters, he argues, is unconnected to previous revolutionary struggles and so the critique of capitalism appears as only one potential framework among others. In such conditions, protests movements like the Spanish 15M and American Occupy Wall Street camps are said to be mostly moralising and reformist. The anarchistic critique that surfaces, he argues, leads to open-ended slogans and the absence of demands. The latter, exploited as 'poetic' features of the protests, indicate that such activists no longer consider the capitalist state to be able to assure their wellbeing and survival. The protests oscillate, therefore, between a desperate plea for redistribution and a confrontational revolutionary position based on the supersession of capital and labour. Rasmussen is sensitive to how the lack of demands also represents a critique of the representative parliamentary politics of the state, with the refusal to take power and the rejection of appointed leaders. However, this stance is mostly defensive, resentment-based, sometimes conservative, populist or even right-wing, or radical-democratic at best. It is not a principled rejection of neoliberal globalisation. While the main problem for the revolutionary working class is the mutual isolation of the protests, Rasmussen is nonetheless optimistic since the various protests in Tunisia, Egypt, Yemen, Oman, Spain, Athens, London and New York did in fact refer to one another and made common cause across classes and national differences. His concern is not so much the particulars of the protests this time, but the basic problems related to production and reproduction. The search for scapegoats plays into a right-wing short-circuiting of the analysis of capitalism. Making the 1% pay its fair share of taxes, or cancelling symbolic debt through the Rolling Jubilee will not solve the fundamental problem and so these alternatives tend to echo the demand that the state concern itself with the reproduction of the labour-capital relation.

The question of 'what is to be done' opens the most exciting part of the book, titled 'Beyond Vanguards, Reformism and Multitude.' Rejecting the Leninist view that class consciousness can be introduced and guided from without, yet maintaining that the important issue for workers is the question of organisation, Rasmussen sets out to disqualify various contemporary left tendencies. He criticises the 2013 *Kilburn Manifesto* of Stuart Hall, Doreen Massey and Michael Rustin for taking a culturalist approach to the British national working class and ignoring political economy. Their theory of collectivity, he argues, which is put forward as an alternative to the neoliberal injunction to individual entrepreneurialism, is reminiscent of 1950s reformist socialism, he says, which attempts to restore the proper balance between the destructive effects of capitalism and the labour movement. Communism, he argues, has always been against the self-negation of the working class and against the idea that it should be put in charge of its own exploitation. Hardt and Negri's 2012 *Declaration* is also addressed and in this case critiqued for replacing the notion of the working class with the idea of the multitude, which, within the terms of a dominant biocapitalism, experiments with new social forms and new ways of being. Whereas Hardt and Negri consider this kind of creative self-production to be inherently communistic, Rasmussen holds that such positivist constructs of class are not so much self-valorising as they are devalorising and denegating, confusing crisis with protest, revolution with counter-revolution. Rasmussen suggests that instead of turning to trendy topics like immaterial labour and the primacy of resistance, it would be better to consider the crisis as the result of the contradictions of capital as well as workers' refusal of neoliberal governance. Rejecting the notion of massism, he explains that capital is not simply opposed to the masses but is a contradiction that creates specific kinds of relations. In this regard the revolution is not strictly immanent to the mode of production and so we should aim to keep radicalism from being dissolved into the new modes and relations of post-Fordist production.

There are flaws in Rasmussen's presentation of Žižek's work that are worth noting. Rasmussen rests his argument against Žižek on one short essay and only with passing reference to Žižek's first book-length treatment of Lenin's writings, *Revolution at the Gates*. He finds that Žižek overestimates the influence of vanguard leadership as well as superstructural political ideas in their ability to direct social change. Capitalist political economy is the product, he argues, of structural necessities in the mode of production and not, as Žižek might suggest, the result of the leadership of people like Mao, Tito or Thatcher. Whereas Rasmussen's argument might seem overly deterministic or 'scientistic,' its contradictions are well taken as fundamental aspects of Marxist dialectics. Žižek himself has many times criticised the limitations of having charismatic and powerful leaders like Hugo Chavez and Fidel Castro. The fact is that his theory of the Discourse of the vanguard Master is different from what Rasmussen makes of it. Žižek has always maintained that what needs to be repeated in Lenin is not the model of the Bolshevik party, but the notion that the potential of an authentic act is not guaranteed and covered over by the big Other, interpreted in the case of Lenin as historical necessity. A Master is not someone who tells us what to do – how to be free – but who, in Žižek's estimation, disturbs us into freedom. It is not an exemplary figure who must be followed or emulated, since, in Lacanian terms, the Master is inherently inconsistent: the Master figure is someone who is exemplary insofar as she or he refuses the situation and refuses the kind of negation that relies on the disavowed underside of the split Law. The Žižekian leader is thus not a demagogue who knows better than the people what is good for them and imposes this against their will. It is someone who takes risks based on a vision of change that others may or may not adhere to.

Rasmussen's singular emphasis on the contradictions of capitalism might be faulted for conforming to what Jacques Rancière describes as Marxist metapolitics, the assumption that the economic infrastructure is the only true site of politics. Or as David Harvey has argued, the capital-labour contradiction is not the sole political explanation of the crises of capitalism. Having said this, it would be false to assume that Žižek is himself entirely removed from this perspective. Against the Foucauldian emphasis on disciplinary biopower, Žižek's Lacanian-Hegelian materialism insists that social reality is not wholly given and moreover that class struggle, regardless of the myriad levels of contradiction, is the foreclosed Real of global capitalism. Whereas classical political economy is focused on the contradictions of the value form, the interpassivity of belief for Žižek brings Lacanian psychoanalysis into the structure of late capitalism. The sublime, religious character of the commodity is a correlate to the emptiness of the rule of capitalism as big Other. Rasmussen and Žižek may thus have more in common than Rasmussen acknowledges. Both of them understand that the revolution 'from each according to his or her ability, to each according to his or her needs' is not a clearly mapped plan but a destruction of the structures of oppression. The communist utopia that lies on the other side of the lower stages of communism and its distribution of goods, focuses, Rasmussen says, on particularity and needs. A minimum programme would therefore begin with a de-monetisation of the economy, altogether transforming the conditions of opression that enslave the working masses.

Defending the revolution

One can only hope that books like Rasmussen's can influence the current manifestations of radical praxis. Since *Crisis to Insurrection* does not directly address engaged art, it is worth disussing further his 2017 article published in the journal *FIELD*, which is edited by Grant Kester and is dedicated to socially engaged art criticism. Rasmussen's 'A Note on Socially Engaged Art Criticism' examines the significance of four areas of critical art practice and their outcomes.[42] In the case of relational aesthetics, as defined and championed by Bourriaud, the emphasis on small-scale utopias based on inter-human realtions that take place mostly within the space of art institutions is deemed by Rasmussen to have become indistinguishable from the art-as-entrepreneur-ialism of the global circuit of cultural tourism. Institutional critique, with its self-critical sociology and immanent approach to the rules of art institutions, became a fixture of contemporary art, giving way to new institutionalism and other kinds of recuperation. Tactical media's playful do-it-yourself guerrilla projects against state and corporate domination privileged an exodus from institutions through social movement networks. Although it experienced set-backs after 9/11 and the war on terror, it made something of a comeback with the wave of protests of circa 2011. However, from the point of view of the theory of the avant garde, tactical media prefers protest strategies to any grand claims for system change.

Having criticised relational art, institutional critique and tactical media, Rasmussen turns to socially engaged art, which he argues has its sources in the interventionist art of the 1960s through to the 1980s, including 'social sculpture,' 'activist art,' 'participatory art' and 'community art.' Placing an emphasis on dialogue but also working outside the confines of the art institution and with non-art audiences, socially engaged art works with social-political relations as a framework for projects. Despite some institutional cooptation, socially engaged art remains a serious direction for politically-minded artists. With regard to the journal *FIELD*, however, Rasmussen questions Kester's programme for socially engaged art criticism, which should, Kester argues, be based on ethnographic fieldwork that is able to assess the relations that artists sustain with local communities and the ways in which practices, as Kester writes in the editorial for the journal, should investigate 'the ways in which power and resistance operate through a manifold of aesthetic, discursive, inter-subjective and institutional factors.'[43] Kester's emphasis on process rather than autonomy extends to his views concerning artists' and theorists' attitudes towards audiences. His emphasis on a kind of participant or dialogical anthropology tends to disallow the insights of ideology critique in favour a 'non-ideological' progressive pragmatism. The purpose of critical theory is to challenge the degradation of life, creativity and work produced by capitalist alienation. In terms of art affecting change, according to Rasmussen, socially engaged art limits itself to consensus-based modes of interaction in a local community context – an 'art of modest proposals' that avoids recourse to meta-narratives of radical anti-capitalism in favour of micropolitics and micro-utopias. In other words, despite his appreciation of contemporary art's social engagement, Rasmussen charges it with an 'insufficiently dialectical' consciousness of the relations between art, politics and capitalism, which results in the confirmation of a neoliberal abandonment of class struggle.

In a response article, titled 'The Limitations of the Exculpatory Critique,' Kester reasserts his defence of socially engaged art, arguing on the one hand that there can be no simple dichotomy between consensus and negation in social processes oriented towards political change, and secondly, that there is often confusion in the analysis of radical art between rhetorical effects that presume a priori knowledge of the politics of a situation and pragmatic effects that test political assumptions through action.[44] Rasmussen's critique of modest gestures, Kester says, prevents distinctions between those practices that link to radical social movements and those that are rather more depoliticised. The crux of their disagreement centres around the question of what constitutes 'real' social change. Against what he perceives as Rasmussen's 'purist,' and as such 'conservative,' hard line against capitalism, Kester develops the concept of the 'exculpatory critique,' which, in summary, faults socially engaged art for providing a veneer of political change for capitalist state regimes and preventing systematic transformations.

Kester, in turn, faults Rasmussen for failing in his work to address the problematic legacy of communist social experiments. Without such a critique as a starting point, it is impossible to fully appreciate the 'capillary' practices of social activism. Ideological purity leads Rasmussen, like Adorno at an earlier moment in history, to privilege avant-garde art and radical theory against pragmatic, diagnostic and prefigurative encounters. This makes Rasmussen similar to Žižek, Kester adds, who warned the OWS protesters at Zuccotti Park that 'carnivals come cheap' and 'what matters is [what happens] the day after.' Kester's charge here is immaterial, since, as we have seen, Rasmussen largely agrees with him that social change is a product of modes and relations of production, and not something that is affected from 'above' by revolutionary theory or by political leaders. In other words, Rasmussen is not an ideologue but rather someone who asserts the Marxist critique of political economy for its materialist veracity. Kester and Rasmussen would in this regard disagree with Žižek's Lacanian-Hegelian theory of non-causal social change and the kind of *non-knowledge* that, for example, conditioned Lenin's choices during the October Revolution.

One of Žižek's main claims is that the left has more or less accepted the Fukuyaman doctrine of the end of ideology. Despite all the back and forth in the exchange between Rasmussen and Kester, which involves their respective writings beyond these two short essays, what compromises Kester's position on this issue, and nothwithstanding his commitment to 'freedom and equality,' as he puts it in his response, is his charge that nowhere does Rasmussen ask himself why working-class people and the poor have not rallied to the cause of the Fourth International but have instead joined the ranks of Islamic fundamentalism and populist neo-fascism. This characterisation of the working class as prone to demagogical manipulation is surprising coming from someone who champions works of community engagement. The rightward drift that we see emerging today is not directly an aspect of the failures of communism, but rather a result of the depradations of global capitalism, which vacillates between the neoliberal centre and the authoritarian right. Both of these actively prevent the emergence of leftist alternatives. Insofar as liberal and postmodern academics conflate all projects for revolutionary macropolitical change with totalitarianism, with top-down theoretical and ideological purism, with class essentialism and with modernism, the art of reformist proposals can be used to ignore and downplay the kinds of radical achievements that have actually contributed more to the emergence of socially engaged art than its practitioners sometimes let on. On this question Claire Bishop is nobody's fool.[45] No wonder then that Kester refers to the 'exculpatory critique' as 'repressive re-sublimation,' which is nothing if not a disavowal of Herbert Marcuse's concept of 'repressive sublimation.' Its opposite is the Freudian notion of repression, which liberal pragmatists associate with terms like 'propaganda' and 'communism,' but not with terms like 'freedom' and 'equality.' Without ideology critique, let alone psychoanalysis, it becomes impossible to think of dialogical aesthetics and related forms of art under neoliberalism as anything less than socially beatific.

Much of the talk about art and revolution that rejects a role for a communist party and state apparatus limits itself to Stalinist fiascos and even in this case, wherever you might find it, one does not typically encounter any degree of complexity concerning the potentials and failures of communist social experiments. I conclude therefore with Rebecca Gordon-Nesbitt's exemplary and helpful study of cultural policy in Cuba: *To Defend the Revolution Is to Defend Culture*.[46] Based on extensive research 'in the field,' the book is designed to propose alternatives to the current global capitalist regimes in which the forms of socially engaged art have emerged as bandaid, if not placebo, solutions to problems that should otherwise be organised through the communal servicing of goods.[47] The question then becomes, would socially engaged art as we know it exist in a future communist society? Or rather, what aspects of socially engaged art would change and what others would remain? Some possible answers to this enigma are provided by Gordon-Nesbitt, who examines the Cuban Revolution as a means to question the state of actually existing cultural production. Her main hypothesis is that there exist possibilities for relations to be created between art and society that are not premised on the profit motive. In the preamble to the book, titled 'Cuba as an Antidote to Neoliberalism,' she states that what motivated her project is the current market fundamentalism that consigns all cultural production to the needs of economic growth, shaping it into an ideological weapon of capitalist globalisation. Readers are richly rewarded as they are immersed in a case study where some of the perennial debates among artists and writers of conscience are worked out in concrete historical circumstances in which a socialist regime attempts to bring into existence the best of what humanist Marxism has promised, along with the necessity of struggle against the results of centuries of colonialism, the pressures of capitalist imperialism and the failures of Soviet Stalinism. As Gordon-Nesbitt makes clear, the political events of the Cuban Revolution are not simply a matter of history, but have implications for the future.

Aside from the introductory texts and a brief conclusion, the book is essentially divided into two parts, with a section discussing the subject of cultural policy in revolutionary Cuba through a historically-specific perspective on theoretical issues, and a second part that follows a more chronological trajectory from the earliest days after the victory of the 26th of July Movement in 1959 to roughly the late 1970s. In this period, 'liberal' and 'orthodox' tendencies vied for primacy, as Cubans interacted with international comrades, leading eventually to the ratification of the revolutionary humanist vision of leaders like Che Guevara and Fidel Castro, whose slogan was 'within the Revolution, everything; against the Revolution, nothing.' The role of militant leadership and of state functions are therefore affirmed not only as a matter of record, but as a point of solidarity by Gordon-Nesbitt, who notes with keen lucidity a meeting of cultural producers at which Fidel intervened by placing his pistol on the table, reminding all those present that the Revolution had been achieved at a great cost and that whatever freedoms had been won by the people of Cuba, artists and intellectuals were mandated with the task to pursue their work in the interest of social, political and cultural transformation and the needs of a socialist society.

Gordon-Nesbitt's affirmation of this social project extends to her critique of the defenders of Tania Bruguera's 'dissident' provocations of Cuban authorities with the 2009 work *Tatlin's Whisper #6* (*#YoTambienExijo* [I also demand]) in 2014.[48] A member of the editorial board of *FIELD*, and a high-profile international artist, Bruguera is criticised by Gordon-Nesbitt for planning a staged arrest in order to solicit accusations of censorship and to promote freedom of speech, an issue that has a long history of precedents in Cuban cultural policy that Bruguera otherwise ignores. As it happens, although Bruguera is associated with socially engaged art, her tactics in this case, and according to Gordon-Nesbitt, have less to do with dialogue with fellow Cubans and are much more in line with the kind of avant-garde negation that Kester rejects. However, in this case, what is negated is the leadership and the Revolution as we know it, as identified by the site that Bruguera chose for her performance: the Plaza de la Revolución.

In the first part of the book, Gordon-Nesbitt takes the broadest view possible on what a radical cultural policy, in any context, should encompass. Beyond the mechanisms of socio-economic support for artists and writers, the relation between culture and the state is shown to be essentially different in a capitalist and a socialist context. Since the enlightenment, the aesthetic has been associated with human emancipation, a notion that has been tailored by different political perspectives and government agencies. Insofar as the US and the UK have associated culture with commerce and economic growth, they ignore United Nations stipulations that art should be supported but not reduced to the status of a consumer good or a site for speculation. The policies experimented with in Cuba provide some ideas on how culture can offer a means beyond socio-economic contradictions. It is significant that the Revolution did not originate in strictly communist circles and that the Cuban communists of the Popular Socialist Party (PSP) only belatedly joined the insurrection, leading to longstanding scepticism towards communism. Rather, the Cuban Revolution was led by new left intellectuals who considered themselves post-Stalinist. Yet, insofar as US aggression was an ever-present danger, ties were maintained with the Soviet Union and Marxism-Leninism was applied to matters of political economy. The flipside to this, however, was a vision of socialism and of a humanist Marxism that sought to protect freedoms and human happiness as well as national cultural characteristics. This took the form of a Marxism influenced by the ideas of the Cuban intellectual José Marti, which were introduced by Che Guevara as a means to devise a continent-wide resistance to imperialism. The goal of freeing people from economic pressure, to overcome alienation and restore individuals' capacity to relate themselves to humanity and nature are keystones of proletarian humanism that were given expression in the creation of a better life in both a material and spiritual sense. While literacy was a first objective of the 26th of July Movement – with Cuba having today the second highest literacy rate and the US and the UK coming in forty-fourth and forty-fifth place – the creation of cultural institutions was undertaken as early as 1961 with the building of national art schools, professional training for art instructors and an outreach programme to rural areas so as to abolish the distinctions between town and country and between manual and intellectual labour. In a short period, the amateur *aficionados* art education campaign would produce more than a million amateur artists within a population of seven million.

Throughout the 1960s, steps were taken in the development of an infrastructure for the administration of Cuban culture. In 1959 the government established the Cuban Institute of Cinematographic Arts and Industries (ICAIC) as well as the Casa de las Américas; in 1961 intellectuals formed the National Union of Cuban Artists and Writers (UNEAC); the pre-Revolutionary Nuestro Tiempo cultural society represented the ideas of the PSP; and the National Council of Culture (CNC) was created in 1961 – a group that Gordon-Nesbitt reproaches for its orthodox misreading of Marxian dialectics and separating art from the historical processes of the Revolution. Gordon-Nesbitt provides a brilliant theoretical and historical elucidation of the pitfalls of ideological orthodoxy. In 1961 the National Art Schools (ENA) were established for training across the disciplines and in 1963 a National Museums Commission was formed, exhibiting art recovered from the elite, building a dozen new museums and touring exhibitions around the island and abroad. All of these institutions were committed to collective consciousness while sustaining creativity, supporting artists, developing pedagogical programmes and engaging with the world though cultural exchanges. In an early statement by Roberto Fernández Retamar, editor of the journal of the Casa de las Américas, the Revolution is described as a process whose course is not exact, but that the Cuban people are immersed in. One can see how different a statement this is from that of artists in the capitalist world who see themselves as an enclave, detached ideologically from the rest of society and at the same time immersed in the culture industries at large.

It was only in 1976 that the CNC was dissolved and replaced by the Ministry of Culture (MINCULT), headed by Armando Hart, a lawyer and former urban guerrilla. The bulk of Gordon-Nesbitt's book, one could say, is dedicated to describing the process that resulted in the creation of MINCULT. Whereas the first part of the book provides an overview of this period, elaborating what was at stake in terms of the ideals of the Revolution and the emancipatory role of culture under socialism, the second section leads the reader into more detailed analysis of the particulars, demonstrating how at every stage the valences of the dialectic, as Fredric Jameson calls it, can lead to very different understandings of what is happening. Gordon-Nesbitt consistently shows how the leadership sought to encourage the freedom of creative expression while at the same time securing the Revolution for future generations. In this process, culture was given an important role in galvanising revolutionary ideas, artists were freed from the laws of supply and demand, subsidies replaced royalties and sales, and property rights for creative works were replaced by state-sponsored dissemination.

Although it is not possible to do justice to all of the events that are related in the book – from Fidel's 'Words to the Intellectuals' after the 1961 *Pasado del Meridiano* controversy, the First National Congress of Writers and Artists (August 1961), the CNC policies of the early 1960s, Che's 1965 text 'Socialism and Man in Cuba,' the [International] Cultural Congress of Havana of 1968 and its many participants, the Padilla Case of 1968–71, the First National Congress of Education and Culture of 1970, the Five Grey Years of military control of culture from 1971 to 1976, and the First Congress of the Cuban Communist Party of 1975 – I would mention that throughout, Gordon-Nesbitt provides a rich and compelling analysis of the relationship between the political vanguard and artistic praxis that could easily be read alongside today's discussions on socially engaged art, art activism, community art, transversal practice, relational and dialogical aesthetics, participatory art and other variants. Her book brings to the fore the problems that we in the capitalist universe might face if some of our political and cultural ambitions were to be realised. The major institutions would be ours – people's museums, universities and ministries – and we artists and intellectuals would have to decide amongst ourselves whether and how we support the Revolution, including its state mechanisms and infrastructures. We would not need to network compulsively or work without pay in order to accrue social capital like so many entrepreneurs of solidarity. Of course, even in the case of Cuba, there was never a moment when struggle was not required and protest against an imperialist foe was not a reality. The lessons of the Cuban experiment are not that liberal traditions are of no use to the Revolution, but that a national culture should not be chauvinistic or elitist, that art and politics cannot be collapsed, nor can they be separated, and that artistic vanguards must work alongside political vanguards and vice versa. *To Defend the Revolution Is to Defend Culture* thus provides Marxist aesthetics with a view of radical ideology and universality that goes beyond sociological and ethnographic reduction and that challenges the free-market models of today's neoliberal bureaucracies.

4

Psychoprotest: dérives of the Quebec Maple Spring

In Canada and Quebec, like in so many other countries where neoliberal policies have been imposed, the level of social inequality has increased dramatically, with virtually all of the income growth between 1980 and 2010 going to the richest one percent of the population.[1] A major part of this project of class restoration is the devolution of state provision, as noticed in the practice of consecutive federal government administrations in the 1990s to disregard budget surpluses and to insist on cutting transfer payments to the provinces – payments that were previously invested in education and other social services.[2] The commoditisation of education in Canada and elsewhere has led to an exponential growth in tuition fees, making student debt a matter of political struggle.[3] In the province of Quebec, however, due to a tradition of social democratic reforms that began in the 1970s, tuition fees for post-secondary education have been relatively low, encouraging students to frequently protest government initiatives to commodify educational services. In 2012, in the context of growing inequality, and after the provincial Liberal government decided to increase tuition fees by seventy-five percent over five years, hundreds of thousands of university, college and senior high school (CÉGEP) students across Quebec declared an unlimited general strike. Beginning in March and through to August, students held marches and organised actions that dramatically transformed the experience of city space.

Claiming a right to the city often entails challenges to the dominant order that result in state repression. The student strike, which almost led to a general social strike, was so well-coordinated that the Montreal police, in an effort to criminalise dissent, transferred its student portfolio to the department of organised crime.[4] Both the provincial government and the Montreal municipality imposed new laws designed to control the improvisational dimension of the demonstrations, giving the police the power to demand protest itineraries and the authority to declare the protests illegal in the case of noncompliance. Aware of the newly defined stakes involved in the radical occupation of city streets, demonstrators and citizen supporters engaged in broad-based yet unplanned street marches. In his recent book on 'rebel cities,' David Harvey argues that over the last decade Henri Lefebvre's idea of 'the right to the city,' the right to create alternative forms of urban life that are less alienated, more playful and more conflictual, has undergone a certain revival.[5] Harvey calls on Marxists to focus on the city rather than the factory as the major site of surplus value production and argues that the ruling elites are especially vulnerable in cities and for this reason are 'gearing up for militarized urban struggles as the front line of class struggle in the years to come.'[6] This perception is consistent with studies that show how neoliberal regimes have begun to shift policing strategy from that of negotiated management towards criminalisation. According to Leanne Serbulo, the purpose of policing in the wake of anti-globalisation protests is no longer the differentiation between 'good' and 'bad' protesters, but the incapacitation of demonstrations through the creation of a climate of fear.[7]

In the spirit not only of Lefebvre, but in particular, of the Situationists, we propose that the student protests of the 2012 *printemps érable* can be productively interpreted in the terms of the Situationist theory of psychogeography. In our case, the Situationist *dérive* is transferred to the terrain of the student demonstrations and the built environment is reconceived to include not only the given city space, but the presence and intervention of municipal and provincial police. Given that the previous Prime Minister of Quebec, Pauline Marois, decided to defuse student anger by stating that opposition to government policy should not turn into a 'psychodrama,' we have termed our application of Situationist psychogeography to street protest *psychoprotest*.[8] We make use of the early writings of the Situationist International and the Lettrist International in order to advance a cultural analysis of protest activity. While the city of Montreal has been working for decades to brand Montreal a city of festivals and urban spectacle, the student psychoprotests revealed the forms of repression that are at work in a system of neoliberal privatisation. In this regard we reject contemporary cultural theoretical perspectives that discount the critique of the spectacle and that work to reduce radical politics to the bogeymen of teleology, totalitarianism and the Stalinist gulag.

The 2012 Quebec student strike

On February 13, 2012, after two years of protests, petitions and occupations, students across Quebec voted to go on a general unlimited strike against the provincial Liberal government's plan to dramatically increase tuition fees.[9] The months following the strike declaration were the most politically intense time in Quebec or Canada in recent memory as the students' demand for a moratorium on tuition fees was representative of a broader struggle against the failed logic of neoliberal policies. This social movement declared itself

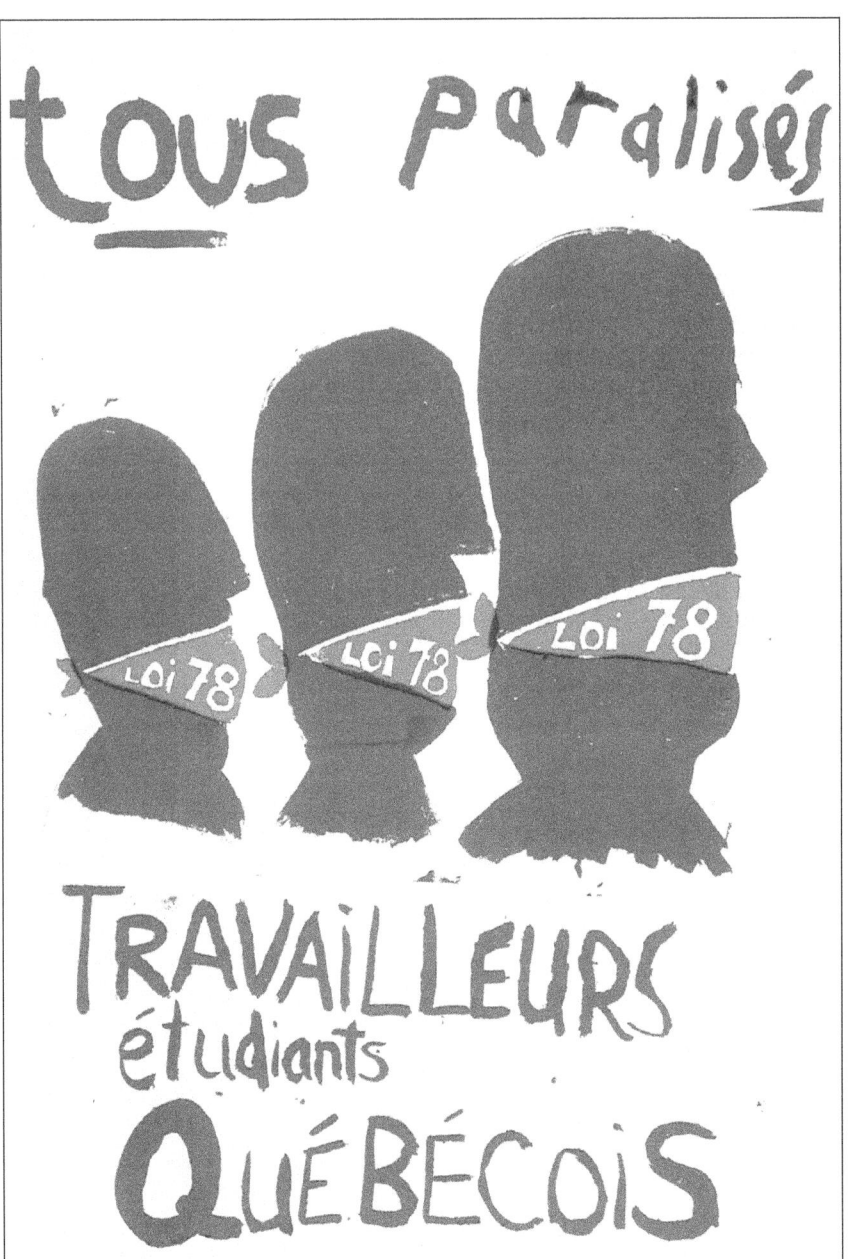

Poster created during the Quebec student strike by the École de la Montagne Rouge, 2012. Courtesy of Guillaume Lépine.

le printemps érable, or Maple Spring, as the Quebec pronunciation of 'Arab' rhymes with *érable*, the French term for maple. The Maple Spring was therefore named in solidarity with the democratic uprisings in the Arab world in 2011 and as part of a global resurgence of popular resistance. The strike ended on September 5, one day after premier Jean Charest was voted out of office and the incoming Parti Québécois leader Pauline Marois followed through on her election promise to cancel the tuition increase. Many considered this victory – however temporary and partial given the larger demand for tuition-free education – to be a direct result of the student mobilisation. Along with the cessation of studies during the course of the strike, students picketed classrooms, took to the streets daily, and engaged in various forms of civil disobedience and direct action.

In light of the government's initial refusal to meet with student representatives and negotiate the terms of the increase, students voted in favour of a general unlimited strike. The strike endured for 206 days, making it the longest student strike in Quebec history. At its peak, 175,000 joined the strike, that is, over half of Quebec's 342,000 post-secondary students. The three major associations that represented the striking students were the Fédération étudiante universitaire du Québec (FEUQ), the Fédération étudiante collégiale du Québec (FECQ) and the Association pour une solidarité syndicale étudiante (ASSÉ). For the duration of the strike, the ASSÉ formed a temporary coalition, La Coalition large de l'Association pour une solidarité syndicale étudiante (CLASSE), which was considered the most radical of the student groups and represented half of the striking students. What distinguished the CLASSE from its more moderate counterparts was its commitment to the principle of free post-secondary education as well as its organisational structure, which was based on direct democratic decision-making by student assemblies during weekly meetings. Instead of representatives, the CLASSE had spokespeople who relayed the decisions of its membership to the government and the public.

While the minimal demand of the striking students was a moratorium on the tuition increase, the more radical demands involved a plan to move towards a tuition-free system. The CLASSE pushed for the realisation of this latter demand by proposing that the government introduce a small 0.7 percent tax on banks that would cover the costs of tuition for all of Quebec. The students defended their position by arguing that higher tuition diminishes accessibility to education and results in larger amounts of student debt. Rather than treat education as an individual consumer investment, the students insist that education is a social good that should be paid for through a progressive tax system. The decision to strike and the street tactics devised by the students were informed by the CLASSE's principle of combative syndicalism. This principle consists of a commitment to the progressive escalation of tactics until an objective is met. The slow escalation of tactics over the two years preceding the strike declaration, from petitions and one-day strikes to a general unlimited strike, conforms to this principle and helps to explain the widespread and sustained engagement in the strike mobilisation.

The student strike became institutionally and politically significant after the establishment of picket lines. These pickets resulted in an effective freeze of teaching activities at most French universities and CÉGEPs. While students struggled to maintain picket lines and control over the strike they also engaged in regular demonstrations of between several hundred to tens of thousands of people. The 22nd day of each month became a massive day of action that attracted the largest demonstrations of support for the student cause. On March 22, for instance, 200,000 students from across Quebec marched in Montreal. Other than the 2003 demonstration against the impending war on Iraq, this was the largest demonstration in Quebec history. Despite the massive turnout, the government refused to negotiate the issue of tuition increase. On April 22, the monthly march coincided with Earth Day and attracted an even larger crowd, estimated at 300,000. The march of May 22 became the largest act of civil disobedience in Canadian history as approximately one hundred thousand demonstrators diverged from the official route in contravention of the special law passed by the government, which criminalised spontaneous protest. Although no arrests were made during this march, the following day the police made a mass arrest by kettling 500 people. These large demonstrations continued until August and September when the crowd numbers dwindled along with the winding down of the strike.

In response to the injunctions aimed at undermining the democratic strike mandate and in light of the government's refusal to negotiate, student tactics shifted towards economic disruption. Demonstrators participated in peaceful civil disobedience by blocking bridges and major streets. Bags of bricks were thrown onto the tracks of the subway system, disabling it for several hours. The office windows of education minister Line Beauchamp were painted red and a few bank windows were broken. The red square, the symbol of the student movement, became increasingly visible across the province and was worn by students, supporters, and even some politicians from the social democratic party Québec Solidaire and the nationalist Parti Québécois. The visual landscape of Montreal was transformed by a proliferation of red flags and banners suspended from balconies and taped to the windows of the homes and businesses of supporters. Just as this happened, however, the level of police violence increased, with the regular deployment of tear gas, stun grenades and baton charges. After some of the worst police violence occurred, students began to stage naked bloc 'maNUfestation' marches in their underwear and with their bodies adorned with slogans in red paint in order to draw the attention of the media and to demonstrate their vulnerability and nonviolent intentions in relation to the heavily armed riot police.

Among all of these creative actions, the most significant in terms of transforming city space were the night marches. After walking out of talks on April 25, the Liberals presented a new plan that would result in an even higher increase than that of the original proposal. From the evening of April 24 onward students began to assemble nightly at 8 p.m. at Place Émilie-Gamelin and led marches throughout downtown Montreal and the surrounding areas until the early hours of the morning. After almost one month of these night marches, and after negotiations broke down, the government introduced a surprise emergency bill that effectively criminalised the strike actions. Bill 78, or Law 12, nicknamed the 'billy club' law, suspended the winter 2012 term at any institution where classes were significantly interrupted by the strike and legislated a change in the fall semester start date in order to accommodate the completion of the winter term in August and September.[10] In addition, the law banned any interruption of classes and any assembly of people within fifty metres of an educational institution. The law criminalised any demonstration of fifty or more people that did not provide its itinerary to police eight hours in advance and instituted steep penalties for any individual ($1,000–$5,000 per offence), student leader ($7,000–$35,000), or organisation ($25,000–$125,000) that broke its provisions, with double the amount for recidivism. Institutions were also allowed to block the transfer of student fees to any student federation or association found to be in violation of the law, effectively incapacitating the students' rights to defend their own interests. Most problematically, the law declared that these penalties would apply not only to those who broke the law, but to student representatives or organisations that did not adequately prevent their members from breaking it. On the same day the City of Montreal introduced a municipal law that banned the wearing of masks at demonstrations.[11] As Law 12 was denounced by the Quebec bar association as well as the United Nations, and as it was unlikely to stand up to constitutional challenge, it appeared to Quebec civil society as an undemocratic measure, however temporary.

On May 18, the night that Bill 78 was passed into law, tens of thousands took to the streets in Montreal in a wilful act of civil disobedience. Police responded by declaring the march illegal and by firing rubber bullets and tear gas into the peaceful crowd. The crowds were so large, however, that they quickly reassembled and marched for hours without further incident. People continued to march every evening with police making a number of arrests. The new law emboldened police to declare the marches illegal before they had even begun and to use unnecessarily coercive tactics. Those who were arrested in Montreal, however, were not actually charged according to the provisions of Law 12, but were instead given fines of over $600 for breaking the highway safety code. By the end of the summer, more than 3,000 arrests had been made in relation to the student strike.

The arrests and police violence temporarily abated in the face of a new phenomenon. Angered by the special law and the contemptuous way that the government had dealt with the students' concerns, citizens across Montreal began at 8 p.m. to bang pots and pans in their neighbourhoods, eventually taking over city streets in their hundreds and thousands in spontaneous marches that violated the unjust law. Unable to contain or follow all of these *manif des casseroles*, the police allowed them to carry on without interference. The night of May 26 marked the high point of these events with tens of thousands of people marching in dozens of groups all over the city. The casseroles continued every night for two weeks and inspired solidarity demonstrations across Canada and in more than seventy cities internationally. In the end the amount that was spent on policing – over $15 million for the Montreal municipality alone – was more than enough to cover the costs of the tuition increase. Such neoliberal state attacks on democracy confirm David Graeber's observation that today's capitalism is more concerned with convincing people that there is no alternative to free-market capitalism than with making itself functional.[12]

Based on the various aspects of the student strike, the idea of psychoprotest as a mutation of psychogeographic dérive applies most specifically to the night marches and the casserole marches, though some aspects of it could also be noticed in the mass demonstrations of the 22nds. Before attending to some of the particulars of these street actions, however, it is necessary to contextualise the concerns of our investigation.

Psychogeography

The Situationist theory of psychogeography was developed in the mid-to-late 1950s as a means to overcome of the limits and failures of previous avant-garde art movements. In this regard we caution against studies that seek to transform psychogeography into a genre category.[13] Against the tendency to historicise, it is necessary to appreciate the significance of Hegelian Marxism to the politics of the Lettrists and Situationists. When the French *Philosophies* group, which included Lefebvre, was courted by André Breton and the Surrealists in 1925, Breton very rudely told them that they should read Hegel before resuming negotiations.[14] The importance of Hegel for Breton, according to Lefebvre, was the combination of unity and struggle within the real; in other words, the significance of Hegel to avant-garde movements was the importance of the idea of alienation as a constructive concept.[15] Alienation is the essential ingredient of what the S.I. would later term 'unitary urbanism,' which itself led to the development of the methods of the *dérive* and *détournement*.

For Lefebvre, the Surrealist avant garde had come to a dead end around 1930 since it translated all struggle into literary alienation. This criticism of Surrealism is famously expressed by Lefebvre in his 1947 *Critique of Everyday*

Life, in which he decries the group for its diversion of interest away from reality, for its belittling of the real in favour of the marvellous, for its attack on everyday life, its extreme aesthetic individualism, and for seeking human redemption in a world of images and poetry.[16] Against the Surrealists' 'fictitious negations,' Lefebvre set out on a critique of capitalist abstraction and the separation of spheres of human activity by proposing a Marxist understanding of everyday life, an approach to culture and politics based on the concept of alienation. If there was to be a revolution, for Lefebvre it would not be an armed struggle, but a revolution of and within the everyday.[17] Lefebvre prefigured the Situationist critique insofar as he advocated the method of Hegelian Marxism in his approach to the alienation of social life. More specifically, Lefebvre gave close attention to the domain of leisure. The critique of everyday life, he argued, is enacted by humans on a regular basis through their leisure activities, which cannot be separated from the everyday aspect of work. Leisure, which includes not only traditional culture but also the mass media, film, radio and television, breaks with everyday routines and liberates people from the realm of necessity. As compensation for the same everyday routines, however, leisure creates artificial needs and illusory contents. Whatever the analysis of culture, Lefebvre insisted that the realm of leisure should be part of everyday social practice and be based on needs that are reversible and provisional. The need to enjoy, he argues, comes into conflict with the need to accumulate and therefore, leisure should include the critique of money and mystification.[18] Regardless of the eventual disputes between Lefebvre and Guy Debord, it is necessary to underline this connection between unity and struggle in the S.I.'s 'desacralisation of culture' and in its affirmation of negation in the need for a revolutionary overthrow of bourgeois tradition.[19]

From out of the postwar alternatives and counter-movements to Surrealism, the Lettrist International, which included Debord, put out a series of statements on urban theory.[20] The first and most important of these was written by Ivan Chtcheglov, a.k.a. Gilles Yvain, in October 1953. Titled 'Formula for a New Urbanism,' the statement declares a break with Dada and Surrealism as lost legacies.[21] The piece is far more imaginative than later formulations, and so, along these lines, the question of play and the critique of 'boring' leisure are foregrounded as means to disrupt the way that modern architecture, modern conveniences and the mechanisation of desires have prolonged the conditions of work. The new world should be more fun and the goal of the avant garde should be to 'carry out an *intensive propaganda* in favor of new desires.'[22] Chtcheglov writes:

> We have already pointed out the need of constructing situations as being one of the fundamental desires on which the next civilization will be founded. This need for *absolute* creation has always been intimately associated with the need to

play with architecture, time and space … The principal activity of the inhabitants [of the new urbanism] will be the CONTINUOUS DÉRIVE. The changing of landscapes from one hour to the next will result in complete disorientation.[23]

In relation to previous European avant-garde movements, Chtcheglov's tract is the first proposal for a new architecture for which play, leisure and imagination are set against boredom, control and regulation. Chtcheglov tends, however, to emphasise poetic power and chance operations at the expense of political analysis. We thus find that the first descriptions of *psychogeography* appear in the Lettrist bulletin as 'game of the week,' with banal Fluxus-like propositions such as 'choose an area, build a house, furnish it, etc.'[24]

The concepts associated with psychogeography were taken up by Debord in a series of far more programmatic statements written between 1955 and 1958. The first of these, 'Introduction to a Critique of Urban Geography,' was produced while he was still a member of the Lettrists.[25] Debord states that the term psychogeography was proposed in 1953 as a materialist perspective on the determinations of life and thought. Its purpose is the search for new ways of life through processes of chance and predictability in the streets.[26] 'Psychogeography,' he writes, 'could set for itself the study of the precise laws and specific effects of the geographical environment, consciously organized or not, on the emotions and behavior of individuals.'[27] His formulation adds the serious element of research to the more playful aspects defined by his comrade. Aware of the architecture of social control that has been effected through urban renewal, and in the postwar period, the transformation of cities to accommodate automobile circulation, Debord wished to spoil the pleasures and the 'pathetic illusions' of happiness and privilege that are promoted by capitalist production. His purpose was to provoke a crisis in advertising spectacle and cinematic happiness by 'turn[ing] the whole of life into an exciting game.'[28] Against overproduction and overaccumulation, the method of psychogeography studies the various ambiances of city space, overcoming the usual, prescribed influences, for instance, between rich and poor neighbourhoods, between commercial and historical zones, and going against the grain of specially designated activities like tourism, sports and shopping.

In his text on 'Methods of Détournement' Debord set the stage for psychogeography as a new avant-garde method designed to overcome the limits of cultural heritage. The method of *détournement* is a kind of parody and educative propaganda.[29] It is brought to bear on city space through the psychogeographic *dérive*. In his first tract as part of the soon to be formed Situationist International, which broke off from the Lettrists in 1957, Debord defines the project of the S.I. as being specific to the critique of urbanism.[30] The new art should be formed at the level of urbanism, he argues, which uses psychogeographical research to study urban development and to propose 'hypotheses on the structure of a situationist city.'[31] Opposed to the conditions of the modern spectacle, with its increase in leisure time and imposition of bourgeois tastes, the method of psychogeographical observation is both a moral choice and a game that negates the element of competition. Its form is the dérive, a practice of strolling that changes the way one perceives the city. In the first issue of the *Internationale Situationniste* journal, Debord defines the dérive as a 'mode of experimental behavior linked to the conditions of urban society: a technique of transient passage through varied ambiances' that 'liberate[s] the tendency toward play,' the 'experimental form' of a 'game of revolution' that is opposed to games that represent a regression to an infantile stage.[32]

As a final, programmatic statement on the theory of the dérive as part of a Situationist study of the effects of the geographic environment, Debord considered the dérive in terms of four elements: chance, scale, duration and terrain.[33] In the process of drifting, one or more people drop their usual work and leisure activities and let themselves be drawn by the different ambiances of the urban terrain. In the process, the play of **chance** is overdetermined and diminished by the psychogeographical relief of the city, with its 'currents,' 'fixed points' and 'vortexes.' One does not simply improvise one's way as one goes, but becomes aware of and attentive to the calculation of possibilities, which Debord says are both relative and absolute. To fully appreciate the method of psychogeography, the determining aspects of city space must be utilised and not simply ignored or disavowed. The dérive is therefore not a practice of transgression or even of direct action. He writes: 'The objective passional terrain of the derive must be defined in accordance both with its own logic and with its relations with social morphology.'[34] Chance, he argues, tends to reduce things to habit and to limited possibilities. Progress therefore lies in breaking away from chance by creating new conditions that are favourable to *revolutionary* purposes. In this regard Debord avoided the aimless strolling and nostalgia of predecessors like Baudelaire, Breton and Aragon.

Nowhere is the difference between psychoprotest and the psychogeographic dérive more evident than on the matter of **scale**. Debord recommends dériving alone or in small groups of two or three people, in particular, people with the same level of political awareness. Since the goal is to achieve certain objective conclusions, the increase of scale to four or five persons diminishes the specificity of the method. Any more than ten people, he contends, causes the group to break up into smaller groups. In this regard, on the other hand, the way that a demonstration of anywhere from 1,000 to 100,000 people tends to involve smaller groupings of individuals, friends and associated parties, may very well have a potential kinship to psychogeography. This affinity is also borne out on the matter of **duration**. The average duration of a dérive is one day, sometimes merging into the night, after which fatigue naturally sets in. While it may, Debord says, last from three to four days, it is more likely limited to a period of three to four hours. At the outer limits, dérives have been known to last two months and according to Chtcheglov, a 1953–54 dérive lasted for three or four months. Chtcheglov adds: 'It's a miracle it didn't kill us.'[35]

Lastly, in terms of **terrain**, the psychogeographer, in the action of studying, may become disoriented by the randomness of wandering. The point of departure, Debord says, does not usually lead far beyond a city or its suburbs; it may be limited to a certain neighbourhood or may remain within one specific location for an entire day. The goal is the calculation of directions of penetration rather than the search for the exotic. The psychogeographer may not know who they will be meeting at the rendez-vous point. They may converse with people not directly implicated in the game and may make unexpected turns. In other words, there is in this avant-garde practice an openness to chance operations that undermine the logic of duty, discipline and obedience to rules. Movement may involve hitchhiking or wandering into spaces that are 'forbidden to the public' and so implies a certain level of civil disobedience or delinquency.

The goal of psychogeography is to discover 'unities of ambiance' – the main zones of influence of the built and symbolic environment – and to fathom their possible transformation. The only known visual representation of

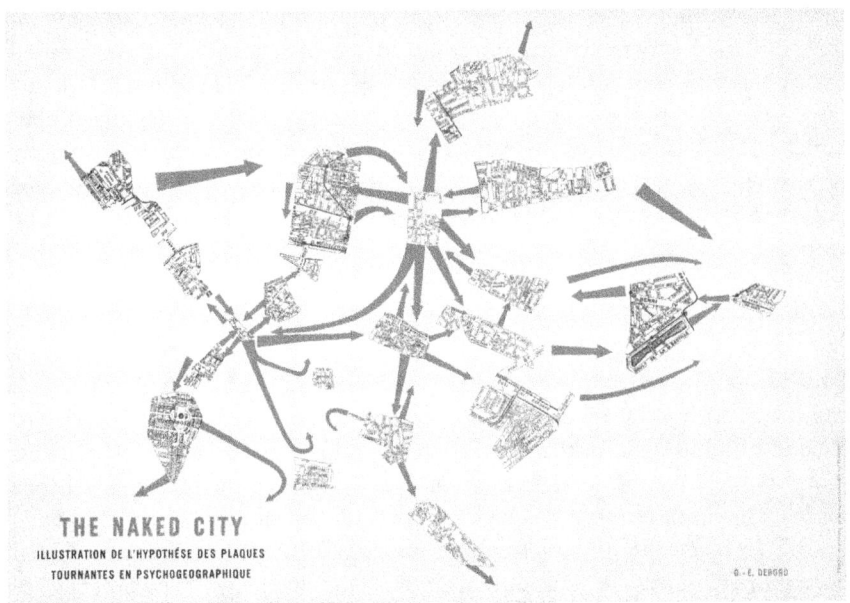

Guy-Ernest Debord, *The Naked City, Illustration de l'hypothèse des plaques tournantes en psychogeographique*, 1957. Sheet, printed in Copenhagen by Permild & Rosengren, 33 x 48 cm. Collection of the Beinecke Rare Book and Manuscript Library, Yale University. With permission from Alice Debord.

unitary urbanism created by the Situationists is Debord's 1957 map of Paris, known as *The Naked City*. The map cuts up city neighbourhoods into a collage of fragmented parts rearranged into a new configuration with large gaps in between and connected by arrows that connote a dance chart, alluding to the importance at that time of new dances influenced by the then popular jazz and rock and roll sounds – not to mention its reference to a 1948 American film noir as well as a book of crime photographs by Weegee. The image enlists the pleasure of popular music and dance as well as the sinister aspects of crime for the purposes of social critique and the construction of a radical perception of urban space. The function of this appropriated map is to propagandise a prac-tice of insubordination of urban directives. While Tom McDonough argues that the dérive's spatial practices reject a totalising view, echoing in the process the distinction made by Michel de Certeau between pedestrian speech acts and the Archimedean view from atop the World Trade Center, we would note that *The Naked City* does in fact present just such a re-totalised, or 'dialectical' depiction based on the re-mapping of human needs and emphasising the results of militant research.[36]

Psychoprotest

In the following psychogeographical notes on the student protests we draw on our combined experience as participants in the marches. We have organised these observations according to the four elements that Debord used to define the dérive. Our purpose here is not to provide an exhaustive description but rather a sketch of some of the ways in which the notion of psychogeography is pertinent to our experience of the protest marches, especially those that occurred while it was still unknown to what extent the special law would be enforced.

1. Chance

Situationist psychogeography is concerned with the determining aspects of city space, with its currents, fixed points and vortexes, leading in the dérive to a game of improvisation that is coordinated with social and not just physical morphology. Like the dérive, protest activity epitomises the breaking of habits for leftist political purposes.[37] The conditions of illegality that were occasioned by Bill 78 made the protests far more intense. While attending to the 'fixed points' of city space, we consider that in this case, such legal fixed points were directly reflected in the slogans that developed. For example, the three chants that were often heard were: '*On est plus que 50!*' (We are more than 50!), which was chanted in a mocking manner and referred to the fact that although the march involved more than fifty demonstrators, no one had notified the police; '*La loi spéciale – on s'en calisse!*' (The special law – we don't give a fuck!); and '*SSPVM – police politique,*' which criticised the Montreal police (Service de police de la Ville de Montréal) for not protecting citizens and for siding with the powerful. Also popular was '*Charest – yoooo hooooooo,*' chiding the Quebec Prime Minister for not meeting with students and daring him to come out of his hiding place. After Charest had told the news media that he had jobs for discontented students up North – referring to his government's plan to subsidise extensive resource extraction in the province's northern regions – the chanting included '*Charest, Dehors! On va't trouver une jobe dans l'Nord!*' (Charest, Out! We'll find you a job up North!). The invention of new marching slogans allowed for a counter-construction of fixed points within the movement itself, focusing on shared meanings and allowing for the creation of new solidarities. By producing and repeating this repertoire of common slogans, the improvisational element was provided with swing and momentum, transforming fear and anxiety into collective moral indignation.

Psychoprotest, unlike psychogeography, takes place under the constant watch of police, who are trained in crowd control. Police tactics seemed at times to be highly organised, while at other times seemed relatively unorganised and casual. Police tactics contribute dramatically to defining the terms of engagement and influence the mood and attitudes of protesters. In terms of legal structure, the fixed point of reference used by the Montreal police was not the provisions of Bill 78 but an excerpt from the Quebec Highway Safety Code that reads:

> No person may, during a concerted action intended to obstruct in any way vehicular traffic on a public highway, occupy the roadway, shoulder or any other part of the right of way of or approaches to the highway or place a vehicle or obstacle thereon so as to obstruct vehicular traffic on the highway or access to such a highway.

An interesting archive of documents in relation to Bill 78's insistence on the provision of protest itineraries is the now defunct website Manifencours (Protestunderway). The site documented the trajectories of the marches and allowed people to post mobile phone pictures while also displaying a live Twitter feed. The dates that were archived on this site are mostly from late April and May 2012.[38] What the itineraries show is the general range of the marches, which remained mostly in the downtown zone, Hochelaga-Maisonneuve, the Plateau, Mile End, Outremont and Little Italy. Using the same streets created as sense of ritual and narrative, allowing new slogans and styles to develop within the march form as an open structure. These improvised itineraries reflect the decision of the students to violate an unconstitutional law designed to dispossess them of their political rights and power. The confrontational aspect of this choice is reflected in a map that began to

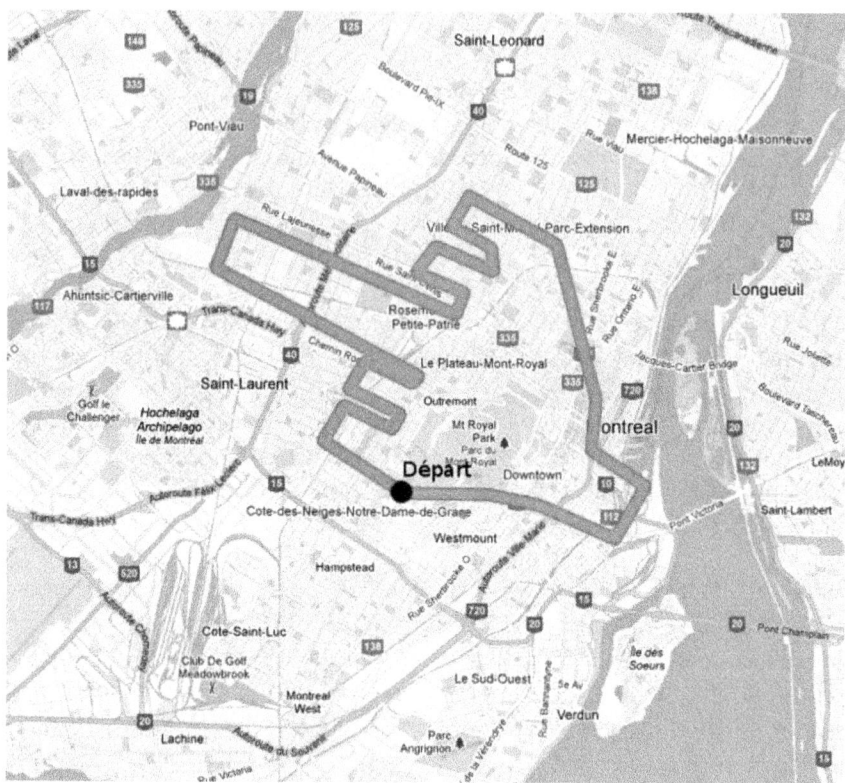

Anonymous GPS map of downtown Montreal and protest itinerary from May
2012 defying the provisions of the 'billy club law.' Source: Internet.

circulate on the Internet sometime in May and which shows a march itinerary
in the form of a 'fuck you' finger. The improvised marches also reflect the
constituent aspect of the demonstrations and the absence of any designated
leaders. In contrast to anti-globalisation marches, there was no stewardship
of the marches, and no designation of green nonviolent and red direct action
zones. The marches broke the circulation habits of downtown streets for
political purposes, creating an emotional intensity designed to maximise the
chances of success for the student strike.

The ludic character of the psychoprotests began to worry city officials,
especially during the planned disruptions of the Grand Prix auto race activities, which spread scepticism concerning what Attila Kotányi defined as the
'racket' and 'protected crime' of officially designated leisure activities.[39] The
experimental living of those who attempted to disrupt the Grand Prix was
a clear denunciation of existing conditions of alienation, materialising freedom by appropriating and disrupting the macho and crime-ridden scene that

reminded people of the corruption charges that plagued the former mayor of Montreal, Gerald Tremblay, and that eventually led to his removal from office. Our experience of the protesting of the Grand Prix was highly uneven. In a daytime demo we marched and casseroled through the racecar displays on Crescent Street without any problems, whereas at night, within a larger group of protesters, we were blocked by police charges, targeted with tear gas and maimed with stun grenades.

While the interventions that affected the Grand Prix were heavily policed, the casseroles were far too popular and broad-based for the police to do anything more than act as chaperones. After the pots and pans began to sound at 8 p.m., we would look for a busy corner. It was never possible to know on any given day how many people would turn out and whether or not the gathering would develop into a march. As we experienced it, people would gather on a street corner, follow the traffic lights and move in unison from corner to corner, cheering while passing one another. After there was enough momentum, people would take the street and completely block car traffic. Once a group started marching, the direction and aim of the demonstration was again very open and directed by the mood of the crowd. The imponderables of chance included the choice to find other groups of supporters, whether or not to remain a small group or coalesce with others, whether to follow the police car escorts or escape them for fun, what casserole groove to get into and how to influence the direction of the entire group. We tended to first follow a nearby march that would wind through the neighbourhoods north of Mount-Royal avenue and then go searching for others near the larger Saint Denis or Saint Laurent boulevards. We would cheer when merging with another group and then start to work our way downtown. On a few occasions the casserole night marches assembled into massive swarms and rivers of demonstrators numbering in the tens and hundreds of thousands.

2. Scale

Debord emphasises the fact that the group of psychogeographers should have the same level of social consciousness. In the case of psychoprotest, the goal is to enhance the level of political awareness as the movement grows in size. The solidarity networks that comprised the student strike were based on assemblies and involved individuals through participation and coordination. Previous strike activism had made the students well-informed of the stakes and the forms of mobilisation. While the duration of the protests influenced the learning process, so did its scale, which included institutional actors, in particular, Amir Khadir, one of the leaders of Québec Solidaire and the only politician who struggled against government and media efforts to delegitimise the students.

Collective goals cannot be limited to one person, however, but are based on dense informal networks that allow people to enter and exit the movement at will. The strike was not about personal change, personal empowerment or identity politics, nor was it a cultural-artistic movement or countercultural movement, but was based on gaining support for a specific issue. Many small groups marched alongside the students, including Profs Contre La Hausse (Professors Against the Tuition Hikes), Mères en Colère (Angry Mothers), La Coalition Opposée à la Tarification et la Privatisation des Services Publics (Coalition Against Tarifs and the Privatisation of Public Services), Occupy Montreal and the anarchist Coalition Large Anti-Capitaliste. All of these groups share an understanding of what is involved in fighting neoliberal austerity. We regret to note the significant absence of labour unions, especially insofar as the students attempted to transform the *printemps érable* into a broad-based social strike. We also disagree with those social movement analysts who consider that the student protests are beyond the labour-capital conflict. Although the students have different class backgrounds, as workers they represent the lowest rungs of the educational system. In this regard the unions of Quebec failed to recognise the student strike as a significant political event.[40]

As the *printemps érable* became significant to the international student movement, the organising CLASSE group attempted to define the scale of the movement by issuing in July the manifesto *Nous sommes avenir* (Share Our Future). That the struggle against neoliberal capitalism is understood by the CLASSE in radical democratic terms, involving a diversity of struggles, including feminism and environmentalism, was confirmed at press conferences given by spokespersons Gabriel Nadeau-Dubois and Jeanne Reynolds.[41] A pragmatic description of the 'associated institutions' that comprise the student movement, and certainly one that would come close to the CLASSE's general social movement outlook, is provided by Harvey's list of non-governmental organisations, anarchist and autonomous grassroots organisations, traditional left political parties and unions, social movements guided by the pragmatic need to resist displacement and dispossession, and lastly, minority and identitarian movements. Harvey considers communist anyone who understands and struggles against the destructive tendencies of capitalism.[42]

Protesting in large numbers allows demonstrators to disrupt routines and also provides an avenue for political involvement beyond elections, merging politics with everyday life. The larger the demonstration, the safer one feels. This was especially true after Bill 78 was put in place. A march could sometimes feel too safe and too large if it attracted those who were not as enthusiastic or committed to demonstrating. In some of the 22nd marches, for example, the focus, energy and collective feeling was diffuse in comparison with the solidarity that was experienced on night marches. The scale also varied depending on government actions. When the government angered people the demonstrations would grow. On the other hand, although the large demonstrations were less cohesive, they were broadly popular, allowing people to enter the political process with a sense of security in numbers and giving public legitimacy to the activities of the hard core as they attempted to shift the terms of the strike to popular struggles.

3. Duration

The duration of the psychoprotests pushes against the limits that Debord describes regarding the duration of dérives. While each separate march would only last a few hours, the student strike endured for many months. The way in which the constancy of the events altered participants' experience of daily life leads us to consider the strike as a collective city-wide dérive that persisted with varying degrees of intensity. Aside from a small core, most participants did not attend every march. The constancy of the dérive was therefore sustained by people attending when they could in what one might consider to be rotating 'shift work.'

The spatial extension of protest also comprised a temporal extension into the evening hours and reconfigured everyday rhythms. The evening start time meant an incursion into leisure time, allowing those who work in the daytime to participate and adding a ludic quality to the nocturnal marches that sometimes included fireworks. The night marches would begin at 8 p.m. at Émilie-Gamelin park and would at times return to this 'home base' at around 10 or 11 p.m., only to start again and continue until midnight or even 2 a.m. Many of these very late marches came to an end without incident when people grew tired and went home. Yet, as the crowd shrank to only a few hundred or a few dozen, the risk of arrest or forced dispersal by the police increased.

Those who became regular participants in the daily and nightly marches experienced a destabilisation of their former daily routines and rhythms. In our case, marching for hours for many evenings in a row, watching the livestream partisan coverage on Concordia University television (CUTV) when we were not marching, and reading news coverage on the strike eventually led to a delirious state of exhaustion. This fatigue would quickly dissipate when on a 'night off' a march would pass by our street and we would find ourselves drawn towards its chanting vortex.

4. Terrain

On the level of terrain the Quebec Maple Spring was more expansive than typical Montreal protests had been. Rather than remain strictly in the downtown core, and rather than orient marches towards a symbolic site of power, the night marches extended into the surrounding neighbourhoods. On particular occasions the night marches would target a site with political significance, as in the May 21 march to Charest's home in the wealthy municipality of Westmount. That night, the behaviour of demonstrators changed dramatically from the respect shown towards residents in Hochelaga-Maisonneuve as compared to that exhibited in Westmount, where pranksters ran across lawns and rang doorbells, a difference that acknowledges Kotányi and Raoul Vaneigem's statement that 'one doesn't live somewhere in the city; one lives somewhere in the hierarchy.'[43] The same march destroyed some of the signage in the downtown 'Quartier des Spectacles,' a managed zone of programmed commercial leisure. More generally, however, the marches did not target any specific site but were oriented towards maintaining a constancy of presence.

Richard Day has argued that recent tendencies in social movements exhibit a different logic from those of the past that were oriented towards a 'politics of the demand.'[44] Social movements that are based on a politics of the demand are reformist and risk reinforcing the legitimacy of existing institutions by appealing to them for particular changes. Day contrasts this with a 'politics of the act,' which describes the rejection of hegemony by localist and anarchist activists who focus on creating alternative ways of life that do not depend on existing institutions. The temporary autonomous zones, informal networks and affinity groups that constitute this form of social struggle are often referred to as horizontalist politics. It is possible to understand certain dimensions of the Maple Spring as exhibiting horizontalist tendencies. The extension of the marches away from physical sites of power could be seen as a rejection of a politics of the demand. The use of social media produced a set of counter-discourses and representations that were unconcerned with the mainstream media news coverage and generated an alternative and autonomous media sphere.

The spatial orientation away from centres of power in a psychoprotest reflects this ideology to a degree, but we would contend that the success and power of the movement was largely due to a dialectical relation between these horizontalist tactics and those that acknowledge the actuality of hegemonic struggle through formal organisations. The question of whether to engage in negotiations with the government was a fraught one within the CLASSE, and the link to the existing power structure was never fully ignored or severed. While the machinery of official negotiations and representative power was perceived from a critical distance on the level of the political consciousness of the student organisations, in practice they were utilised and played with strategically. Maintaining this link gave legitimacy to the students' position while also displaying the unwillingness of the government to respond to democratic demands.

The orientation of the night marches outwards from downtown into the mixed and residential neighbourhoods had the effect of producing an interpellation of city residents. The marches addressed the public street-by-street, district-by-district, and offered people an immediate opportunity to take part, if only by cheering the marchers or dismissing them. We can recall one young woman in a downtown pizza parlour giving us marchers two big 'fuck you' fingers, as if to indicate that she was unafraid of our collective power. What this demonstrates is the way the street marches became a diffuse medium of address through which the students cultivated an image of cheerful collectivity that contradicted the image of violent protesters that was disseminated elsewhere. We contend that the casserole marches would not have emerged had people not witnessed the students march through their neighbourhoods and been interpellated by them through this spatialised address. A night march in early May that stands out in our memory was one that took us through the southeast of the Plateau. We marched through normally quiet residential streets and were received with supportive enthusiasm from the people who watched us from doorways and balconies. This was an exhilarating experience for those among us who are used to protesting in downtown Montreal and are accustomed to receiving blank or hostile looks from shoppers. Only a few weeks later the casseroles would begin in these same residential streets.

Conclusion

Having considered the affinities between the Situationists' theory of psychogeography and the dérives of the student psychoprotests, one cannot help but wonder about the relevance of the S.I. to the events of May 68 and how this might relate to the *printemps érable*. Beyond their politically revolutionary goal of overcoming aesthetic alienation and the hold of the spectacle on the everyday, the Situationists dedicated themselves to an avant-garde critique of the bureaucratic power of the Stalinist communist parties. However, in their reflections on the student protests that were published in the September 1969 issue of *L'Internationale Situationniste*, the S.I. argued that May 68 was not a student movement but a revolutionary proletarian movement.[45] 'Stalinists!' ran one of the slogans, 'Your sons are with us!'

In Quebec in 2012, and among contemporary social movements in general, there is far less interest in the notion of a revolutionary proletariat and in a vanguard leadership than there had been as late as the 1960s. Regardless, this is exactly what was provided in the form of the ASSÉ and the CLASSE, with their weekly assemblies, organised structure and philosophy of combative syndicalism. Of the 300 books that were published on the subject of the 1968 strike in France the following year, the S.I. argued that only a handful of these were worth reading. In general, they argued, the books either misinformed readers or falsified the facts. In 1969 the French Larousse dictionary added an entry for the term *situationniste* that effectively reduced the S.I.'s revolutionary politics to youthful protest and the problem of generation gap. In today's context the generational conflict is replaced by the problems of intersectionist theory, with the radical democracy that advocates the equivalence between struggles based on race, class, gender and sexuality.

We consider that distinctions need to be drawn between Situationist psychogeography, psychoprotest, and contemporary postmodern and post-structuralist theories whose anti-foundationalism and critique of the subject disallow the notion of social totality. It would seem that in these times of global social mobilisation, earlier cultural critiques of Marxist urban geography have been radically displaced. Alain Badiou and Slavoj Žižek, for example, are only two of the most prominent advocates of a communist turn in the context of neoliberal globalisation. Whereas Ernesto Laclau and Chantal Mouffe's theory of radical democracy renounced the objective grounding of superstructural struggle in the economic base, defining the economy as a discursive site, their approach did not repoliticise capitalism. According to Žižek, the postmodern game of plurality makes it necessary that 'we do *not* ask certain questions (about how to subvert capitalism as such, about the constitutive limits of political democracy and/or the democratic state as such),' and thereby avoid the question of 'the political act proper.'[46]

Žižek's thinking is consistent with both psychogeography and psychoprotest insofar as it is grounded in a theory of capital as the concrete universal and insofar as it posits a revolutionary subject that is willing to break with this order. Žižek argues further that the contingency of plural political struggles is not opposed to the totality of capital, but rather that the latter shapes the very conditions of emergence for the myriad of shifting political subjectivities. In this regard, the diverse social movements that participated in the psychoprotests of the *printemps érable* represent the inherent conflictual nature of neoliberal global capitalism. The excessive policing and systematic repression of the Quebec strike was part of a global capitalist offensive that produces the now common features and determining aspects of a global ideological landscape that today's psychoprotesters must learn to subvert.

Badiou's thinking, in contrast to Žižek's, is consistent with the aims of psychoprotest insofar as it makes connections between being and event, between being as a science of multiplicity and event as the basis of a truth procedure. The significance of structural change is not what we can know in terms of reality, but what is new in the situation. Being and event are not external to one another, but articulated through the impasse of being itself. Badiou's metapolitics, which resists all forms of representational politics, opposes politics and culture to economic calculation. Politics must not be considered against an eternally fixed notion of capitalism. His work therefore shifts the terms of totalisation and negation. According to Bruno Bosteels, in Badiou's metapolitics the subject is 'a fragment of the sustained enquiry into the consequences of an event for a possible universal truth.'[47] From this we derive the simple understanding that not everything is political, and by the same token, not everything is of aesthetic significance. Politics is an art of the impossible that favours a truth that is universally the same for all, an art that can organise a generic equality. In our estimation, it is communism that defines the intelligibility of the psychoprotests of the 2012 student strike.

5

The unrealised extravagance of the avant garde: Test Dept and the subsumption of labour

We will not take money in taxes from those who work hard and pay it out to those who don't ... We are trying to roll back the tide of Socialism.
– Prime Minister Margaret Thatcher, February 1, 1980

Around the world, we see a rise of populism, nationalism and protectionism. We see the great positive forces of free trade, economic liberalism and the rules-based order which sustains them under threat ... That's why as Conservatives, we are on a renewed mission to fight and win the battle of ideas and to defeat socialism today as we have defeated it before.
– British Prime Minister Theresa May, February 7, 2018

Writing about Isabell Lorey's *State of Insecurity*, Sarah Charalambides argues that with regard to the newly defined immaterial creative class faction promoted by neoliberal governance, there is no Stakhanovite equivalent of the model worker and that instead the condition of insecurity in a risk society – precarity – names diverse situations that cannot come under a unifying identity based on production processes. She asks: 'Can precarisation be used as a shared name for diverse situations?' 'Is it possible to articulate alliance without falling back upon identity, without flattening or homogenising precarious situations?'[1] Such questions regarding the state of intellectual and artistic labour in the age of austerity inform the context of reception of *Test Dept: Total State Machine*, a comprehensive study of the work of the British industrial music group Test Dept.[2] Authored by three core members of the group, Graham Cunnington, Angus Farquhar and Paul Jamrozy, and edited by industrial music and Neue Slowenische Kunst specialist Alexei Monroe, as well as sociologist and author Peter Webb, *Test Dept* covers the formation of the group, its social context of emergence in the South London of Thatcherite Britain, its various undertakings in the praxis of art and political activism, and its eventual dissolution as it diversified into new projects. Reflecting the visual media focus of Test Dept, the book is lavishly illustrated and resembles more a magazine layout than a standard monograph. Dynamic visual graphics adorn disparate kinds of texts, beginning with a scholarly essay by Monroe and diverging into new articles by band members on the various stages of their work, texts by and about collaborators, interviews, snippets of music reviews, diary entries, police files, samples of song lyrics presented as broadsheets, and archival documents and photos. The whole is completed with a useful discography and timeline.

The principal motifs and the continuing relevance of the work of Test Dept are addressed in the introduction by Monroe, who argues against monumental historicism and suggests that avant-garde breakouts in sonic and artistic innovation create their own utopian constellations. This approach allows Test Dept to be discussed both in relation to those ontogenetic peers who worked contemporaneously to them – Cabaret Voltaire, Throbbing Gristle, SPK, Einstürzende Neubauten, 23 Skidoo, This Heat, Art Deco, Laibach – but also in relation to phylogenetic comrades like Kazimir Malevich, the Soviet filmmakers Dziga Vertov and Sergei Eisenstein, the popular campaigner Anatoly Lunacharsky, the graphic designer El Lissitzky, Arseny Avramov and his *Symphony of Factory Sirens*, Nikolai Roslavets and his atonal soundscapes, Alexander Mosolov and his factory machine music, Hans Eisler's 'Blast Furnace' soundworks, Henryk Górecki and his musical laments, and Andrei Tarkovsky, with his dystopian wastelands. This historical junction is mediated by the very specific materials that are used by the group: sounds that come from disused shipyards and by hammering away at scraps of metal; oil drums, steel piping, petrol tanks, water tanks and lorry suspension springs used as idiomorphic percussion instruments; foghorns, factory sirens, recordings of political speeches, mainstream media and military drills – all of these a 'sonic weaponry,' according to Monroe, wielded against Thatcherite common sense.[3] Going to the core of the undertaking, Monroe quite rightly identifies this choice of materials to be the main contradiction: the fact that Test Dept sought to show political solidarity with industrial workers precisely at the time when heavy industry and whole manufacturing towns and regions were in the process of disappearing forever from the UK. This contradiction tends, however, to lead to a dissociation of aesthetics and choice of materials from the group's anarcho-socialist political commitments. If one focuses only on Test Dept's use of relentless industrial imagery and sounds, one ignores the alignment of these motifs with a distinctly leftist socio-political critique. Monroe here introduces a further mediation to the central contradiction of the choice of industrial materials, that of 'discipline as a corrective force.'[4] Proposed originally by the industrial music group Throbbing Gristle as a means to counter commercial conformity and liberal laissez-faire, Test Dept pushed the constructivist and Stakhanovite denotations of discipline into avant-garde sublations of art and life, understood in terms of dialectical praxis rather than the pretence of a premature synthesis or already achieved goal. This implied, according to Monroe, rejecting 'micro-political aesthetics and tactics' and instead going 'to the people,' those who are most oppressed, including those workers of the former eastern bloc countries, to spark emancipatory resistance.[5] The basis for this bridging of art and life was physical labour, the disciplined and precise performance of percussive action on unyielding metal, mixed with vocal appeals, commands and trumpet blasts, as well as projections of fragments of industrial reality to audiences of youths, blue-collar workers and poor communities that had for generations been dominated by the ruling class, their petty-bourgeois hangers-on and police henchmen.

With Monroe's introduction in mind, the rest of the book reads like something of a challenge. One is encouraged to sift through the archive of the Test Dept adventure to find what is useful to anyone involved in the struggle against Thatcherism, which continues unabated in these days of austerity, destruction of social programmes, kowtowing to American militarism and support of fascists in European countries and elsewhere. One soon discovers, according to band member Paul Jamrozy, that the group started out in 1981 as an effort to carry on the 'unfinished business' of punk music, looking to Burrundi drummers for inspiration on how to properly carry out an hour-long programme of machine-like 4/4 rhythm. These mates were South London squatters, disaffected and unemployed, and this was the time of the Brixton riots, when domestic police began to use military tactics in their enforcement of UK-style Reaganomics. Needless to say, not everything in this scrapyard will find an immediate utility. Their first manifesto, for instance, 'Beating the Retreat,' is pure Soviet futurism – a brash celebration of the destructive forces of efficiency and the cold logic of technology. Unusable as a piece of political wisdom, it nevertheless defines the background against which the group would forge a collectivism that is reminiscent of the Scratch Orchestra. The group lived communally, split their earnings equally and refused all individual identification, fighting the glitz and glamour of the popular music industry.

Test Dept's use of Stakhanovite imagery, of sweaty young men in grey work clothes hammering away with heavy tools and wooden batons at sundry and unwieldy pieces of metal was hardly at this time strictly aesthetic. At issue was not only 'labour' in the broadest sense of the term, but the dead labour it rested upon. The war over the Falkland Islands in 1982 was an indication of the desperate measures to which Thatcher would resort in order to rekindle the dream of empire. The real targets, however, were the unions, especially the miners, who had numbered 750,000 in the years after WWII, but were down to about 3,000 after Thatcher had successfully closed most of the mines. In order to show solidarity with these workers, Test Dept had understood their touring as a contemporary version of the red 'agit trains' on which Vertov had cut his teeth as a filmmaker and editor. According to Jamrozy, '[w]hen TD got involved with the Miners' Strike, we drew parallels with what were classified as the "Red" or "Educational Trains" and what the Russian

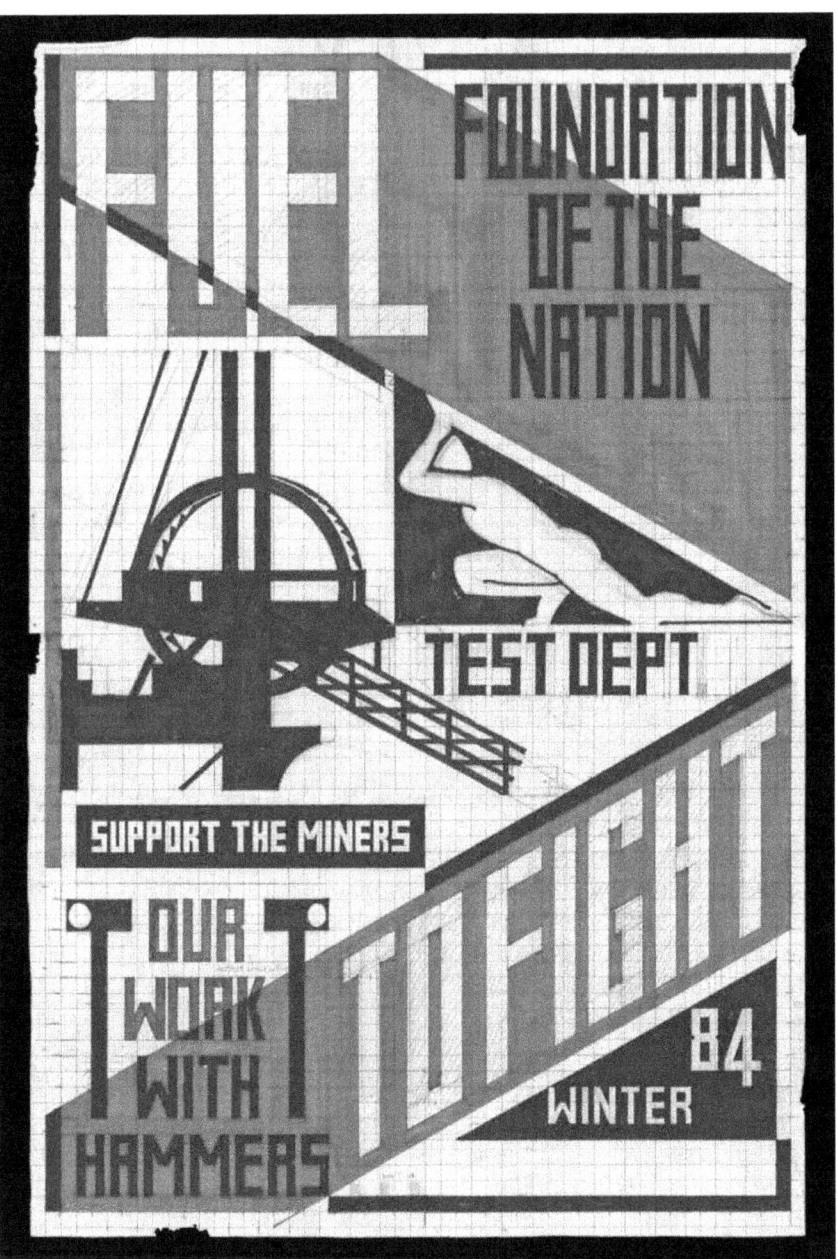

Brett Turnbull, Fuel to Fight poster design for the 1984 Miners Support Tour.
Courtesy of and © Test Dept.

futurists were doing 70 years previously.'⁶ The 'battle bus,' as they called it, travelled to various mining towns, eventually making alliances with the newly formed South Wales Striking Miners' Choir and with the Kent activist miner Alan Sutcliffe, whose passionate speeches accompany the thrashing intensity of the music on the 1984 album *Shoulder to Shoulder*. Test Dept travelled to Yorkshire, Durham, Northumberland and Glasgow, playing in site-specific locations rather than mainstream venues. TD filmman Brett Turnbull would shoot footage of the strike and show this material at concerts in the next town, producing on-the-spot agitational material, which, as late as the TD/ SD30 performance at the AV Festival in Newcastle in 2014, remained useful as a method to teach resistance. Solidarity meant joining picket lines, raising money for the cause and sharing drinks with the strikers. Older miners and their families who were not accustomed to industrial music would find ways to relate to the concerts, either through familiarity with the materials of heavy industry, the hard work involved in the performance, or the projected images of people like themselves who were otherwise rarely heard on radio or seen on television. The rhetoric of the early single 'Total State Machine' – One Voice, One Will – would raise people's spirits in anger, a proposition that was tested in the mid-1980s in Poland and other East European countries where the same visuals were presented to workers of a supposedly enemy ideology. Of course there Test Dept had to hide their intentions and their film footage from the state police, playing unannounced or in one instance as a form of payment to the families of workers at a bus repair factory.

There is a great deal more in *Test Dept: Total State Machine* that could be used to bridge the gap between an early 1980s moment of proletarian post-punk bruitisme and today's creative class digitariat, least of all, a certain number of petty-bourgeois 'deviations' like pagan festivals, heritage baiting and digressions into the expanded body consciousness of rave and club culture. While throughout the 1980s Test Dept mostly kept to the script of revolution- ary praxis, supporting striking newspaper workers, the Anti-Poll Tax Unions and the Polish Solidarity movement, by the early 1990s their efforts to remain relevant to audiences changed to a somewhat more flexible and flocculent Michel Serres-inspired 'break from the realpolitik of theory' wherein the remix of digital sounds corresponds loosely to the bricolage of identities.⁷ In his essay contribution to the book, Marek Kohn points out that a survey conducted in the UK in 2011 found that 'less than a quarter of the population described themselves as working class.'⁸ Test Dept adjusted accordingly. The lyrics to the 1995 jazzy dance tune 'Timebomb,' for instance, declares that 'love is sacred,' and calls on listeners to 'do the right thing,' 'respect the world we live in' and 'open your minds.' Nothing could be further from the 1984 track 'Total State Machine,' with its agit-lyrics 'Use Every Means,' 'Means of Control,' 'Means of Production,' 'Marching Boots,' 'Marching Orders,' 'One

Voice! One Will!' On the whole, *Test Dept* mostly charts this journey from Bolshevik classicism to what Jordi Blanchar refers to as 'new frameworks' that signal a shift away from 'a uniform body' towards a Hardt and Negri-inspired 'multitude acting together to defend what is common.'[9]

This shift of emphasis by Test Dept from revolutionary proletarian politics to nomadic anarchism brings the reader back to the aesthetic question that is addressed in the epigraph of Monroe's introduction, a quotation from Peter Bürger's 2010 essay 'Avant-Garde and Neo-Avant-Garde: An Attempt to Answer Certain Critics of *Theory of the Avant-Garde*.' The words from Bürger read: 'Measured against their goals and the hopes that they carried, all revolutions have failed: this fact does not lessen their historical significance. But it is precisely in its extravagance that the project of the avant-garde serves as an indispensable corrective to a society foundering in its pursuit of egotistical goals.'[10] This reference to Bürger yields more than is at first apparent since in the early 1980s it was not Bürger's assessment of 1970s pluralism that might have been most relevant to the emergence of this group but instead the material that is addressed by Jochen Schulte-Sasse in his foreword to the 1984 English translation of *Theory of the Avant-Garde*.[11] Schulte-Sasse begins with an assessment of Renato Poggioli's 1962 study of the 'modernist' avant garde, which Poggioli defines as a cult of novelty and of the strange that is set against realist representation, understood as prosaic convention. This modernist definition of contradiction within bourgeois, technological society, however, is a rather blunt instrument and does not allow for very fine distinctions to be made between aestheticism, romanticism, symbolism, avant-gardism and postmodernism. At best, according to the author, it allows for a summary distinction from commercialism and conformism.

For Schulte-Sasse, the advantage of Bürger's work over Poggioli's is that it is both more historically specific and more sociologically relevant, outlining, not unlike Fredric Jameson's essay on postmodernism, three separate phases to bourgeois culture and society. The story begins with the severance of cultural production from its dependence on the market. This break with the system of patronage allows for the development of the sphere of autonomy, a form of negativity that prefigures a utopian future but that in the present signals absolute confrontation. In the work of Herbert Marcuse and Theodor Adorno, however, writing almost one hundred years after the first anti-academic avant-garde works of the nineteenth century, the institution of autonomy has become a form of compensatory affirmation.[12] The contradiction between negation and affirmation leads to various modernist innovations, such as musical dissonance, literary anti-narrative and visual abstraction – revolts in style that result in semantic atrophy, a situation that Bürger considers inherent to the 'institution art,' understood as a space of bourgeois self-critique shorn from radical confrontation of the contradictions of this same society. This is what makes the appearance of Bürger's book in English translation relevant to the discussion of the emergence of Test Dept out of New Cross in the world of South London squats and co-ops: the fact that this Stakhanovite work was being tested at the time of the rise of postmodern academic theory.

For Bürger, the value of art can only be gauged in relation to notions of social value and society as a whole, and not only with regard to its intellectual class. There is thus no such thing as purely aesthetic experience. In this regard Test Dept's work should not be divided, as it is oftentimes in the book, between aesthetic and political revolution; rather, these two elements should be seen as co-terminous features of a superstructural expression of social change. This is in stark contrast to the theories of postmodernists like Roland Barthes, Julia Kristeva, Jacques Derrida, Michel Foucault, Gilles Deleuze, Jean-François Lyotard and Jean Baudrillard, who focused on modernist texts as means to deconstruct norms and ideological closure. According to Schulte-Sasse, such reading practices were premised on 'social inconsequentiality.'[13] In fact, given their status as avatars of today's post-political left, such inconsequentiality, with its indeterminate, undecidable, impossible and aleatory 'reality effects,' was worn like a badge of honour for fear of being responsible for further catastrophes. Postmodern theory was both post-enlightenment and post-revolutionary, declaring the end of the historical subject as defined by the meta-narratives of Marx and Freud. In stark contrast, Bürger championed the historical avant gardes for their presumption that art could effectively and *dialectically* lead back into social life. On the other hand, Bürger castigated the neo-avant gardes of the 1960s and 1970s for surrendering to institutional capture, a phenomenon described by Adorno and Horkheimer's thesis on the 'culture industry' and which Bürger referred to as 'false sublation.' For Bürger, the success of the neo-avant gardes of postwar art, from New Realism and Pop art to minimalism and conceptualism, was subsumed by capitalist institutions. The long and the short of it for Schulte-Sasse is that modernist as well as postmodernist analyses of solid and fluid, metaphysical closure and deconstruction, or what today we might readily refer to as the paradigm of social constructionism, have very little bearing on social totality and political ideology. Paradoxically, such art and theory reflects rather than resists society, in part, because it mistrusts the world. Nothing could be further from the words of Alan Sutcliffe in *Shoulder to Shoulder*, the miner who wants to say 'a few words about the strike' and 'make an honest appeal to everyone in our community.' Such words are not pre-theoretical. The call for support on the picket lines and denunciations of the magistrate is the most advanced theory of its time, perhaps no more but certainly no less than talk of phallocentrism, symbolic exchange and rhizomes. The problem with the latter concepts is not their efforts at estrangement and understanding of excess, but their dependence on what they deconstruct, which, according to Schulte-Sasse, makes them irrelevant.[14] Despite the goodwill of the theorists themselves – even if some stridently professed their pessimism – their theories failed to relate to social justice and social value. The process of endless demystification that they proposed vacillates between relativity and trumped up claims of validity – a theory of the false consciousness of meta-narratives, doxa and the logos, dressed up in the new clothes of structure and discourse.

The conclusion for Bürger is that avant-garde art and theory should seek to reproduce the social totality rather than the minutiae of historicist reconstruction.[15] In this regard, Marx's *Grundrisse* and *Capital* are not merely theories of production, and not merely theories of labour value, but theories of the relations of domination, understood contradictorily in terms of the colonisation of human desires.[16] In this sense, according to Schulte-Sasse, Bürger reflects on the material (realist) and not only abstract (positivist, identitarian) conditions of possibility of historical categories like art and labour. Bürger's conclusion is that the neo-avant gardes both protested and protected the status quo.[17] Their transgressive hostility to the ideals of the bourgeoisie reflected those same ideals. In contrast, genuine avant-garde artists do not isolate themselves, but while attacking the institutionalisation of art, seek to integrate art with life, contributing to the establishment of new norms based in emancipatory social justice. In this respect Test Dept's inaugural manifesto, 'Beating the Retreat,' remains somewhat aestheticist. It allowed Test Dept to come into visibility but it otherwise obscured the bourgeois weapon of neoconservative ideology. Nor did it adequately address the social function of music; it rather distinguished the band from its predecessors and contemporaries in the Pop universe. On the other hand, it is this ambiguity that brought Test Dept closest to its Slovenian counterpart Laibach. Confusing to fans as well as detractors, both groups had their activities monitored by the secret police – in the case of Test Dept by the same DDR officer responsible for the files of the writer Christa Wolf. Laibach never clearly identified with or against various political regimes, but kept a distance from concrete political activism, allowing for misinterpretation of their motives and mining avant-garde genealogies through a 'retrogarde' ideological position.[18] In contrast, Test Dept made use of industrial aesthetics in order to engage directly in social contexts of production and with various communities of struggle, effectively reflecting on the end of an epoch. In this regard the work of Test Dept offers us something beyond the institutionalisation of aesthetic praxis and even beyond the realm of 'industrial' as a music genre.

The crux of the matter, then, is that the situation today has changed so dramatically for both art and labour that we no longer look to postmodern theory except as itself a somewhat 'retrogarde' set of tools for intellectual and cultural production. This post-postmodern condition is partly what frames the contexts of production and reception of *Test Dept*. With regard to the question of precarity, what the current conjuncture of biopolitical activism seeks to understand and make into a basis for radical political organisation is the shift from Bürger's thesis on the 'false sublation' of art into culture industry and creative industry to a somewhat more up-to-date analysis of the 'real subsumption of labour.'[19] According to Marxist theory, the formal subsumption of labour occurs when labour power is exchanged for wages and exploited for surplus value profit. In the industrial mode of production, labour exploitation is 'formal' since the labour process has not yet been completely transformed by machines, and so surplus value depends on the ability of the capitalist to extend the working day, reduce workers' wages and increase the speed of work. In this context, labour is provided only enough resources to reproduce itself. The capitalist seeks to lessen the contradiction between labour and capital by revolutionising the processes of production, which contributes to surplus value but without requiring more from labour. The capitalist survives competition by investing in technological automation and intensifying management, which leads to the 'real subsumption' of labour. While the real subsumption of labour revolutionises what can be expected from one worker in a day, it reduces the amount of variable capital that is spent on workers' wages and consequently reduces the amount of capital that can be transformed into surplus, since the source of value according to the labour theory of value is human labour, or what Marx referred to as the organic composition of capital. As competition and automation reduce the valorisation process, rates of profit decline and more of the labour force is made redundant. On the one hand, beyond the money nexus, this freeing up of time is the realisation of human dreams of emancipation from toil and drudgery, but on the other hand, the pauperisation of the labour market creates a crisis in production since there is also a reduced ability to consume what is produced. In order to compensate for this situation in which labour has been made redundant by innovation, capitalism looks to the growth of the tertiary sector, with new services made available in education, culture, leisure, advertising, health, administration, social welfare, security, and so on – a new 'post-industrial' labour market that satisfies new needs and defines workers in terms of consumer identities rather than their place in the division of labour. In the most recent phase of the real subsumption of labour, the shift from Fordism to post-Fordism places a great deal of emphasis on the computer technologies and digital information that facilitate the financialisation of the economy, a further shift away from profits based on the industrial mode of labour exploitation.

Although mechanisation promises to free people from drudgery, the working day for many people extends well beyond the forty-hour work week. As David Graeber notes in his essay 'On the Phenomenon of Bullshit Jobs,' countless new jobs are created every day to keep populations working overtime.[20] The service sector in today's developed West accounts for about three quarters of employment, effectively replacing productive work, which is otherwise transferred to so-called developing economies. Workers in these fields are the same people, mentioned earlier, who do not identify as working-class. The paradox is that even as more and more people spend their time performing non-productive activities, such uses of time are somehow factored back into the production process and circulation of capital, invisibly extending the working day to 24/7 and making the minutiae of daily existence into something that is calculable and exchangeable. The consequence of this is that it becomes all the more difficult, as Graeber points out, to provide an objective measure of the social value of labour, especially the kind of industrial labour that was embodied in early Test Dept performances. Productive labour, even in the high-tech industry, is increasingly outsourced to offshore factories and maquiladoras. Meanwhile, in the developed West, corporate CEOs earn 300 times more than the average employee. The social and ideological function of the political class that does the bidding of corporate capitalists is to find ways to siphon the combined social wealth of the majority into the pockets of the billionaire class. For example, the austerity policies of the European Union caused the Greek economy to shrink by twenty-five percent, unemployment to rise to twenty-seven percent, and youth unemployment to rise to sixty percent. The population of Greece was asked in the referendum of July 4, 2015, to decide if this undemocratic social vision should be allowed to dominate government policy. Even if the answer should be a no-brainer, the population nevertheless seemed to be divided, at least according to mainstream media. One reason for this confusion is the fact that many people in this country dedicated to tourism effectively do not know the value of their activity. When bikini-clad Miss Tourism Planet models are not hired to send the message that 'Greek tourism is not in crisis,' right-wing populism and tabloids fill the void by drawing on sentimental notions of the nobility of hard work and the paying of one's debts. When workplace pressure can be used to exert political influence, however, like the Syriza government's closing of banks in the lead-up to the referendum, people complain. Yet at the same time the population tolerates the continued evisceration of unionised work, those jobs that have 'a clear social value,' as Graeber puts it, wherever one might find them.[21]

In this context, the image of heroic labour discipline that was wielded by Test Dept in the early to mid-1980s is indeed quixotic. To come back to Charalambides' article, the normalisation of precarisation anticipates disobedience to neoliberal capitalism. However, as readers of the work of Karl Polanyi have argued, it is not self-evident that the forms of insurgency will be progressive. With regard to Greece, the European establishment toyed with the idea of orchestrating a coup d'état similar to the installation of the Abdel Fattah al-Sisi regime in Egypt. The politics of precarity that Charalambides and Lorey allude to has yet to take place since most people still understand work in terms of a former 'formal subsumption.' Like the proverbial cartoon cat that has unknowingly walked off a precipice but failed to look down, the working masses in the post-industrial West remain in a state of suspended animation. As Charalambides rightly says: 'precariousness is not something autonomous that exists in itself in an ontological sense.'[22]

Given the conditions of structural inequality, the reality principle of precarity seeks compensatory illusions of various sorts. Such fantasmatic substitutes are increasingly the order of the day in the field of socially engaged art, in which social and political activism is rapidly replacing the concern with 'Art.' According to Gregory Sholette, in an essay on the 'delirium' of social practice, art has taken a social turn precisely at the moment when the system of state governance is no longer adequately managing broad social, structural and ecological problems.[23] This makes for a neat analogy to the situation encountered by the members of Test Dept in the early 1980s. What then might we take from their choice to explore the outmoded for its ability to explode the continuum of the present? Sholette argues that contemporary art is the avant garde and social realism of capital.[24] While financialisation accompanies the exponential growth of the art market, it is worth distinguishing between the primary economy of artists who live from the sale of their work and the equally value-generating secondary economy of precarious artists that Sholette refers to as 'dark matter.'[25] The conundrum facing this dark matter is, on the one hand, the question of political organisation, which tends to focus on reformist reallocation of resources, with many calling for a living wage as a human right, and on the other hand, what I would emphasise with my notion of the 'brave new avant garde' as the pretence of autonomous collectives to be able to withdraw from the field of cultural production.[26] Sholette makes the important observation that such a withdrawal implies making common cause with workers and activists outside the distinct sphere of art – a process that is definitional to Bürger's theory of the historical avant garde and that leads Sholette to now refer to social practice art as 'the unconfirmed major contender for an *avant-garde redux*.'[27] However, the 'choreography of social experiences,' which covers the range of practices from apolitical flash mobs, relational hanging around and file sharing, to more politicised orchestrations such as Occupy Wall Street, Strike Debt, Liberate Tate/Platform and Gulf Labor, is now a feature of what I have addressed as real subsumption. One need not see these phenomena in a cynical way as mere expressions of the neoliberal injunction to participate and network, and even, if you want to survive in the secondary economy, collectivise. Certainly, these phenomena are generative of political use values. Regardless, such art workers tend to perform reparative social work more loosely, with less accountability, less institutional permanence and job security, and with possibly less professional know-how than people employed in traditional social service jobs, no matter how expert one might become in the course of fieldwork. In many cases, artists become professionalised on the basis of one or more university degrees in fine arts, with proven ability to work collaboratively with communities and with expectations of the requisite skills and nomadic flexibility. Once their qualifications are established they are offered temporary, part-time jobs and project work at substandard non-union wages, that is, if they are not simply asked to do what they do for free: work for work's sake. The rest are either employed in universities or become small-scale entrepreneurs.

Idealism runs deep and one should not underestimate it, but one should also attend to ideology. Sholette's best guess for the success of social practice is that it resolves intolerable contradictions in the art world by inverting art's privileged hermeneutic into its heterogeneous social materials.[28] The simple production of the social, attributed by Sholette to the performance theory of Shannon Jackson, comes to resemble the relation between things that is acknowledged by the thesis of real subsumption, only this thing is now increasingly immaterial and leads from specific concrete demands to an ambiguous atmosphere of interpersonal and affective collaboration in the best of cases but sometimes also to volatile pseudo-conflict. Despite the real ideological gains made by the grassroots left, the general tendency is for the question of class conflict at the heart of the labour-capital relation to dissolve into anti-statist and anti-capitalist post-politics. Here I agree with Sholette that social practice must tarry with the delusion of political effectiveness.

A broader consideration of the post-enlightenment conditions of semio-capitalism might further explore the way that Oskar Negt and Alexander Kluge's theory of experience today comes closer to a surrealist world of intoxication, mediated by a Žižek-derived notion of the weakening of the function of the big Other. Insofar as Test Dept's performances resemble the work of Laibach, they very interestingly touched on the question of belief in a world of contradictions. This was particularly acute as they toured their Stakhanovite sounds and images in former Eastern European countries. Why perform industrial labour for those who do it for a living? In his essay, Sholette suggests à la 'Theses on Feuerbach' that the free gifts of today's social practice artists are sacrifices to an absent god, and god, he says, 'is of course society itself, defined as a project of collective good, from each according to her ability, to each according to his need,' which Sholette contrasts to the selfishness of Capitalism 2.0.[29] This, however, misses Marx's main point that capitalist exploitation is not only a moral matter of greed but takes place even when people have the best intentions. It misses the point of Marx's *Capital* wherein the absent god takes the pernicious form of money. It further misses the mark of some of the ideas that we could find in Freud. For Sholette, the answer to the question of whether art should merge with life can only come from the grassroots and the quest for social justice. In other words, it is less a matter of ideology. Despite Sholette's promising reference to Viktor Shklovsky's 'optimism of delusion,' much of what he proposes as change is premised on the proliferation of relatively autonomous acts of resistance and a measure of resentment.[30] In the case of the July 2015 Greek referendum we find a similar problem of politicisation but from the opposite end of the political spectrum, where the question of ideology is avoided by members of the Eurogroup, who reduce politico-ideological decisions to a matter of technical administration without political consideration.[31] Even leftists are divided about the political outlook of Syriza, and communist groups were not surprised when after the referendum Syriza approved the EU's brutal austerity measures as the best hope for reforming the system. Spain's Podemos is now encountering similar problems. For such reasons I wholeheartedly agree with Sholette that political acts are delirious; not only are they not grounded in political economy but sometimes they cannot be fully grounded in political reason. A political act, Žižek argues, is a wager that can only be assessed retrospectively.

Marx's theory of socially necessary labour time today meets the problem of production and distribution on a global scale. It is, because of this, all the more necessary to adapt the ideology of labour value that was developed under Fordist social relations to today's international division of (digital) labour.[32] Insofar as labour is integral to the reproduction of capital, the social coordination of production rather than the production of wealth is increasingly definitional to any situation that could lead to a post-capitalist political economy.[33] Regardless, the question of politics and therefore of class antagonism remains.[34] For good and bad, the real subsumption of labour is part and parcel of the exponential growth of social practice art. As Sholette argues, such practices can no longer remain unseen by institutional discourse. The work of Test Dept can today be received as an earlier instance of social practice, an older brother in the permanent revolution. In the context of the subsumption of living labour, it is a truth that only a collective effort can dismantle the relations of domination. To cite Alan Sutcliffe once again: Down with the police state! Victory to all working people in struggle throughout the world!

6

No strawman for the revolution

The most helpful definition of avant-garde art we have today, one that is adequate to contemporary forms of socially engaged art and to the global political economy of culture as we know it, is that proposed by John Roberts in *Revolutionary Time and the Avant-Garde*.[1] While Roberts' theory has some affinity with Jacques Rancière's work in the sense that he first distinguishes between the ontology of art and the heteronomy of non-art, he further proposes that art's worldly materials are part of art's 'ontology of conceptualisation,' an 'end of art historicity' that understands art as not only adisciplinary and non-identitarian, but reflexive and experimental, a post-art condition that opens radical avant-garde art practices to knowledge of its history, and its failures, as well as to techniques of mass production. Art's extended conceptualisation often eludes the interest of activist artists, even if it is inherent to activist art. Just as Marx and Engels criticised the idealism of utopian socialists, one should be wary of efforts to model the theory of the avant garde on an ethnography of activist self-conception, or alternately, on theories of socially engaged art that limit themselves to practical goals simply because such pragmatism is often suited to the working conditions and outlook of activists. We should therefore reject the separation of pragmatic art and radical theory insofar as unmediated approaches to social reality allow art institutions and funding bodies to more easily tolerate social projects in the traditional terms of bourgeois reformism or as an adjunct to neoliberalisation. In this regard Roberts distinguishes avant-garde art from the primary economy of the art market but also from the bohemian attitudes of the creative class. The post-art condition of the avant garde implies collective struggle and oppositionality as the basis of democratisation.

One small modification that I would make to Roberts' theory of art's ontology of conceptualisation is the Lacanian-Žižekian notion of the Real as an epistemological-ontological mediation, or ontological failure, as Slavoj Žižek puts it, the transposition of an epistemological obstacle into the thing itself and therefore the inability to fully know the art 'thing.' In this regard the only pre-Kantian, Spinozist bit of naive reality that it is necessary to maintain is that of *objet a*. This pre-transcendental gap affords us the concept of revolution as deadlock, castration, social difference or antagonism. It also provides us with various other Lacanian approaches such as the dialectical mediation of the problems of symbolisation and social relation. This helps to develop an understanding of why it is, as Roberts puts it in relation to Theodor Adorno, that art is never simply reducible to non-art. Given this, the added problem is that non-art has no further ontological consistency and historicity itself is pressured by forms of subjectivisation, which in the work of Alain Badiou has been developed in terms of truth procedure and fidelity to the event.

The question of ontological failure is not merely a matter of individual pathology but is essential to theories of ideology that impact cultural and political praxis. Foremost on the activist agenda is the ecological threat, which all would agree must be made a priority for collective action. McKenzie Wark addresses Žižek's work in his writings on the Anthropocene.[2] For Žižek, the issue of global warming is not one that can be solved by limiting one's analysis to the social forces and relations of production. Whereas Wark proposes a new kind of proletarian culture, one might wonder what the potential is for a new Proletkult today. For this I turn to recent writings by Sven Lütticken and Yates McKee and address the shift from the 1960s to the present, from the Situationists to Occupy Wall Street, where transformations to cultural praxis raise important questions concerning the effectiveness of the current forms of organisation. The status of the Lacanian Real and the virtuality of subjectivity have been an irritant to activists who look to social mediation and non-art heteronomy as the basis for social and political practice. In order to question some of the intellectual trends of the new art activism, Žižekian dialectics and in particular his recent turn to the Discourse of the Master can help contribute to the redefinition of a contemporary vanguard art and politics.

Beyond the Anthropocene myth

In *The Spectacle of Disintegration*, McKenzie Wark returns to Guy Debord's 1967 book *The Society of the Spectacle* in order to gauge the metabolic rifts that have affected the ecosphere since the time when the spectacle could be neatly divided into two Cold War camps: the concentrated spectacles of the totalitarian East, with its images of leaders like Lenin, Stalin, Mao and Che, and the diffuse spectacle, with its endless parade of movie stars and fashion models.[3] By 1988, the same year that Claude Lefort had thought to diagnose the failure of May 68, Debord had written his *Comments on the Society of the Spectacle* and according to Wark considered that the diffuse spectacle had not simply won out but harboured forms of concentration through the integrated power of a shadow state plutocracy. For a more recent version of such diffusion and concentration, Wark proposes that what we are confronted with today is a 'disintegrating spectacle' in which state mechanisms can no longer be managed with any pretence to strategic popular interest. The spectacle of disintegration, he argues, is immune to all of the myriad single issue problems we throw at it: 'The disintegrating spectacle can countenance the end of everything except the end of itself. It can contemplate with equanimity melting ice sheets, seas of junk, peak oil, but the spectacle itself lives on.'[4]

Single issues are not all the same, however, since for Wark, writing in *Molecular Red*, the condition of the biosphere signals the key metabolic rift and the main terrain of struggle.[5] After all of the revolutionary and liberation movements of the last three centuries, the theme of the Anthropocene – a Marxian universal history adjusted to twenty-first century environmental end times – brings us to the last line of defence: the Carbon Liberation Front. Against solutions to the climate crisis that focus solely on the market, technology, individual choice, or romantic anti-modernism, the CLF seeks to integrate these different levels of economic, political, technical and cultural analysis and transform the totality of their arrangements. This of course also entails changing ourselves, but more importantly, it includes the Marxist strategy of identifying labour as a central category of experience and politics. With regard to this self-transformation, Wark proposes a kind of 'queer' theory of metabolic change produced by expanding the capitalist productivity through which subjective and social life is changed beyond the 'normal' state of things. In his review of *Molecular Red*, Žižek agrees that the rift in nature also signals a rift within humanity, but that in this respect Wark does not go far enough with his theory of alienation since the modern science of particle physics and quantum waves teaches us that there is no rhizomatic, micro-level or queer metabolism that can be elevated into a reality of last resort.[6] The productive interruption of shared life is not an expression of low-level positivity but of negativity, a cut in reality raised to the infinite power of Understanding and the Real that is obfuscated by the multiplicity of social conflicts, which alone and in their multiplicity cannot be explained in their own terms. The Anthropocene thus becomes an apparatus through which we attempt to account for the complexity of today's forces and relations of production.

By focusing on the economic base and taking from this some implications for ideology, Wark's hack of what Andreas Malm calls the 'Anthropocene Myth' is consistent with the Marxist notion of universal history and asserts that the carbon-based economy is coextensive with the capitalist mode of production.[7] The fact that we are dealing with an ideological problem that takes the form of denial can be noticed in the simultaneity of awareness of global warming and the growth in global emissions, which tripled from the 1990s to the 2000s, with most of this expansion due to foreign investment in commodity production and surplus extraction in China, where a grow-ing population is a source of cheap labour and where communist dirigisme guarantees labour discipline. Beyond production, there is unevenness also in consumption, where the average North American wastes one thousand times more than those in sub-Saharan Africa. Carbon exploitation is therefore a direct result of class exploitation and with this Malm disputes the myth of any Anthropocene narrative that lays blame on an undifferentiated species-thinking and humanity-bashing.

Given the overwhelming evidence, one might wonder why the Anthropocene Myth persists. But the question is posed backwards: it is because of the overwhelming evidence of man-made change under conditions of exploitation and overproduction that the myth emerges. In a lecture on 'Ecology as the New Opium of the Masses,' Žižek lists ecology as one of the major antagonisms that poses a threat to the infinite expansion of market logic. He argues: 'In spite of the infinite adaptability of capitalism, which, in the case of an acute ecological catastrophe or crisis, can easily turn ecology into a new field of capitalist investment and competition, the very nature of the risk involved fundamentally precludes market solutions.'[8] The radical implication of the environmental threat is that it no longer holds that whatever we do, history will go on. The twist in Žižek's argument is that it is today's excluded, the newly proletarianised in China and the Third World, the Palestinians trapped behind apartheid walls, and the millions of slum dwellers in South America, Mexico City, Africa, India and Southeast Asia, who today directly stand for universality. It is their reality that poses a threat to state control of the market. Without considering this excluded domain, he argues, ecology loses its subversive edge. The problem, then, is that one can fight for ecology but not question the ideological conditions that separate the Included and the Excluded.

Ecology, as it currently stands in liberal and social democratic discourse, allows us to ignore the true universality. Fear of radical political solutions but-tresses a post-political biocapitalism that seeks to leave behind old ideological struggles. The way that this political fear is displaced, however, is through fear of environmental disaster, which becomes a global ideology, a new opium for the masses based in a dread of real change. The upshot, for Žižek, is that we should accept the contingency of our existence and the utter groundlessness of nature.[9] However, the radical contingency of choice implies that we could, for fear of the necessary change, make the wrong decision and choose to act in a self-destructive manner. Today, Žižek argues, the real problem is believing in and assuming responsibility for this radical uncertainty: 'we find ourselves constantly in the position of having to decide about matters that will funda-mentally affect our lives, but without a proper foundation in knowledge.'[10] Belief in ecological catastrophe and the inevitability of neoliberal governance come to function in terms of fetishistic disavowal: we believe in it and we don't believe in it. In this, Žižek asserts, we have a way of understanding not only ideology, but culture, which relies on a big Other, a social unconscious or superego, that does not know. In contrast to the function of the analyst, who acts as the 'subject supposed to know,' the elementary rule of culture, according to Žižek, is to know when and how to *not* know, to not notice, or 'to go on and act as if something which happened did not happen.'[11] From this point of view, we must come to believe that the catastrophe is possible since we do not have the knowledge that would allow us to make the qualified choice that betrays the fact that no real choices are on offer.

This is a fundamentally different argument from Wark, who proposes that the abolition of capital would not automatically solve all of our problems since we would still need to 'provide energy and shelter and food for seven billion people without *completely* destabilizing planetary metabolic systems.'[12] From this perspective, the question of alienation is posed in terms of a materialist reduction to questions of survival and necessity, bypassing the terms of analysis that Žižek is noted to have introduced in such texts as *For They Know Not What They Do: Enjoyment as a Political Factor*.[13] Contrary to Wark's fearful presentation of Žižek as an authoritative figure to be displaced, the essence of Lacanian psychoanalysis is always to insist that there is no big Other, which leads to various states of transference, fantasy, repression, and so on. Insofar as Wark suggests that the question of gap, along with the Real and social antagonism, is where Žižek's 'philosophy revs its engines' and 'anticipates an open road,' since such thinking is 'not amenable to empirical inquiry,' he obviates both psychoanalysis and dialectics. We might find the sources of this rejection in the work of Gilles Deleuze, for whom, as Badiou explains, politics was never a matter of ideology. Rather, according to Badiou, Deleuze's transcendental metaphysics and open road of rhizomatics, becoming, molecular rifts, folds and paradigm shifts, were derived from Nietzsche and Bergson. As Badiou put it best, this 'vitalist terrorism'

> presupposes the consensual nature of the very norm that needs to be examined and established, to wit, that movement is superior to immobility, life superior to the concept, time to space, affirmation to negation, difference to identity, and so on. In these latent 'certainties,' which command the peremptory meta-phorical style of Deleuze's vitalist and anti-categorical exegesis, there is a kind of speculative demagogy whose entire strength lies in addressing itself to each and everyone's animal disquiet, to our confused desires, to everything that makes us scurry about blindly on the desolate surface of the earth.[14]

As an example of how this plays out in Wark, we find that he considers all speculative thought to be 'molar' abstraction. 'Philosophy,' he writes, 'is that which has the capacity to reduce differences to the same.'[15] His concern, further, is that the kind of 'high theory' that someone like Žižek practices is able to decide what kinds of differences matter, like for instance class antagonism over and above the antagonism between labour and nature. Wark writes:

> From this point of view, Žižek borrows from philosophy a certain authority-gesture, where causal chains stop at a peak term beyond which there can be no questioning. Only that last term is no longer the God or the Goddess [Mother Earth], and still less Man, but the Void. Everything ascends and descends from this key term, of which the philosopher is the guardian. The Subject, the Object, even the Subject's encounter with the Other are always antagonisms riven by the self-same impossibility. The philosopher's self-appointed task is to show how any and all labors encounter the same limit of which the philosopher is the keeper of the essential names.[16]

If this is true then those names are primarily the Imaginary, the Real and the Symbolic, with the many other attendant terms derived from Freud and from Lacan – *objet a*, *jouissance*, the unconscious structured like a language, drive, the four discourses, etc. The essence of the void for Žižek is the question of fantasy and ontological limitation that is at the heart of all ideology, as well as all subjective, material and symbolic structures. This represents for Lacan a dialectics of subject and *objet a*, and therefore hardly a reduction of difference to sameness; in fact, the opposite is closer to being accurate, so long as one accepts along with difference the problem of negation. Just as theory rejects both relativism and absolutes, Lacanianism rejects both absolute identity and absolute difference, which are different ways to avoid symbolic castration. Subjectivity is a 'subject effect' and function of the gaze as big Other, an impersonal symbolic order and set of social rules that are impossible for the subject to fully assimilate, in particular, since such rules are themselves inconsistent. For Žižek, the abolition of capital could not solve all of our problems since for psychoanalysis our subjective relationship to the world and vice versa 'makes sense only against the background of this absolute unknowableness.'[17] Žižek provides a description of this in terms of Lacan's theory of the subject of the signifier, which dislodges Wark's false assumption that in Žižek's thinking the gap is situated specifically between labour and nature:

> Nature is simply unknown, its unknowableness is epistemological, whereas the Other *qua* another person is ontologically unknowable; its unknowableness is the way its very being is ontologically constituted, disclosed to us. Freud already had a presentiment of this when he wrote about a 'foreign kernel' [*fremdes Kern*] in the very midst of our neighbour [*Nebenmensch*]: the Kantian unknowable 'Thing-in-itself' is ultimately man himself.[18]

For Lacan, the subject's alienation in the Other is transposed into the Other itself. Žižek locates dialectical materialism in this irreducible difference between subject and object, and not as Wark proposes, in either the sameness or absolute opposition between the two. Nor are subject and object in Lacan what Wark elsewhere refers to as 'pre-constituted categories.'[19] Against Wark's view of the Lacanian subject as an absolute, it is better and perhaps easier to understand it as a concept similar to what Marx understood as the proletariat, not the complementary subaltern to bourgeois ideology, but a subject with no proper place in its edifice – in other words, a lack that causes the bourgeoisie to assume it can impose even more exploitation. In this regard, Wark's counter-cultural stance towards master signifiers avoids the ways in which oppositions are means to contain antagonism and to impose empirical content where there is lack.

So what does Wark propose for metaphysical thought, or for what he refers to as a Bogdanovian realism of sensations and media theory? Wark looks not only to the effects of humankind as a geological force transforming the planet, but to a humankind that is able to control and alter the infrastructural mode of production and social relations of production. He defines the Carbon Liberation Front as 'a poetics and technics for the organization of knowledge' and takes as his reference point the work of the Soviet scientist, philosopher and fiction writer Alexander Bogdanov.[20] Expelled from the Bolshevik Party in 1909, largely as a result of his disputes with Lenin, Bogdanov, according to Wark, held that philosophy, oriented to the needs of the working class and its organic intellectuals, could become effective in reorganising the relationship of labour and knowledge. The specialised knowledge of science and social science could be integrated with everyday life and philosophy in its reorganisation of nature. Echoing Žižek's view that ideology is not merely constituted by abstract ideas, but is the very basis of everyday life, which designs propositions and makes them practically inhabitable as rules and rituals, Wark recovers Bogdanov for the spectacle of disintegration insofar as Bogdanov understood how ideology motivates organisational labour. For Bogdanov, writing in *The Philosophy of Living Experience*, labour is subsumed within a totality that is greater than itself and comes into being as it resists and seeks to repurpose nature.[21] In its experiments with nature, labour comes to a new understanding of causality, viewing energy as the outcome of the human transformation of carbon sources. Inspired by Bogdanov's alternative ecological vision, notably in his science-fiction novel *Red Star*, the contemporary novelist Kim Stanley Robinson proposes in his 'Mars Trilogy' that the Bogdanov position, represented by the character Arkady Bogdanov, is not to carve out a space of refuge within the existing totality, but to expand and transform the modes of organisation, making into a general condition the 'most advanced forms of collaborative labour.'[22] Such utopian visions, according to Wark, bring into existence new structures of feeling and a new boundary against exploitative and militarised forms of life. While in Bogdanov's *Red Star* the Martians had not yet achieved a new organisational social formation, the seeds of the future might be contained in the current struggles, which for Bogdanov, in his day, were found in the proletarian art movement of Proletkult.

Precarity and postcontemporaneity

What sites of possibility are there for Proletkult in the age of social media networking, creative industries and biopolitical protest? I will limit myself here to the reflections of two contemporary theorists of the politicisation of culture: Sven Lütticken and Yates McKee. In his essay on 'cultural revolution,' Lütticken wonders how the Leninist call for a socialist culture has been transformed since Debord appropriated this idea in the 1960s and shifted the terms of discussion from the takeover of state power to those of an avant-garde excavation of the promise of communism.[23] His concern is to address the idea of cultural revolution as a problematic term but also as a productive concept with the potential to shift the discussion on contemporary political art away from both institutional critique and art activism. His approach relies on the much maligned model of base and superstructure, with the implication that the field of art and the field of politics are distinct aspects of the superstructure – an understanding that is often implicit within the intellectual or academic strands of institutional critique but ignored in the more voluntarist camps of art activism. Less convinced of the total subsumption of labour than many autonomist thinkers, Lütticken proposes that a new class composition comprised of students, intellectuals, artists and bohemians might serve as a catalyst for new forms of revolutionary action.

Among several sources of ideas, Lütticken mentions the importance of Herbert Marcuse for a countercultural theory of the proletariat. In an unpublished text from circa 1970, Marcuse notes that the popular forms of countercultural rebellion might be useful in 'preparing the soil' for political revolution, that is, if it were not for the fact that they tend, rather, and insofar as the working class is now absorbed into a white-collar class of salaried employees, technicians and service workers, to integrate the sphere of cultural production into the sphere of the capitalist structural revolution.[24] In this regard the manifest revolutions of collective social action in response to the contradictions of capitalism were mixed and mired in cultural forms of revolt. As 1960s prosperity turned to 1970s economic crisis, this same culture was increasingly corporatised and by the 1990s artistic labour itself became the model of work for the new creative economy. Undeterred, French postmodern theorists held that libidinal economies and micropolitics could successfully sabotage dominant forms in such a way that the molecular revolution made the vanguard party redundant. The significance of this shift in the 1970s and 1980s is that such formations as micropolitics, punk and autonomedia were economical as much as they were cultural. Micro-practices were internal to the acceleration of capitalist change – a permanent counter-revolution.[25] For Lütticken, these formations may very well be part of today's art world establishment but they did contain the 'seeds of the future' mentioned earlier. He writes: 'When compared with the ongoing structural revolution of which they are part, and against which they react, such manifestations may appear fitful, faltering and contradictory. Yet in their excessive and doomed splendour, they form illuminating constellations: Benjaminian fireworks.'[26]

By the 1990s artists and intellectuals largely sought individual roads to success as cultural entrepreneurs. Reacting to neoconservative backlash, they put forward a new cultural politics of representation that struggled according to a mostly superstructural definition of culture. Today, this entrepreneurial model reaches a limit and Lütticken gives as examples the culture of permanent auditioning and volunteering in which, in 2013, 1,600 people applied for a cloakroom job at the Rijksmuseum, and 19,000 people applied for a few posts as attendants at the Prado.[27] Insofar as people refuse to identify as a class but rather as a multitude or an angry crowd, there is no social project to which the term cultural revolution might refer. Instead, the current forms of collaboration and self-organisation such as Occupy Wall Street, comprised of lumpen freelancers, artists and intellectuals, rely on a narrow class identification that is rather, in Lütticken's estimation, an assemblage or montage of temporarily connected 'sub-classes' and 'ex-classes' who are prey to the overwhelming privatisation of economic capital in the hands of the upper class. Small and informal counter-institutions that are concerned with sustainable forms of exchange are nevertheless operating in a situation in which they exploit themselves to an even higher degree than in the past and act as innovators of an informational primitive accumulation. Hacking capitalism's informational revolution, as Edward Snowden has done, might warrant the status of folk hero, but it remains for Lütticken a form of institutional critique, a liberal politics performed by the biopolitical outcasts of today's surveillance society. If the biocapitalist watchword for sustainability is recycle, the same might be said for today's cultural revolution, with its re-use of avant-garde and neo-avant-garde strategies. Such neurotic repetitions, according to Lütticken, need nevertheless to be read as symptoms of a potentially liberating break from teleological certainty.[28]

One such tactical break from inevitability is the 'postcontemporary' art of Strike Debt, as defined and described by Yates McKee.[29] In his analysis of what he terms the 'revolutionary struggle' of Strike Debt, McKee follows Peter Bürger's well-known formula that the goal of the historical avant gardes was the sublation of art into life.[30] McKee considers that the work of Strike Debt represents an altogether 'new' programme of politicised art.[31] In my own jargon, and given the fact that such activist work as Strike Debt is being

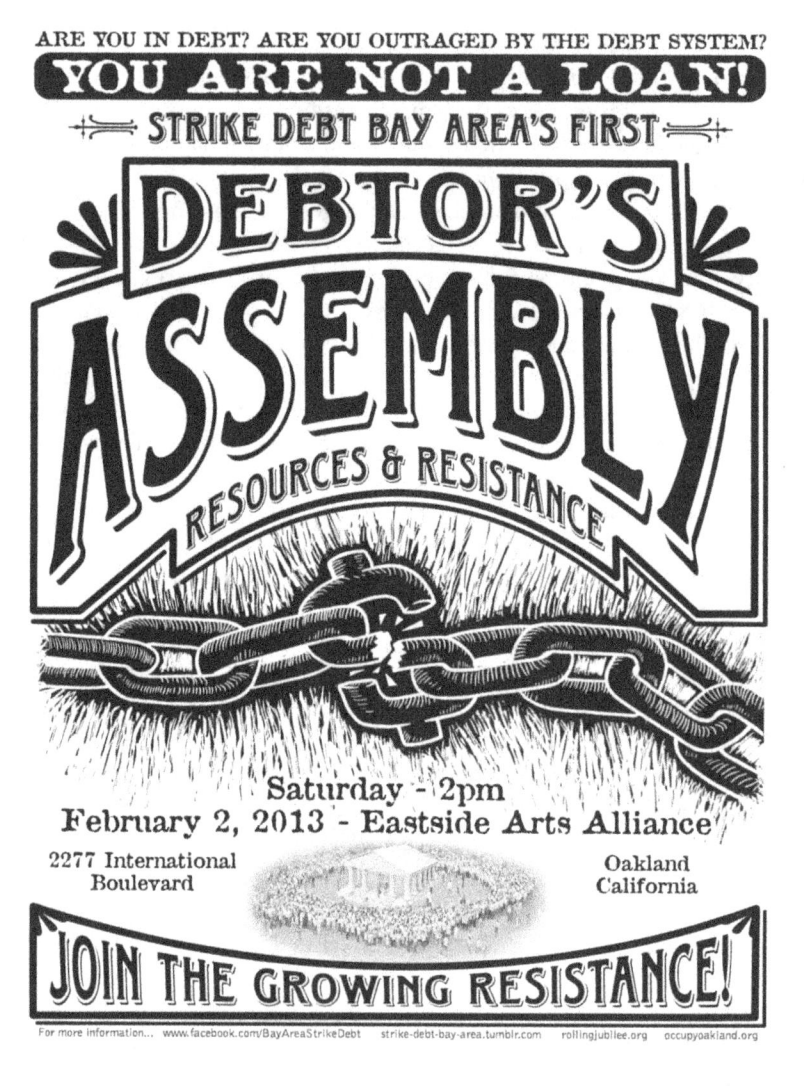

Poster for Strike Debt Bay Area Debtors' Assembly, Oakland, California, February 2, 2013. Strike Debt Bay Area is a local chapter of Strike Debt, an international movement of groups working to build popular resistance to all forms of unjust debt. The assembly created a space to rethink debt as a political platform for collective resistance and action. Design by Sandy Sanders. Courtesy of Strike Debt Bay Area.

produced on this side of the anti-globalisation movement and after 9/11, the war on terror, and after the widespread awareness of workerist concepts in the cultural field, one could refer to this kind of practice as not simply 'activist,' but more complexly as 'post-political bio-activism.' The point of this kind of grassroots community art is to be effective in real life and to not waste time with too much concern for theory or art world consecration. The effort to escape art and theory into politics is in many ways a strength, especially for the artists themselves. It is a weakness, however, insofar as this kind of work separates activism from class struggle. One might wonder where the vanguardism comes in exactly if the most effective tactic of Strike Debt has been to make socially progressive use of the secondary debt market, an idea put forward by the artist and organiser Thomas Gokey.[32] For McKee, however, the main innovative principle of postcontemporary art is not the Rolling Jubilee itself – the raising of funds as an example of 'microtopian' alternative economies – but the conceptualisation of the artist as an organiser, someone who facilitates assemblies, devises strategies and tactics, designs propaganda, stages performances, delivers workshops, cultivates alliances and administers media platforms.[33] None of these practices would in and of themselves be considered artistically relevant if it was not for the fact that in the case of both Occupy Wall Street and Strike Debt, a large number of organisers also happen to be artists whose creativity is essential to the movement. Such artists may be supported by institutions, but they take their cues from the new forms of political subjectivity.

In contrast to the avant-gardist stance cultivated by some artists to exploit art world values for the promise of potential or future social effectivity, Strike Debt does not focus on art tactics such as irony, defamiliarisation or critical autonomy, but rather distances itself from any concern with genre classifications such as 'socially engaged art' and from contemporaneity in art and culture. What is important is what happens in terms of social effectiveness. Moreover, what is important is the social bond of solidarity that is created in the process. As McKee puts it, Strike Debt could be seen to be a biopolitical laboratory for self-management and freeing of the commons.[34] The cooperative nature of such projects extends from a single set of issues to the whole of organic subjectivity; activists want not only to solve a particular problem, but, in the tradition of both bohemian subcultures and Soviet personalism, to penetrate the soul and bring the whole of personhood into the unfolding of the movement.

Given all of the lifestyle concerns and anti-authority patterns that coincide with the rising hegemony of the petty-bourgeois habitus, it makes complete sense that artists today are particularly drawn to participatory political engagement. The forms of anti-authority struggle are only apparent, however, insofar as they do not put forward a political programme and rely on indeterminate criteria of moral discipline.[35] As a defensive rather than inclusive measure, albeit one with the tactical advantage of flexibility and imperviousness to demobilisation, the space of activism becomes a scene for insiders rather than members. Some of the features of this appeal, according to McKee, would include attention to language, affect and imagination oriented towards love, caring and mutual aid. The enlistment of the affect of caring corresponds in some ways to Michel Foucault's notion of biopower as the extension of care through capitalist institutions. For the most part, and so that the 'evil' of state power can be avoided, the focus on labour as the key to ideology within capitalist social relations is replaced by the figure of the multitude. In terms of the Marxian presuppositions of people like Sylvia Federici, Michael Hardt and Antonio Negri, the custodial impulses of biopower are not in themselves to be eliminated but rather further socialised. While this contemporary attention to affect might seem to revisit the idealism of the late 1960s, it adds to this a desire to go beyond the countercultural critique of 'the system' and put forward a strategic vision that would be better able to challenge the prevailing economic and political hegemony. In the case of Strike Debt, 'witness testimonies' and 'conversion narratives' form the shared experience of crippling student, credit card, health care and mortgage debt. Strike Debt builds an affective space of care against the predatory practices of Wall Street and large banks that is based on mutual concerns and that raises the spectre of an 'Invisible Army of Defaulters' that could act cohesively and strategically against the corruption of moneyed interests, thereby prefiguring non–capitalist social bonds.[36]

McKee's postcontemporary art resembles Wark's Bogdanovian proletarian art movement and Lütticken's neo-provotarian formations, but with the added feature of a characteristically American grassroots populism. However, as Žižek has observed, the tragedy of such anarchist populism is that despite its critique of authoritarian rules it tends to create microtopian enclaves with their own forms of authority and charismatic personalities. Žižek suggests that the anti-hierarchical and consensus-based organisational principles of social movement activists often rely on unwritten rules and unacknowledged sources of authority, preventing awareness of the pretence to equality. In this the new forms of activist organising evade questions of representation. 'In order to safeguard this equality,' Žižek argues, 'you have a more sinister figure of the master, who puts pressure on the others to safeguard the purity of the non–hierarchic principle.'[37]

Confronting freedom

For some time now Žižek has been interested in the way that Lacan's Discourse of the Master can help distinguish between an authentic master and a false master. The real master is more terrible in a sense than the political leader – say, someone like Stalin – insofar as they do not tell people how to act and what to obey, but confronts them with their own freedom.[38] Žižek's recent development of the Lacanian Discourse of the Master has met with expected resistance and is addressed from the point of view of anarcho-communism by Mikkel Bolt Rasmussen in an article titled 'Is the Revolution Going to Be Communist?'[39] The purpose of Rasmussen's text is to defend the theory of revolution from three deviations: a vanguard political leadership, which he associates with Žižek's idea of the Master; Stuart Hall, Doreen Massey and Michael Rustin's reformist *Kilburn Manifesto* (and with this the focus on wealth redistribution by social democratic parties); and Hardt and Negri's optimism concerning the multitudes' refusal of neoliberal capitalism. I will not address the latter two as neither of these proposes the need for or function of a political vanguard. I am mostly concerned to understand what Žižek implies by the figure of a Master, and this, as part of his recent approach to the theory of the vanguard. Insofar as I myself have written about the artistic avant garde in terms of Lacan's Discourse of the Analyst, and also about the way that the rejection of vanguard functions leaves us within the biocapitalist cycle of resistance and repression, it is my interest to understand why it is that the Lacanian Master rather than the Lacanian Analyst acts best as a figure for the vanguard.

For the purposes of political effectivity, Rasmussen's article glosses over what it is that Žižek understands by the Master. The passage on Žižek in his text is brief and somewhat misleading – even if in some sense it also understands what Žižek is concerned with. While Žižek's position is associated by Rasmussen with that of Lenin's theory of the vanguard party, it should be mentioned that what Žižek retains the most from Lenin is his rejection of the notion of teleology and Lenin's view that the laws of History are not automatically written into or guaranteed by the necessity of a dialectical overcoming of capitalism through proletarian negation.[40] The situation that Lenin confronted in Russia was the relative absence of advanced relations of industrial production and the possibility of enlisting peasant forces. At the moment of betrayal by bourgeois allies, it was deemed necessary by the Bolsheviks to develop an alternative party apparatus so as to save the revolution. These were contingencies that implied that the reality of the situation was not altogether closed, and that there was a possibility of acting in these circumstances in ways that were not predetermined. It is this idea of an 'authentic act' that does not fall under pre-given laws of causality and necessity that interests Žižek in his Lacanian-inspired approach to post-transcendental dialectics, and thus his rejection of various forms of contemporary historicism, materialism and deconstruction. The question of how the Discourse of the Master pertains to the function of a political vanguard relates very specifically to his ongoing effort to rehabilitate a theory of dialectical materialism against the overwhelming intellectual status quo. Like it or not, it is this status quo that forms the blockadia of certitude that has shaped much contemporary activism. It should in this regard be acknowledged the extent to which Žižek and Badiou have almost single-handedly led theory out of the post-structuralism of the 1980s and 1990s, which had consigned the avant garde and cultural revolution to a Fukuyaman position on the inevitability of capitalism.

According to Rasmussen, Žižek argues that we need a Master rather than a Deleuzian leaderless multitude. In this regard Žižek is said to oppose horizontality, endless deliberation, episodic protests and network-based organisation without leaders. This in other words represents a critique of the notion of direct democracy. So much is more or less accurate. For some reason, however, Rasmussen then adds: 'Žižek uses a problematic idea of the political subject as an individual and shows a remarkable lack of trust in the critical potential of the mass, as well as complete disregard for history.'[41] The critique of 'spontaneism' is well-rehearsed on the revolutionary Marxist left and there is no reason why Rasmussen should attribute this to Žižek in particular. What is unexpected is how from this Rasmussen assumes that, hypothetically speaking, Žižek would consider neoliberalism to be the product of Thatcherite leadership rather than the outcome of restructuring in the 1970s. Rasmussen wrongly assumes that Žižek would consider Thatcher to be a Master, with the person of Thatcher standing in for the agency behind neoliberal ideology, as though ideology is not operative at the level of the economic base, or among the masses, for that matter. Rasmussen opts for the overdetermining aspects of social relations and the economic base over any 'great wo/man' theory of history, which as such misses the point of Žižek's argument. For Rasmussen, Thatcherism was the outcome of material historical forces rather than the leadership that gave us neoliberalism. His conclusion is that Žižek's work is indifferent to structural constraints and 'does not engage in a meaningful critique of political economy.'[42] Wrapped up in this assertion are the stakes of political agency and the possibility of political solidarity. Rasmussen then draws his conclusions from the above findings – summed up in between the lines as Žižek's focus on ideology over and against the economic base – and uses these to account for Žižek's recent emphasis on the Discourse of the Master. Žižek, he argues, defends the idea of a strong leader and of a leftist authoritarian party, a repetition of Lenin's vanguard model. This is perhaps not so bad when we consider that Wark considers Žižek's communist project 'a peculiarly perverse version of Stalinist apologetics.'[43]

As I mentioned previously, Žižek has always maintained that what needs to be repeated in Lenin is not the model of the party that the Bolsheviks created, but the notion that the potential of an authentic act is not guaranteed and covered over by the big Other, interpreted here as the determinations of the Historical situation. Without this Lacanian-Hegelian understanding of what Žižek implies in his approach to materialism there is no basis for further discussion. Rasmussen's dismissal adds insult to the spectacle of Žižek insisting repeatedly that twentieth-century revolutionary experiments are definitely a thing of the past. With regard to the need for radical change, however, Žižek is not satisfied to write arcane texts that will take three decades to filter into the zeitgeist. And so we discover that his discussion of the Discourse of the Master is presented as a prologue to *Absolute Recoil*, but also in a simplified popular version in *Trouble in Paradise*, interpreted through accessible references to the Batman movies.[44]

Žižek's approach in these books is not altogether new, however, and we find one version of it in his contribution to the second volume of *The Idea of Communism*, which indeed calls for both leadership and a political programme.[45] The question of the Master enters in this discussion through Žižek's response to Ayn Rand's view that the left's vaunted abolition of private property and elimination of the profit motive would require even greater organisational control of the economy from above. While this argument is put forward by an arch-conservative, it clears the table from the half-measures of reformism and responds immediately to the rhetoric of the multitude. Žižek's reply to Rand is that such domination, if it is to be worthy of the name communism, would have to be a communist organisation of the relations of production and political economy. This would be a necessary corrective to the present global capitalism, which does not afford any possibility for civil freedom and democracy but relies increasingly on exclusion, torture and brutality.[46] Žižek rejects the one-party rule of contemporary China and so it is clear that what he understands by a communist party is not one that serves economic power but one that serves an emancipatory left universality.

Insofar as Žižek broaches the issue of agency and political mass subject, the question that he asks is properly dialectical, meaning historicist as well as, in a Lacanian sense, resistant to historicism, relativism and vulgar reduction. What do we do after so many of the protests of 2011 and 2012 have been rolled back? Žižek adds to the questions of enlightenment, universal history and mode of production the fact that the cultural studies of the 1980s and 1990s have largely failed as a response to neoliberal capitalism and so there is today a need to re-emphasise class struggle. The question for him is not what do we not want, usually defined as revolutionary violence and state control, but more simply, what do we want: 'What social organization can replace the existing capitalism? What types of new leaders do we need? What organs, including those of control and repression? The twentieth-century alternatives did not work, obviously.'[47] He adds: 'the open-ended debates will have to coalesce not only in some new Master Signifiers, but also in concrete answers to the old Leninist question "What is to be done?".'[48] The idea of a Master does not necessarily represent an individual like Hugo Chavez, for example, but can be applied to a political process like the Bolivarian Constitution, a new set of social institutions that allow the mass of the excluded to become more self-sufficient and also to have political influence. Insofar as Žižek has repeated on several occasions that he does not consider the Venezuelan model under Chavez, or the indigenous perspective of Evo Morales, to be radical enough, it is some wonder that he even acknowledges them. His approach is to focus on the emancipatory potential within *any* situation.

In *Absolute Recoil*, Žižek explains that Lacan's Master is a vanishing mediator 'who delivers you to the abyss of your freedom' since we cannot directly accede to what it is that we want, and so, to what is to be done, without some external *objet petit a*.[49] There is no absolute escape from the virtuality of the big Other. Žižek's point is that there is no pure immanence to political economy without ideological remainder. There is always in effect some notion of the big Other that is operative in society, however unconscious it may be. A Master is not someone who tells us what to do in the same way that symbolic representations tell us how to enjoy; it is rather an agent who, in Žižek's estimation, disturbs us into freedom. In the present democratic conjuncture, we are compelled to accept capitalist domination as a free choice and deterritorialisation as opportunity. There is no freedom in this. The Master, in contrast, is not an exemplary figure who must be followed or emulated, since, in Lacanian terms, the Master is inherently inconsistent. The Master figure is exemplary insofar as he or she refuses the situation and refuses the kind of negation that relies on the disavowed underside of the obscene Law. The Master is not a demagogue, Žižek adds, who 'pretends to know better than the people themselves what people really want (what is really good for them) and enforces it on them even against their will.'[50] Seen in these terms, Žižek's Master comes full circle to describe, despite himself perhaps, the effectiveness of such unaccountable 'anarchist' actors whose 'propaganda of the deed' may not represent an actual, effective solution to today's problems, but whose exemplary act of will and rejection of the status quo inspires other similar acts of solidarity.

The conclusion that Žižek draws from his analysis of the Master is consistent with Lacan's discussion of the Four Discourses in his seminars from the late 1960s.[51] The relation of transference between the Master and the Slave in the Discourse of the Master is one of impossibility. The Master here simply embodies the Law that is inevitably always suspended. The specific place of the 'slave' is in the field of knowledge and the function of the big Other. For Žižek, this Lacanian view of knowledge implies that 'freedom cannot be handed down to us by a benevolent master but has to be won through hard struggle.'[52] This, one has to say, is not the conclusion of Žižek's research, but only a starting point for cultural revolution, not unlike and no more simple than Marx's study of the commodity.

Žižek concludes his passage on the Master in *Absolute Recoil* with the assertion that the Master 'is not a subject supposed to know' and 'not a subject of transference.'[53] In this regard one may wonder how it is possible for the subject in the Discourse of the Master to 'traverse the fantasy' and move on to organisation rather than dwell in psychosis. It is worth noting that for Lacan one must pass through the Discourse of the Master in order to then move towards the Discourse of the Analyst, but that effectively there is no end to the movement of *objet a* in the various schema. The advantage of the Discourse of the Master is that it is also a Discourse on the Master and as such may be a useful way to think about politics as a field that is different from other superstructures.

Insofar as we are speaking of Lacanian rather than Foucauldian and Deleuzian versions of discourse, the Discourse of the Master is one that must be passed through – it cannot be avoided – and so Žižek is honest to his project to incorporate this figure into his philosophy. With regard to the Master, there is something very specific that Žižek wishes to develop in relation to the network of signifiers that will confront us in our efforts to overcome the limits of the permanent counter-revolution. As for the masses and the subjective agency that Rasmussen mentions, the point of radicality that Lacan addresses is the possibility of a subject to emerge from the system of knowledge and master signifiers, and also from the system of the pure signifier and its status as a vanishing mediator. Insofar as master signifiers mediate the figures of production, Lacan's dialectics offer an alternative to the immanentism of today's metaphysical materialism and as such provide some of the elements necessary to the theory of avant-garde art and cultural revolution.

Abolish class society (a useful May 68 slogan)

Given the new and emerging class compositions, it is necessary for today's service workers and precarious to finds ways to renew class politics, and for this to happen, vanguard functions will be required. Beyond playful subversion and culture jamming, the cultural revolution this time will need to sidestep the contradictions that Wark identifies as the conflation of the integrated and diffuse spectacles. Rather than be captivated by this disintegrating reality, we need to keep in mind the radical uncertainty of any situation and the need to face radical conclusions. As Žižek likes to say, the light at the end of the tunnel is just another train approaching. The left needs to turn this perspective around and be that train.

7

Beyond socially enraged art

Since the early 2000s, many of the art practices that were formerly implicit under the umbrella term of 'critical art practices' have in one way or another become resources for a more comprehensive and vanguard socially engaged art. Despite the many different versions of social practice art, the basic operative principle of 'SEA' is that art can be used to bring about progressive social change and social justice. At the same time that this politicised art has expanded exponentially and taken root institutionally, leftist politics since the rise of resistance movements against neoliberalism call for radicalised constituent politics that displace to a great extent the 'cultural politics of representation' of postmodern cultural studies.[1] It is not enough, as Jacques Rancière has it, to assert art's weak ability to change the world through the singularity of its objects and the transformation of attitudes.[2] There is a politics to aesthetics, but at the limits of that proposal, the question remains: what politics? For Rancière, a politics of aesthetics should not be focused on avant-garde mobilisation, as proposed for instance in Ben Davis' call for a new cultural front.[3] Even Alain Badiou, a paradoxical figure in this art and politics equation, warns about the ontological difference between an art of representation and an art that anticipates change.[4] Such a militant art, however, connected as it may be to a 'stronger ideology' that is not compatible with neoliberal capitalism, presumes a difference from the category of politics, separated through Badiou's notion of truth procedure from Marxist political economy.[5]

With the idea of praxis around the categories of art and politics, we might consider what remains of the idea of cultural revolution. From the side of politics, the idea of revolution is not one that is popular with today's prefigurative politics because of its assumption of a heavy-handed, top-down and violent imposition of change. In this respect, Susan Buck-Morss calls for a commonist rather than communist transition. In the terms of commonists, according to Buck-Morss, neither art nor politics has an ontological specificity. There is no particular way of being-in-the-world, only concrete contingencies and specific solidarities.[6] For communists, in contrast, the dialectical approach to autonomy makes art a fully historicised and contradictory category, pressured by the totality and the vicissitudes of class struggle. As Kim Charnley has correctly noted, activist art often relies on the prestige of 'art' in order to open a political space.[7] In contrast to thinkers like Grant Kester and Rancière, according to Charnley, an art whose self-understanding confronts its social reality is one that does not abandon the notion of avant-garde confrontation.[8] The populist assumption within socially engaged art that the 99% is directly opposed to the various ideological state apparatuses, plutocracy and corporate domination is one that can suppress politics rather than deepen it. As Badiou puts it:

> the Occupy Wall Street movement's slogan 'We are the 99%,' with its supposed capacity to unite people, is completely empty. The truth is that what we call the West is full of people who though not constituting part of the 10% that make up the ruling aristocracy, do however provide globalised capitalism with a petty-bourgeois support troop, the famous middle class, without which the democratic oasis would have no chance of survival.[9]

Badiou calls on people in the West to engage in cultural revolution by shaking off the false perception that the current struggle is between the economic calculations of western regimes and reactive fundamentalisms and fascisms; the true contradiction is between these two options and the missing third: the free association of egalitarian symbolisation based on common rules.[10] We can move beyond the closed loop of power and resistance, or resistance and reaction, by reintroducing the concept of the avant garde.[11] In these terms, today's socially engaged art could be oriented towards the task of cultural revolution.

The current context of social practice suggests that rather than socially engaged art, the predominant modality among artists today is an activist-oriented socially *enraged* art that corresponds by and large to an end of ideology post-politics. Badiou's study of Maoism has something to offer those who wish to confront the limits of today's art activism. I bring these thoughts to bear on the January 2015 symposium of Artist Organisations International, an event that explored the idea of creating a confederation of engaged art collectives from around the world. With this I hope to provide a glimpse into the prospects for cultural revolution in the current artistic and political conjuncture.

Socially enraged art

We do not know what the new communism will be except to say that it will not be the old one of Soviet modernism. But so much was already part of the programme of the Situationist International, with their neither Moscow nor Washington policy. Gerald Raunig opened a once timely essay in *Artforum* with the reflections forty years after the fact of Gilles Deleuze on May 68.[12] For Deleuze, the last great eruption in Western Europe was the opposite of a Leninist rupture and separation from capitalist society, paradigmatically announcing the beginning of a new sequence. In Deleuzian terms, this 'event' corresponds to a multiplicity of becomings rather than linear striations and fixities, least of all André Glucksmann's view that Nicolas Sarkozy was somehow an heir of 68.[13] How then to capture the ambiguities of becoming, in particular, against 'hasty journalism' and the 'repressive order' of 'academic historicism'? For Raunig, the importance of this event is its 'potential for recompositions and uncustomary concatenations' beyond the state and beyond constituted efforts to take power, to transform sites like the university, the factory and the street into non-places where change becomes possible.[14] This rebellious disabling of institutions, according to Raunig's reading of Claude Lefort's contribution to the multi-authored book *La Brèche, Premières réflexions sur les événements*, is one of emotional outburst: 'Instead of being "engaged," they were, famously, "enraged".'[15] On this most crucial question regarding programme, leadership and organisation, Raunig reduces Situationist dialectics to anarchist agonism: 'They refused to channel their rage into the available political parties or labor unions and instead used Situationist and other artistic-*cum*-political methods to call for a thoroughly political objective: *L'imagination au pouvoir*.'[16] The rest reads like a legacy of disorder and disagreement on the left: for Lefort a breach, but one without lasting effects; for the official polity something best forgotten; and for Raunig, a process of becoming within the commercial regimes of neoliberal governance, or, enraged self-organisation rather than engaged organisation, leading to new breaches. In these terms, even if revamped with transversal molecules, most of what today goes by the term socially engaged art should rather adopt the more accurate moniker of *socially enraged art*.

Cultural revolution is ordinary

In his essay on 'cultural revolution,' Sven Lütticken describes how the avant gardes of the 1960s took up the term cultural revolution, which by 1967 and 1968 had acquired Maoist connotations. This tainted the concept for some, he writes, while increasing its appeal for others.[17] In his work on Badiou's post-Maoism, Bruno Bosteels explains that the culturalisation of politics that Lütticken describes was in fact possible since the cultural and ideological freedom afforded artists in the 1970s and 1980s was largely due to 'the perceived ineffectiveness of the overall movement as a *political* phenomenon.'[18] Bosteels adds: 'few commentators fail to recognise the astonishing expansion to which the political playing field is subject in the late sixties and early seventies, with the result that "cultural revolution" becomes a generic term to a large extent cut loose from its concrete moorings in the sequence of events in China.'[19] It is worth examining this sequence for a better appreciation of what is involved in this concept.

In an essay from 2002 titled 'The Cultural Revolution: The Last Revolution?' Badiou provides a detailed analysis of the 'disturbances' that shocked communist China between the years 1965 and 1976, and more specifically, from the period May 1966 to September 1967.[20] The term 'cultural,' as it is defined in the Sixteen Points Decision that was drafted by the Central Committee of the Cultural Revolution Group (GPCR), which was led by Mao Zedong in his attacks against conservative bureaucratic forces within the Communist Party, and which was recognised by the student-led Red Guards, asserted that the Cultural Revolution sought to 'change people in what is most profound' and that the term 'cultural' in this case referred broadly to the concepts civilisation, ideology and superstructure.[21] For Badiou, the Cultural Revolution in China is the last revolution insofar as it is the last effort, after the invention of the Leninist vanguard party, to create a new form of politics that could be defined in terms of proletarian class struggle. This particular sequence of what he elsewhere refers to as the communist hypothesis is an important lesson in the failure to revolutionise the party-state. Despite the outcome, this failure must not be thought to discredit the idea of communism and of the political activity of the working masses. It is significant for communism especially as it represented a critique of Stalinism, the forced collectivisation of peasants and the litany of purges and executions within the party. In contrast, the Cultural Revolution represents a real struggle both between the party-state and the masses, and within the party-state itself, a struggle in relation to which those forces that were loyal to Mao and Maoism acknowledged the legitimacy of autonomous political organisations outside the party-state apparatus. By condoning revolts in universities and factories, and within the party itself, Mao aroused the masses to continue the proletarian class struggle against the reconstitution of the bourgeoisie at the level of the communist party apparatus.

It is clear from this that the Mao cult of personality provided the conditions for radicalisation at the base rather than the kind of top-down oppression that communist leadership is commonly associated with. It is significant also that Maoism was more pronounced among the anarchistic elements of the student extreme left than among labour groups, even though these too in late 1966 followed Mao in opposing 'economism' and 'material incentives' in favour of political consciousness.[22] For all this, however, Mao was also very critical of the student extremists insofar as their outrage did not, according to Badiou, create an affirmative space for the positive creation of a new politics.[23] The limit of Maoism, on the other hand, was its contradictory association of political mobilisation at the base with the stabilisation of the party-state as the representative of the working class. Mao's effectiveness as cult leader, paradoxically, was this very contradictoriness with regard to the notion of guarantees and assurances.

Mao, Badiou says, is the political leader who struggles against conservative elements within the establishment, who speaks truths and encourages dissent. He represents not a known source of political authority and vested interests but an irreducible element. As Badiou puts it: '"Mao" is the name of a paradox: the rebel in power, the dialectician put to the test by the continuing needs of "development," the emblem of the party-state in search of its overcoming, the military chief preaching disobedience to the authorities.'[24]

While Badiou is today convinced that emancipatory politics calls for the elimination of the party-state, anarchism for him remains a shadow of the former communisms in which politics were tied to class struggle. If socially enraged art is anything on the order of politics, it is a refraction of the more generalised dualism of masses versus state. Still, it remains a task for all workers to struggle against the semblance of antagonism – the kinds of adventurist politics that seek empowerment (*embourgeoisement*) for only some kinds of individuals and specific groups.[25] If the Chinese Cultural Revolution was truly the last revolution to invent a new political situation because its politics was effective at the level of the nation and beyond, what social experiments do today's autonomous mass movements contribute to the politics of class struggle? Politics, as Bosteels says of Badiou's suspension of the party-system and consequent search for an adequate form of political organisation, must be more than sporadic protests and demonstrations.

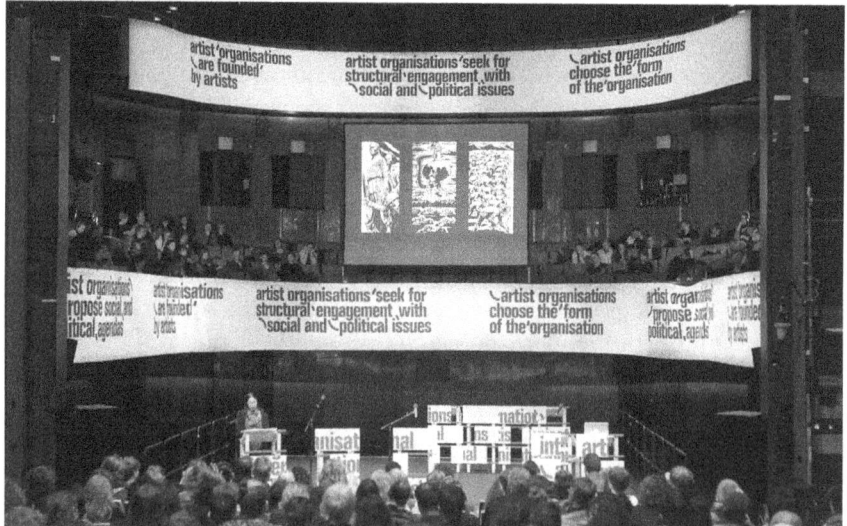

Lisa Ito of Concerned Artists of the Philippines on the panel 'Propaganda & Counter-Propaganda' at Artist Organisations International, HAU Theatre, Berlin, January 9–11, 2015. Initiated by Florian Malzacher, Jonas Staal and Joanna Warsza. Photo by Lidia Rossner. Courtesy of Artist Organisations International.

One more effort, comrades

As a thought experiment into what might cultural revolution and avant-garde art mean today, I would like to offer some reflections on the January 2015 meeting of Artist Organisations International (AOI), which to my mind is one of the most significant art world events since the 2010 Creative Time Summit. I say this knowingly since this event, as well as the proposed umbrella group AOI, organised by artist Jonas Staal along with curator Joanna Warsza and dramaturg Florian Malzacher, could in some respects be considered a form of avant-garde artwork. In fact, the worry that Staal and the organisers would act as unacknowledged leaders caused participants to question the city and country in which the event took place, the theatre in which it was held, the agit-prop look of the stage design and the sources of funding involved. Sensitive to the use of the term 'International' in the founding gesture of AOI, Dmitry Vilensky of the collective Chto Delat coyly asked if the organisers were thinking of AOI as some new kind of Trotskyist party. There should have been no need to worry about this, however, since the frameworks of pro-letarian politics, socialism and communism were rarely mentioned during the symposium. Indeed, despite the use of the term 'International,' the organisers and participants avoided any call for artists to come together under a unifying political or ideological banner.

So what was proposed at this symposium that would make it different from the corporate model of Creative Time and from the various biennales that have adapted to artists' demands for social engagement? One of the purposes of AOI was to address the shift from ephemeral project work – the type of institution-based projects that were discussed by Andrea Fraser in the mid-1990s as 'service work,' and characterised by Gregory Sholette and Nato Thompson as 'interventionist art' – to the development of long-term infrastructures, and thus the name Artist Organisations.[26] This tendency towards extradisciplinary self-institutionalisation explains the choice of artists who were invited: Concerned Artists of the Philippines, Immigrant Movement International, Jewish Renaissance Movement in Poland, Zentrum für Politische Schönheit, Artist Association of Azawad, Chto Delat, School for Engaged Art, Büro for Antipropaganda, Performing Arts Forum, Artists of Rojava, Forensic Architecture, Silent University, Gulf Labor, HudRada, International Institute of Political Murder, Laboratory of Insurrectionary Imagination, Etcétera (Errorist International), Haben und Brauchen, Institute for Human Activities, Schoon Gonoegl! and WochenKlausur. It could be said that the substance of the event came from the presentation of the various social struggles involved, the development of methods to engage creatively and effectively with social reality, and the lively interaction between the moderators, the presenters, the respondents and the audience. It is not possible in this context to address all of this material and all of the different refractions of the subjects that occurred through the discussions.[27] On the whole, the different themes that were chosen for the panels – Propaganda and Counter-Propaganda, State and Statelessness, Violence and Non-Violence, Solidarity and Unionising – proved to be somewhat innocuous as organising concepts and tended to function as they do in art magazines and biennales: a means to avoid discussing the ideological framework of the proposed organisation. In this regard, some of the moderators were very helpful, but some others, who are more invested in so-called criticality, were quite obviously unable and possibly unwilling to offer constructive insights. In this respect, Charles Esche was very effective as the mediator of the final debate, helping to keep the focus on the political potential of the event rather than dwelling on indeterminacy and the dangers of cooptation.

There is one particular organisational feature of AOI that would allow us to consider this work as avant-garde, and that is the distinction between activist anti-institutionality on the one hand, referred to here as socially enraged art, and institutional affirmation on the other, in relation to which most major institutional spaces have become neoliberalised in one way or another. AOI performs what Roberts refers to as a 'metastasis' of art and politics, escaping neither the demands of art nor those of politicisation. Roberts provides a very elaborate account of metastasis as specific to conditions of labour within capitalism. In contrast to those who consider autonomy to be a luxury that is unwarranted in a 'permanent state of emergency,' or as many of the AOI participants indicated, in the pressing context of climate change, Roberts holds that political praxis and art praxis, in the productive form of metastasis, 'offer[s] a place of memory, a set of relations, modes of cognition and learning and mapping, that provides a different space of encounter between praxis, critique and truth – a place that sustains an open and reflective encounter between art and the totalising critique of capitalism.'[28] In the words of the organisers, who are equally concerned with collective objectification and intellectual labour, 'artist organizations bring forward a social/political agenda that connects the fields of ethics and aesthetics. Rather than a medium merely "questioning" and "confronting" the world, the artist organisation situates itself in the field of daily political struggle.'[29] Neither a political party, nor an artists' union, AOI, according to Staal, would work to demand that institutions adopt the ethical stances of engaged artists and build a 'structural solidarity' that would allow for meaningful engagement with other existing organisations while envisioning the ideal of a 'common world.'

It should be said that the refrain among both the participants and audience members about changing 'the world' is by and large ameliorist and reformist insofar as it is not more specific about already existing radical left critiques. In this regard it becomes possible for art world commentator Andrea Liu, the founder of a social practice fellowship programme in New York, to write that 'the strengths of the conference were its openness to critique, dissensus, and agonism to the point of uncivil hostility at times from audience members, and its incessant self-examination and deconstruction of the premise of the event itself,' only to congratulate moderator Margarita Tsomou for suggesting that the notion of an 'organisation' seemed, in Liu's words (and not Tsomou's, based on my interpretation), 'an old-fashioned classical leftist conception of the rational centered subject that has been surpassed by the Occupy Wall Street post-representative trope of the "swarm" and the nameless, formless "multitude" catalyzed by social media.'[30] In the epigraph to her review, Liu reiterates moderator Maria Hlavajova's citation of the somewhat cliché statement by Antonio Gramsci that the old is dying and the new cannot be born, with the chaser: now is the time of monsters. The review fails to remark that quite unlike Gramsci, she and Hlavajova are using this statement against the radical left. To her credit, Hlavajova knows enough about what is happening in social practice art to see that the new creative class 'recompositioning' that is underway requires more than the openness of relationality and that collaboration and participation today function as neoliberal injunctions. But Liu seems to think like moderator Ekaterina Degot that the participants in the event are, in Degot's words, 'in the wrong play,' 'reluctant to repeat some sort of left-wing political rhetoric' since 'the situation has changed' and 'it's time to find some different language.' Because of this, Liu fails to notice that Tsomou in fact spoke of preventing solidarity from being a strictly artistic gesture and that although swarms explode the concept of organisation, there is a real need for sustainability, as noticed in Greece and Spain with the reorientation of social movements around leftist political party organisations. Syriza and Podemos are perhaps the kinds of monsters that Gramsci and Tsomou are talking about, now shifted to DiEM25, the Democracy in Europe Movement initiated by Yanis Varoufakis. Tsomou suggested that artists' organisations were in fact questioning the more fashionable concepts of activism and intersectionality. Her questions were: How do we organise? How do we become protagonists who are able to suggest organisational tools?

Given the range of positions presented during the symposium, it is not impossible to imagine that Liu genuinely came away with an overall view of the event as the collective endorsement of a leaderless and formless multitude. All the talk about artists 'making a world' rather than 'questioning the world' (Staal) risks a discursive overinflation of knowledge in terms of the production of subjectivity through 'social construction.' On the whole this was not a problem for the organisers, but it does point to certain tendencies among socially enraged artists. Many of the assembled and someone like Liu would have much to learn from Lisa Ito of the Concerned Artists of the Philippines, who defined CAP as the organisational result of cultural revolution. However, if I was to do like Liu and take away from this event my own view of it, not only would I emphasise the Zentrum für Politische Schönheit (Center for Political Beauty) project of over-identification with activist NGO art – *Kindertransporthilfe des Bundes* – and curator Christoph Gurk's critique of the limitations of the AOI paradigm, which was based on a critique of activist 'anti-intellectualism' and a focus on the 'fantasmatic character' of 'real politics,' but I would do so in order to stress how both these presentations gave an indication of the limitations of their presuppositions concerning the ontological frame of 'art.' Refusing to instrumentalise aesthetics, CPB and Gurk were nevertheless unable to provide an adequate rationale for their rejection of artistic political organisation. In other words, not only did they appear unable to reach across the aisle to their activist comrades, but they failed to further demonstrate how fantasy underscores the structure of both art and politics. With this in mind, they could have acknowledged the radical openness of an engaged artists' International. If Liu's activist multitude finds an ally in the technocratic moderators' Discourse of the University, then the Germans' Discourse of the Master of Art has its counterpart in the AOI's avant garde as Analyst, since, to put things in Lacanian terms, the organiser, or curator-Father (invoked during the proceedings), is always a castrated Father. The Analyst, more than the Master, not only confronts you with your freedom, but helps you to realise that if you do not organise yourselves, no one will.[31]

If an artist organisations International was not a presupposition of the conference, the presentations by Zentrum für Politische Schönheit and Gurk did something to reveal that the meetings could indeed be oriented to such an outcome, as Vilensky was correct to point out. They also demonstrated, however unintentionally, some of the finer points of revolutionary struggle. On the one hand, Zentrum für Politische Schönheit's refusal of the status of activist indirectly reminded participants of what is otherwise a comfortable stance in the institutionalised art world. On the other, Gurk's critical-institutional or 'discursive' orientation echoed the concerns of what we might refer to as the bourgeois and petty-bourgeois bureaucratic elements within the AOI meetings and outside of it in the mainstream art world.

In an essay that discusses the organisational situation faced by the American anti-war movement in 1968, Brian Holmes mentions the theory of the revolutionary leader Amílcar Cabral, who argued that petty-bourgeois functionaries should be allowed to develop in the direction of their natural inclination as an intermediary bourgeoisie, eventually committing suicide as a class so that it can be reborn in its popular aspirations.[32] It is good then that art world functionaries were invited to the event, so that they too could learn from the experience but also so that they could react and pronounce themselves. Citing the research of Barbara and John Ehrenreich on the professional-managerial class, Holmes mentions that the PMC tends to be subordinate to the capitalist

imperative of accumulation, but it also establishes its own autonomy, generating hostilities to both the capitalist and the working classes. Its professional
aspirations, educational qualifications, ethical standards and commitment to
public service have nevertheless been significant to the development of the
new left and activist movements since the 1960s.[33] Despite this, we should
point out that such cadres within and around social practice art circles are
hardly well-trained trade unionist apparatchiks or 'radicals-in-the-professions,'
but somewhat disorganised elements. Their objections to leftist ideology defy
the purpose of an event that proposes the name International.

At the outset, the local or specific struggles of each of these artist organisations may also represent different political and ideological interests, with
links to bourgeois state power, NGOs, social movements or popular struggles. According to revolutionary theorist Régis Debray, the Trotskyist notion
of 'dual power,' which links popular actions – agitations, protests, strikes,
occupations – through a network of committees – in this case, a confederation
of artist organisations – can place added pressure on the resources of such
groups, a problem mentioned by the delegates from Azawad and that Noel
Douglas argued could be addressed through design intelligence. It can also
divert attention from already existing activity into ineffective organisational
busyness. The point of any added organisational effort, then, must be to
emphasise the socialist character of cultural revolution, from control of the
means of production to challenging state power. Such a confederation would
no doubt risk setbacks to local efforts.[34] Given the conflicting class aspirations
and the local nature of the various organisational structures, an artist organisations International would presume that a challenge to ruling-class control is
even possible at this moment. In the words of Debray, who wrote about the
coordination of guerrilla cells during the Cuban Revolution, the 'dual power'
proposed by Trotskyism leads by exploiting the weaknesses of local struggles.[35]
The example of Fidel Castro in Cuba, in contrast, was to challenge orthodoxy
by proposing that a vanguard can act independently of a Marxist-Leninist party.

If anything of value to AOI can be derived from Debray's study of guerrilla
warfare in Latin America, it would be that independent organisations should
not become dependent on an umbrella group, but that such a group, nevertheless useful, should have a solid leadership structure and plan of action that
recognises the potential need and inevitability of change in elected leaders.
Whereas member groups would carry on their local, autonomous struggles,
the umbrella group would provide ad hoc solidarity, educational and communicational assistance, and political influence among establishment institutions,
as Debray says, 'to raise one's voice and to impose oneself on the stage of
power.'[36] All strategy, political analysis and direct action, however, would
depend on a shared ideological horizon. For the time being, given the reluctance of cadres to support radical leftist ideology, it might be enough to follow

the lead of the Zapatistas and expand the points of struggle against neoliberal capitalism, while at the same time discussing deeper philosophical questions. In certain circumstances, it may well be that local, autonomous struggles could act as the unofficial leadership of the prospective International. However, it should be kept in mind that a politics that impacts national and state politics is destined to encounter imperialist repression. A further consideration is that in the case of institutional cooptation or backlash, the creation of an AOI could temporarily hamper the proliferation of artist organisations. In the long run, however, the goal is to encourage the proliferation of social engagement, both artistic and political.

Another resulting problem could be, as Debray describes it, 'rivalry among competing organizations or a petty bourgeois sentiment of frustration in the face of an established vanguard,' leading to 'ineffectual dispersion.'[37] In contrast to Debray's study, the particular advantage that artist organisations have in comparison with guerrilla forces is that they do not require a common military or artistic doctrine and training, and so the notion of a central command alters radically. Strikes against Empire can more easily be a part of local efforts and offer a diversity of types of action where dispersion or organisational initiatives strengthen the common struggle rather than lead to problems of control and command. Further, the phenomenon of art world 'personalities' (or even artists who work independently) can be an added benefit to political influence since we are concerned here with morale and propaganda rather than warfare. And because these are not electoral platforms, there is no need to worry about the manipulation of appearances. Unlike street protests, for instance, there is no need for the martyrdom of getting arrested in acts of civil disobedience or direct action. The confused mixture of class interests in the age of biopolitical protest does not change the fact that all classes have a stake in the destruction of neoliberal capitalism, a reality that should nullify the need for endless and excessive deliberation and propose some 'diagonal' forms and methods of organisation as well as the tactical independence of member groups.

The challenge for an AOI therefore would be to establish campaigns and actions that transcend the specific interests of various member organisations. The interest in an AOI is that member groups would have more to think about than their own survival, a question that extends beyond the revolutionary's motto of *Patria o Muerte* to that of the Situationist notion of living underground.[38] The question in the 1960s in Asia and in Latin America was therefore the same one we could ask today: how to think revolution with or without a party? Before this question can be answered, the question of class alliance and class politics must be acknowledged and it is clear that an AOI cannot function effectively under bourgeois and petty-bourgeois leadership. The petty-bourgeois class must, in Cabral's terminology, and as cited by both

Debray and Holmes, 'commit suicide as a class in order to be restored to life as revolutionary workers.'[39]

If the characteristic of the now hegemonic class of the global petty bourgeoisie is to refuse not only national but all class belonging, it would indeed be difficult to identify forms of hijacking, blackmail, provocation and sectarianism, but we can for the time being consider unproductive those aspects of consensus decision-making that play to the whims of cranks and cynics, as for example those audience members who most hysterically ranted that they want to 'change the world' without offering useful and principled points of action. Lorenzo Pezzani of Forensic Architecture made the valid point, based on the ideas of Rodrigo Nunes, that vanguard functions can be achieved by striking a balance between openness and closure, without attempting absolute horizontality.[40] As Antonio Negri also says, 'it's really urgent that we organise politically' and that 'we bring a political vertical out of the horizontality of the movements: one that's able to express strength and political programmes.'[41] Such opportunistic animosity, as was found for instance in many OWS camps, leads to dead ends. Process is easily exploited by cliques and provocations that seek to delay negotiations with polemics that do not raise the level of class struggle. Solutions to serious structural problems such as those based on gender and race inequality need therefore to be agreed upon and made into explicit principles of the organisation as a whole or otherwise abandoned or deferred.

Another aspect of petty-bourgeois opportunism that ignores the class aspects of struggle is technocratic managerialism. With regard to the question of political organisation and cultural revolution, we could refer to the technocratic attitude as 'right deviationism.' An example of this can be noticed in architecture theorist Felicity Dale Scott's essay ' "Vanguards".'[42] The point of her use of scare quotes in her title is to caution against, as she puts it, heroic narratives on the left that have a naive approach to social issues. The example she gives is the contrast at the Yale School of Art and Architecture in the late 1960s between the design solutions of idealistic students and the protocols of new computer and information technologies. The students' protest activities against white privilege and urban renewal schemes eventually led to the suspension of classes and the closure of the architecture programme. Scott interprets this in Foucauldian terms to propose that the students were not realistic enough about the matrix of power within which architecture is imbricated. Rather than 'silence such troubles' as 'the rules of law,' 'management techniques' and 'morality,' Scott proposes that the students should rather have learned to 'engage with' those forces of power that inform architecture's ideological, economic and technological parameters.[43]

Scott either misses or ignores the fact that the purpose of vanguards is precisely to interrupt the cycle of power and resistance that Foucault instrumentalised in his theory of power/knowledge. Her example of politically effective organisation is therefore blinkered.[44] We could also propose, however, a critique of 'left deviationism,' which in similar terms limits what is imaginable as leftist organisation. David Graeber makes the interesting claim that Foucault's equation of power with knowledge fails to consider how power, in the form of bureaucracies that avoid the 'interpretive labour' of knowing and understanding people, can be an agency of violence. Bureaucratic power is therefore synonymous with absurdity, stupidity and non-knowledge, avoiding debate, clarification and negotiation.[45] For Graeber, rather than embrace bureaucracy, as Scott suggests, the left needs to develop a critique of bureaucracy that is substantially different from that of the right, which simply serves to expand the scope of neoliberal ideology's collapse of private capital and the public interest. His practical suggestion comes from his experience in the global justice movement and its elaboration of new forms of democratic process based on assemblies and spokescouncils that carry out collective projects. He considers such anarchist organising 'the first major leftist antibureaucratic movement,' and proposes that the Arab Spring, *indignados* and Occupy Wall Street are the best examples of the May 68 slogan '*l'imagination au pouvoir*' come to life.[46]

The point of movements from below, according to Graeber, is that they have understood the Situationist lesson of lowering one's ambition and scope to the level of everyday acts of creative subversion, avoiding the seizure of state power and thus avoiding the creation of new rules and regulations. For Graeber, the cultural revolution will not be a single moment of rupture, like a civil war for example, but a slow-building cumulative movement towards a world without capitalism, which he argues requires overcoming habituated laziness and the violent stupidity of bureaucracy. Graeber echoes Žižek's maxim that what is important is not the day of carnivalesque protest but what happens the morning after, in other words, the more or less enduring characteristics of new social infrastructures and values. Graeber leaves us to understand, however, that May 68, the Arab Spring and OWS are more radical and lasting events in terms of social experiences than events like the Chinese Cultural Revolution or the Cuban Revolution, which resorted to violent armed struggle and which eventually led to state centralism. He proposes that the 'new, emerging conception of revolution' that comes from insurrectionary moments makes use of imagination to throw open the horizons of possibility.[47] Graeber's version of relative structurelessness, however, leads to a politics of bad infinity, or bad affinity, insofar as issues like climate change, the socialisation of capital, employment policy, energy policy, health care, and so on, require enormous organisational systems and planning. It serves no one to castigate the struggles that produced something like communist political projects and the welfare state in terms of violence, stupidity, laziness or fear of play. Graeber is aware of this but he nevertheless wants to encourage a political theory based in small autonomous movements and collectives, and in the case of AOI, he would perhaps recommend that everyone should go their separate ways. What I would like to suggest is that although Graeber's approach would reverse Scott's opportunistic *problématique*, which is simply imposed by the state of things, and which is highly exploitative and therefore unacceptable, his ontologised Manichaeism of subversion and countercultural anti-bureaucracy mostly plays the alternative new left against the radical old left and precludes a supersession of organisational programme. It leaves out, for instance, the programme of Cornelius Castoriadis and the group *Socialisme ou Barbarie* who did not call for the dissolution of revolutionary parties but for a change in their bureaucratic mechanisms so that they could become open to direct election and subject to instant recall, so that they could better serve the principle of equality rather than, as Graeber would have it, greater transparency within a 'Marxist-Leninist' administration. But of course Graeber is concerned with the avoidance of state power. This is not necessarily an issue for an artists' organisation and even he admits the need for autonomous spaces to engage with larger social systems.

It seems inevitable that a confederated organisation would avoid the fet-ishisation of consensus-based horizontality, that it would adopt organisational instruments and structures of decision-making that could, for example, involve majority vote within an anti-capitalist politics, creating new possibilities for the mobilisation of collective political power. One of the concerns of the AOI participants was with the term International, which evoked for some the spectre of nationalism. It would be worth retaining this term, however, as it relates very specifically to the major success of the First International, the 1871 Paris Commune, an event that most leftists have not too much difficulty agreeing about. Despite the fact that the word International is rooted in the word nation, there is, according to Kristin Ross, nothing about the frame of the nation-state that characterises this popular insurrection. 'Under the Commune,' she argues, 'Paris wanted to be not the capital of France but an autonomous collective in a universal federation of peoples. It did not wish to be a state but rather an element, a unit in a federation of communes that was ultimately international in scale.'[48] The social and political ideals that perme-ated the event of the Commune were the result of years of popular discussions and debates within associations, committees, meetings, reunions and clubs during the last days of the Second Empire. Their purpose was to coordinate social intelligences against a government of corrupt traitors. Disidentifying with the imperialist nation-state and its middle-class authority, these meetings were international, with participants from around the globe who were admit-ted into the ranks of commune citizenship. The decentralised and multi-tiered structure of the Commune affirmed a politics directed against the state and in favour of a Universal Republic set against liberal parliamentary bureaucracy and its apparatus of state violence. The Commune was also the first widespread movement to combat gender-based inequality, creating jobs for women and instituting equal pay for equal work. What at that time stood in the way of even the word International was counter-revolution, which associated the cultural revolution with the misery it struggled against.

In this sense, to return to the AOI event, Gurk's wariness about the pragmatism that he hears coming from socially enraged artist 'good guys' is not one that should be separated from his 'dialectics of the real and reality.' The call for action coming from artists effects a very real call from the official and unofficial structures of today's art scene. This is not simply a missed encounter. To understand the fantasmatic character of the real in the form of enraged art refers not only to the 'suturing' of meaning as something through which artists 'elude their own ambitions and privileges' within the 'self-imagination of neoliberal capitalism.' Where, Gurk asks, 'is the fantasy in the political and the political in fantasy?' The answer to this is more troubling than he seems to imply since there is no unified place from which to ask such questions. And this is why pragmatism is not necessarily the best description of a genuinely socially engaged art and why terms like cultural revolution, International, vanguard and avant garde retain their traumatic quality, even and especially to the ears of today's petty-bourgeois left. Such terms, as opposed to the socially enraged art that often assumes it operates outside of ideological parameters, aim directly at the symptom and its repressed signifiers.

8

The only game in town

Slavoj Žižek likes to tell an old Soviet joke about the character Rabinovich, in which someone asks if Rabinovich, who is sceptical about the Soviet government, won a new car in the state lottery. A state official responds: 'In principle, yes, he did. Only it was not a car but a bicycle, it was not new but old, and he did not win it, it was stolen from him.'[1] The story is reminiscent of Henri Lefebvre's suggestion that around the 1960s and 1970s, Marxism had lent its passport of historical and dialectical materialism to various other kinds of struggle, from anti-colonialism to feminism and now queer theory. Once the various struggles became accustomed to thinking like Marxist materialists they did not want to return the passport but keep it for themselves. To extend the metaphor, and the story, they became postmodern, rejecting dialectics and universality as 'masculinist' and redefining critical theory along non-Marxist lines. So, in principle, yes, today's social constructionists are materialists, only they are not post-transcendental, they are naive materialists; this is nothing new, and they did not borrow dialectical materialism, they reduced it to fodder for undergraduate courses. One thinks here of the fate of teachers of Marxism-Leninism in the former German Democratic Republic in Phil Collins' *marxism today (prologue)*. One political economist became a banker and another set up a dating service. In Collins' 2010 film *use! value! exchange!*, an elite GDR economics school is now a business school. Collins also takes interest in what is happening in his native Great Britain, where the new left and political dissent have been exchanged for continental philosophy and the Internet.

A similar conclusion regarding the fate of Marxist dialectics is drawn by Johanne Lamoureux in her synopsis on the concept of the avant garde. Since Marxism has informed most of the discussions on the avant garde, she argues, and since Marxists consider art and culture to be superstructural, determined for the most part by capitalist social contradictions, most Marxist critics reject the forms of contemporary art as inadequate to the concept of the avant garde. One exception to this, Lamoureux says, are the kinds of strategic collaboration

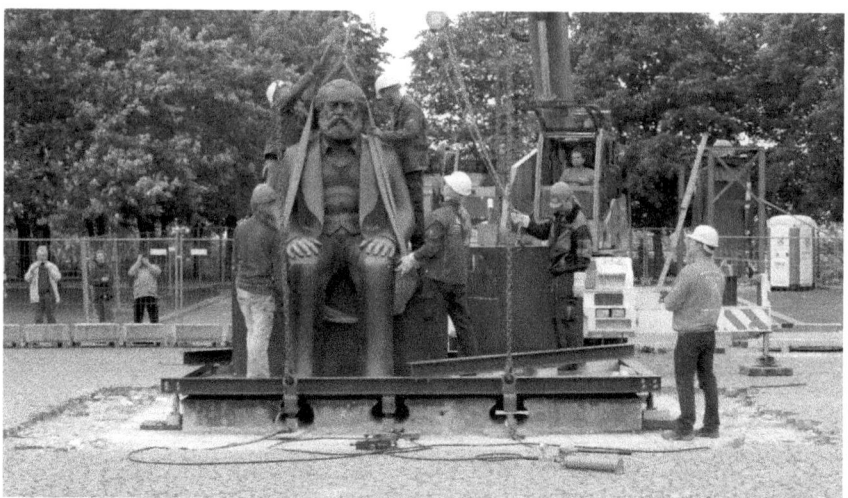

Phil Collins, *use! value! exchange!*, 2010. HD video projection with 5.1 surround sound, 21 minutes. German with English subtitles. Courtesy of Shady Lane Productions, Berlin and Tanya Bonakdar Gallery, New York.

that are at play in various forms of 'criticality,' like feminism and post-colonial theory, as well as 'fluid identity positions' that test not only the boundaries of art but of non-artistic institutions as well. Whether such critical projects are labelled avant-garde, she argues, is less important than their influence on socio-political conditions.[2] Lefebvre, for his part, considered that what is new in terms of avant-gardism may in fact simply be retro.[3] In terms of the dialectic between the particular and the universal, Lefebvre denounced any political action that did not improve class relations, especially acts of violence and terrorism that exacerbate social conflicts and allow authorities to increase repression. Revolutionary violence must be distinguished from any action that is designed to frighten people into submission and should instead encourage action and critical reflection. Although the problem of global technocracy has any number of determinations, he said, nothing is predetermined at the outset – the revolution is to be reinvented and the party is to be remade.[4]

One question for today's avant-garde art and politics is whether there can be something like a revolutionary gender or sexuality or an ethnically or nationally particular Marxism-Leninism-Maoism. The question itself is complicated by the dialectical insight that there is no particularism that is not mediated by universality. This issue is the subject of *Contingency, Hegemony, Universality*, a landmark text that seems by and large to have gone unnoticed or has been ignored by academic cultural studies, even though it set an intellectual standard for conversations around Marxism and post-structuralism.[5] In this book, Judith Butler, Ernesto Laclau and Slavoj Žižek address the incompleteness of identity and the way that dislocations of the self, as addressed by various philosophers, from G.W.F. Hegel to Michel Foucault and Jacques Derrida, are essential to the project of hegemony, as defined by Antonio Gramsci and taken up by radical democracy.

The three interlocutors agree that universality is a contested site and always incomplete. Butler emphasises the question of exclusions, associating universality with reciprocal recognition, conditioned by customary practices. In most cases, the universal is exposed as a false universal, or what she refers to as an 'annihilating universal' of discontinuities and dispossession. For Butler the abstract universal of negation must become a concrete universal in the performative iteration of cultural norms, defined as the social and structural dimensions of the habitus of the body, which is open to new articulations and subject to contaminating reuses and misuses since no claim is exclusively particular or universal.[6] Laclau, for his part, argues that multicultural pluralism and hegemonic struggle deny the right to the universal since minority rights can only be formulated as universal rights. For Laclau, the category of the universal is neither neutral nor indifferent, nor is it the distorted expression of particular interests. Rather, it is an empty place that is always already hegemonised by a contingent, particular content, making it a battleground for which particular groups fight for hegemony. Because there are no shared norms, there are no norms that become distorted or resemanticised through performative displacements.[7] Žižek, for his part, emphasises how the Real, defined in Lacanian terms, makes it impossible to establish fixed subject positions and so maintains the gap between the universal and social life. There are no shared norms because there are no norms that can function as regulative ideas, even for subjects themselves.

Žižek's main point of contention with Butler and Laclau, or with the proponents of micropolitical identity struggles, is that they accept capitalism as 'the only game in town' and as the basis, the price to pay, for the pursuit of identity agendas.[8] The repression of class politics in the new left mantra of 'race, class, gender and sexuality' limits class struggle to the assessment of how it is that capitalism creates sexist and racist oppression. Micropolitics avoids a politics based on the contestation of capitalist social relations. Postmodern post-politics thus results in the ideological displacement of class antagonism for other markers of social difference, which come to stand in for the sufferings produced by capitalism. Through political correctness, Žižek argues, economic causes are replaced by the focus on sexism and racism. The resulting state apparatus ceases to be a state in the full sense of its universal or Hegelian notion. What one encounters instead is the concrete universality of capitalist relations, which positivises the ideological field as the impossible big Other that pulls the strings of social life. In other words, the impossibility of society is positivised and made into an external obstacle. The inability to confront capitalism as the concrete universal is then displaced to solving the limited and partial problems of the abstract universal, an anti-utopian reformism and radical democratic gradualism that brings into effect the short circuit of the concrete universal of capital with the particulars of identity.[9] The difficulty of this, from the perspective of Hegelian philosophy, is that the particular is the other of the universal.[10] Any given particular is only ever an other and never a self. Politically and culturally speaking, a particular can be universal only as a matter of solidarity or as part of the genericity of a truth, and never as a matter of substance, which is often missed by chauvinistic proponents of hegemonic contestation. In other words, a particular becomes not simply 'in itself' but 'for itself' when it is universal.

The widespread influence of postmodern identity politics is symptomatic of global capitalist hegemony. The aim of radical praxis is not to ignore or downplay the different forms and histories of oppression and certainly not to avoid matters of redress. Its focus, however, is the possibility of solidarities to be constructed around a universal project of emancipation. For this to be possible, it is necessary to understand the imbrication of class struggle with identity struggles. Some signs of hope could be thought to be coming from the institutionalised art world. In the following I relate insights drawn from the 2015 *Das Kapital Oratorio* to the political limits of the Black Lives Matter and MeToo movements as forms of 'victim politics.' In contrast to Simon Critchley's notion of an 'ethics of commitment' and Nizan Shaked's particularist and identity-based approach to conceptual art's 'synthetic proposition,' I draw on Marxist theory in order to better appreciate the limits of postmodern pluralism as a means to confront the problems of global capitalism.

Prole art threat

Judith Butler's notion of the performative iteration of norms was given a Marxist inflection in the 2015 art world intervention by Okwui Enwezor. Enwezor was the curator of *All the World's Futures*, the 56th edition of the Venice Biennale, which took place between May 9 and November 22, 2015, at the Giardini della Biennale and the Arsenale. The curator's press statement for this event is socially mindful, stating that '[t]he world before us today exhibits deep divisions and wounds, pronounced inequalities and uncertainties as to the future.'[11] The main page of the Biennale website also includes a short presentation by its chairman, Paolo Baratta, who says that the various aspects of the event are designed to formulate aesthetic judgements on contemporary art, that is, following the demise of the avant gardes. Despite this well-rehearsed obituary, which otherwise knows nothing of the avant-garde concept of self-sublation, Baratta cites Walter Benjamin's notion of the angel of history, stating that the Biennale hosts 'dialectical images,' and then in a more futurist fashion, that he is glad that every two years 'a new storm of energy drives us "irresistibly into the future".'[12] Such a pseudo-dialectical image, observing the disasters that will shape future art events, might very well emblematise the signal contribution of the curator, who hosted for seven months in the ARENA exhibition space of the Central Pavilion, an 'epic' live and continuous reading, or oratorio, of all three volumes of Karl Marx's *Das Kapital*. These texts were read by trained actors who were directed by filmmaker Isaac Julien. Notwithstanding Baratta's disclaimer, the work of several well-known avant-garde artists was also presented during the Biennale, including projects by Gulf Labor, Jeremy Deller, Tania Bruguera, Charles Gaines, Sergei Eisenstein, Steve Reich, Chris Marker, Hans Haacke, Thomas Hirschhorn, Isa Genzken, Marcel Broodthaers, Alexander Kluge, Nancy Holt, Robert Smithson, Adrian Piper, Coco Fusco, Marco Fusinato and Ousmane Sembène. Two of the participating avant-gardists, Harun Farocki and Chantal Akerman, have since passed away. One could mention as well the fact that the 2015 Creative Time Summit was held at the Biennale, August 11–13, with keynote presentations by Achille Mbembe, Antonio Negri, Amy Goodman and Gregory Sholette/Gulf Labor.

If one considers the avant garde to consist of those who struggle on the front lines of anti-capitalism, the focus of the Biennale should perhaps not be

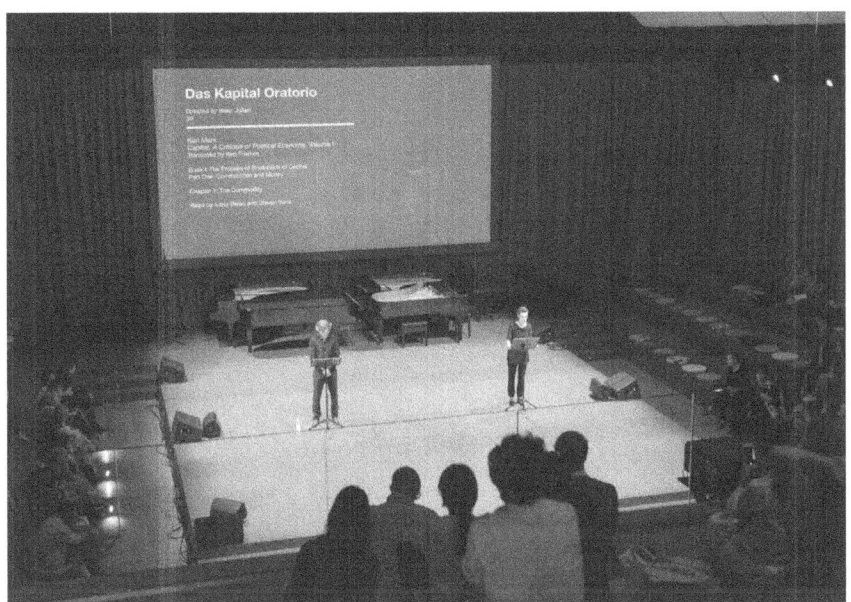

Isaac Julien, *DAS KAPITAL Oratorio*, ARENA, Padiglione Centrale, Giardini, 56th International Art Exhibition – la Biennale di Venizia, *All the World's Futures*. Photo by Andrea Avezzù. Courtesy of la Biennale di Venizia.

the *Das Kapital Oratorio*, but *Das Kapital* itself, its continuing relevance as a text of engaged scholarship and political manifesto. Capital as such, according to Enwezor, is the dramatic preoccupation of our time and modernity. He lists in relation to this 'the predations of the political economy,' 'the rapacity of the financial industry,' 'the commodification of natural resources' and 'the growing structure of inequality.'[13] He then says in his press statement that the spectres not of Marx but of *capital* will be felt through the live readings, nonstop, every day, for seven months. This was to be supplemented by songs, discussions, plenaries and film screenings. He mentions Louis Althusser and Étienne Balibar, who write at the start of their 1965 book, *Reading Capital*, that in the past the ideas of Marx were known through his interpreters, Engels, Kautsky, Plekhanov, Lenin, Luxemburg, Trotsky, Stalin and Gramsci. However, for this project, Marx's ideas would not be interpreted by the leaders of workers' organisations, but by theatre ensembles, contemporary intellectuals, students and members of the public.

Enwezor's interest in the full account of *Capital* echoed David Harvey's 2013 posting of the online course for volume two of *Capital*, as well as Harvey's 2014 book *Seventeen Contradictions*. In an atypical act of showmanship, Enwezor called on people to read, or to listen to, all four volumes of *Capital*, 'to the letter.'[14] By this time, Harvey's online course on *Capital* volume one had been screened by more than one million viewers and translated into more than forty-seven languages.[15] Enwezor concluded that the readings should not be performed to build class consciousness or develop a labour politics, but so that 'the reader and listener will be able to find in them new-born the experience of a reading,' 'shifting from the guttural enunciation of the voice and physical manifestations between artworks and the public.'[16] In other words, what Enwezor was proposing was a Rancièrian 'distribution of the sensible' of the Marxist corpus. This was less a call for organisation around leftist parties and labour unions, and more an aesthetics that reflects the deterritorialisations caused by twenty-first century global capitalism, as described for instance in Michael Hardt and Antonio Negri's *Empire*:

> Empire establishes no territorial center of power and does not rely on fixed boundaries or barriers. It is a *decentered* and *deterritorialized* apparatus of rule that progressively incorporates the entire global realm within its open, expanding frontiers. Empire manages hybrid identities, flexible hierarchies, and plural exchanges through modulating networks of command.[17]

Similarly, Enwezor's emphasis on the grain of the voice and the physical manifestations of the body relates the deterritorialising aspects of capital to particularity and embodiment. It takes the art world's interest in body politics and fuses this with a performative aestheticisation of Marx's critique of political economy.

At the outset Enwezor does not appear to be Marxist in any particular sense of the word. An article published in *The Guardian* by Charlotte Higgins finds him stating: 'I don't think that Marx, had he lived, would have wanted capitalism to end.'[18] According to this report, Enwezor has not himself read all of the first volume of *Capital*, let alone the other volumes. The value of Marx is as a symbol of the capacity of artists and intellectuals, in Enwezor's words, 'to question prevailing orthodoxies, especially political orthodoxies.'[19] This is maybe not so bad in times when a country like Ukraine, now under American tutelage, is imposing up to five-year sentences for people who are caught singing The Internationale.[20] Enwezor adds: 'If you look at authoritarian regimes, the first people they want to ban are artists and writers.'[21] Higgins concludes her article with an acknowledgement of the geographical spread of the Biennale, one of the most diverse on record, with participating artists from Cameroon, Ghana, Congo, Nigeria, Jordan, Iraq, Palestine and Syria. She finishes with the inevitable question to Enwezor himself as a prominent black curator on the situation for black artists and the conditions of institutional racism. He replies: 'It is the same for women and other groups in society for which there is a reflexive limit set on what they can and cannot do. You have to keep asking yourself, how does one get past it, how does one get around it?'[22]

Enwezor's approach to the *Das Kapital* oratorio asserts identity, or embodiment, in the context of a renewed left radicalism. Surely, the emancipatory principles of Marxism should be able to address the voices of the many. But the difficulty of the issue, for a Marxist, and possibly for Enwezor as well, is that it is capital that today embodies the universal. We can get a glimpse of this contradiction in Harvey's 'Listen, Anarchist,' a reply to Simon Springer in which Harvey mentions how in the late 1960s and 1970s the radical movement was mixed with anarchists, Marxists, anti-imperialists, feminists, ecologists, anti-racists and fourth-worldists – that is, even if there were few women and people of colour in the academic profession.[23] The doors of the profession were pushed open, he says, revealing what had been oppressive yet hidden in politics. The struggle for leftists in academia was to publish with a superior level of academic sophistication, and twice as much, or perish. Those who had no taste for radical academic pedagogy chose activism. Whatever radicalism remained in academia by the late 1980s was dominated by the postmodern turn – with the ideas of Foucault, Baudrillard, Deleuze and Guattari displacing Marx – as well as the forms of identity politics based on race, gender and sexuality.

According to Harvey, his 1989 book *The Condition of Postmodernity* elicited tremendous criticism from radical feminists. In this he was not alone; so were other Marxist geographers criticised: Fredric Jameson, Edward Soja and Mike Davis most prominently. Rosalyn Deutsche's critique of Jameson's theory of postmodernism, for instance, in her 1990 essay 'Men in Space,' is exemplary of this critique. Deutsche writes:

> Because he disavows the importance of other social relations, Jameson confuses capital's fragmentation with 'fragmentations' caused by challenges – from feminists, gays, lesbians, post-colonials, antiracists – to the types of discursive power Jameson himself exercises: universalizing thought, essentialist discourses, constructions of unitary subjectivity. Such challenges expose Jameson's fragmentary unity as a fiction from the start and he responds by silencing them. Accordingly, he has dispelled any doubts about the nature of 'cognitive mapping' by revealing that he actually meant it to be a code phrase for 'class consciousness,' thereby definitively wiping feminism off the map of radical social theory.[24]

Harvey is also taken to task for failing to account for the materiality of the signifier and its contestatory uses in late capitalist culture. While Harvey considers the postmodern city to be the image of capital, this vision, for Deutsche, is not related to contingencies of viewership. What he does not want to see, she contends, is the partiality of his position; he desires instead a particularism that can function as the equivalent of a universalising discourse. Deutsche further argues that Harvey denies his own specificity in his book *The Urban Experience* when he admits to feeling a voyeuristic pleasure in seeing the city 'as a whole' from the highest possible vantage point, thereby claiming to square off bravely with the fully objective view that is not afforded by the view from the ground. The total view of the city figures as an emblem for the critical practice of *metatheory*, which prioritises the spatial-dialectical method of historical materialism as the master-narrative of global culture.

The radical geographers' spatial-dialectical method is attributed to Lefebvre, who in the late 1960s and early 1970s developed a Hegelian-Marxist challenge to structuralism by spatialising the historical emphasis in dialectical materialism. The crux of Deutsche's critique, however, can be said to be the function of vision in relation to subjectivity and social space. Her critique thus addresses the implausibility of the meta-theoretical 'view from nowhere.' Post-structuralist theorists like Deutsche challenge the concrete universal of capital with the abstract universal of embodiment. What is at issue is not so much the idea that the social theories of Jameson and Harvey are flawed, but rather that their claims to seeing the totality disavows the ways that vision relates to discursive complexes. The point is not that feminist authors like Deutsche deny Marxist claims, but that they wish to emphasise counter-discourses and different aspects of social structuration.[25] Deutsche insists on the use by feminists of psychoanalytic theories of visual pleasure, the scopic drive and fetishism – psychic processes that help secure an illusory sense of subjective wholeness. Countering reflectionist theories of representation, she argues that much writing in urban theory maintains itself by subordinating feminist scholarship and by producing illusions of coherence, or what Lefebvre referred to as 'illusions of transparency.'[26] Feminist scholarship, however, risks a different form of illusion: the illusion of maintaining oneself in a relation of desire, excluding the dimension of metapolitics. The subsequent problem is not the materialist unmasking of the unstable character of signification and subjectivity, but rather the encounter with the Real of illusion, fantasy and fetishism, which allows no possibility for an unconflicted and fully 'material' encounter with 'other' spaces.

At one time in the late 1990s it was considered enough to 'culturalise' politics and assert how reality is socially constructed, thereby supplementing the gesture of denaturalisation with the particulars of one's micropolitical agenda of empowerment. So as to not appear myopic about one's difference politics it was then necessary to link all the forms of oppression in a chain of equivalences, usually based on genealogies of marginalisation by an ominous 'normality,' 'block of discourse' or 'phallogocentrism.' The arguments of radical feminism, however, have not been settled by the pluralisation, hybridisation and diversification of the 'bodies that matter,' which in today's new materialisms, post-humanism and animal studies, go all the way down to the microphysics of the atom.

Does the claim of a situated subjectivity not equally result in a fantasy of immanence, marked by an impossible appropriation of life's contingencies? The greater problem is that the opposition between contingent and universal is inherent rather than extraneous to biocapitalism. Deutsche's best effort in this regard was to acknowledge particularity and not explain it away. She related this to Homi Bhabha's definition of masculinism as the basis for a singular social consciousness:

> Masculinism as a position of social authority is not simply about the power invested in the recognizable 'persons' of men. It is about the subsumption or sublation of social antagonisms; it is about the repression of social division; it is about the power to authorize an 'impersonal' holistic or universal discourse on the representation of the social.[27]

Such singular consciousness, however, was never a strong claim among those who defended class struggle and the subject of the unconscious. Despite the affirmation by radical democracy of the equivalence of the forms of struggle, the problem of class inequality did not disappear in the 1980s and 1990s but increased exponentially, covered over in academia by an opportunistic 'agonism in the public sphere.'

In light of this recent history, Harvey's affirmation of identity struggles can be thought to be either a simple add-on to his focus on Marxist geopolitics, or a slight shift away from the notion of a revolutionary working class. Either way, one has to admit that the continuing relevance of Marx disturbs the dominant neoliberal hegemony. The Marxist corpus, including its socialist experiments, has to this day a retroactive necessity of singular note. And so, after two decades of anti- and alter-globalisation, according to Harvey, the Marxist critique of political economy is once again on the agenda. Yet social movements are more interested in putting together new compositions and dispersed concatenations of anti-capitalism. In this situation, the convenient caricature of a dogmatic orthodox leftist, Harvey says, is someone who believes that a vanguard party will lead the working class through a period of dictatorship to that of a communist state and potentially the end of history.[28] He argues that thanks to the sophistication of intellectuals like Georg Lukács, Antonio Gramsci and Raymond Williams, it is no longer necessary for leftists to be embarrassed by this stereotype. His main claims against this caricature, however, are not the ideas of contemporary radical thinkers like Alain Badiou and Žižek, who are the only two intellectuals to have renewed dialectical materialism after post-modernism.[29] Žižek has in fact proven to be more aware than previous waves of Lacanians that the instability of subjectivity is one of the means through which capital maintains its moorings. If one is to change this, one must move away from narratives concerning the intolerance towards the 'stranger within ourselves,' or what Žižek defines as the 'pseudo-psychoanalytic drama of the subject unable to confront its inner traumas.'[30] The politically correct zeal with

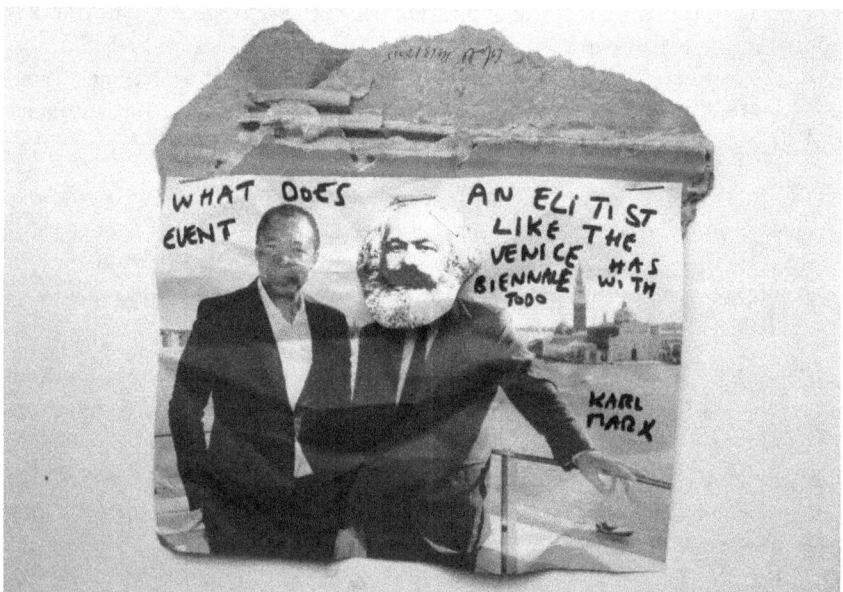

Thierry Geoffroy/Biennalist, *'What Does an Elitist Event Like the Venice Biennale Has to Do with Karl Marx?'*, 2015. Mix-media, cardboard and paper, 10 x 13 cm. Courtesy of Thierry Geoffroy.

which cultural studies have dealt with sexism, racism and colonialism has also operated, Žižek argues, as a defence against awareness of one's identifications with social mobility and middle-class elitism.

Why should Harvey be invited to chat with Enwezor during the marathon reading of *Das Kapital*? Why is it now safe for the elite art world to rehabilitate a Marxist like Harvey? Of course there is no simple answer to this, but one possible explanation is that his participation would address the difference between Harvey and someone like Žižek, who, as it happens, was invited to headline the Neue Slowenische Kunst's utopian State in Time splinter pavilion at the 2017 Venice Biennale.[31] For Harvey, the challenge to leftism is not post-modern cultural studies, which he would otherwise criticise as non-scientific anti-foundationalism, but is internal to Marxism itself, and in particular, to the disparity between the different volumes of *Capital*. This internal crisis of Marxist-Leninist politics, does not necessarily make the case for Enwezor, however, since the internal contradictions of capitalism spill over into forms of oppression that are not reducible to the contradictions of capital. In an article about his book, *Seventeen Contradictions*, Harvey writes:

> Finally, there is the question of gender and sexual preferences which are universal in the ways that questions of race, ethnicity, religion, nationalism and the like are not. The nature of gender and sexual preference questions varies immensely, however, from one part of the world to another … The autonomous development of these other contradictions – expressive of some version of the fluctuating role of human alterity within capitalism in general – cannot be reduced to functions of the inner contradictions of capital … But then neither can the contradictions of capital be reduced to questions of race, gender, national identity, queer theory or the like. This simple fact also establishes something else important. To be anti-capitalist is not necessarily to be an anti-racist, anti-nationalist feminist/queer theorist … By the same token, to be a feminist/queer theorist or anti-racist is not necessarily to be anti-capitalist … The street battles in Ferguson Missouri in recent times … were not anti-capitalist in their content (although certain individuals and groups may have been so) even as their form is hard to understand without invoking class position. There are, however, plenty of intensely pro-capitalist anti-racists and feminists and queer theorists in the world … Much of the left used to believe that all anti-colonial struggles were anti-capitalist but the actual history of post-colonial political economy belies such an assumption.[32]

As Harvey also states,

> While the capital-labour contradiction is unquestionably a central and foundational contradiction of capital, it is not – even from the standpoint of *capital* alone – a primary contradiction to which all other contradictions are in some sense subservient. From the standpoint of *capitalism*, this central and foundational

contradiction within the economic engine constituted by capital clearly has a vital role to play, but its tangible manifestations are mediated and tangled up through the filters of other forms of social distinction, such as race, ethnicity, gender and religious affiliation so as to make the actual politics of struggle within capitalism a far more complicated affair than would appear to be the case from the standpoint of the labour-capital relation alone.[33]

Harvey considers what it means to be anti-capitalist – a term that is sometimes as depoliticising as the equally expedient terms anti-patriarchy and anti-racism. He argues that the contradictions of capitalism require a reading of all of Marx's texts and a willingness to question their applicability to our times. His recent focus on how the contradictory unity of production and realisation, supply and demand, is spread across volumes one and two of *Capital* could be seen, for instance, in the neoliberal trend towards wage repression, which was compensated by the inflation of credit and led to the 2008 financial crisis that was tempered by more bailout credit. Or in another instance, the Apple corporation does not generate all of its surplus from production in China, but makes large profits from sales in the US, potentially making consumer politics in this and similar cases a key component of class struggle. Harvey argues that such problems decentre notions of class struggle and define a broader terrain of anti-capitalism. On the other hand, as John Smith has argued, the globalised exploitation of labour leads to a 'GDP illusion' wherein value added productivity is directly related to the exploitation of labour and the expropriation of surplus value by transnational corporations.[34] The unproductive labour displayed at the Biennale is directly derived from the surplus labour of productive workers. Consumption is not the same as production. We are therefore back to Benjamin's aphorism that every document of civilisation is at the same time a document of barbarism.

The contradictions of capital do not transcend the need to struggle against all forms of oppression. Harvey adds, however, that struggles against oppression do not transcend the contradictions of capital. One is left to wonder whether or not the contradictions of capital can be understood at all without attending to matters of gender, race and sexuality. Is Harvey mostly tolerant of moral struggles while giving greater attention to the more serious and difficult matter of the cognitive mapping of the political economy of the world system? By the same token, from the other side of things, is Enwezor merely acknowledging the salience of Marx today so that he can otherwise ignore the role of culture in the globalisation of surplus extraction? And does his focus on embodiment merely reiterate the art world platitude that there is no outside to capital? Certainly, that is the mandate of an institution that is as capitalised as the Venice Biennale, and yet, which can be politically repurposed as much as any other institution. The Biennale is not only, as one commentator put it, 'a bog of moneyed hypocrisy.'[35] But then, as Žižek commented after his participation in the 2017 Biennale, there is something deeply suspicious about an event that is fully part of the capitalist machinery but that plays the game by proclaiming self-critically that it is fighting capitalism.[36] How then can the *Das Kapital Oratorio* be said to be Marxist, and how can Harvey be said to have acknowledged in his thinking the philosophical and psychoanalytic problems of subjectivity that Deutsche and others raised in the 1990s?

One of the problems with the *Oratorio* is that it plays all too easily into the kind of cultural studies social constructionism that presumes we can privilege particularism against universalism. This for example, is the case with Malik Gaines, whose book, *Black Performance on the Outskirts of the Left*, argues that 'flesh as the material of form' undermines universalist sensibilities.[37] Gaines focuses on race, gender and sexuality as models of antagonism and as what he considers to be the basis for a 'vanguard of negativity,' also defined as 'the avant-garde of difference.'[38] Differences, according to him, have exceeded Marxist theory insofar as the pluralism of race and gender interferes with class orderings. Marxist analysis, he argues, is incapable of addressing the interrelation of capitalism and white supremacy. Against this, Gaines opts for Laclau and Mouffe's logic of contingency and the plural forms of resistance that destabilise and decentre the left. Any international Marxist project and class project could thereby be faulted for the 'appropriation of black bodies' and for determining the 'universal relevance' of local conflicts. Marxism is thus for him a masculinist and colonialist discourse.[39] Gaines opts instead for a 'black transnational network' that cannot be associated with rights discourse or a specific political organisation and common economic condition, but that is understood rather as a 'place of imagination where different models of being and belonging can be performed.'[40]

Reporting on the 56th Venice Biennale, Gaines celebrates the *Das Kapital Oratorio* and related works, such as Emeka Ogboh's 'Song of the Germans,' for which the German national anthem was sung in ten African languages. He applauds the way that the 'insidiously aural' orchestration of sounds favoured transnationalism, combining the 'flexible communicative powers' of sound with visuality.[41] Oddly enough, Gaines associates his discussion of black futures and collective potential with an image of Michelle Obama in the company of Joan Jonas, the American artist who represented the US at the Biennale. The presence of Obama is indirectly equated with the diversity of the performers of the *Oratorio*. In his interpretation of Enwezor's project, Gaines perceives difference in terms of disruption rather than solidarity and internationalism. Certainly, Michelle Obama is not a person who represents leftist politics, even if she does represent diversity.

Gaines mentions in his discussion that Isaac Julien, who directed the live readings of *Capital*, had previously created a two-channel video titled *Kapital*, which was on view in Venice. In this 2013 piece, Julien interviews David Harvey in the company of an audience. In his description of the Q&A that follows the interview, Gaines mentions that Harvey addresses the relationship between the universal dimension of capital and the particularities of variables like wages, rents and interest rates, and well as the singular as the place of individual consumption. From the audience Stuart Hall challenges Harvey and suggests that his concepts do not adequately describe contemporary conditions, and that he should give more attention to questions of consumption and social reproduction. Hall argues that Marx's *Capital* favours masculine industrial production and that his notion of the proletariat is obsolete, least of all because it does not address issues of gender and race. Harvey replies that one can only examine the ways that capital is gendered or racialised; one cannot use race or gender to theorise capitalist economics. Gaines proposes no further analysis of capital or of capitalism and takes this as proof enough that Marxism needs to be subjected to a greater degree of indeterminacy and must acknowledge the limits of economic science for politics, which is not determined by something like surplus value and rates of profit, but by the balance of social forces, which Gaines defines as the 'concrete conjuncture.'[42]

If Gaines correctly states the idea that Marxism has no knowledge of the future, his rejection of 'prognostication' by economics does not address the usefulness of Marx's approach to theories of economic crisis. As well, despite the rhetoric of indeterminacy, Gaines' emphasis on identity does not make his politics less reductive. His desperation in this regard is reflected in his appeal to armed resistance. His hope, he writes, is that in the future gay guerrillas will match the strength of the Taliban or the PLO. In the case of the Taliban, he confuses revolutionary struggle with fundamentalism, thereby undermining the position of radical democracy that he otherwise claims to endorse. He also ignores how it is that capitalist imperialism is responsible for both of these armed movements. His notion of solidarity abandons the question of state socialism and with it any possible challenge to global capitalism. He takes courage in W.E.B. Du Bois' assessment in 1961 that capitalism is doomed to self-destruction. His strategy, then, is to simply wait out this eventuality or to accelerate it though various forms of disruption. In a sense it seems to Gaines that the simple fact of blackness is enough to constitute a revolutionary politics.

Gaines' stance is not uncommon in contemporary intersectionist and decolonial struggles, in which class struggle is made to compete with various other forms of anti-oppression. The issue for Marxism is the disparity that is implicit in the way these issues are addressed. On the one hand, from a historical point of view, the anti-globalisation movement and movement of the squares had made important steps away from postmodern micropolitics and initiated a re-engagement with the struggles of the macropolitical left. As Žižek put it in the early 2000s:

[I]n the postmodern 'anti-essentialist' discourse regarding the multitude of strug-gles, 'socialist' anti-capitalist struggle is posited as just one in a series of struggles ('class, sex and gender, ethnic identity'…), and what is happening today is not merely that the anti-capitalist struggle is getting stronger, but that it is once again assuming the central structuring role. The old narrative of postmodern politics was: from class essentialism to the multitude of struggles for identity; today, the trend is finally reversed.[43]

From a theoretical point of view, the solidarity that is expressed by activists has certain fault lines. What Gaines and what many post-structuralist cultural theorists and activists oppose is what Jacques Rancière refers to as the order of police, which is contrasted to the less ontologically homogenous category of politics. In the short circuit between universal and particular, the equality of all voices defines democratic inclusion as an unconditional demand. Politics therefore come into conflict with the policing of society. In his summary of Rancière's *Dissensus* (1995), Žižek distinguishes between three kinds of politics. *Archi-politics* refers to an organic conception of community that pre-vents politics and polices the homogeneity of the social space. Democratic deliberation, and to a certain extent the kinds of pluralist agonism promoted by thinkers like Mouffe, defines a *para-politics* that depoliticises politics by turning it into a police logic, making debate and struggle an inherent aspect of social processes, and which therefore prevents an explosion of political chaos. Political correctness is typical of such police politics. A Marxist *meta-politics* accepts political conflict but limits 'real' politics to macropolitical issues of eco-nomic regulation. Žižek adds to this a fourth category of *ultra-politics*, which depoliticises conflict by foreclosing politics outright as a conflict between 'us' and 'them.'[44] Žižek distinguishes multiculturalism from revolutionary politics insofar as identity struggles against oppression seek a polity in which everyone can share the same rights and responsibilities. The concept of culture wars is therefore a misnomer. Class struggle, in contrast, is a fight for the eradication of bourgeois capitalist class relations and for the eradication of class society. It is not a fight for the eradication of bourgeois people since neither the proletariat nor the capitalist class is perceived as a category of identity.

Žižek's version of the short circuit between the universal and the particular makes the proletariat into a singular that stands in for the universal, which is the basis of Marxist politics. While commentators like Gaines consider that proletarian labour is a masculine category that is part of an outmoded industrial mode of production, the transition to capitalism is itself hardly a *fait accompli* and continues today through the expropriation of land and through the dec-imation of public sector provisions, contributing to pauperisation through debt servicing, falling wages, unemployment and under-employment. In Iraq alone, in the aftermath of a bloody colonial war that left more than one million dead, more than three million peasants moved to cities. The process of urban migration is especially noticeable in China, the world's second largest economy after the US, where, since the economic reforms of 1992, there has been a significant expansion of the proletarian class and new middle class. Chinese proletarianisation is due in large part to the transformation of areas cultivated by subsistence farming families into large-scale farming enterprises that are developed through practices of expropriation. Internationally, mass migrations caused by poverty and civil wars account for nearly twenty percent of the underclass of metropolitan areas. Industrialisation has been especially intense in countries like Malaysia, Sri Lanka, Korea, Tunisia and Morocco, where women workers are substituted for men. Since the 1990s, the transition to capitalism can be said to contribute increasingly to the proletarianisation of women, especially in Latin America, the Carribean and Southeast Asia. The globalisation of female labour is less intense in the Middle East, however, where lower rates of foreign direct investment have kept women out of the world market. The 1979 Revolution in Iran, for example, limited female employment and the kinds of proletarianisation seen in Southeast Asia and Latin America. Lower levels of industrialisation, thanks largely to oil revenues, have resulted in lower levels of proletarianisation. In contrast, countries that are dedicated to export industries and that experience higher levels of foreign direct investment participate more intensely in a global division of labour. Slum cities in developing economies and the casualisation of labour in the economic centres place pressure on national economies as large-scale industry contributes to the fragmentation of the global working class, which is drawn increasingly towards religious and ethnic regression and mafia-type patronage. According to Karl Heinz Roth, proletarianisation, with its increasingly transcultural and multicultural identifications, has become the single most important factor of a new global class composition.[45] Proletarianisation and the expansion of informal work is accompanied by the rise of a salaried international petty-bourgeois class, the expansion of the private sector and the development of managerialism. Among the different possibilities of political regression in this context, and one that can potentially harm the anti-capitalist movement, is a tendency to project fears and anger onto anyone who represents the interests of the working class.

If postcolonial struggles and Third Worldism were once a solution to imperialism, the nationalisation of wealth is increasingly a thing of the past in a world of globalised production. The suppression of labour mobility makes it such that so-called developing countries have no chance of achieving the living standards that are enjoyed in the global North. Underdevelopment contributes to immiseration as more people, and more women than ever before, are pushed into the world market, which increased by more than one billion people since the 1980s.[46] Much of this workforce is unprotected, unregulated, informal and unorganised. Women workers, according to Smith, who are employed by transnational corporations because they are more easily exploited, have far more in common with male workers than with the parasitic coercion of business elites, state authorities and criminal gangs. The fall in labour's share of wealth throughout the neoliberal era is the result, he argues, of capitalism's desperate efforts to stave off economic crises by increasing the exploitation of labour and nature. The current logic of nationalism and protectionism is a veneer for the destruction of the remaining rights and freedoms of organised workers. Regardless of whether neoliberal capitalism functions through surplus-value extraction, through monopoly capital or through the privatisation of commons, capitalism is prone to imperialist competition and increasing violence between, as Lenin defined them, oppressed and oppressor nations.

One could say, paradoxically, that the growing reserve army of precarious, unemployed, underemployed and redundant workers is one of the factors contributing to the inability of the left to move away from identity politics. In the global North, as post-Fordism increasingly makes subjectivity and sociality the basis for the organic composition of capital, that is, the ratio between dead labour and living labour, people are increasingly called upon to transform their subjectivity and affect into an asset.[47] If histories of colonial and gender oppression can be transformed into means to invest in oneself, this is not only due to education and higher standards of living, but also to the intensity of exploitation, the cheapening of automation, offshoring, lower wages, overpopulation, the ecological crisis and the destruction of resources.[48] As Michael Henrich puts it, the question of class is frowned upon today, even by politicians, in favour of the various forms of oppression based on gender, race and sexuality. In a post-political world, these subjectivities do not constitute class societies, but middle classes made up of employees and entrepreneurs. The problem, he adds, is that the working classes do not possess a better or more privileged perception of capitalist relations than do the middle classes.[49] Given that capital itself is the real barrier to capitalist production, the more complicated level of this question, from a Marxist perspective, is how it is that difference and subjectivity are increasingly becoming the raw materials of labour exploitation.

Against victim politics

People who have been subjected to racialised or gendered violence and discrimination may not want to hear that identity struggles are part of the logic of multinational capitalism, especially not from white, European males.[50] It is nevertheless necessary for social movement artists and activists to address the ways that contemporary capitalism integrates people into the social order through 'capture devices' like race and gender. Against postmodern

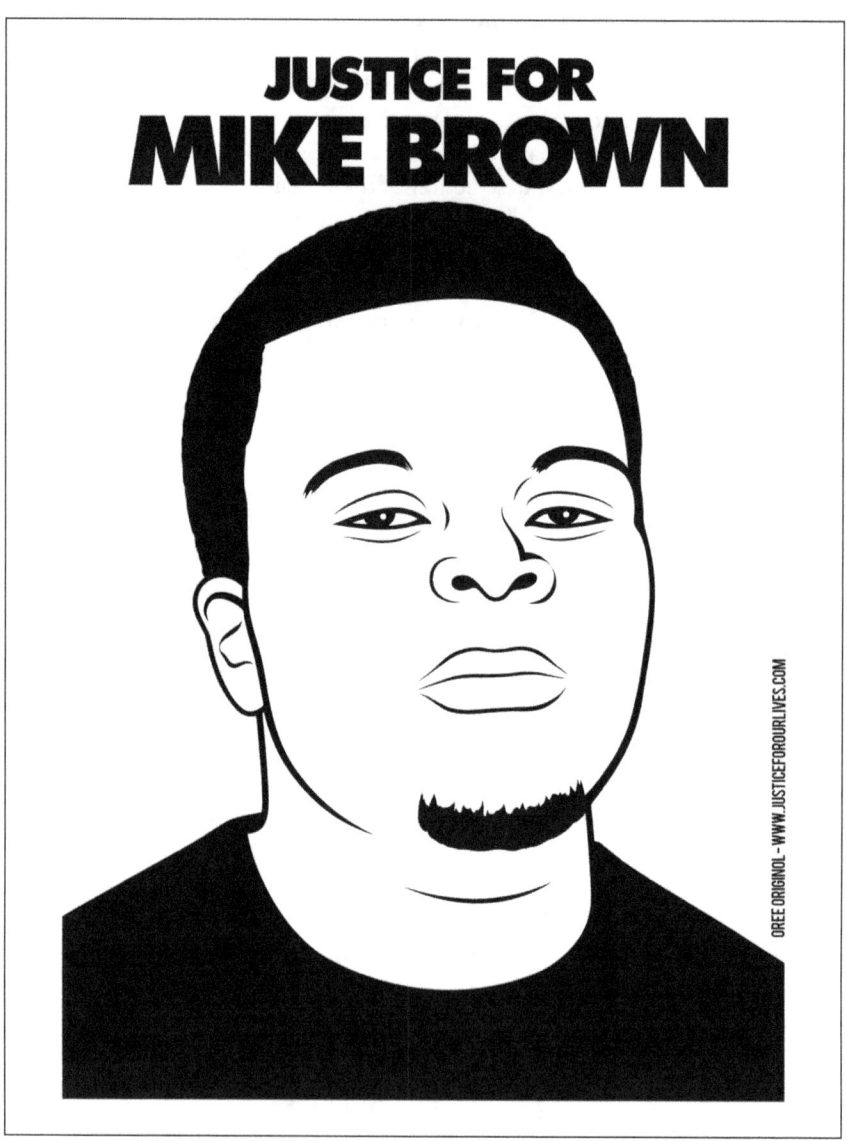

Oree Originol, *Justice for Our Lives (Justice for Mike Brown)*, 2014–ongoing. Portrait series of people from marginalised communities who have lost their lives due to police violence and as a result of racism. Courtesy of Oree Originol and www.justiceforourlives.com.

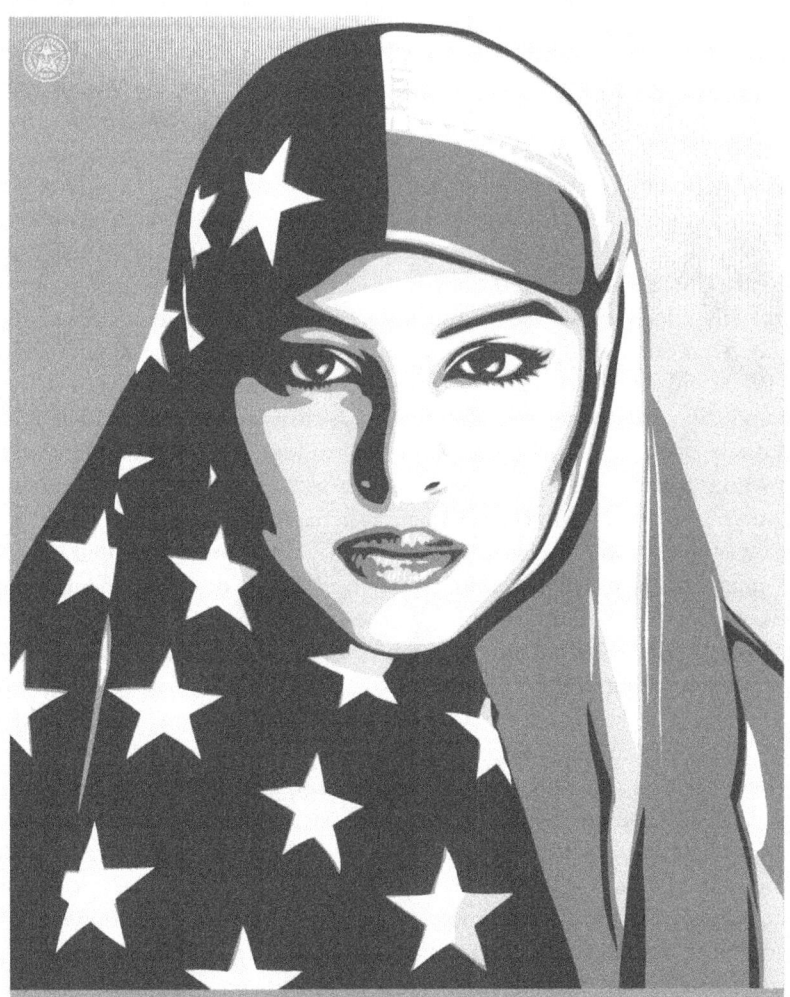

Shepard Fairey, *WE THE PEOPLE (Greater Than Fear)*, 2017. Print made in honour of the 2017 Women's March on (Trump) Inauguration Day against nationalism, bigotry and intolerance. Artwork by Shepard Fairey and by Ridwan Adhami, commissioned and in collaboration with Amplifier.org. Courtesy of Shepard Fairey.

contingency, which leaves us with little more than technocracy and antagonism, Badiou proposes that for all its fiascos the thinking of the twentieth
century was a thinking that had the courage to view humanity as a universal
political project.[51] Consequently, Badiou argues: 'We must ... concede nothing to the negative and victimary definition of man.'[52] Badiou proposes that
politics cannot be founded on identity, and especially not on one's identity as
a victim. What then do Badiou's suggestions allow us to think about the Black
Lives Matter and MeToo movements?

At a London Critical Theory Summer School event, which took place
July 10, 2015, the feminist scholar Jacqueline Rose argued that if there was
no patriarchy in society, we would not need feminism, and if patriarchy was
completely effective, we would not have feminism.[53] She adds, further, that
radical feminism monopolised the question of violence against women in
the 1970s and 1980s because it was neglected by Marxist and psychoanalytic
feminists. She offers a corrective to this by discussing how Melanie Klein had
nevertheless theorised how infant boys need to repudiate feminine identification with the mother. Men's violence against women is therefore more asocial
than men's violence against other men. Whereas men are meant to fight and
go to war against other men, male violence against women is hidden because
it is mixed with an unconscious repudiation. Rose does not mention the
repudiation of male identification with the father as a feature of heterosexual
socialisation. Her research, all the same, seeks to provide a gender analysis of
the psychic distribution of violence.

As Rose's interlocutor, Žižek responded by rejecting the effort to build an
ethics on identifications that predate the socialisation process – any hope for
humanity will be one that is thoroughly socialised. We become human, he
argued, and not simply gendered, through various kinds of denaturalisation.
The problem for radical feminism is that it is simply inadequate to consider
the persons of men to be guilty in advance, for instance, for their primordial
repudiations. Žižek therefore emphasises the divided nature not only of subjectivity but of reality. Rose concluded with the idea that feminism was in
danger of being hijacked by the human rights discourse of western powers
in their invasions of Afghanistan and other countries and that laws against
anti-social behaviours can turn into laws against political protest. Feminism is
always therefore available for rightist appropriation and can be used to divert
attention from the forms of exploitation inequality that combine the attack on
welfare with neoliberalism. But the fact that violence against women is on the
agenda at all, she said, is thanks to feminism. We could say the same thing for
other civil rights movements within the context of radical democracy. The
problem, however, is the extent to which the progressive and conservative
approaches to the question of oppression are now two sides of the same
neoliberal horizon.

The political stakes of this discussion are addressed in a short article by Seth Ackerman in *Jacobin* magazine. Ackerman remarks upon the 2016 US presidential campaign in which, on July 18, 2015, at a Netroots Nation conference, Democratic presidential candidates Bernie Sanders and Martin O'Malley were shouted down by Black Lives Matter activists who objected to O'Malley's statement that 'black lives matter, white lives matter, all lives matter.' The activists in the room wanted the candidates to admit that racism is a problem in the US and wanted to know what they would do about it. In response to this, Hillary Clinton told a *Washington Post* reporter: 'Black lives matter. Everyone in this country should stand firmly behind that. We need to acknowledge some hard truths about race and justice in this country, and one of those hard truths is that racial inequality is not merely a symptom of economic inequality.'[54] Ackerman criticises Clinton for pandering to what black activists want to hear, that racial animosity is a structural problem in its own right, and argues that Clinton does not want to account for the ways that racism is in fact symptomatic of economic inequality.

The impunity of political processes, from policing and border security to war, feeds the current politics of neoliberalism insofar as people become cynical about authority. Lack of faith in institutions and ideals does not require truth to be revealed since the truth itself appears non-ideological. In this regard, a movement like Black Lives Matter appears to be non-ideological, even when it is articulated with black nationalism, anarchism and other social movements like OWS, as was the case for instance in the 2012 Million Hoodie March for Trayvon Martin. The organisational aspects of BLM were from the start mediated by civil rights organisations, who were motivated to repeal Stand Your Ground and to eradicate racial profiling and police violence. Yet the sizeable black middle class gave the movement a vertical composition that is unlike the civil rights struggles of the 1950s and 1960s, with even the federal government investigating violations.[55] The message on the part of neoliberal politicians is thus divided between the correct political response, which is fully known, and the obscene command to obey – to articulate Black Lives Matter within the dominant neoliberal capitalist logic, as seen for instance in BLM accepting $100 million from the Ford Foundation and Borealis Philanthropy.

Today's politics of impunity is designed to secure the consent of the ruled. Yet the ruled must at the same time be convinced that their domination is the price to be paid for their freedom. This relationship of domination defines biocapitalism. Biocapitalism is not a simple matter of hegemonic consent, however, since it requires as a core feature the post-political view that ideological opposition is a thing of the past. In biocapitalism the dominant strains of academic identity politics, which are evident in the Black Lives Matter and MeToo campaigns, are complexly subtended by the politics of austerity and impunity. In this sense today's authoritarian politics take the form of a 'bipartisan' technocratic management of 'complex systems' that would by themselves appear to be only arbitrarily serving the interests of the wealthy plutocracy. Insofar as victim politics occlude the collective organisation of the radical left, typically ruled out in advance as totalitarian and anti-democratic, solutions must therefore be made consistent with the neoliberal order. In terms of American history, the perception that the radical left is a threat to capitalism is a matter of pure ideology since class conflict in the US has been overshadowed by ethnic and religious conflict. According to Richard Hofstader, violence in the US tends to emerge as citizen-versus-citizen violence, often encouraged by establishment elites against abolitionists, religious groups, political radicals, labour organisers and racial minorities. Hofstadter does not make the case for anti-capitalist revolution, however, but rather makes the point that most social reforms in American history – child labour laws, wage-hour regulation, industrial safety, workers' compensation, collective bargaining, social security, medicare – were brought about through nonviolent militancy, education and through official political channels.[56] Even these, however, should be conceived in relation to international struggles.

In the context of neoliberalism, the question is whether identity-based politics can deliver the kinds of reforms that were obtained by previous waves of civil rights and social democracy. In *The Courage of Hopelessness*, Žižek criticises the pathos of universal solidarity as a kind of false solidarity and 'ideological theatre of shadows.' When disaster strikes, he argues, we need to think about what conditions contribute to or create these problems and what political-ideological projects emerge in response to them.[57] Too often, one is satisfied to apportion blame as a means to dissolve antagonisms. For instance, an anonymous social movement activist discusses the kinds of problems that victim politics can give rise to with regard to the 'call-out culture' that they have experienced in activist groups. The faulty premises and effects of call-outs, this person says, include: non-transformative reverse violence; the homogenisation and ghettoisation of minority groups; lack of educative follow-up and resource-sharing on complex social problems; the conflation of queer/trans/women's spaces with everyplace; the exploitation of the uneven development of political awareness as a strategy of exclusion; the failure to negotiate discomfort and disagreement and its elevation into threat and safety issues; the elevation of marginality into privilege; the inflation of the political salience of the kinds of sex one has or the conflation of queer with radical; the avoidance of class issues and specific social demands in favour of interpersonal animosity; and the use of call-outs and exclusion as a kind of show trial mentality without frameworks of accountability.[58]

A show trial mentality has to some extent developed alongside the legitimate demands of the MeToo campaign. Beginning around October 2017, and led by the mainstream press, the MeToo movement emerged after an article in the *New York Times* reported on the allegations of sexual harassment against Hollywood producer Harvey Weinstein. This was followed by other reported accusations against men with public profiles, including Kevin Spacey, Louis C.K., Al Franken, James Toback, Jeffrey Tambor, Dustin Hoffman, Charlie Rose and James Franco, not to mention countless politicians. Critiques of the campaign have divided into two sets of problems. One response has to do with reactions against the moral panics and puritan hypocrisy that could result as a consequence, as argued for instance by the one hundred signatories of a comment published on January 9 in the French newspaper *Le Monde*. Signed by Catherine Deneuve among others, the comment defends promiscuity and a refusal of the role of victim.[59] This side of the issue has to date received fairly little attention as it requires a degree of sophistication – for instance, to argue against something like the law that has been drafted in Sweden that would require written consent prior to a sexual encounter. The other issue has to do with the right to due process and the presumption of innocence of the accused, as argued for instance by Matt Damon in comments he later retracted.[60] For some, the fact of being found guilty without even any charges being laid recalls the problems of witch-hunts, show trials and mob rule, as argued for example by Canadian writer Margaret Atwood.[61] Such critiques result in an almost immediate backlash as failure to support the women who are coming out with their testimonies.

The MeToo campaign has extended to the art world, not only in accusations against artists like Chuck Close and Bruce Weber, and executives like art dealer Anthony d'Offray, *Artforum* publisher Knight Landesman and curator Jens Hoffmann, but also in the questioning of works by canonical artists like John William Waterhouse, Egon Schiele and Balthus.[62] Kate Winslet's role in Woody Allen's *Wonder Wheel* would seem to have been passed up for a 2018 Oscar nomination on the basis of the disputed matter of Allen's relationship to Dylan Farrow.[63] Once we begin to proscribe deviant artworks on the basis of moral criteria, where does censorship end? What other artworks have to be censored and artists blacklisted in order to defend public morality? Beyond the specific issues of the MeToo campaign, the question of embodiment that was mentioned by Enwezor and Gaines can become a means to reject all objective or universal evaluative criteria for works of art. The same goes for science and politics. The issue, then, is the way in which accusations and misdeeds get transformed into politics, policy and procedure. Moral panics are not a new phenomenon and have been exploited historically by the forces of political reaction to attack the vulnerable. In 1955, fourteen-year-old Emmett Till was murdered for having been falsely said to have whistled at a white woman. It is ironic then that activists in the art world objected so strongly to the showing of Dana Schutz's painting of a deceased Emmett Till at the 2017 Whitney Biennale, accusing Schutz and the curators of exploiting and appropriating

Black trauma for profit. Activists called for the work to be destroyed. While not denying the issues, Coco Fusco challenged the puritanical anti-intellectualism that reduced the Schutz affair to a matter of moral condemnation.[64]

It is not altogether surprising that the MeToo campaign should find a great deal of support on the part of the neoliberal establishment, from the mainstream media as well as celebrity victims of wrongdoings, like IMF chief Christine Lagarde, most of whom have no real concern for the fate of working-class women. Politicians like Franken are asked to leave their jobs on the basis of allegations of negligible sexual misconduct while politicians who authorise the murder of civilians can be considered allies. Insofar as it is not based in leftist theory and practice, the sum total of victim politics is a shift of the political spectrum towards the right. Another dimension of this shift is the way in which the tactics of leftist protest have been recuperated by the mainstream.

The over-inflation of lifestyle as one of the only spaces in democratic life where some margin of social change is allowed reflects the more general conditions of neoliberalism's combination of flexibilisation with power. The gradual erosion of democratic processes in the US since 9/11 has been pursued through the creation of the Department of Homeland Security, leading to the establishment of the PATRIOT Act, which increased government spying and led to the Authorization to Use Military Force as well as the Military Commissions Act, which, in the case of an attack similar to 9/11, provides measures for the suspension of the American Constitution with a military government. The strengthening of police powers and the assault on democratic rights that have been instituted since the early 2000s have led to the progressive weakening of the separation between executive, legislative and judicial powers. The Guantánamo Bay prison camp as well as 'black sites' around the world are another consequence of the 'war on terror,' along with the Obama administration's extension of drone warfare, targeted and extrajudicial killings, extraordinary rendition, no-fly lists and crackdown on whistleblowers. These powers have been used by the Trump administration to curtail immigration and to increase the military budget. All of this gives a picture of the impunity that corresponds with austerity and reflects the fact that violence in the US is directly associated with economic inequality. In 2017 alone, there were 345 mass shootings in the US. In response to the school shooting in Parkdale, Florida, in February 2018, both Democrats and Republican politicians proposed increasing police powers. When students met with Trump to discuss gun control, the President responded by proposing that teachers and staff should be armed with concealed weapons and that schools should be better fortified.

According to a report issued by the University of Michigan in June 2014, wealth inequality doubled in the United States during the period 2003 to 2013, the same period in which civil liberties, social security, education, health care, unemployment benefits and industrial policy were being cut, slashed and squandered. In this time period, the median American household lost more than thirty-five percent of its wealth, while the lowest twenty-five percent of the working poor and unemployed lost over sixty-three percent of its wealth. In contrast, the richest five percent of Americans have seen their wealth grow by fourteen percent, that is, from $1.2 to $1.35 million.[65] A picture of how these trends impact the lives everyday people can be seen in the story of Eileen DiNino, the mother of seven children who was found dead in her Pennsylvania jail cell on June 7, 2014. DiNino had been imprisoned because she was unable to pay the $2,000 truancy fines that were imposed on her because some of her children did not attend school classes. In 2009 the School District of Lebanon, Pennsylvania, had collected more than $500,000 from poor families like DiNino's. In Ferguson, where Michael Brown Jr. was killed by police, court fines nearing $2.5 million account for ten percent of the city's revenue. Although the US has only five percent of the world's population, it has twenty-five percent of the world's prison population – a number that is double that of Russia, the next highest incarcerator. Nearly twenty-five percent of black men in the US have spent some time in prison. Without the capacity to exploit the black workforce, government turns to segregation strategies and policing.

The 'hands up don't shoot' slogan that was an early hashtag of Black Lives Matter emphasised vulnerability and nonviolent tactics. The particularist logic of victim politics gradually shifted from #BlackLivesMatter to the dozen or so similar hashtags that followed, including BlackGayLivesMatter, BlackTransLivesMatter and BlackDifferentlyAbledLivesMatter, all of which were eventually countered by #alllivesmatter.[66] With #policelivesmatter the NYPD assimilated victim politics for its own purposes. The stance of victim was brought to an extreme with the 'Je suis chien' campaign. Echoing the 'Je suis Charlie' slogan that appeared after the *Charlie Hebdo* shootings in 2015, people posted social media hashtags to honour the death of a police dog during a raid in a Paris suburb. Even if all crimes are equally reprehensible, police crimes are more pernicious because they are made by the people who are entrusted with the responsibility to uphold the law. The structural unevenness of the politics that condition victim politics was noticed in the response to Michelle Obama's media meme of May 2014, in which she held up a cardboard sign that says #BringBackOurGirls, referring to the kidnapping of 276 girls by the Nigerian terrorist group Boko Haram in April 2014. The complexity of this conflict was soon revealed, as were the plans of the US government to make use of this campaign – in a manner not unlike the Kony 2012 campaign that went viral in social media – to increase its military presence and economic control of Africa, partly as a response to Chinese investment on the continent. The American state also supports the government in Nigeria, which indirectly supports and funds the Boko Haram. The meme was soon détourned by pranksters who had Obama's sign stating all manner of obscene, connoted messages, including 'Nothing will bring back the children murdered by my husband's drone strikes.'

The misdeeds of police officers and politicians do not outweigh the need for institutions to reproduce themselves: the logic of police and state violence is therefore inscribed, on the one hand, in the exceptional status of the state's monopoly on violence, and on the other, in the kinds of institutions these have become. The problem, however, is not only that the Law protects those in power, but that the Law itself is inconsistent, supported by myriad unstated rules that prescribe the ways in which it is acceptable to break them. The shared guilt that is involved in protecting legal and constitutional rights is mirrored in the protests against political inaction. This situation is overdetermined by the domination of the corporate state, the dysfunctional justice system, the prison-industrial complex, the military-industrial-entertainment complex and the class inequality that overwhelmingly affects the lives of the poor in the US and elsewhere.

The political system cannot be corrected solely by demands for democratic accountability. The current parliamentary-capitalist constraints must also be challenged. However, when this system is contested, either by civil disobedience or by acts of terrorism, governments and media respond by exploiting the fear and confusion of the public to build support for more authoritarian control. In this context, victim politics do not substitute for a conscious political project.[67] Building bridges between communities, civil rights groups as well as state and federal organisations does not adequately address questions of class inequality among women or blacks. According to the Endnotes collective, a new activist class of leaders now makes use of social media to avoid traditional organisational models. They tend to be college educated, relatively affluent, technically savvy, and get involved in activism as part of a career plan in the non-profit and non-governmental sector. Identification with victims is a matter of 'elective sympathy' and choice. Once in power, such leaders typically opt for better ways to police surplus populations. On the whole, capital seeks access to cheap labour and neoliberal capital is prepared to undermine collective bargaining and destroy social programmes in order to solve its fiscal crises.[68] Despite diminishing opportunities for the many, the visible signs of female and black mobility, for example, in Hollywood films and in government positions, help to build faith that the system works. On the other side of this, expressions of solidarity among the increasingly immiserated masses cannot be thought of as the solution to a political impasse. Victim politics are in some ways what Žižek describes as both 'defense-formations' that cover over the void of the 'failure to intervene effectively in the social crisis' and 'proof *a contrario* of the possibility of the authentic proletarian revolution.'[69]

Universal abstraction

It is necessary for progressive politics to find a civilisational route that does not rely on either the criminality of today's neoliberal state regimes or a citizenry of victims. Insofar as victim status becomes a kind of ontology, gender and race cannot be made to correspond with revolutionary class struggle. This is perhaps one of the reasons why Stephen Bannon, the former strategy advisor to Trump and former chairman of the 'alt-right' Breitbart News Network, said in a 2017 interview with *The American Prospect* that 'the longer [the Democrats] talk about identity politics, I got 'em. I want them to talk about racism every day. If the left is focused on race and identity, and we go with economic nationalism, we can crush the Democrats.'[70] According to Žižek, liberal multiculturalists do not fight against the bigotry of the right by addressing the class dimension – direct political struggle – but by repressing it further through calls for endless self-culpabilisation. One of the contradictions of the liberal left and its solution to the problem of incompatible ways of life is therefore an 'excessive sensitivity to the Other's pain and humiliation.'[71]

Such solidarity-through-guilt is the basis of Simon Critchley's notion of an 'ethics of commitment,' as developed in his 2007 book *Infinitely Demanding*.[72] Critchley calls on activists to reject nihilism in favour of 'ethical subjectivity.' Equating revolutionary vanguardism with nihilism and normative ethics, he proposes instead an infinitely demanding hetero-affectivity that he knows no subject can ever respond to fully, but that alters the sovereignty of autonomy in favour of the Other's demand. To protect from masochistic self-persecution by this superego ethics, Critchley appeals to the sense of humour as an alternative to the tragic-heroic paradigm. His 'ethics of discomfort' is proposed as an alternative to the economistic reductionism of Marxism and is defined instead as a Gramsci-influenced hegemonic contestation that is active rather than passive, and that is formed out of the shifting compositions of subaltern classes.

Capitalism of course can accommodate an ethics of hetero-affectivity. Žižek draws from this the pessimistic conclusion that today's left, anarchist or not, is unable to offer an alternative to global capitalism. If nothing new or revolutionary can emerge from capitalism's compulsive self-overcoming, then radical politics is left with the following options: 1) accept the ultimate triumph of capitalism and fight for social democratic emancipation within its rules; 2) accept this framework but resist it at the level of its interstices; 3) accept the futility of resistance and wait patiently for outbursts of violence that can shake the system; 4) defend what remains of the welfare state and withdraw into cultural studies; 5) limit the problems of capitalism to questions of technology and instrumental reason; 6) focus on everyday practices of subversion rather than tackle capitalism and state power; 7) shift from anti-capitalism to struggles for

hegemony as a process of discursive rearticulation; 8) shift the analysis of capitalism from Fordism to post-Fordist immaterial labour, thereby emphasising
the conflict between the relations and forces of production.[73] The repression
of class struggle and the lack of a radical left position results in the rise of the
multiplicity of 'new antagonisms,' which presume that cultural diversity is
co-extensive with economic equality.

Žižek's difference from Critchley is the view he takes from Lacan that the
superego is not a moral agency but an imperative. In contrast to discursive
anti-humanism, in which the subject is an effect of structures, the Lacanian
version of anti-humanism finds that the subject precedes subjectivisation and
is defined by the negativity of death drive rather than the supergo demands of
desire.[74] The Lacanian subject neither adapts to its environment nor co-evolves
with it. The subject is always in some way a failure of subjectivisation, as
Critchley seems to appreciate. However, if Critchley embraces failure, Žižek
opines that the subject is not equivalent to failure either. In other words, the
Lacanian ontology of the subject never coincides with the heteronomy of
practical reason, as is the case for instance in Jodi Dean's notions of the communist horizon and crowd communism.[75] Ethics and aesthetics thus function
as means to protect us from exposure to the Real.

Lacanian and Hegelian approaches have not only been misinterpreted by
Critchley; they are missed entirely in Nizan Shaked's book on *The Synthetic
Proposition* of conceptual art.[76] Making use of Mary Kelly's notion of the
synthetic proposition, which criticises the analytic presuppositions of certain
strands of conceptual art, Shaked gives an account of the ways that conceptualism made use of political subject matter, especially the kinds of identity
politics that were articulated in the 1970s in the practices of artists like Adrian
Piper, David Hammons, Hans Haacke and Martha Rosler, and more recently
in the work of Renée Green, Silvia Kolbowski, Daniel Joseph Martinez, Lorna
Simpson and Charles Gaines. Not unlike Critchley, Shaked celebrates the
kinds of practices that destabilise identity and the notion of a coherent speaking
subject – claims for art practice that are somewhat apposite after Freud and
Lacan. Her stated goal is to synthesise art and identity politics into larger
political coalitions of solidarity.[77] Also like Critchley, and like much postmodern theory, Shaked deceptively plays the notion of the universal against the
particular. Wishing to synthesise formal concerns with the politics of identity,
Shaked obviates several problems from the perspective of a theory of the avant
garde: the problem of negation and incommensurability in dialectics; questions
relating to hegemony and mediation by capital; the problem of the historicity
of class struggle, especially with regard to global petty-bourgeois ideology; the
neoliberal impasse and the rise of the far right.

Žižek's argument is not that identity formations do not define the subject
of the unconscious and the social order, but that the fluidity of identity is not

incompatible with neoliberal capitalism, as noticed for instance in the way that New York state law now recognises thirty different classifications for sexual identity. The future of politics cannot therefore be based in efforts to get rid of the male/female antagonism since subjectivity has no objective correlate. It is not a moot point, therefore, as Shaked suggests, that identity politics is not revolutionary.[78] Shaked tries to counter this argument by stating that identity politics cannot be accused of perpetuating oppression or of facilitating neoliberalisation. She argues, moreover, that Žižek is not averse to seeing his position as multiculturalist, arguing in his essay on 'Multiculturalism, or, the Cultural Logic of Multinational Capitalism' that he is against organic notions of community, the ideology of neoliberal capitalism, and leftist critical theorists who reject liberal multiculturalism at the same time as fundamentalist populism. What such critical theorists point to, Žižek argues, is the domain of the political and of active citizenship through ideological and political rearticulation. Shaked suggests that in this Žižek seems to be alluding to the cultural studies of Stuart Hall. However, Shaked leaves out of her discussion Žižek's argument that such critical leftists ignore how populism is a result of global capitalism. The victories of the remaining social democratic parties, like Labour in the UK, or the Democratic Party in the US, give the misleading impression that they represent an alternative to neoliberal rule, which can be ignored insofar as they stand for the rejection of parochialism in favour of enlightened liberal democracy, respect for human rights, women's rights, ethnic minorities, and so on.[79] Žižek's main point is that the effort to keep open the multicultural space of 'the political' operates against the background of global capitalism.

Žižek's question is not how to avoid populism, but 'how are we to reinvent political space in today's conditions of globalization?'[80] He writes: 'The politicization of the series of particular struggles that leaves intact the global process of Capital is clearly not sufficient.'[81] Žižek further argues that what we should reject is the 'post-ideological' opposition between universal and particular. Against the liberal centre and against post-politics, we should, he says, assert a leftist suspension of the ethical. One could possibly say the same thing with regard to aesthetics. One does not eliminate the level of neutrality and form but one takes sides in the name of the universality that one struggles for. The antagonism between universal and particular is therefore immanent to the universal itself, and today, to the conflict between the concrete universality of capital and the impossible demands of an abstract universality of democratic inclusion. The resulting politics is not one of recognition or of ethical subjectivity, but one of identification with the symptom as the point of exception. A further question Žižek asks is why is it that culture has become the privileged site for the reflexivity of political struggles?

The children of Gramsci and Pepsi

Making a case for the commitment of political artists, Shaked cites Bruce
Robbins, who argues that people today are seduced by the writings of authors
like Žižek, Badiou, Rancière, and Hardt and Negri, because revolution, as
opposed to the difficult work of reform, possesses an occult and messianic
mystique.[82] Such a statement would hardly come as a shock to those who work
in the field of Marxist political economy, for whom the study of the value
form and the movement of capital have never been considered uncomplicated,
especially not for any corresponding communist politics. This applies to the
work of the late Ellen Meiksins Wood, whose 1995 book *Democracy Against
Capitalism* has only become more pertinent with time.[83] Her premise is that
postmodernists' emphasis on contingency and hostility to totalising concepts
prevents them from thinking capitalism as a social system. Meiksins Wood
criticises not only the cultural studies shift from political economy to the study
of discourses, texts and identities, but also the kinds of deterministic Marxist
theory that are compatible with capitalist ideology. She calls on Marxists
to pursue the critique of political economy so as to better understand the
historicity and specificity of capitalism. This implies a rejection of structuralist
approaches to base and superstructure that would allow the economic to
be understood independently of the political. The Althusserian concepts of
overdetermination, relative autonomy and social formation are consequently
charged for replacing Stalinism's mechanical determinism with an uneasy synthesis, which serves to repudiate causation, replacing class struggle with the
autonomy of culture, and material production with discursive construction.
Despite the limitations of Meiksins Woods' emphasis on historicity, from a
Lacanian view at least, she is correct to criticise the academic left for returning
to metaphysical materialism. The aspect of her work that is particularly useful
here is her discussion of the concept of civil society and of identity issues in
relation to the renewal of revolutionary consciousness.

At the outset, Meiksins Wood does not consider Marxism to be a technique or a method, but rather a 'mode of analysis' that is focused on the
kind of political action that could change society and capitalist ideology. The
organised left has by and large reduced political struggles to economic issues,
thereby protecting capitalist relations of production as the form of society in
the abstract. By focusing on the mode of production and therefore on the
question of labour, Marxism distinguishes capitalism from earlier modes of
production, from the slave economies of ancient Greece and the serfdom of
the feudal middle ages. The notion of citizenship in modern liberal democracies destroys social relations of bondage in favour of property relations. The
sovereign individual is formally free and equal to all others in the political
community. Propertyless wage labourers become interchangeable units of

labour power, abstracted from identity and traditional communal customs. Modern citizenship therefore devalues the political sphere in favour of the economic domain but allows for freedom from communal repression. Formal political equality coexists with class inequality, she argues, and so the notion of democratic citizenship is inherently anti-democratic.[84] The balance of power in favour of the propertied oligarchy and against the popular power of citizens is embodied in democratic and 'representative' institutions. In the case of US federalism, the inclusive and universalistic concept of 'we the people' is indifferent to particularisms and tempers revolutionary culture with the notion of active citizenship. Democracy does not represent the balance of class power but is defined as rule by the wealthy. Civil rights therefore represent access on the part of marginalised and excluded groups, women and former slaves, into this 'passive' and 'inconsequential' definition of citizenship as the safeguard of constitutional rights.

Capitalist democracy protects economic power from politics, bringing an end to history. The postmodern world can thus be conceived as a patchwork of multiple and shifting social relations, with class being the basis of only one of many kinds of struggle. What replaces class struggle, Meiksins Wood argues, is not identity politics but rather the concept of civil society, which, insofar as it 'embraces a wide range of emancipatory aspirations' transforms into 'a whole set of excuses for political retreat' and an 'alibi for capitalism.'[85] The concept of civil society understands society as distinct from state authority and is historically indistinguishable from property relations. Like democracy, the concept of civil society is premised on the distinction between the economy and the political. Whereas in the seventeenth century, civil society was identified with the state, Hegel associated civil society with bourgeois society and the modern economy, allowing for the emergence of the particularities of individual autonomy and the universality of the state. Marx, in turn, emphasised the particularistic class interests that define both the state and civil society. Gramsci, for his part, defined civil society as a terrain of class struggle against capitalism. The use of Gramsci on the left today tempers his anti-capitalism with a sense of the danger of state power, defined as repressive and ideological apparatuses, especially in the case of communist regimes. New social movements, Meiksins Wood says, strengthen non-governmental institutions but weaken resistance to capitalism. The kinds of agonism that are promoted by radical democrats on the basis of formal democracy ignore capitalist economic relations as the determining feature of social relations. Pluralism and diversity are instead made the primary good of a free society, along with ecology and anti-war movements.

Meiksins Wood's argument is not that class is the only principle of social stratification. The issue is how 'non-class identities' function within the totalising logic of capitalism. Radical democrats who claim Gramsci as an influence do not deny the effects of capitalist relations. The question is rather how the concept of civil society becomes specific to capitalism and whether capitalism is better than socialism in securing civil liberties and autonomy. Grassroots power from below, she argues, preserves market coercion. Consumer choice secures the interests of billionaires. In advanced capitalist countries, the question of oppression has become focused on gender relations, homophobia, racism and anti-immigrant sentiment. Meiksins Wood contends that these forms of oppression are the essence of civil society under capitalism.[86] She identifies three common features that condition the success of intersectionist radical democracy, cultural studies and postmodern difference politics: the probing of subjectivity beyond political opinion; the presumption that universal principles cannot accommodate the plurality of identities and lifestyles; and the view that the totality is not capitalist but heterogeneous. The left is consequently expected to build power on the basis of difference and the multiplicity of forms of oppression, replacing vanguard politics and aesthetics with a polity that treats all oppressions equally. Not unlike Žižek, Meiksins Wood argues that the theories and politics of difference cannot incorporate class difference because class relations, unlike race and gender relations, are inherently antagonistic. Moreover, class equality means abolishing class relations and capitalism. The abolition of gender inequality would not and could not abolish the system of gender difference. Her conclusion is that unlike class struggle, sexual and racial equality are not incompatible with capitalism: 'The first point about capitalism is that it is uniquely indifferent to the social identities of the people it exploits.'[87] Capitalism has a positive tendency to dilute identities based on race and gender, in part, because it seeks to integrate people into labour and consumer markets. As well, capitalism subjects all forms of identity to *its* requirements; it can reinforce inequalities, just as it did in the case of slavery and the bourgeois ideology of separate spheres, but it can also promote racial and gender equality in the interests of capitalist exploitation. Differences are immaterial to the notions of abstract labour and human capital. Capitalism can therefore co-opt or discard particulars at will. Although it has no specific structural necessity for racial or sexual oppression, capitalism seeks to divert identity struggles away from anti-capitalist struggles. Capitalism, in short, cannot promote class equality.[88]

Without denying the moral claims that are the basis of the current trends within identity struggles, the politicisation of culture emphasises how it is that class struggle has a more universal reach and greater capacity to advance emancipatory interests and enhance autonomy beyond the requirements of the market. People were rightfully incensed by the 2017 Pepsi commercial in which celebrity model Kendall Jenner reperformed an iconic photograph from a 2016 Black Lives Matter rally in Baton Rouge protesting the shooting death of Alton Sterling. The question for vanguard art and politics is how to combat the drift of democracy towards the extreme right and rethink the postmodernist rejection of universality and class struggle. After the wave of protests associated with anti-globalisation and the movements of the squares we have been beset with right-wing counter-movements associated either with political parties of the far right or with 'countercultural' versions that are referred to as the 'alt-right.' As cultural theorist Angela Nagle has proposed in *Kill All Normies*, the cultural conservatives who fought on the wrong side in the culture wars from the 1960s to 1990s have been replaced by a 'vanguard,' as she calls it, of teenage gamers, anime lovers, *South Park* conservatives, anti-feminist pranksters and Internet trolls.[89] According to Nagle, the love of transgression for its own sake makes it difficult to distinguish people who are in it for 'the lulz' from the political correctness of campus politics. This combination of an anti-establishment attitude with political confusion helps to account for the success of politicians like Donald Trump and Marine Le Pen.

If we want to redeem what is worthwhile in liberal democracy we need to establish a new left based on international agreements, the control of banks, ecological standards, workers' rights, universal health care and protections for minorities. For this to happen, Žižek argues, today's left-liberals need to focus on their own shortcomings, much as liberal capitalism did when it was faced with the challenge of the international socialist movement.[90] In the case of the US, his argument is best exemplified by Thomas Frank, whose 2016 book, *Listen, Liberal*, argues that despite economic recovery and productivity advances since the banking crisis of 2008, none of the benefits have gone to ordinary people whose lives have no chance of improvement at the level of wages and income.[91] The reversal of the American trajectory of prosperity cannot be compensated by more work and effort. Meanwhile, the owners of Walmart now possess more wealth than the bottom forty percent of the US population. Frank's argument is that the Democratic Party has for the last four decades abandoned the middle (read: working) class in favour of capital and the interests of billionaires.

Not unlike Nagle, Frank points out how civil rights achievements like gay marriage, the removal of Confederate flags and the election of a black president have all received the support of corporate America and were celebrated by the mainstream press as Democratic triumphs, gaining with such policies the support of young people, minorities and middle-class professionals. How is it then that the same Democrats have lost control of the White House, Congress and the Supreme Court? Is it appropriate to blame the white working class, as some do, especially when most of Trump's support comes from the white middle class? Frank's thesis is that as courageous as they may be on diversity issues, the Democrats do not believe they can do anything when it comes to economic democracy. Beyond the hierarchy of economic power, the Democrats are equally afflicted, he argues, by the hierarchy of merit, learning and status, replacing the 'party of the people' with a party that is obsessed with professional status and the values of the well-graduated 'creative class' who monopolise knowledge. He argues that the Democrats have ceased to be concerned with the interests of working people and have dedicated themselves to the concerns of the upper-middle-class meritocracy.

The conundrum of the postmodern left is made succinct in the official portraits of the former US President and First Lady. Kehinde Wiley's portrait of Barack Obama has him seated in a chair in front of a wall of green foliage from which emerge blue Kenyan irises, Hawaiian jasmine and Chicago chrysanthemums. Amy Sherald's painting shows Michelle Obama wearing a dress with what seems to be an avant-garde or Bauhaus-style design. Not only does the designer of the dress, Michelle Smith, associate the cotton poplin that the dress is made from with 'workers' clothes,' but the Spring 2017 Milly collection it was selected from by Michelle Obama is dedicated to human rights, racial equality and LGBT equality. The patterns are not avant-garde, however, but are inspired by early twentieth-century African-American Gee's Bend quilts. The 'flatness' of Sherald's painting, if one recalls T.J. Clark's discussion of Édouard Manet's *Olympia*, and the starkness of the 'wallpaper' background in Wiley's work, if one thinks of Žižek's discussion of Jacques-Louis David's *The Death of Marat*, allow us to consider the question of ontological incompleteness in the anamorphic shift between identity and class issues. If we can relate the work of David and Manet to histories of class struggle, Wiley's and Sherald's work would seem to have more to do with civil rights. As with Manet's Olympia, the Obamas' blackness is in their embodiment and not in the flowers and designer accessories.[92] In Žižek's analysis, the negativity in question relates rather to the inability to represent the People in the figure of the political leader. In this case, the gap between the People and their representatives is filled in with neoliberal celebrations of African-American success. This gap is redoubled by the transposition of the failure of Obama to do anything of political significance into the ornamentations of postmodern painting. Universality has been converted into a substance that fills the ideological void in the dominant social order.[93] What such post-political representation asserts, to put things in Lacanian terms, is that there it no ideological relationship. The Obamas' blackness matters as neoliberal post-politics.

The function of art in today's biocapitalism is to produce and reproduce the new forms of non-ideological struggle within the ranks of the global petty-bourgeois class, with its competing activist and professional factions. Any hope of social change, in my view, will come from a break with this order of intra-class conflict and will involve the totality of the social space and consciousness. Such a break will inevitably encompass vanguard functions. An art that breaks with the conditions that call it into being is not an art of transgression but rather an art of negation.[94] Art's reflection on its conditions of possibility includes the critiques of capitalist democracy that have come from the artistic and political avant gardes. This encompasses a critique of the categories of art and politics.

How can we explain the radical deficit in the realm of art production and reception? Boris Groys argues that the postmodern aesthetic sensibility rejects everything universal and therefore rejects communism. The postmodernist politics of cultural diversity, in contrast, is a taste formed by the market and is a taste for the market.[95] Consequently, the universal projects of enlightenment and communism are no longer possible because they are commercially inoperative. Yet, Groys argues, only universal politics and universal culture are truly democratic. Similarly, Badiou argues that all genuine events in the realm of art and politics are universal because a truth is the same for everyone.[96] His philosophy is one means to solve the riddle of the multiplicity of identity and the universality of events in art and politics. Further, his notion of the ontology of being, which was developed in accordance with Lacanian psychoanalysis and set theory, is that subjectivity is infinitely multiple. Beyond this level of ontology, and beyond the relativism of bodies and languages, humans sometimes act in fidelity with events that create new situations in the realms of art and politics. The consequent universalism that he describes is not concerned to make peace with the status quo but neither is it given to nihilistic destruction. Access to such universality requires a step beyond the victimary definition of humanity that is the basis for much of today's culturalised politics. A truth procedure, such as the event of communism or the avant garde hypothesis, deploys the genericity of the true, producing sameness, equality and emancipation. Fascism, in contrast, produces difference: the master race as absolute difference. The universality of communism therefore has its key concepts: class struggle, revolution and the abolition of private property. This does not imply conformity nor the elimination of autonomy. Rather, the avant garde's end of art and end of politics provides the conceptualisation of a universality beyond today's biocapitalism. No solidarity without autonomy. No autonomy without solidarity.

Notes

Introduction: a thousand contradictions

1 See David Harvey, *A Brief History of Neoliberalism* (Oxford: Oxford University Press, 2005). The Group of Eight (G7), the World Trade Organisation and the International Monetary Fund are the main institutions that represent the member nations whose concentrated wealth and military power have been the basis for neoliberal policy since the 1970s. Neoliberal reforms to trade and public policy seek to deregulate and devolve government responsibility for welfare state provisions against poverty, sickness, unemployment and ecology. The privatisation and corporatisation of the public sector has consistently met with protests on the part of citizens' movements and anti-globalisation activists since the late 1990s. Governments since then, along with the support of corporate-owned media, have increasingly sought to criminalise protest.

2 Alain Badiou, *The Return of History: Times of Riots and Uprising*, trans. Gregory Elliott (London: Verso, [2011] 2012); Slavoj Žižek, *The Year of Dreaming Dangerously* (London: Verso, 2012). See also my essay, 'Culture and the Communist Turn,' in Marc James Léger, *The Neoliberal Undead: Essays on Contemporary Art and Politics* (Winchester: Zero Books, 2013), 17–37.

3 Peter Bürger, 'Avant-Garde and Neo-Avant-Garde: An Attempt to Answer Certain Critics of *Theory of the Avant-Garde*,' *New Literary History* 41:4 (2010): 695–715.

4 Marc James Léger, 'Welcome to the Cultural Goodwill Revolution: On Class Composition in the Age of Classless Struggle,' in *Brave New Avant Garde: Essays on Contemporary Art and Politics* (Winchester: Zero Books, 2012), 82–99.

5 Pierre Bourdieu, *Distinction: A Social Critique of the Judgement of Taste*, trans. Richard Nice (Cambridge: Harvard University Press, [1979] 1984), 318–71.

6 See Peter Bürger, *Theory of the Avant Garde*, trans. Michael Shaw (Minneapolis: University of Minnesota Press, [1974] 1984).

7 Gregory Sholette, *Dark Matter: Art and Politics in the Age of Enterprise Culture* (London: Pluto Press, 2011); Richard Florida, *The Rise of the Creative Class, And How It's Transforming Work, Leisure, Community and Everyday Life* (New York: Basic Books, 2002).

8 The French sociologist Bernard Lahire has provided empirical data on the predominance today of the petty-bourgeois habitus across different class factions. See Tony Bennett, '*Habitus Clivé*: Aesthetics and Politics in the Work of Pierre Bourdieu,' *New Literary History* 38:1 (2007): 201–28.

9 John Roberts, *Revolutionary Time and the Avant-Garde* (London: Verso, 2015), 1.

10 See Jacques Rancière, *Aesthetics and Its Discontents*, trans. Steven Corcoran (Cambridge: Polity Press, [2004] 2009).

11 Marc James Léger, 'Introduction: 1 + 1 + a,' in *Drive in Cinema: Essays on Film, Theory and Politics* (Bristol: Intellect, 2015), 1–25. Gene Ray, 'On the Conditions of Anti-Capitalist Art: Radical Cultural Practices and the Capitalist Art System,' *Transversal* (November 2006), http://eipcp.net/transversal/0303/ray/en. For a critique of class reductionism and an analysis of the distinction between class being, class standpoint, class attitude and class culture, see Alain Badiou, 'The Autonomy of the Aesthetic Process (1965),' *Radical Philosophy* 178 (March/April 2013): 32–9.

12 Slavoj Žižek, 'It's the Political Economy, Stupid!' in Gregory Sholette and Oliver Ressler, eds. *It's the Political Economy, Stupid: The Global Financial Crisis in Art and Theory* (London: Pluto Press, 2013), 17.

13 See BAVO, eds. *Cultural Activism Today: The Art of Over-Identification* (Rotterdam: Episode Publishers, 2007) and 'The Spectre of the Avant-Garde,' *Andere Sinema* 176 (2006): 24–40. See also Marc James Léger, 'The Subject Supposed to Over-Identify: BAVO and the Fundamental Fantasy of a Cultural Avant Garde,' in *Brave New Avant Garde*, 100–26.

14 Léger, *Brave New Avant Garde*, 76.

15 The four discourses are defined in Jacques Lacan, *The Seminar of Jacques Lacan, Book XVII: The Other Side of Psychoanalysis, 1969–1970*, trans. Russell Grigg, ed. Jacques Alain Miller (New York: W.W. Norton, [1991] 2007). For Lacan's discussion of the Discourse of the Capitalist, see Jacques Lacan, *Lacan in Italia, 1953–1978 / Lacan en Italie, 1953–1978* (Milan: La Salamandra, 1978).

16 Dave Beech, *Art and Value: Art's Economic Exceptionalism in Classical, Neoclassical and Marxist Economics* (Leiden: Brill, 2015).

17 Franco 'Bifo' Berardi, *The Uprising: On Poetry and Finance* (Los Angeles: Semiotext(e), 2012), 9.

18 Cited in Marc James Léger, 'Bruce Barber and the Parenthetical Suspension of Performance,' in Bruce Barber, *Performance, [Performance] and Performers*, ed. Marc James Léger (Toronto: YYZ BOOKS, 2007), 19.

19 Gene Ray, 'Culture Industry and the Administration of Terror,' in Gerald Raunig, Gene Ray and Ulf Wuggenig, eds. *Critique of Creativity: Precarity, Subjectivity and Resistance in the 'Creative Industries'* (London: MayFly Books, 2011), 167–79.

20 See Lee Baxandall, ed. *Marx and Engels on Literature and Art* (New York: International General, 1974).

21 Georg Lukács, 'Narrate or Describe?' in *Writer and Critic, and Other Essays* (London: Merlin Press, 1970), 110–48.

22 Roberts, *Revolutionary Time and the Avant-Garde*, 1–3.

23 See George Yúdice, *The Expediency of Culture: The Uses of Culture in the Global Era* (Durham: Duke University Press, 2004).

24 Roberts, *Revolutionary Time and the Avant-Garde*, 32–3.
25 Alain Badiou, *The Communist Hypothesis*, trans. David Macey and Steve Corcoran (London: Verso, 2010), 40.
26 Slavoj Žižek, *Trouble in Paradise: From the End of History to the End of Capitalism* (London: Allen Lane, 2014), 181.
27 Alain Badiou, 'Does the Notion of Activist Art Still Have Meaning?' Lecture presented at the Miguel Abreu Gallery, New York City, 13 October 2010, www.lacan.com/thevideos/10132010.html.
28 Badiou, 'Does the Notion of Activist Art Still Have Meaning?'
29 Badiou, 'Does the Notion of Activist Art Still Have Meaning?'
30 Badiou, 'Does the Notion of Activist Art Still Have Meaning?'
31 Žižek, *Trouble in Paradise*, 185.
32 Žižek, *Trouble in Paradise*, 185.
33 Slavoj Žižek, 'Answers Without Questions,' in Žižek, ed. *The Idea of Communism 2: The New York Conference* (London: Verso, 2013), 203.
34 Žižek, 'Answers Without Questions,' 204.
35 Jacques Derrida, *Spectres of Marx: The State of Debt, the Work of Mourning, and the New International*, trans. Peggy Kamuf (New York: Routledge, [1993] 1994).
36 Francis Fukuyama, *The End of History and the Last Man* (New York: Avon Books, 1992), xv.
37 Derrida, *Spectres of Marx*, 80.
38 Derrida, *Spectres of Marx*, 81–3.
39 Derrida, *Spectres of Marx*, 37–9.
40 The United States Government Accountability Office announced in a January 2013 report to Congress that the 2008 financial crisis cost the US economy more than $22 trillion. See www.gao.gov/assets/660/651322.pdf. See also the website Costs of War, http://costsofwar.org, and 'Marx popular amid credit crunch,' *BBC News* (20 October 2008), http://news.bbc.co.uk/2/hi/7679758.stm.
41 David Harvey, *The Enigma of Capital and the Crises of Capitalism* (Oxford: Oxford University Press, 2010), 90. See also Sam Gindin and Leo Panitch, *The Making of Global Capitalism: The Political Economy of American Empire* (London: Verso, 2013).
42 Harvey, *The Enigma of Capital*, 93.
43 István Mészáros, *The Challenge and Burden of Historical Time: Socialism in the Twenty-First Century* (New York: Monthly Review Press, 2008), 82.
44 Bruno Bosteels, 'The Leftist Hypothesis: Communism in the Age of Terror,' in Costas Douzinas and Slavoj Žižek, eds. *The Idea of Communism* (London, Verso, 2010), 35.
45 Bosteels, 'The Leftist Hypothesis,' 38. See also Nancy Fraser, 'Against Anarchism,' *Public Seminar* 1:1 (9 October 2013), www.publicseminar.org/2013/10/against-anarchism/#.VL6lNsaJndn.
46 Bosteels, 'The Leftist Hypothesis,' 41.
47 Michael Hardt, 'The Common in Communism,' in Žižek and Douzinas, eds. *The Idea of Communism*, 143–4.
48 Étienne Balibar, 'Communism as Commitment, Imagination, and Politics,' in Žižek, ed. *The Idea of Communism 2*, 14.

49 Balibar, 'Communism as Commitment, Imagination, and Politics,' 15.

50 Balibar, 'Communism as Commitment, Imagination, and Politics,' 22.

51 Balibar, 'Communism as Commitment, Imagination, and Politics,' 23.

52 Balibar, 'Communism as Commitment, Imagination, and Politics,' 26.

53 Slavoj Žižek, 'The Barred One,' in *Incontinence of the Void: Economico-Philosophical Spandrels* (Cambridge: The MIT Press, 2017), 11–50.

54 On the depoliticisation of Gramsci by the new left and by cultural studies, see Perry Anderson, 'The Antinomies of Antonio Gramsci,' *New Left Review* (November/December 1976): 5–78, and Timothy Brennan, *Wars of Position: The Cultural Politics of the Left and Right* (New York: Columbia University Press, 2006).

55 Chantal Mouffe, 'Artistic Activism and Antagonistic Spaces,' *Art & Resesarch: A Journal of Ideas, Contexts and Methods* 1:2 (Summer 2007): 1–5.

56 Ernesto Laclau and Chantal Mouffe, *Hegemony and Socialist Strategy: Towards a Radical Democratic Politics* (London: Verso, 1985).

57 See Slavoj Žižek, 'Over the Coalition Rainbow!' in *The Parallax View* (Cambridge: The MIT Press, 2006), 359–65, and Žižek, 'Multiculturalism, or, the Cultural Logic of Multinational Capitalism,' in *The Universal Exception: Selected Writings, Volume Two*, eds. Rex Butler and Scott Stephens (London: Continuum, 2006), 151–82. See also Walter Benn Michaels, *The Trouble with Diversity: How We Learned to Love Identity and Ignore Inequality* (New York: Holt, 2006).

58 Slavoj Žižek, 'Class Struggle or Postmodernism? Yes Please!' in Judith Butler, Ernesto Laclau and Slavoj Žižek, *Contingency, Hegemony, Universality: Contemporary Dialogues on the Left* (London: Verso, 2000), 90–135. See also Žižek, 'The "Dream Work" of Political Representation,' in *The Year of Dreaming Dangerously*, 19–34.

59 Slavoj Žižek, *The Courage of Hopelessness: Chronicles of a Year of Acting Dangerously* (London: Allen Lane, 2017) eBook, 121–2.

60 Slavoj Žižek, *Absolute Recoil: Towards a New Foundation of Dialectical Materialism* (London: Verso, 2014), 218.

61 On the question of an avant-garde 'traversal of the fantasy,' see Slavoj Žižek, 'The Enlightenment in Laibach' (1994), in Zdenka Badovinac, Eda Čufer and Anthony Gardner, eds. *NSK from* Kapital *to* Capital: *Neue Slowenische Kunst, An Event of the Final Decade of Yugoslavia* (Ljubljana/Cambridge: Moderna galerija/The MIT Press, 2016), 205–12. See also Jacques Lacan, *The Seminar of Jacques Lacan, Book XIV: The Logic of Phantasy, 1966–1967*, trans. Cormac Gallagher, www.lacaninireland.com/web/wp-content/uploads/2010/06/14-Logic-of-Phantasy-Complete.pdf, 9.

1 Alter-globalisation, revolutionary movement and the state mode of production

1 For a study of the anti-democratic ideology of neoliberal institutions, see Maude Barlow and Tony Clarke, *Global Showdown: How the New Activists Are Fighting Global Corporate Rule* (Toronto: Stoddart, 2001).

2 Nicos Hadjinicolaou, 'On the Ideology of Avant-Gardism,' *Praxis* 6 (1982): 38–70.

3 Raymond Williams, *Politics of Modernism: Against the New Conformists* (London: Verso, [1987] 1989), 35.

4 See for example, David Byrne, *Bicycle Diaries* (New York: Viking, 2009) and Morrissey, *Autobiography* (London: Penguin Classics, 2013).

5 Mikkel Bolt Rasmussen, 'A Note on Socially Engaged Art Criticism,' *FIELD: A Journal of Socially-Engaged Art Criticism* 6 (Winter 2017), http://field-journal.com/issue-6/a-note-on-socially-engaged-art-criticism.

6 Oliver Ressler, 'A World Where Many Worlds Fit. A section on the counter-globalisation movement for the Taipei Biennial 2008, curated by Oliver Ressler,' *Transversal* (3 September 2008), http://transform.eipcp.net/correspond ence/1220542296#redir; Oliver Ressler, 'Curator's Statement,' in *A World Where Many Worlds Fit/Un monde dans lequel plusieurs mondes s'inscrivent* (Lennoxville: Foreman Art Gallery/Bishop's University, 2010), 3–4.

7 Michael Hardt and Antonio Negri, *Empire* (Cambridge: Harvard University Press, 2000). For an introduction to Italian workerism, also known as autonomist Marxism and post-operaismo, see Sylvère Lotringer and Christian Marazzi, eds. *Autonomia: Post-Political Politics* (Los Angeles: Semiotext(e), 2007).

8 Isabell Lorey, 'Governmentality and Self-Precarization: On the Normalization of Cultural Producers,' *Transversal* (January 2006), www.eipcp.net/transversal/1106/lorey/en.

9 See Emma Dowling, Rodrigo Nunes and Ben Trott's introduction to the special issue on 'Immaterial and Affective Labour' in *Ephemera: Theory & Politics in Organization* 7:1 (February 2007), www.ephemerajournal.org/sites/default/files/pdfs/7–1ephemera-feb07.pdf.

10 See Paolo Virno, *A Grammar of the Multitude: For an Analysis of Contemporary Forms of Life* (New York: Semiotext(e), 2004).

11 See the chapter on 'Co-operation' in Karl Marx, *Capital: A Critique of Political Economy, Volume 1*, trans. Ben Fowkes (London: Penguin, [1976] 1990), 450. See also Maurizio Lazzarato, 'Construction of Cultural Labour Market,' *Framework* 6 (January 2007), http://eipcp.net/policies/cci/lazzarato/en.

12 Luc Boltanski and Eve Chiapello, *The New Spirit of Capitalism*, trans. Gregory Elliot (London: Verso, [1999] 2006).

13 Slavoj Žižek, *First as Tragedy, Then as Farce* (London: Verso, 2009), 51–5.

14 See the *Left Views* interview with Hugo Blanco in 'Hugo Blanco: Indigenous People are the Vanguard of the Fight to Save the Earth,' *Socialist Voice* (13 October 2009), www.socialistvoice.ca/?p=701.

15 Slavoj Žižek, *The Plague of Fantasies* (London: Verso, 1997), 28.

16 See 'John Holloway and Alex Callinicos Debate,' organised by the British Socialist Workers Party, *YouTube* (7 July 2008), www.youtube.com/watch?v=2liVjkA 30T4. See also Costas Douzinas and Slavoj Žižek, eds. *The Idea of Communism* (London: Verso, 2010); Slavoj Žižek, ed. *The Idea of Communism 2: The New York Conference* (London: Verso, 2013); Alex Taek-Gwang and Slavoj Žižek, eds. *The Idea of Communism 3: The Seoul Conference* (London: Verso, 2016).

17 See issue 1 of the journal *Turbulence*, 'What would it mean to win?,' http://turbulence.org.uk/turbulence-1/.

18 See Brian Holmes, 'Answer to *Chto Delat* Questionnaire,' (2008), formerly available at http://brianholmes.wordpress.com.

19 Karl Marx, *Grundrisse: Foundations of the Critique of Political Economy (Rough Draft)*, trans. Martin Nicolaus (London: Penguin, 1973), 101.

20 See Alain Badiou, 'One, Multiple, Multiplicities,' in *Theoretical Writings*, trans. and eds. Ray Brassier and Alberto Toscano (London: Continuum, 2006), 68–82.

21 Two of the editors of *Turbulence*, Tadzio Mueller and Michal Osterweil, are featured in *What Would It Mean to Win?* Also featured are John Holloway and Emma Dowling.

22 Obama cited in Dave Zirin, 'Chicago 2016? Why Obama's wrong to boost Olympic bid,' *rabble.ca* (1 October 2009), http://rabble.ca/news/2009/10/chicago-2016-why-obamas-wrong-boost-olympic-bid.

23 John Jordan, 'Diary of a Revolution,' *The Guardian* (25 January 2003), www.guardian.co.uk/world/2003/jan/25/argentina.weekend71.

24 Franco 'Bifo' Berardi, 'Ten Years After Seattle, One Strategy, Better Two, For the Movement Against War and Capitalism,' *InterActivist Info Exchange* (29 August 2009), http://interactivist.autonomedia.org/node/12965.

25 John Holloway, *Change the World Without Taking Power: The Meaning of Revolution Today* (London: Pluto Press, 2002).

26 See Alex Callinicos, 'How Do We Deal with the State?' in the *Revista Herramienta* online debate concerning Holloway's *Change the World Without Taking Power* (no date), www.herramienta.com.ar/debate-sobre-cambiar-el-mundo/presentacion-e-indice-de-articulos.

27 See Slavoj Žižek, 'Revolutionary Terror from Robespierre to Mao,' in *In Defense of Lost Causes* (London: Verso, 2008), 183.

28 Luke Stobart, 'Letter from Venezuela,' *Socialist Review* (October 2009), http://socialistreview.org.uk/340/letter-venezuela.

29 Henri Lefebvre, *De L'État, Tome II: De Hegel à Mao par Staline (La théorie 'marxiste' de l'état)* (Paris: 10/18, 1976).

30 Lefebvre, *De L'État, Tome II*, 129.

31 Henri Lefebvre, *Hegel – Marx – Nietzsche, ou le royaume des ombres* (Tournai: Casterman, 1975).

2 A brief history of Occupy Wall Street

1 See Ben Davis, 'How a Canadian Culture Magazine Helped Spark Occupy Wall Street,' *Blouin Artinfo* (5 October 2011), www.artinfo.com/news/story/38786/how-a-canadian-culture-magazine-helped-spark-occupy-wall-street?comment_sort=desc. See also Rod Mickleburgh, 'Anti-Wall Street protests take off thanks to a Canadian idea,' *The Globe and Mail* (4 October 2011), www.theglobeandmail.com/news/world/americas/anti-wall-street-protests-take-off-thanks-to-a-canadian-idea/article2191364/.

2 See 'Occupywallstreet Orientation Guide,' *Adbusters* (16 September 2011), www.adbusters.org/action/occupywallstreet/occupywallstreet-orientation-guide/.

3 Paul B. Farrell, 'America's Tahrir Moment: Does the American Left have the guts to pull this off?' *Adbusters Blog* (6 September 2011), www.adbusters.org/action/occupywallstreet/does-the-american-left-have-the-guts-to-pull-this-off/. See also

Joseph E. Stiglitz, 'Of the 1%, by the 1%, for the 1%,' *Vanity Fair* (May 2011), www.vanityfair.com/news/2011/05/top-one-percent-201105.

4 Nathan Schneider, 'Who Will Occupy Wall Street on September 17?' *Huffington Post Blog* (14 September 2011), www.huffingtonpost.com/nathan-schneider/occu py-wall-street_b_961374.html.

5 Henri Lefebvre, *The Critique of Everyday Life, Volume 1*, trans. John Moore (London: Verso, [1947] 1991); Ben Highmore, *Everyday Life and Cultural Theory: An Introduction* (London: Routledge, 2002).

6 Jodi Dean, 'Claiming Division, Naming a Wrong,' *Theory & Event* (online supplement) 14:4 (2011), http://muse.jhu.edu/journals/theory_and_event/v014/14.4S. dean01.html.

7 Dean, 'Claiming Division, Naming a Wrong.'

8 Sarah Ledesman, 'Romney Compares Occupy Wall Street to "Class Warfare",' *Neon Tommy* (4 October 2011), www.neontommy.com/news/2011/10/romney-compares-occupy-wall-street-class-warfare.

9 Jeremy White, 'Occupy Wall Street Denounced by Cain, Romney as "Class Warfare",' *International Business Times* (6 October 2011), www.ibtimes.com/occu py-wall-street-denounced-cain-romney-class-warfare-321650.

10 Nicos Poulantzas, *Les classes sociales dans le capitalisme aujourd'hui* (Paris: Editions du Seuil, 1974), 195.

11 Leon Trotsky cited in William Keach, 'Introduction,' in Trotsky, *Literature and Revolution* (Chicago: Haymarket Books, 2005), 11.

12 See Bill Van Auken, 'Mayor Bloomberg backs mass arrests of Wall Street protesters,' *World Socialist Web Site* (4 October 2011), www.wsws.org/articles/2011/ oct2011/wall-o04.shtml. See also 'Michael Bloomberg: Occupy Wall Street is trying to destroy jobs,' *The Guardian* (8 October 2011), www.guardian.co.uk/ world/2011/oct/08/bloomberg-occupy-wall-street-jobs.

13 Warren Buffett, 'Stop Coddling the Super-Rich,' *The New York Times* (14 August 2011), www.nytimes.com/2011/08/15/opinion/stop-coddling-the-super-rich. html.

14 Paul Ryan cited in Dominic Rushe, 'Obama's millionaire tax is class war, say Republicans,' *The Guardian* (18 September 2011), www.guardian.co.uk/world/20 11/sep/18/obama-millionaire-tax-war.

15 Paul Ryan cited in Rushe, 'Obama's millionaire tax is class war, say Republicans.'

16 John Boehner cited in Rushe, 'Obama's millionaire tax is class war, say Republicans.'

17 Stephanie Condon, 'Obama: "This is not class warfare – It's math",' *CBS News* (19 September 2011), www.cbsnews.com/news/obama-this-is-not-class-warfare-its-math/.

18 'Bipartisan corporatism: "Class War!",' *The Economist* (20 September 2011), www. economist.com/blogs/democracyinamerica/2011/09/bipartisan-corporatism-2.

19 Patrick Martin, 'The many frauds of the "Buffett Rule",' *World Socialist Web Site* (26 September 2011), www.wsws.org/articles/2011/sep2011/pers-s26.shtml. See also '20 Facts About U.S. Inequality that Everyone Should Know,' Stanford

Center for Poverty & Inequality (2011), https://inequality.stanford.edu/publica tions/20-facts-about-us-inequality-everyone-should-know.

20 Stiglitz, 'Of the 1%, by the 1%, for the 1%.'

21 Stiglitz, 'Of the 1%, by the 1%, for the 1%.'

22 David Harvey, 'Their Crisis, Our Challenge,' *Red Pepper* (March 2009), www. redpepper.org.uk/Their-crisis-our-challenge/.

23 Harvey, 'Their Crisis, Our Challenge.'

24 James Laxer, 'Income and wealth inequality: An underlying cause of the crash,' *rabble. ca* (23 December 2009), http://rabble.ca/blogs/bloggers/james-laxer/2009/12/ income-and-wealth-inequality-underlying-cause-crash.

25 Thomas Frank, *Listen, Liberal, or, What Ever Happened to the Party of the People?* (New York: Metropolitan Books, 2016).

26 David Graeber cited in Karen McVeigh, 'Wall Street protesters: over-educated, under-employed and angry,' *The Guardian News Blog* (19 September 2011), www. theguardian.com/world/2011/sep/19/wall-street-protesters-angry.

27 'David Graeber: The Debt of the American Poor Should Be Forgiven,' *Democracy Now* (19 September 2011), www.democracynow.org/2011/9/19/david_grae ber_the_debt_of_the. See also David Graeber, *Debt: The First 500 Years* (New York: Melville House, 2011).

28 See for example, Ari Lipsitz and Rebecca Nathanson, 'Is This What Democracy Looks Like? Observing the Launch of Occupy Wall Street,' *The Village Voice* (19 September 2011), www.villagevoice.com/2011/09/19/is-this-what-democracy- looks-like-observing-the-launch-of-occupy-wall-street/.

29 Kalle Lasn cited in Michael Saba, 'Wall Street protesters inspired by Arab Spring movement,' *CNN* (17 September 2011), www.commondreams.org/headline/ 2011/09/17–1.

30 Kalle Lasn cited in Ilana Greene, 'Invading Wall Street: Who Did It?' *Forbes* (19 September 2011), www.forbes.com/sites/ilanagreene/2011/09/19/invading- wall-street-who-did-it/.

31 Micah White cited in Jenny Uechi, 'Adbusters' "Occupy Wall Street" modeled on Egypt protests,' *The Vancouver Observer* (19 September 2011), www.vancouver observer.com/blogs/world/2011/09/19/adbusters-occupy-wall-street-modeled- egypt-protests.

32 Some of these included: www.meetup.com/USDaysOfRage, www.occupywall street.org, wearethe99percent.tumblr.com and http://anonops.blogspot.com. For commentary, see D.E. Wittkower, 'Wall Street Protests: Will the Revolution Be Tweeted?' *The Wall Street Journal* (19 September 2011), http://blogs.wsj.com/ speakeasy/2011/09/19/wall-street-protests-will-the-revolution-be-tweeted/.

33 Noam Chomsky cited in Velcrow Ripper, 'The revolution will be tweeted,' *rabble.ca* (26 September 2011), http://rabble.ca/blogs/bloggers/velcrow-rip per/2011/09/revolution-will-be-tweeted.

34 Michael Moore cited in Velcrow Ripper, 'The revolution will be tweeted.'

35 'Michael Moore: "Occupy Wall Street will only get bigger",' *rabble.ca* (28 September 2011), http://rabble.ca/rabbletv/program-guide/2011/09/best-net/ michael-moore-occupy-wall-street-will-only-get-bigger.

36 ' "Something Has Started": Michael Moore on the Occupy Wall St. Protests That Could Spark a Movement,' *Democracy Now* (28 September 2011), www.democra cynow.org/2011/9/28/something_has_started_michael_moore_on.

37 'Cornel West on Occupy Wall Street: It's the Making of a U.S. Autumn Responding to the Arab Spring,' *Democracy Now* (29 September 2011), www.dem ocracynow.org/blog/2011/9/29/cornel_west_on_occupy_wall_street_its_the_ makings_of_a_us_autumn_responding_to_the_arab_spring.

38 Suzy Khimm, 'Congressional Democrats embrace Occupy Wall Street,' *The Washington Post – Wonkblog* (5 October 2011), www.washingtonpost. com/blogs/ezra-klein/post/congressional-democrats-embrace-occupy-wall- street/2011/10/05/gIQAEvNIOL_blog.html.

39 See Andy Kroll, 'Video: Obama: Occupy Wall St. "Expresses the Frustrations the American People Feel",' *Mother Jones* (6 October 2011), http://motherjones.com/ mojo/2011/10/obama-biden-occupy-wall-street.

40 Naomi Klein, 'Naomi Klein speaks at Occupy Wall Street,' *rabble.ca* (7 October 2011), http://rabble.ca/columnists/2011/10/naomi-klein-speaks-occupy-wall-str eet.

41 Slavoj Žižek's speech at OWS, http://muse.jhu.edu/journals/theory_and_event/ v014/14.4S.zizek.html.

42 Mark Read, 'Mic Check! Notes on How the Mo(ve)ment talks and learns from itself during the American Autumn,' *Journal of Aesthetics and Protest* (October 2011), http://joaap.org/webspecials/read.html.

43 Barbara Adams, 'Notes from the Periphery,' *Journal of Aesthetics and Protest* (October 2011), http://joaap.org/webspecials/Adams_periphery.html.

44 See McKenzie Wark's distinction between 'drum circle' ambiences and 'chanters' in 'Zuccotti Park, a psychogeography,' *Verso Books Blog* (6 October 2011), www. versobooks.com/blogs/735.

45 Aidan Rowe, 'Politics Averted: Thoughts on the "Occupy X" Movement,' *Workers Solidarity Movement* (12 October 2011), www.wsm.ie/c/politics-avert ed-occupy-movement.

46 Rowe, 'Politics Averted.'

47 Immanuel Wallerstein, 'Occupy Wall Street is the most important political hap- pening in America since 1968,' *Verso Books Blog* (18 October 2011), www.verso books.com/blogs/752.

48 Joseph Kishore, 'Amidst police crackdowns, widespread public support for Occupy movement,' *World Socialist Web Site* (27 October 2011), www.wsws.org/arti cles/2011/oct2011/occu-o27.shtml.

49 Patrick Martin, 'A day of international action against Wall Street,' *World Socialist Web Site* (17 October 2011), www.wsws.org/articles/2011/oct2011/pers-o17. shtml.

50 On this subject, see Manissa Maharawal, 'Standing Up,' in Astra Taylor and Keith Gessen, eds. *Occupy! Scenes from Occupied America* (London: Verso, 2011), 34–40.

51 'Occupying Washington Square Park With Angela Davis,' *Seismologik* (1 November 2011), formerly available at www.seismologik.com.

52 See Slavoj Žižek, 'A Leftist Plea for Eurocentrism,' in *The Universal Exception: Selected*

Writings, Volume Two, eds. Rex Butler and Scott Stephens (London: Continuum, 2006), 183–208. See also Žižek, 'Tolerance as an Ideological Category,' *Critical Inquiry* 34 (Summer 2008): 660–82.

53 See Oskar Negt and Alexander Kluge, 'On the Dialectic Between the Bourgeois and the Proletarian Public Sphere,' in *Public Sphere and Experience: Toward an Analysis of the Bourgeois and Proletarian Public Sphere*, trans. Peter Labanyi et al. (Minneapolis: University of Minnesota Press, [1972] 1993), 54–95.

54 Slavoj Žižek, 'Multiculturalism, or, the Cultural Logic of Multinational Capitalism,' in *The Universal Exception*, 171.

55 Slavoj Žižek, *The Parallax View* (Cambridge: The MIT Press, 2006), 361.

56 Ken Knabb, 'The Awakening in America,' *InterActivist Info Exchange* (16 October 2011), http://interactivist.autonomedia.org/node/32866.

57 Franco 'Bifo' Berardi and Geert Lovink, 'A Call to the Army of Love and to the Army of Software,' *InterActivist Info Exchange* (12 October 2011), http://interactivist.autonomedia.org/node/32852.

58 Michael Hardt and Antonio Negri, 'The Fight for "Real Democracy" at the Heart of Occupy Wall Street,' *Foreign Affairs* (11 October 2011), www.foreignaffairs.com/articles/136399/michael-hardt-and-antonio-negri/the-fight-for-real-democracy-at-the-heart-of-occupy-wall-street.

59 Hardt and Negri, 'The Fight for "Real Democracy" at the Heart of Occupy Wall Street.'

60 Slavoj Žižek, *In Defense of Lost Causes* (London: Verso, 2008), 342.

61 Žižek, *In Defense of Lost Causes*, 343.

62 See Slavoj Žižek, 'Thinking the Occupation.' Lecture delivered at St. Mark's Bookshop, NYC, 26 October 2011, https://cdn.shopify.com/s/files/1/0069/6232/files/SlavojZizek_St.Marks_102711.pdf.

63 See J. Nicole Jones, 'Six Questions for Slavoj Žižek,' *Harper's* (11 November 2011), http://harpers.org/archive/2011/11/hbc-90008306.

64 Yates McKee, *Strike Art: Contemporary Art and the Post-Occupy Condition* (London: Verso, 2016), 5, 17.

3 Vanguardia

1 Brian Holmes, 'Extradisciplinary Investigations: Toward a New Critique of Institutions,' in *Escape the Overcode: Activist Art in the Control Society* (Eindhoven, Neth.: Van Abbemuseum, 2009), 98–109.

2 Renato Poggioli, *The Theory of the Avant-Garde*, trans. Gerald Fitzgerald (Cambridge: Harvard University Press, [1962] 1968), 53.

3 Martin Jay, *Marxism and Totality: The Adventures of a Concept from Lukács to Habermas* (Berkeley: University of California Press, 1984), 10.

4 Maurizio Lazzarato, 'Construction of Cultural Labour Market,' *Transversal* (November 2006), http://eipcp.net/policies/cci/lazzarato/en.

5 Siegfried Kracauer, *The Salaried Masses: Duty and Distraction in Weimar Germany*, trans. Quintin Hoare (London: Verso, [1930] 1998); C. Wright Mills, *White Collar: The American Middle Class* (New York: Oxford University Press, 1953).

6 John Roberts, *Revolutionary Time and the Avant-Garde* (London: Verso, 2015), 23.

7 Tiqqun, *Preliminary Materials for a Theory of the Young-Girl* (Los Angeles: Semiotext(e), 2012).

8 Jen Delos Reyes, 'What Are We Trying to Get Ahead of? Leaving the Idea of the Avant-Garde Behind,' *Blade of Grass* (24 September 2014), www.abladeofgrass.org/growing-dialogue/growing-dialogue-the-latest-thing-2-2/.

9 Lane Relyea, *Your Everyday Art World* (Cambridge: The MIT Press, 2013).

10 Eric Cazdyn and Imre Szeman, *After Globalization* (Oxford: Wiley-Blackwell, 2011).

11 Gene Ray, 'Toward a Critical Art Theory,' in Marc James Léger, ed. *The Idea of the Avant Garde – And What It Means Today* (Manchester: Manchester University Press, 2014), 135. Ray has more recently questioned the limits of critical theory as a means to resist domination. See Ray, 'Writing the Ecocide-Genocide Knot: Indigenous Knowledge and Critical Theory in the Endgame,' *documenta 14* (2017), www.documenta14.de/en/south/895_writing_the_ecocide_genocide_knot_indigenous_knowledge_and_critical_theory_in_the_endgame.

12 Gerald Raunig, *Art and Revolution: Transversal Activism in the Long Twentieth Century*, trans. Aileen Derieg (Los Angeles: Semiotext(e), 2007).

13 BAVO, eds. *Cultural Activism Today: The Art of Over-Identification* (Rotterdam: Episode Publishers, 2007).

14 Pierre Bourdieu, *Contre-feux: Propos pour servir à la résistance contre l'invasion néo-libérale* (Paris: Éditions Raisons d'agir, 1998), 119.

15 Slavoj Žižek, *The Parallax View* (Cambridge: The MIT Press, 2006).

16 Gregory Sholette, *Dark Matter: Art and Politics in the Age of Enterprise Culture* (London: Pluto Press, 2011).

17 Gregory Sholette and Oliver Ressler, eds. *It's the Political Economy, Stupid: The Global Financial Crisis in Art and Theory* (London: Pluto Press, 2013).

18 Gregory Sholette and Oliver Ressler, 'Unspeaking the Grammar of Finance,' in Sholette and Ressler, eds. *It's the Political Economy, Stupid*, 11.

19 John Roberts, 'The Political Economisation of Art,' in Sholette and Ressler, eds. *It's the Political Economy, Stupid*, 63.

20 Roberts, 'The Political Economisation of Art,' 64.

21 Grant Kester, *The One and the Many: Contemporary Collaborative Art in a Global Context* (Durham: Duke University Press, 2011).

22 Kester, *The One and the Many*, 9–10.

23 Kester, *The One and the Many*, 123.

24 Michel Foucault, 'Two Lectures,' in *Power/Knowledge: Selected Interviews and Other Writings, 1972–1977*, trans. Colin Gordon et al., ed. Colin Gordon (New York: Pantheon, 1980), 80.

25 Miwon Kwon, *One Place After Another: Site-Specific Art and Locational Identity* (Cambridge: The MIT Press, 2002), 152.

26 Grant Kester, *Conversation Pieces: Community + Communication in Modern Art* (Berkeley: University of California Press, 2004), 160.

27 Critical Art Ensemble, *Digital Resistance: Explorations in Tactical Media* (Brooklyn: Autonomedia, 2001), 24.

28 Critical Art Ensemble, *Disturbances* (London: Four Corners Books, 2012).

29 Critical Art Ensemble, *Disturbances*, 158.

30 Brian Holmes, 'Three Keys and No Exit: A Brief Introduction to Critical Art Ensemble,' in Critical Art Ensemble, *Disturbances*, 11–12.

31 See Nato Thompson and Gregory Sholette, eds. *The Interventionists: Users' Manual for the Creative Disruption of Everyday Life* (North Adams/Cambridge: MASS MoCA/The MIT Press, 2004); Nato Thompson, ed. *Living as Form: Socially Engaged Art from 1991–2011* (New York/Cambridge: Creative Time Books/The MIT Press, 2012).

32 Nato Thompson, *Seeing Power: Art and Activism in the 21st Century* (Brooklyn: Melville House, 2015).

33 Thompson, *Seeing Power*, 72.

34 Thompson, *Seeing Power*, 80.

35 Thompson, *Seeing Power*, 49.

36 Yates McKee, *Strike Art: Contemporary Art and the Post-Occupy Condition* (London: Verso, 2016).

37 McKee, *Strike Art*, 5–6.

38 McKee, *Strike Art*, 81, 156.

39 McKee, *Strike Art*, 238.

40 Mikkel Bolt Rasmussen, *Crisis to Insurrection: Notes on the Ongoing Collapse* (Brooklyn: Minor Compositions, 2015).

41 Rasmussen, *Crisis to Insurrection*, 58.

42 Mikkel Bolt Rasmussen, 'A Note on Socially Engaged Art Criticism,' *FIELD: A Journal of Socially Engaged Art Criticism* 6 (Winter 2017), http://field-journal.com/issue-6/a-note-on-socially-engaged-art-criticism.

43 Grant Kester cited in Rasmussen, 'A Note on Socially Engaged Art Criticism.'

44 Grant Kester, 'The Limitations of the Exculpatory Critique: A Response to Mikkel Bolt Rasmussen,' *FIELD: A Journal of Socially Engaged Art Criticism* 6 (Winter 2017), http://field-journal.com/issue-6/mikkel-bolt-rasmussen.

45 See Claire Bishop, *Artificial Hells: Participatory Art and the Politics of Spectatorship* (London: Verso, 2012).

46 Rebecca Gordon-Nesbitt, *To Defend the Revolution Is to Defend Culture: The Cultural Policy of the Cuban Revolution* (Oakland: PM Press, 2015).

47 On this subject, see Fredric Jameson, *An American Utopia: Dual Power and the Universal Army*, ed. Slavoj Žižek (London: Verso, 2016).

48 Rebecca Gordon-Nesbitt, 'Whose Side Are You On? Response to Coco Fusco ("The State of Detention: Performance, Politics, and the Cuban Public" (*e-flux*, 3 January 2015),' *Mute* (29 January 2015), www.metamute.org/community/your-posts/whose-side-are-you-response-to-coco-fusco-'-state-detention-performance-politics-and-cuban-public'-e-flux-0.

4 Psychoprotest: dérives of the Quebec Maple Spring

1 See Armine Yalnizyan, 'The Rise of Canada's Richest 1%,' *Canadian Centre for Policy Alternatives* (1 December 2010), www.policyalternatives.ca/publications/reports/rise-canadas-richest-1.

2 Avi Lewis, 'Students of the World Unite: Nothing to Lose But Everything.' Lecture presented at the University of Lethbridge, Alberta, 14 February 2006.
3 Student strikes against rising tuition have been particularly acute in Chile, Honduras, Columbia, Brazil, Italy, Greece and the UK. In the United States, the government now receives approximately $50 billion in annual revenue from student loan interest, an amount that is equal to the combined profits of the four largest US banks. For information on the significance of student debt to the Quebec struggle, see Andrew Gavin Marshall, 'Student Strikes, Debt Domination, and Class War in Canada,' *Andrewgavinmarshall Blog* (17 April 2012), http://andrewgavinmarshall. com/2012/04/17/student-strikes-debt-domination-and-class-war-in-canada-class-war-and-the-college-crisis-part-4/.
4 André Frappier, Richard Poulin and Bernard Rioux, *Le printemps des carrés rouges: Lutte étudiante, crise sociale, loi liberticide, démocratie de la rue* (Montréal: M éditeur, 2012), 14.
5 David Harvey, *Rebel Cities: From the Right to the City to the Urban Revolution* (London: Verso, 2012), xi.
6 Harvey, *Rebel Cities*, 131.
7 Leanne Serbulo, 'This Is Not a Riot: Minimization, Criminalization and the Policing of Protest in Seattle Prior to the 1999 WTO Shut-Down,' in Jeff Shantz, ed. *Protest and Punishment: The Repression of Resistance in the Era of Neoliberal Globalization* (Durham: Carolina Academic Press, 2012), 111.
8 Robert Dutrisac and Lisa-Marie Gervais, 'Le Sommet sur l'enseignement supérieur – Désaccord persistant sur les droits de scolarité, "Essayons de réfléchir au fait qu'il faut sortir de ce psychodrame," dit Pauline Marois,' *Le Devoir* (26 February 2013), www.ledevoir.com/politique/quebec/371878/desaccord-persistant-sur-les-droits-de-scolarite.
9 For a more detailed chronology than is provided here, see Cayley Sorochan, 'The Quebec Student Strike: A Chronology,' *Theory & Event* 15:3 special supplement (Summer 2012), http://muse.jhu.edu/issue/26026.
10 The details of Law 78 are available on the Quebec government website: www2. publicationsduquebec.gouv.qc.ca.
11 The municipal mask law P-6 is still in effect today and a similar law, titled Bill C-309, was passed by the federal Conservative government in June 2013.
12 See David Graeber, *The Democracy Project: A History, A Crisis, A Movement* (New York: Spiegel & Grau, 2013).
13 This is the case in Merlin Coverley's *Psychogeography* (Harpenden, Herts: Pocket Essentials, 2006).
14 Rémi Hess, *Henri Lefebvre et l'aventure du siècle* (Paris: A.M. Métailié, 1988), 45.
15 Henri Lefebvre, *Le temps des méprises* (Paris: Editions Stock, 1975), 48–50.
16 Henri Lefebvre, *The Critique of Everyday Life, Volume 1*, trans. John Moore (London: Verso, [1947] 1991), 110–12.
17 According to Ben Highmore, this approach to gradual and reformist revolution allowed Lefebvre to have a 'more amenable relationship with government agencies and institutions.' See Highmore, *Everyday Life and Cultural Theory: An Introduction* (London: Routledge, 2002), 142.

18 Lefebvre, *Critique of Everyday Life*, 92.
19 See Tom McDonough, 'Introduction: Ideology and the Situationist Utopia,' in McDonough, ed. *Guy Debord and the Situationist International* (Cambridge: The MIT Press, 2002), ix–x.
20 On the relation between Situationism and Surrealism, see Mikkel Bolt Rasmussen, 'The Situationist International, Surrealism, and the Difficult Fusion of Art and Politics,' *Oxford Art Journal* 27:3 (2004): 365–87.
21 Ivan Chtcheglov, 'Formula for a New Urbanism,' [1953] in Ken Knabb, ed. *Situationist International Anthology* (Berkeley: Bureau of Public Secrets, [1981] 1995), 1.
22 Chtcheglov, 'Formula for a New Urbanism,' 3.
23 Chtcheglov, 'Formula for a New Urbanism,' 3–4.
24 See *Potlatch* 1 and 2 (1954).
25 Guy Debord, 'Introduction to a Critique of Urban Geography' (originally published in the Belgian journal *Les Lèvres Nues* 6 (September 1955)), in Knabb, ed. *Situationist International Anthology*, 5–8.
26 Debord, 'Introduction to a Critique of Urban Geography,' 5.
27 Debord, 'Introduction to a Critique of Urban Geography,' 5.
28 Debord, 'Introduction to a Critique of Urban Geography,' 6.
29 Debord, 'Methods of Détournement' (originally published in *Les Lèvres Nues* 8 (May 1956)), in Knabb, ed. *Situationist International Anthology*, 9.
30 Guy Debord, 'Report on the Construction of Situations and on the International Situationist Tendency's Conditions of Organization and Action' (prepared for a conference in Italy in 1957), in Knabb, ed. *Situationist International Anthology*, 17–25
31 Debord, 'Report on the Construction of Situations,' 23. As the first significant example of psychogeographical research, see Abdelhafid Khatib, 'Essai de description psychogéographique des Halles,' *Internationale Situationniste* 2 (December 1958): 13–17. A three-day dérive is also mentioned as part of an S.I. exhibition at the Stedelijk Museum in Amsterdam in 1959 in 'Die Welt Als Labyrinth,' *Internationale Situationniste* 4 (June 1960): 5–7.
32 Debord, 'Preliminary Problems in Constructing a Situation' (published in the *Internationale Situationniste* 1 (June 1958)), in Knabb, ed. *Situationist International Anthology*, 44.
33 See Guy Debord, 'Theory of the Dérive' (written in 1956 and published in the *Internationale Situationniste* 2 (December 1958)), in Knabb, ed. *Situationist International Anthology*, 50–54. We prefer the term terrain in this case to Knabb's use of the word space.
34 Debord, 'Theory of the Dérive,' 50.
35 Ivan Chtcheglov, 'Letters from Afar,' *Internationale Situationniste* 9 (August 1964) cited by Knabb in an editor's note, in Knabb, ed. *Situationist International Anthology*, 373.
36 Thomas F. McDonough, 'Situationist Space,' *October* 67 (Winter 1994): 59–77. Michel de Certeau, *The Practice of Everyday Life*, trans. Steven Rendall (Berkeley: University of California Press, 1984).
37 According to della Porta and Diani, protests represent 'nonroutinized ways of

affecting political, social, and cultural processes.' Donatella della Porta and Mario Diani, eds. *Social Movements: An Introduction*, second edition (Oxford: Blackwell, 2006), 165.

38 The site http://manifencours.diametrick.com is now defunct.

39 Attila Kotányi, 'Gangland and Philosophy' (published in the *Internationale Situationniste* 4 (June 1960)), in Knabb, ed. *Situationist International Anthology*, 59.

40 The failure to pursue the social strike is described in detail by Frappier et al., *Le printemps des carrés rouges*.

41 See 'Nous sommes avenir: Manifeste de la CLASSE,' July 2012, http://issuu.com/ asse.solidarite/docs/manifeste_classe/3, also available in English as 'The CLASSE Manifesto: Share our future,' *rabble.ca* (12 July 2012), http://rabble.ca/blogs/blog gers/campus-notes/2012/07/classe-manifesto-share-our-future.

42 See David Harvey, *The Enigma of Capital and the Crises of Capitalism* (Oxford: Oxford University Press, 2010), 253–59. For an analysis of social movements in Québec, see Francis Dupuis-Déri, ed. *Québec en mouvements. Idées et pratiques militantes contemporaines* (Montréal: Lux, 2008).

43 Attila Kotányi and Raoul Vaneigem, 'Elementary Program of the Bureau of Unitary Urbanism,' in Knabb, ed. *Situationist International Anthology*, 65.

44 Richard Day, 'From Hegemony to Affinity: The Political Logic of the Newest Social Movements,' *Cultural Studies* 18:5 (September 2004): 716–48.

45 'The Beginning of an Era,' in Knabb, ed. *Situationist International Anthology*, 225–56 (originally from *Internationale Situationniste* 12 (September 1969). On the contributions of the Situationists to the events of May 68, see René Viénet, *Enragés et situationnistes dans le mouvement étudiant* (Paris: Gallimard, 1968).

46 Slavoj Žižek, 'Class Struggle or Postmodernism? Yes Please!' in Judith Butler, Ernesto Laclau and Slavoj Žižek, *Contingency, Hegemony, Universality: Contemporary Dialogues on the Left* (London: Verso, 2000), 98–9.

47 Bruno Bosteels, *Badiou and Politics* (Durham: Duke University Press, 2011), 25.

5 The unrealised extravagance of the avant garde: Test Dept and the subsumption of labour

1 Sarah Charalambides, 'Precarity as Activism,' *Mute* (1 July 2015), www.metamute. org/editorial/articles/precarity-activism. See also Isabell Lorey, *State of Insecurity: Government of the Precarious*, trans. Aileen Derieg (London: Verso, 2015).

2 Graham Cunnington, Angus Farquhar and Paul Jamrozy, *Test Dept: Total State Machine*, eds. Alexei Monroe and Peter Webb (Bristol: PC Press, 2015). Thanks to Alexei Monroe for making this book available to me for review and for his corrections to a draft version of this text.

3 Alexei Monroe, 'Introduction,' in *Test Dept: Total State Machine*, 2.

4 Monroe, 'Introduction,' 3.

5 Monroe, 'Introduction,' 5.

6 Test Dept, 'The Revolutionary Camera: A Conversation Between Paul Jamrozy and Brett Turnbull,' in *Test Dept: Total State Machine*, 24.

7 Michel Serres cited in Paul Jamrozy and Gray Cunnington, 'Nomadic Frequencies:

In Conversation with Russ MacDonald (Frequency Nomad) and (Agent) Simon Hyde,' in *Test Dept: Total State Machine*, 320.

8 Marek Kohn, 'The Industrial Revolution: The Social and Cultural Context in Britain from the 1970s to the Present Day,' in *Test Dept: Total State Machine*, 85.

9 Jordi Blanchar, 'From "New World Order" to "Crisis": Recalling a 1991 Test Dept Event in Brixton and the Evolution of the Social and Political Climate that Has Evolved Since that Time,' in *Test Dept: Total State Machine*, 328.

10 Peter Bürger cited in Monroe, 'Introduction,' 1.

11 See Jochen Schulte-Sasse, 'Theory of Modernism versus Theory of the Avant-Garde,' in Peter Bürger, *Theory of the Avant-Garde*, trans. Michael Shaw (Minneapolis: University of Minnesota Press [1974] 1984), vii–xxxix.

12 Schulte-Sasse, 'Theory of Modernism versus Theory of the Avant-Garde,' x.

13 Schulte-Sasse, 'Theory of Modernism versus Theory of the Avant-Garde,' xii.

14 Schulte-Sasse, 'Theory of Modernism versus Theory of the Avant-Garde,' xxiii.

15 Schulte-Sasse, 'Theory of Modernism versus Theory of the Avant-Garde,' xxxiii.

16 Schulte-Sasse, 'Theory of Modernism versus Theory of the Avant-Garde,' xxx.

17 Schulte-Sasse, 'Theory of Modernism versus Theory of the Avant-Garde,' xxxv.

18 See in *Test Dept: Total State Machine*: Angus Farquhar, 'Test Dept European Network Tour,' 94–113; Laibach, 'Anglo-Slowenische Freundschaft,' 118; and Alexei Monroe, 'Laibach/Test Dept Perspectives,' 118–19.

19 See Nathan Brown, 'The Distribution of the Insensible,' *Mute* (28 January 2014), www.metamute.org/editorial/articles/distribution-insensible.

20 David Graeber, 'On the Phenomenon of Bullshit Jobs,' *Strike!* (17 August 2013), http://strikemag.org/bullshit-jobs/.

21 Graeber, 'On the Phenomenon of Bullshit Jobs.' The Greeks voted sixty-one percent in favour of the No option in the referendum, giving the left-wing Syriza party a better standing to refuse the austerity policies of the Troika. The failure of Syriza to do so reflects Greece's status as one of the failing economies of the Eurozone since its exports are among the least complex and so cannot compete with the cheap labour of poor countries. Like Portugal and Spain, Greece is affected by the European Union's colonial relation to emerging nations. The Eurozone's solution to Greece's economic status is labour productivity and wage repression, which belies the notion of a post-industrial economy. See John Smith, *Imperialism in the Twenty-First Century: The Globalization of Production, Super-Exploitation, and the Crisis of Capitalism* (New York: Monthly Review Press, 2016), 88, 90, 183.

22 Charalambides, 'Precarity as Activism.'

23 Gregory Sholette, 'Delirium and Resistance after the Social Turn,' *FIELD: A Journal of Socially Engaged Art Criticism* 1 (Spring 2015): 97, http://field-journal.com/wp-content/uploads/2015/05/FIELD-01-FULL-ISSUE.pdf.

24 Gregory Sholette, *Delirium and Resistance: Activist Art and the Crisis of Capitalism*, ed. Kim Charnley (London: Pluto Press, 2017), 212.

25 Gregory Sholette, *Dark Matter: Art and Politics in the Age of Enterprise Culture* (London: Pluto Press, 2011).

26 See Marc James Léger, *Brave New Avant Garde: Essays on Contemporary Art and*

Politics (Winchester: Zero Books, 2012) and *The Neoliberal Undead: Essays on Contemporary Art and Politics* (Winchester: Zero Books, 2013).

27 Sholette, 'Delirium and Resistance after the Social Turn,' 106.
28 Sholette, 'Delirium and Resistance after the Social Turn,' 108.
29 Sholette, 'Delirium and Resistance after the Social Turn,' 128.
30 Sholette, 'Delirium and Resistance after the Social Turn,' 114.
31 See Slavoj Žižek, 'Slavoj Žižek on Greece: This is a chance for Europe to awaken,' *New Statesman* (6 July 2015), www.newstatesman.com/politics/2015/07/Slavoj-Zizek-greece-chance-europe-awaken.
32 Christian Fuchs, *Digital Labour and Karl Marx* (New York: Routledge, 2014), 286.
33 Paul Mason makes use of the labour theory of value as a basis for understanding its gradual disappearance in a more fully automated, 'zero marginal cost' world in *Postcapitalism: A Guide to Our Future* (London: Penguin Books, 2015).
34 According to the Endnotes collective, '[t]he only revolutionary perspective afforded by the current cycle of struggles is that of the self-negation of the proletariat and the concomitant abolition of capital through the communisation of relations between individuals.' See 'The History of Subsumption,' in *Endnotes* 2 (April 2010), https://endnotes.org.uk/issues/2/en/endnotes-the-history-of-subsumption. For both a use and a critique of communisation theory, see Nick Dyer-Witheford, *Cyber-Proletariat: Global Labour in the Digital Vortex* (London/Toronto: Pluto Press/ Between the Lines, 2015).

6 No strawman for the revolution

1 John Roberts, *Revolutionary Time and the Avant-Garde* (London: Verso, 2015).
2 See McKenzie Wark, 'Žižek and me,' *Public Seminar* (4 June 2015), www.public seminar.org/2015/06/zizek-and-me/#.WRYqGVLMyHo.
3 McKenzie Wark, *The Spectacle of Disintegration* (London: Verso, 2013), 2.
4 Wark, *The Spectacle of Disintegration*, 3. See also Mark Fisher, *Capitalist Realism: Is There No Alternative?* (Winchester: O Books, 2009).
5 See McKenzie Wark, 'Molecular Red: Theory for the Anthropocene (On Alexander Bogdanov and Kim Stanley Robinson),' *e-flux journal* 63 (March 2015), www.e-flux.com/journal/molecular-red-theory-for-the-anthropocene-on-alex ander-bogdanov-and-kim-stanley-robinson/. See also McKenzie Wark, *Molecular Red: Theory for the Anthropocene* (London: Verso, 2016).
6 Slavoj Žižek, 'Ecology Against Mother Nature: Slavoj Žižek on *Molecular Red*,' *Verso Blog* (26 May 2015), www.versobooks.com/blogs/2007-ecology-against-mother-nature-slavoj-zizek-on-molecular-red.
7 Wark, 'Molecular Red.' See Andreas Malm, 'The Anthropocene Myth,' *Jacobin* (30 March 2015), www.jacobinmag.com/2015/03/anthropocene-capitalism-cli mate-change/.
8 Slavoj Žižek, 'Censorship Today: Violence, or Ecology as a New Opium of the Masses.' Lecture presented at the Jack Tilton Gallery, 26–28 November 2007, www.lacan.com/zizecology1.htm. See also Slavoj Žižek, *Living in the End Times* (London: Verso, 2010). The activist journalist Naomi Klein mentions how

investors are aware of the fact that climate change threatens capitalist ideology. She adds that even climate scientists are reluctant to discuss the political and economic implications of their work. Her hope lies with what she calls a 'blockadia' of 'transnational conflict zones.' She adds that a bloackadia has no need for the rejection of institutionalisation, leadership and programmatic demands, a stance that she argues is a luxury that today's social movements can no longer afford. On the other hand she rejects the role of revolutionary vanguards, which she associates with violence and undemocratic practices. See Naomi Klein, *This Changes Everything: Capitalism vs. The Climate* (Toronto: Alfred A. Knopf, 2014), 294.

9 This in fact is the basis of the social ecology movement. See for example, Murray Bookchin, *Remaking Society* (Montreal: Black Rose Books, 1989).

10 Žižek, 'Censorship Today: Violence, or Ecology as a New Opium of the Masses.'

11 Žižek, 'Censorship Today: Violence, or Ecology as a New Opium of the Masses.'

12 Wark, 'Žižek and me.'

13 Slavoj Žižek, *For They Know Not What They Do: Enjoyment as a Political Factor* (London: Verso, [1991] 2008).

14 Alain Badiou, 'One, Multiple, Multiplicities,' in *Theoretical Writings*, trans. and eds. Ray Brassier and Alberto Toscano (London: Continuum, 2006), 70.

15 Wark, 'Žižek and me.'

16 Wark, 'Žižek and me.' A similarly unsubstantiated 'attack meme,' pretending to distinguish the 'queer' Bogdanov from the 'patriarchal' Lenin is put out by Wark in a different text, where he writes: 'We need another worldview ... that works as low theory extracted from worker and hacker practices, rather than a high theory trying to legislate about them from above. It is not hard to see here what infuriated Lenin about Bogdanov. For Bogdanov, both proletkult and tektology are experimental practices, of prototyping ideas and things, trying them out, modifying them. There's no correct and controlling über-theory, as there is in different ways in Lenin or Lukács. There is more of a hacker ethos here, rather than of the authoritarian worldview one still finds in a Lenin or a Lukács or in parody form in Žižek, where those in command of the correct dialectical materialist worldview are beyond question.' One is tempted to reply, according to the familiar discussion by Žižek, that the traditional father is less authoritarian than the permissive postmodern father, not to mention potentially also less capitalist. The free choice – for example between Bodganov and Lenin – that is presented by the postmodern father is not simply imposed, say, through a well-reasoned and substantiated argument, but one that we should simply prefer, thereby emphasising the logic of choice that is a feature of capitalist reflexivisation. Žižek elsewhere compares this logic to the hacker ethos and its basis in symbolic mandates. 'Believing there is a code to be cracked,' Žižek says, 'is of course much the same as believing in the existence of some Big Other: in every case what is wanted is an agent who will give structure to our chaotic lives.' In this case, the official choice is Bogdanov, but the big Other is Lenin. Consequently, 'Žižek and me' should rather be read as 'Žižek or me.' Those who might still prefer Žižek and his Lacanian reading of Hegel are guilty in advance of authoritarianism. See McKenzie Wark, 'Digital Labor and the Anthropocene,' *DIS Magazine* (no date, c.2015), formerly available

at http://dismagazine.com/disillusioned/discussion-disillusioned/70983/mcken-zie-wark-digital-labor-and-the-anthropocene/; and Slavoj Žižek, 'You May! Slavoj Žižek writes about the Post-Modern Superego,' *London Review of Books* 21:6 (18 March 1999), www.lrb.co.uk/v21/n06/slavoj-zizek/you-may.

17 Žižek, *For They Know Not What They Do*, 199.

18 Žižek, *For They Know Not What They Do*, 200.

19 McKenzie Wark, 'Notes on Žižek's Absolute Recoil,' *Public Seminar* (28 November 2014), http://www.publicseminar.org/2014/11/notes-on-zizeks-absolute-recoil/#.Va00-3iJndl.

20 Wark, 'Molecular Red.'

21 On this subject, see also Henri Lefebvre, *Dialectical Materialism*, trans. John Sturrock (Minneapolis: University of Minnesota Press, [1940] 2009).

22 Wark, 'Molecular Red.'

23 Sven Lütticken, 'Cultural Revolution: From Punk to the New Provotariat,' *New Left Review* 87 (May/June 2014): 115–31.

24 See Herbert Marcuse, 'Cultural Revolution' (c.1970), discussed in Lütticken, 'Cultural Revolution,' 117.

25 Lütticken, 'Cultural Revolution,' 119–22.

26 Lütticken, 'Cultural Revolution,' 122.

27 Lütticken, 'Cultural Revolution,' 125.

28 See Sven Lütticken, 'Secrecy and Publicity: Reactivating the Avant-Garde,' *New Left Review* 17 (September/October 2002): 129–48.

29 Yates McKee, 'DEBT: Occupy, Postcontemporary Art, and the Aesthetics of Debt Resistance,' *The South Atlantic Quarterly* 112:4 (Fall 2013): 784–803.

30 McKee, 'DEBT,' 798.

31 Despite this claim, Suzanne Lacy outlined some twenty years ago already a 'critical language for public art' and 'art activism' in her anthology on 'new genre public art.' See Suzanne Lacy, ed. *Mapping the Terrain: New Genre Public Art* (Seattle: Bay Press, 1995). For a genealogy of politicised art practice, focused also in this case on the notion of the art strike, see Gregory Sholette, 'Art Out of Joint: Artists' Activism Before and After the Cultural Turn' (2015), www.academia.edu/15087437/Art_Out_of_Joint_Artists_Activism_Before_and_After_the_Cultural_Turn.

32 McKee, 'DEBT,' 793.

33 McKee, 'DEBT,' 784.

34 McKee, 'DEBT,' 798.

35 For a critique of Occupy Wall Street along these lines, see Saroj Giri, 'Communism, Occupy and the Question of Form,' *Ephemera* 13:3 (2013): 577–601, www.ephemerajournal.org/contribution/communism-occupy-and-question-form.

36 McKee, 'DEBT,' 793.

37 Doug Henwood and Charlie Bertsch, 'I am a Fighting Atheist: Interview with Slavoj Žižek,' *Bad Subjects* (February 2002), http://bad.eserver.org/issues/2002/59/zizek.html. Žižek's focus on questions of leadership does not address other of kinds of problems as they were confronted for instance in the US in the 1960s by Students for a Democratic Society and the Student Nonviolent Coordinating Committee. These experiences also find that consensus-based organisation often

sacrifices decision-making ability, political effectiveness, general public interest, as well as lack of expertise due to rotating leadership. See Francesca Poletta, 'How Participatory Democracy Became White: Culture and Organizational Choice,' *FIELD: A Journal of Socially Engaged Art Criticism* 1 (Spring 2015): 215–54, http://field-journal.com/wp-content/uploads/2015/05/FIELD-01-Poletta-HowDem ocracyBecameWhite.pdf.

38 For a simplified version of his argument, see 'LUX PRIZE 2014: Slavoj Zizek on Class Enemy,' *YouTube* (5 December 2014), www.youtube.com/watch?v=gw _2LWULIdk.

39 Mikkel Bolt Rasmussen, 'Is the Revolution Going to Be Communist?' *Mute* (6 February 2015), www.metamute.org/community/your-posts/revolution-goi ng-to-be-communist.

40 On this see Slavoj Žižek, 'Afterword: Lenin's Choice,' in Žižek, ed. *Revolution at the Gates: A Selection of Writings from February to October 1917* (London: Verso, 2002), 167–336. What is interesting about this text is that it associates the party with the Discourse of the Analyst and the function of truth and so in this regard there is a slight shift of emphasis in Žižek's recent work. See also Slavoj Žižek, 'The Fetish of the Party,' in *The Universal Exception: Selected Writings, Volume Two*, eds. Rex Butler and Scott Stephens (London: Continuum, 2006), 67–93. Note also that in his accentuation of the psychoanalytic concept of drive, Žižek's theory of the subject comes closest to the Discourse of the Hysteric, whose goal it is to understand the cause of subjectivisation. In this Žižek distinguishes his work from Badiou's work, which relies on a distinction between democratic and dialectical materialism that Žižek tends to avoid. See Slavoj Žižek, 'Toward a Unified Theory of Four Discourses and Sexual Difference,' in *Incontinence of the Void: Economico-Philosophical Spandrels* (Cambridge: The MIT Press, 2017), 87–110.

41 Rasmussen, 'Is the Revolution Going to Be Communist?'

42 Rasmussen, 'Is the Revolution Going to Be Communist?'

43 Wark, 'Notes on Žižek's Absolute Recoil.'

44 See Slavoj Žižek, *Absolute Recoil: Towards a New Foundation of Dialectical Materialism* (London: Verso, 2014) and *Trouble in Paradise: From the End of History to the End of Capitalism* (London: Allen Lane, 2014).

45 Slavoj Žižek, 'Answers Without Questions,' in Žižek, ed. *The Idea of Communism 2: The New York Conference* (London: Verso, 2013), 177–205.

46 Žižek, 'Answers Without Questions,' 197.

47 Žižek, 'Answers Without Questions,' 198.

48 Žižek, 'Answers Without Questions,' 198.

49 Žižek, *Absolute Recoil*, 45.

50 Žižek, *Absolute Recoil*, 46.

51 Jacques Lacan, *The Seminar of Jacques Lacan, Book XVII: The Other Side of Psychoanalysis, 1969–1970*, trans. Russell Grigg, ed. Jacques-Alain Miller (New York: W.W. Norton, [1991] 2007).

52 Žižek, *Absolute Recoil*, 47.

53 Žižek, *Absolute Recoil*, 47.

7 Beyond socially enraged art

1 See for example, *Art After Modernism: Rethinking Representation*, ed. Brian Wallis (New York: The New Museum of Contemporary Art, 1984).

2 Jacques Rancière, *Aesthetics and Its Discontents*, trans. Steven Corcoran (Cambridge: Polity Press, [2004] 2009), 21. For an example of theory that reduces the social and political significance of art to that of heterodox singularities, see Nathalie Heinich, *Le Paradigme de l'art contemporain: Structures d'une révolution artistique* (Paris: Gallimard, 2014).

3 Ben Davis, *9.5 Theses on Art and Class* (Chicago: Haymarket Books, 2013).

4 Alain Badiou, 'Does the Notion of Activist Art Still Have a Meaning?' Lecture presented at the Miguel Abreu Gallery, New York City, 13 October 2010, www.lacan.com/thevideos/10132010.html.

5 Alain Badiou, *Handbook of Inaesthetics*, trans. Alberto Toscano (Stanford: Stanford University Press, [1998] 2005).

6 See Susan Buck-Morss, 'A Commonist Ethics,' in Slavoj Žižek, ed. *The Idea of Communism 2: The New York Conference* (London: Verso, 2013), 60–1.

7 Kim Charnley, 'Dissensus and the Politics of Collaborative Practice,' *Art and the Public Sphere* 1:1 (2011): 50.

8 Charnley, 'Dissensus and the Politics of Collaborative Practice,' 51. For Grant Kester's critique of vanguardism, see Kester, *The One and the Many: Contemporary Collaborative Art in a Global Context* (Durham: Duke University Press, 2011); 'The Sound of Breaking Glass, Part I: Spontaneity and Consciousness in Revolutionary Theory,' *e-flux journal* 30 (December 2011), www.e-flux.com/journal/the-sound-of-breaking-glass-part-i-spontaneity-and-consciousness-in-revolution ary-theory/; and 'The Sound of Breaking Glass, Part II: Agonism and the Taming of Dissent,' *e-flux journal* 31 (January 2012), www.e-flux.com/journal/the-sound-of-breaking-glass-part-ii-agonism-and-the-taming-of-dissent/.

9 Alain Badiou, 'True and false contradictions of the crisis,' *Verso Blog* (29 May 2015), www.versobooks.com/blogs/2014-alain-badiou-true-and-false-contradic tions-of-the-crisis.

10 Alain Badiou, 'La crise: vraie et fausse contradiction du monde contemporain,' *Libération* (13 April 2015), www.liberation.fr/politiques/2015/04/13/la-crise -vraie-et-fausse-contradiction-du-monde-contemporain_1240409.

11 Marc James Léger, 'Introduction: 1 + 1 + a,' in *Drive in Cinema: Essays on Film, Theory and Politics* (Bristol: Intellect, 2015), 1–25.

12 Gerald Raunig, 'On the Breach,' *Artforum* 46:9 (May 2008): 341–3.

13 Raunig, 'On the Breach,' 342.

14 Raunig, 'On the Breach,' 342.

15 Raunig, 'On the Breach,' 342. See Cornelius Castoriadis, Claude Lefort and Edgar Morin, *La Brèche. Premières Réflexions sur les événements* (Paris: Fayard, 1968). See also Situationist International, 'The Beginning of an Era,' in Ken Knabb, ed. *Situationist International Anthology* (Berkeley: Bureau of Public Secrets, [1981] 1995), 225–56, and René Viénet, *Enragés et situationnistes dans le mouvement étudiant* (Paris: Gallimard, 1968).

16 Raunig, 'On the Breach,' 342.
17 Sven Lütticken, 'Cultural Revolution: From Punk to the New Provotariat,' *New Left Review* 87 (May/June 2014): 115.
18 Bruno Bosteels, 'Post-Maoism: Badiou and Politics,' *Positions* 13:3 (Winter 2005): 586.
19 Bosteels, 'Post-Maoism,' 589.
20 Alain Badiou, 'The Cultural Revolution: The Last Revolution?' *Positions* 13:3 (Winter 2005): 481–514.
21 Badiou, 'The Cultural Revolution,' 489, 494.
22 Badiou, 'The Cultural Revolution,' 496.
23 Badiou, 'The Cultural Revolution,' 495.
24 Badiou, 'The Cultural Revolution,' 506.
25 See for example Badiou's axiom according to which '[t]he universality of truths rests on subjective forms that cannot be either individual or communitarian,' in 'Democratic Materialism and Materialist Dialectic,' in *Logics of Worlds: Being and Event, 2*, trans. Alberto Toscano (London: Continuum, [2006] 2009), 9.
26 See Andrea Fraser, *Museum Highlights: The Writings of Andrea Fraser*, ed. Alexander Alberro (Cambridge: The MIT Press, 2005) as well as Nato Thompson and Gregory Sholette, eds. *The Interventionists: Users' Manual for the Creative Disruption of Everyday Life* (North Adams/Cambridge: MASS MoCA/The MIT Press/, 2004).
27 The proceedings of the event from 9–11 January 2015, which took place at Hebbel am Ufer Theatre, Berlin, Germany, are available at https://vimeo.com/user36179003.
28 John Roberts, *Revolutionary Time and the Avant-Garde* (London: Verso, 2015), 35.
29 From the website http://www.artistorganisationsinternational.org.
30 Andrea Liu, 'Report: Artist Organisations International Conference,' *Afterimage* 42:6 (May/June 2015): 3. Against this notion that activists have moved or should move away from organisation, see Astra Taylor, 'Against Activism,' *The Baffler* 30 (March 2016), https://thebaffler.com/salvos/against-activism. See also Malcolm Gladwell, 'Small Change: Why the Revolution Will Not Be Tweeted,' *The New Yorker* (4 October 2010), www.newyorker.com/magazine/2010/10/04/small-change-malcolm-gladwell.
31 Slavoj Žižek, 'Afterword: Lenin's Choice,' in Žižek, ed. *Revolution at the Gates: A Selection of Writings from February to October 1917* (London: Verso, 2002), 167–336.
32 Brian Holmes, '1968 in the USA: Political Crisis in the Keynesian-Fordist Economy,' *Continental Drift* (2011), https://brianholmes.wordpress.com/2011/11/08/1968-in-the-usa/.
33 Holmes, '1968 in the USA.'
34 See Régis Debray, *Revolution in the Revolution? Armed Struggle and Political Struggle In Latin America*, trans. Bobbye Ortiz (New York: Grove Press, 1967), 37–8.
35 Debray, *Revolution in the Revolution?* 39.
36 Debray, *Revolution in the Revolution?* 80.
37 Debray, *Revolution in the Revolution?* 80.
38 See Raoul Vaneigem, *The Revolution of Everyday Life*, trans. Donald Nicholson-Smith

(London: Rebel Press, [1967] 2001) and Alain Badiou, *Philosophy for Militants*, trans. Bruno Bosteels (London: Verso, [2011] 2012).

39 Debray, *Revolution in the Revolution?* 112.

40 On this matter, see Rodrigo Nunes, 'Organisation of the Organisationless: Collective Action After Networks,' *Mute* (20 May 2014), www.metamute.org/editorial/books/organisation-organisationless-collective-action-after-networks.

41 Antonio Negri, 'Charlie Hebdo, fear and world war: two questions for Toni Negri,' *Verso Blog* (21 January 2015), translated from a January 23 article in *Dinamo Press*, www.versobooks.com/blogs/1814-charlie-hebdo-fear-and-world-war-two-questions-for-toni-negri. See also Jerome Roos, 'An Interview with Toni Negri: From the refusal of labour to the seizure of power,' *Roar* (January 2015), https://roarmag.org/essays/negri-interview-multitude-metropolis/.

42 Felicity Dale Scott, ' "Vanguards",' *e-flux journal* 64 (April 2015), www.e-flux.com/journal/vanguards/.

43 Scott, ' "Vanguards".'

44 For a critique of the ways in which Foucault's late work approaches neoliberal ideology, see Daniel Zamora and Michael C. Behrent, eds. *Foucault and Neoliberalism* (Cambridge: Polity Press, [2014] 2016).

45 David Graeber, *The Utopia of Rules: On Technology, Stupidity and the Secret Joys of Bureaucracy* (Brooklyn: Melville House, 2015), 65–6.

46 Graeber, *The Utopia of Rules*, 31, 82, 100.

47 Graeber, *The Utopia of Rules*, 97–100. Graeber approvingly refers to the work of the collective Crimethink, a group that David Harvey associates with Murray Bookchin's notion of 'lifestyle anarchism.' In contrast to Graeber, Harvey mentions that most of the mutual aid societies that gave rise to anarchism were based on shared commons, rules and codes of behaviour. See David Harvey, 'Listen, Anarchist!' *davidharvey.org* (10 June 2015), http://davidharvey.org/2015/06/listen-anarchist-by-david-harvey/#more-1871.

48 Kristin Ross, *Communal Luxury: The Political Imaginary of the Paris Commune* (London: Verso, 2015), 11–12.

8 The only game in town

1 Slavoj Žižek, 'Freud Lives!' *London Review of Books* 28:10 (25 May 2006), www.lrb.co.uk/v28/n10/slavoj-zizek/freud-lives.

2 Johanne Lamoureux, 'Avant Garde: A Historiography of a Critical Concept,' in Amelia Jones, ed. *A Companion to Contemporary Art Since 1945* (London: Blackwell, 2006), 207.

3 Henri Lefebvre, *Le temps des méprises* (Paris: Éditions Stock, 1975), 20.

4 Patricia Latour and Francis Combes, *Conversation avec Henri Lefebvre* (Paris: Messidor, 1991), 100–13.

5 Judith Butler, Ernesto Laclau and Slavoj Žižek, *Contingency, Hegemony, Universality: Contemporary Dialogues on the Left* (London: Verso, 2000).

6 Butler, Laclau and Žižek, *Contingency, Hegemony, Universality*, 22.

7 Butler, Laclau and Žižek, *Contingency, Hegemony, Universality*, 58–9.

8 Butler, Laclau and Žižek, *Contingency, Hegemony, Universality*, 94.

9 Butler, Laclau and Žižek, *Contingency, Hegemony, Universality*, 100–1. One could say that such a positivisation of capitalism is the premise and limitation of Wendy Brown's approach to neoliberalism as a process of marketisation and monetisation of social life. See Wendy Brown, *Undoing the Demos: Neoliberalism's Stealth Revolution* (Cambridge: The MIT Press, 2015). In relation to the limits of discourse theory for radical praxis, see Heiko Feldner and Fabio Vighi, *Žižek Beyond Foucault* (New York: Palgrave Macmillan, 2007).

10 G.W.F. Hegel, *The Science of Logic*, trans. George DiGiovanni (Cambridge: Cambridge University Press, [c.1812–1831] 2010).

11 See Biennale Arte, *All the World's Futures* (2015), www.labiennale.org/en/art/exhibition/56/.

12 Biennale Arte, *All the World's Futures*.

13 Biennale Arte, *All the World's Futures*.

14 Biennale Arte, *All the World's Futures*.

15 See 'Reading Capital,' the online courses on *Capital* volumes one and two taught by Harvey, http://davidharvey.org/reading-capital/. See also David Harvey, *Seventeen Contradictions and the End of Capitalism* (Oxford: Oxford University Press, 2014).

16 See Okwui Enwezor, 'Introduction: All the World's Futures.' Curatorial statement for *All the World's Futures* (2015), www.labiennale.org/en/art/exhibition/enwezor/.

17 From Michael Hardt and Antonio Negri's *Empire* (Cambridge: Harvard University Press, 2000), xii, cited in Okwui Enwezor, 'Reckoning with Empire,' *Artforum* 48:2 (October 2009): 175.

18 Enwezor cited in Charlotte Higgins, '*Das Kapital* at the Arsenale: How Okwui Enwezor Invited Marx to the Biennale,' *The Guardian* (7 May 2015), www.theguardian.com/artanddesign/2015/may/07/das-kapital-at-venice-biennale-okwui-enwezor-karl-marx.

19 Cited in Higgins, '*Das Kapital* at the Arsenale.'

20 Niles Williamson, 'Ukrainian Government Blacklists Russian Actors and Musicians,' *World Socialist Web Site* (10 August 2015), www.wsws.org/en/articles/2015/08/10/ukra-a10.html.

21 Cited in Higgins, '*Das Kapital* at the Arsenale.'

22 Cited in Higgins, '*Das Kapital* at the Arsenale.'

23 David Harvey, '"Listen, Anarchist!" A personal response to Simon Springer's "Why a Radical Geography Must be Anarchist",' *davidharvey.org* (10 June 2015), http://davidharvey.org/2015/06/listen-anarchist-by-david-harvey/#more-1871.

24 Rosalyn Deutsche, 'Men in Space,' *Artforum* 28:6 (February 1990): 23. See also Rosalyn Deutsche, *Evictions: Art and Spatial Politics* (Cambridge: The MIT Press, 1996).

25 Deutsche's work was influenced at this time by feminist psychoanalysis and by the radical democracy of Laclau and Mouffe. See Ernesto Laclau and Chantal Mouffe, *Hegemony and Socialist Strategy: Towards a Radical Democratic Politics* (London: Verso, 1985).

26 Henri Lefebvre, *The Production of Space*, trans. Donald Nicholson-Smith (Oxford: Blackwell, [1974] 1991).

27 Homi Bhabha cited in Rosalyn Deutsche, 'Surprising Geography,' *Annals of the Association of American Geographers* 85:1 (1995): 172.

28 Harvey, ' "Listen, Anarchist!" '

29 See Alain Badiou, *Philosophy and the Event (with Fabien Tarby)*, trans. Louise Burchill (Cambridge: Polity, [2010] 2013) and Slavoj Žižek, *Less Than Nothing: Hegel and the Shadow of Dialectical Materialism* (London: Verso, 2012).

30 Slavoj Žižek, 'The Prospects of Radical Politics Today,' in *The Universal Exception: Selected Writings, Volume Two*, eds. Rex Butler and Scott Stephens (London: Continuum, 2006), 239.

31 See Jela Krečič, ed. *The Final Countdown: Europe, Refugees and the Left* (Vienna: Wiener Festwochen, 2017). See also the NSK Biennale website, http://nsk-state-pavilion.org.

32 David Harvey, 'The Most Dangerous Book I Have Ever Written: A Commentary on *Seventeen Contradictions and the End of Capitalism*,' *davidharvey.org* (9 May 2015), http://davidharvey.org/2015/05/the-most-dangerous-book-i-have-ever-written-a-commentary-on-seventeen-contradictions-and-the-end-of-capitalism/#more-1866.

33 Harvey, *Seventeen Contradictions and the End of Capitalism*, 42.

34 See John Smith, *Imperialism in the Twenty-First Century: Globalization, Super-Exploitation, and Capitalism's Final Crisis* (New York: Monthly Review Press, 2016).

35 Some of these criticisms are due to the fact that the oratorio of *Das Kapital* was being directed by filmmaker Isaac Julien and that Julien's personal project in Venice at the Palazzo Malipiero-Barnabò was sponsored by the Rolls Royce Motor Car Company. See Natalie Hegert, 'Capital and Contradiction: Okwui Enwezor's 2015 Venice Biennale,' *The Huffington Post* (21 May 2015), www.huffingtonpost.com/mutualart/capital-and-contradiction_b_7347796.html.

36 Slavoj Žižek, 'The Courage of Hopelessness.' Lecture delivered at the Wiener Festwochen, 20 May 2017, uploaded by Ippolit Belinski on *YouTube* (23 May 2017), www.youtube.com/watch?v=aNlW3HnNqlk.

37 Malik Gaines, *Black Performance on the Outskirts of the Left: A History of the Impossible* (New York: New York University Press, 2017), 198.

38 Gaines, *Black Performance on the Outskirts of the Left*, 3.

39 For a critique of the ways in which postcolonial theory and subaltern studies have undermined leftist solidarity, see Vivek Chibber, *Postcolonial Theory and the Specter of Capital* (London: Verso, 2013).

40 Gaines, *Black Performance on the Outskirts of the Left*, 17.

41 Gaines, *Black Performance on the Outskirts of the Left*, 182.

42 Gaines, *Black Performance on the Outskirts of the Left*, 191.

43 Slavoj Žižek, *Iraq: The Borrowed Kettle* (London: Verso, 2004), 98.

44 Slavoj Žižek, 'The Lesson of Rancière,' in Jacques Rancière, *The Politics of Aesthetics: The Distribution of the Sensible*, trans. Gabriel Rockhill (London: Continuum, [2000] 2004), 71.

45 See Karl Heinz Roth, 'Global Crisis – Global Proletarianisation – Counter-Perspectives' (21 December 2008), www.wildcat-www.de/en/actual/e068roth_crisis.html.

46 Smith, *Imperialism in the Twenty-First Century*, 113.

47 A symptom of this is the 2016 decision in the US by the National Labor Relations Board that employers (like T-Mobile) could not oblige employees to be constantly positive at work.

48 Shane Mage, 'Response to Heinrich – In Defense of Marx's Law,' *Monthly Review* (1 December 2013), https://monthlyreview.org/commentary/response-heinrich-defense-marxs-law/.

49 Michael Heinrich, *An Introduction to the Three Volumes of Karl Marx's* Capital, trans. Alexander Locascio (New York: Monthly Review Press, [2004] 2012), 13–14, 79.

50 Slavoj Žižek, 'Multiculturalism, or, the Cultural Logic of Multinational Capitalism,' in *The Universal Exception*, 151–82.

51 Alain Badiou, *The Century*, trans. Alberto Toscano (Cambridge: Polity Press, 2007).

52 Alain Badiou, *Ethics: An Essay on the Understanding of Evil* (London: Verso, [1993] 2001), 16.

53 'London Critical Theory/Summer School 2015,' *YouTube* (14 July 2015), Part 1 of 4, www.youtube.com/watch?v=TaR7riRmgm4.

54 Hillary Clinton cited in Seth Ackerman, 'Yes, Racism Is Rooted in Economic Inequality,' *Jacobin* (29 July 2015), www.jacobinmag.com/2015/07/hillary-clinton-democatic-primary-sanders-netroots/.

55 Endnotes, 'Brown v. Ferguson,' *Endnotes* 4 (October 2015), https://endnotes.org.uk/issues/4/en/endnotes-brown-v-ferguson.

56 Richard Hofstadter, 'Reflections on Violence in the United States,' (1970) in *The Baffler* 28 (July 2015), http://thebaffler.com/ancestors/reflections-violence-united-states.

57 Slavoj Žižek, *The Courage of Hopelessness: Chronicles of a Year of Acting Dangerously* (London: Allen Lane, 2017) eBook, 320–1.

58 Anonymous, 'Things That Anarchists Say to Me in Private But Never Repeat Publicly,' *anarchistnews.org* (2 August 2015), www.anarchistnews.org/content/things-anarchists-say-me-private-never-repeat-publicly.

59 The comment in *Le Monde* was criticised by the otherwise neoliberal French Socialist Party for defending the right to inconvenience others as a kind of freedom of promiscuity. It also received criticism for its neoliberal stance, which could also be interpreted in relation to post-feminist politics. See for example, Françoise Vergès, 'La liberté d'importuniter est une ode à l'idéologie néolibérale,' *Le nouveau magazine littéraire* (17 January 2018), www.nouveau-magazine-litteraire.com/idees/liberte-dimportuner-est-une-ode-ideologie-neoliberale. See also the website https://metoomvmt.org.

60 Yohana Desta, 'Matt Damon Apologizes for His #MeToo Comments: "I Am Really Sorry",' *Vanity Fair* (16 January 2018), www.vanityfair.com/hollywood/2018/01/matt-damon-hollywood-reckoning-apology.

61 Ashifa Kassam, 'Margaret Atwood faces feminist backlash on social media over

#MeToo,' *The Guardian* (15 January 2018), www.theguardian.com/books/2018/jan/15/margaret-atwood-feminist-backlash-metoo.

62 See for example, Priscilla Frank, 'In the #MeToo Era, Do These Paintings Still Belong In a Museum?' *The Huffington Post* (14 December 2018), www.huffingtonpost.ca/entry/museums-me-too-sexual-harassment-art_us_5a2ae382e-4b0a290f0507176.

63 Meleka Ryzik and Brooks Barnes, 'Can Woody Allen Work in Hollywood Again?' *The New York Times* (28 January 2018), www.nytimes.com/2018/01/28/movies/woody-allen-dylan-farrow.html.

64 Coco Fusco, 'Censorship, Not the Painting, Must Go: On Dana Schutz's Image of Emmett Till,' *Hyperallergic* (27 March 2017), https://hyperallergic.com/368290/censorship-not-the-painting-must-go-on-dana-schutzs-image-of-emmett-till/. See also Coco Fusco's article on the sexual mores of the art world, 'How the Art Worlds, and Art Schools, Are Ripe for Sexual Abuse,' *Hyperallergic* (14 November 2017), https://hyperallergic.com/411343/how-the-art-world-and-art-schools-are-ripe-for-sexual-abuse/.

65 See Fabian T. Pfeffer, Sheldon Danziger and Robert F. Schoeni, *Wealth Levels, Wealth Inequality, and the Great Recession*, University of Michigan, 23 June 2014, http://web.stanford.edu/group/scspi/_media/working_papers/pfeffer-danziger-schoeni_wealth-levels.pdf.

66 On this see, George Yancy's interview with Judith Butler, 'What's Wrong With "All Lives Matter"?' *The New York Times* (12 January 2015), http://mobile.nytimes.com/blogs/opinionator/2015/01/12/whats-wrong-with-all-lives-matter/?_r=3&referrer. See also the website http://blacklivesmatter.com.

67 See 'Slavoj Žižek on the Charlie Hebdo massacre: Are the worst really full of passionate intensity?' *New Statesman* (10 January 2015), www.newstatesman.com/world-affairs/2015/01/slavoj-i-ek-charlie-hebdo-massacre-are-worst-really-full-passionate-intensity.

68 Endnotes, 'Brown v. Ferguson.'

69 Slavoj Žižek, *Welcome to the Desert of the Real: Five Essays on September 11 and Related Dates* (London: Verso, 2002), 23.

70 Robert Kuttner, 'Steve Bannon, Unrepentant,' *The American Prospect* (16 August 2017), http://prospect.org/article/steve-bannon-unrepentant.

71 Žižek, *The Courage of Hopelessness*, 360, 365, 380–1.

72 Simon Critchley, *Infinitely Demanding: Ethics of Commitment, Politics of Resistance* (London: Verso, [2007] 2008).

73 Slavoj Žižek, *In Defense of Lost Causes* (London: Verso, 2008), 337–8. See also Žižek, 'Resistance Is Surrender,' *London Review of Books* 29:22 (15 November 2007), www.lrb.co.uk/v29/n22/slavoj-zizek/resistance-is-surrender.

74 Žižek, *In Defense of Lost Causes*, 342–3.

75 Jodi Dean, *The Communist Horizon* (London: Verso, 2012) and Dean, *Crowds and Party* (London: Verso, 2016).

76 Nizan Shaked, *The Synthetic Proposition: Conceptualism and the Political Referent in Contemporary Art* (Manchester: Manchester University Press, 2017). See also Simon

Critchley, 'Violent Thoughts about Slavoj Žižek,' *Naked Punch* 11 (10 November 2008), 3–6.

77 Shaked, *The Synthetic Proposition*, 8.

78 Shaked, *The Synthetic Proposition*, 36.

79 Žižek, 'Multiculturalism, or, the Cultural Logic of Multinational Capitalism,' 176.

80 Žižek, 'Multiculturalism, or, the Cultural Logic of Multinational Capitalism,' 176.

81 Žižek, 'Multiculturalism, or, the Cultural Logic of Multinational Capitalism,' 176.

82 Shaked, *The Synthetic Proposition*, 148.

83 Ellen Meiksins Wood, *Democracy Against Capitalism: Renewing Historical Materialism* (Cambridge: Cambridge University Press, 1995).

84 Meiksins Wood, *Democracy Against Capitalism*, 214.

85 Meiksins Wood, *Democracy Against Capitalism*, 238.

86 Meiksins Wood, *Democracy Against Capitalism*, 256.

87 Meiksins Wood, *Democracy Against Capitalism*, 266.

88 Meiksins Wood, *Democracy Against Capitalism*, 270.

89 Angela Nagle, *Kill All Normies: Online Culture Wars From 4Chan and Tumblr to Trump and the Alt-Right* (Winchester: Zero Books, 2017) eBook, 11.

90 Slavoj Žižek, 'We Must Rise from the Ashes of Liberal Democracy,' *In These Times* (3 March 2017), http://inthesetimes.com/article/19918/slavoj-zizek-from-the-ashes-of-liberal-democracy.

91 Thomas Frank, *Listen, Liberal, or, What Ever Happened to the Party of the People?* (New York: Metropolitan Books, 2016).

92 See T.J. Clark, *The Painting of Modern Life: Paris in the Art of Manet and His Followers* (Princeton: Princeton University Press, 1984), 146.

93 Slavoj Žižek, *Disparities* (London: Bloomsbury, 2016), 368–71.

94 John Roberts, 'Art and Its Negations,' *Third Text* 24:3 (May 2010): 290.

95 Boris Groys, 'Beyond Diversity: Cultural Studies and Its Post-Communist Other,' in *Art Power* (Cambridge: The MIT Press, 2008), 150.

96 Badiou, *Philosophy and the Event*. See also Badiou, *Saint Paul: The Foundation of Universalism*, trans. Ray Brassier (Stanford: Stanford University Press, [1997] 2003) and Badiou, *Infinite Thought: Truth and the Return to Philosophy*, trans. Oliver Feltham and Justin Clemens (London: Continuum, 2004).

Index

Ackerman, Seth 199
Adbusters 45, 47, 54
Adorno, Theodor 92, 98, 107, 139–40, 148
Althusser, Louis 184, 208
Anthropocene 149–50
anti-anti-art 5–6, 8
anti-art 5–6, 8
anti-art art 5–6, 8
anti-globalisation 27, 31, 36–7, 43, 114, 126, 157, 192, 211
Art Workers' Coalition 96
Artist Organisations International 169–74, 177–8
ATSA 28
avant garde, the 2–3, 5–9, 11, 13, 15–16, 20–2, 27–8, 30, 35, 44, 67, 68–72, 78, 81, 87–8, 92, 97, 102, 110, 119–21, 135, 139–41, 144, 147, 155, 163–6, 169, 179–80, 182–3, 213

Badiou, Alain
    activist art 14–15, 164
    event 132, 213
    Maoism 166–8
    The Return of History 2
    vitalism 39, 152
Balibar, Étienne 19–20
Bannon, Stephen 205
Barber, Bruce 22–3
BAVO 7, 74–7
Beech, Dave 9–10

Begg, Zanny 27, 37, 39
Benjamin, Walter 72, 182, 190
Berardi, Franco 10, 40, 64
Bhabha, Homi 188
Bishop, Claire 87–8, 98, 108
Black Lives Matter 66, 93, 99–100, 182, 199, 201–4, 210
Blanco, Hugo 34–5
Bogdanov, Alexander 153–4
Boltanski, Luc 34, 102
Bosteels, Bruno 18, 132, 166, 168
Bourdieu, Pierre 3–4, 9, 93
Bourriaud, Nicolas 87, 98, 106
Bruguera, Tania 109
Buck-Morss, Susan 164–5
Bürger, Peter 70, 139–42
Butler, Judith 84, 181

Cabral, Amílcar 172, 173
Callinicos, Alex 37, 40–1
capitalism 6–7, 16–21, 33–7, 40–1, 47–50, 59–60, 65, 79, 84, 86, 91–8, 102–8, 119, 128, 132, 142–5, 150, 159, 160–1, 181–95, 205, 207–13
Carbon Liberation Front 149, 153
Castro, Fidel 105, 109, 173
Cazdyn, Eric 71
Charalambrides, Sarah 134, 143–4
Charnley, Kim 165
Chavez, Hugo 105, 161–2
Chiapello, Eve 34, 102

Chomsky, Noam 55
Chtcheglov, Ivan 120–1
civil society 209
class politics 5, 7, 12–14, 16, 19–20, 21, 25,
    31, 34–7, 48–53, 59–65, 93, 101–8,
    114, 143, 145–6, 163, 167–8, 173–5,
    181, 187, 189, 210–13
CLASSE 116, 128, 130–1
Clinton, Hillary 199
Collins, Phil 179–80
commons 19, 86
communism 13, 15–16, 18–21, 33, 35–7,
    67, 103–5, 108, 154, 159, 161, 165,
    167, 213
Communist Manifesto, The 19
community art 7, 10–11, 31, 87–9, 106, 157
Courbet, Gustave 72
Creative Time 98, 169
Critchley, Simon 205–6
Critical Art Ensemble 82, 89–91
cultural revolution 154–5, 164, 166
Cultural Revolution (China) 166–8

Das Kapital Oratorio 182–5, 191
Davis, Angela 61–2
Davis, Ben 164
Day, Richard 130
Dean, Jodi 47–8, 206
Debord, Guy 120–4, 127, 148
Debray, Régis 173–4
de Certeau, Michel 79, 124
Degot, Ekaterina 171
Deleuze, Gilles 39, 72, 151, 165–6
Deller, Jeremy 93–5
Delos Reyes, Jen 70
dérive 121–3
Derrida, Jacques 16–18
Deutsche, Rosalyn 185–6
dialectical materialism 71, 152, 159, 179,
    186, 188
dialectics 25, 68, 72, 74, 79–80, 107, 135,
    140, 161, 165, 180
dialogical aesthetics 7, 87, 98, 107–8,
    112
Douglas, Noel 28, 173

Engels, Friedrich 19, 147
Enwezor, Okwui 182–5, 189
Esche, Charles 170
EuroMayDay 31–3
Expósito, Marcelo 28

feminism 185–7, 198
Forensic Architecture 175
Foucault, Michel 74, 89, 158, 175–6
Fox, Renée 86
Frank, Thomas 211–12
Fukuyama, Francis 16–17
Fusco, Coco 202

Gaines, Malik 191–3
Gerschner, Petra 28, 41
globalisation 24, 27, 31, 33, 39, 42, 47, 71,
    75, 102, 109, 132, 190, 194
Gordon-Nesbitt, Rebecca 108–12
Gradecki, Jennifer 86
Graeber, David 53–4, 84, 142–3, 176–7
Gramsci, Antonio 21, 171, 205, 209
Groys, Boris 213
Guattari, Félix 72
guerrilla warfare 173–4
Guevara, Che 109–10, 112
Gulf Labor 96, 100, 144
Gurk, Christof 172, 178

Hadjinicolaou, Nicos 30–1
Hall, Stuart 104, 192
Hardt, Michael 19–20, 31, 64–5, 104, 159,
    184
Harvey, David 18, 51–2, 114, 184–90, 192
Hegel, G.W.F. 7, 13, 17, 22, 39, 42–3, 105,
    119, 181–2, 184, 206, 209
Heinrich, Michael 195
Hlavajova, Maria 171
Hofstadter, Richard 200
Holloway, John 37, 40
Holmes, Brian 37, 42, 68, 91, 172–3, 175
Horkheimer, Max 92, 140

identity politics 181–2, 185–7, 189–90,
    192–3, 195, 200, 206–7, 213

Institute for Applied Autonomy 82
Ito, Lisa (Concerned Artists of the
    Philippines) 171–2

Jay, Martin 68
Jordan, John 28, 40
Julien, Isaac 191–2

Kester, Grant 87–8, 106–8
Kilburn Manifesto 104
Klein, Naomi 58
Kluge, Alexander 63, 145
Knabb, Ken 64
Kotányi, Atilla 126, 130
Kwon, Miwon 89

Lacan, Jacques 8–9, 20, 22, 25, 75, 105,
    147–8, 151–3 158–9, 160–3, 172, 181,
    188, 206, 213
Laclau, Ernesto 21, 132, 180–1, 191
Laibach 141, 145
Lamoureux, Johanne 179–80
Lazzarato, Maurizio 69
Lefebvre, Henri 42–4, 114, 119–20, 180
Lefort, Claude 148, 166
Léger, Marc James 5, 7
Lenin, V.I. 159–60
Liu, Andrea 170–1
Lorey, Isabell 33, 134, 143
Lovink, Geert 64, 79
Lukács, Georg 12
Lütticken, Sven 154–5, 166

Malm, Andreas 149
Maoism 167–8
Maple Spring (Quebec) 113–19, 124–33
Marcuse, Herbert 108, 139, 152
Martin, Patrick 60–1
Marx, Karl 10, 12, 33–4, 37, 39, 146, 184–5,
    191–2
Marxism 10, 13, 22, 33–4, 37, 41, 43, 64, 68,
    69, 84, 109–10, 119–20, 179–80, 185,
    189, 191–2, 205, 208
masculinism 187
May 1968 131–2, 148, 163, 166, 176

McDonough, Tom 124
McKee, Yates 97–101, 155, 157–8
Meiksins Wood, Ellen 208–10
Mészáros, István 18
MeToo 199–202
Miners' Strike 136, 138
Monroe, Alexei 134–6
Moore, Michael 55–6
Mouffe, Chantal 21, 84, 132, 191, 193
multitude 31, 33–4, 37, 39, 64, 69, 98, 102,
    104, 139, 155, 158–61, 171–2, 193

Nagle, Angela 211
Negri, Antonio 19–20, 31, 37, 64–5, 104,
    139, 175, 184
Negt, Oskar 63, 145
neoliberalism 1–2, 52–3, 69, 95, 109, 195,
    202, 214
Not An Alternative 65

Obama, Barack 40, 50, 58, 212
Obama, Michelle 191, 203–4, 212
Occupy Wall Street 16, 45–67, 97–101, 165,
    176
Ogboh, Emeka 191
over-identification 75–6

Paris Commune 72, 177–8
petty bourgeoisie 3, 5–9, 14, 36–7, 48–9,
    63, 65, 69–70, 80, 136, 138, 157, 165,
    172, 174–5, 178, 194, 206, 212, 215
Poggioli, Renato 68, 139
Political Art Documentation/Distribution
    79–80
post-colonialism 63, 180, 186, 189
post-Fordism 19, 33–4, 68–70
postmodernism vi, 2, 17, 20–1, 24–6, 31,
    34–6, 42, 88–9, 102, 108, 132, 139–41,
    154, 179, 181–2, 185–6, 192–3,
    208–13
post-politics 24, 26, 34, 39, 59, 93, 101, 145,
    165, 181, 207, 212
Poulantzas, Nicos 48
precarity 10–11, 18, 81, 134, 155
Pritchard, Stephen 70

proletarianisation 194
PublixTheatreCaravan 73–4
psychogeography 121–31
psychoprotest 124–31

radical democracy 21, 132
radical geography 185–7
Rancière, Jacques 5–6, 105, 147, 164, 184, 193
Rasmussen, Mikkel Bolt 31, 101–8, 159–60
Raunig, Gerald 71–4, 165–6
Ray, Gene 5–6, 11, 71
Read, Mark 59
Rebel Clown Army 29
relational aesthetics 1, 5, 7, 31, 98, 106, 112, 144, 171
Relyea, Lane 70
Ressler, Oliver 27–8, 31, 37, 39, 84–7
Roberts, John 5, 13, 86, 147–8, 170
Rolling Jubilee 99, 104, 157
Rose, Jacqueline 198
Ross, Kristin 177
Roth, Karl Heinz 194
Rowe, Aidan 59
RTMark 27–8

Saint-Simonianism 30
Sanders, Bernie 13–14, 199
Schutz, Dana 201–2
Scott, Felicity Dale 175–6
Scratch Orchestra 136
Sekula, Allan 28
Serres, Michel 138
Shaked, Nizan 206–8
Sherald, Amy 212
Sholette, Gregory 5, 28, 30, 77–87, 144–5
Shulte-Sasse, Jochen 139–41
Situationist International 36, 119–24
Smith, John 190, 195
Socialisme ou Barbarie 177
socially engaged art vi, 1–2, 6–7, 13–14, 16, 24–6, 28, 31, 67, 70, 75, 78, 89, 92–3, 97–8, 106–10, 112, 144, 147, 157, 164–6, 178
Sorochan, Cayley 24, 113–33

Staal, Jonas 169–71
Stakhanovism 134, 136, 145
Stalinism 12, 42
Stiglitz, Joseph 47, 50–1
Strike Debt 155–8
subRosa 83
subsumption of labour 142
Sutcliffe, Alan 138, 140, 146
Syriza 143, 146
Szeman, Imre 71

tactical media 79, 106
Temporary Services 92
Test Dept 134–46
Thatcher, Margaret 136, 160
Thompson, Nato 91–7
Throbbing Gristle 135
Tiqqun 70
transversalism 5–6, 68, 71–5, 77, 96, 112, 166
Trotsky, Leon 48
Trump, Donald 17–18, 211
Tsomou, Margarita 171
Turbulence 37–8
Turl, Adam 4
Turnbull, Brett 138

universalism 15, 20–1, 26, 34, 36, 39, 41–2, 44, 62–3, 72, 81–2, 84, 103, 112, 132–3, 149–50, 161, 179–82, 185–7, 191–3, 198, 200–1, 205–7, 209–13

Vaneigem, Raoul 130
vanguard 13–15, 23–4, 105, 188
Velthius, Olav 81
Venice Biennale 182–4, 189–92
Vila, Nuria 28
Vilensky, Dmitry 28, 169, 172
violence 16, 20, 42–3, 62, 74, 100, 117, 119, 161, 170, 176, 180, 195, 198–200, 202–5, 231

Wallerstein, Immanuel 60
Wark, McKenzie 148–9, 151–4
West, Cornel 56–7

Wiley, Kehinde 212
Williams, Raymond 31
World Where Many Worlds Fit, A 27–30

Yes Men 77

Žižek, Slavoj
  blackmail 6, 21
  class struggle 64
  The Courage of Hopelessness 21, 200
  ecology 150–2

ideology 22
multiculturalism 63, 207–8
Occupy Wall Street 58, 66
ontological failure 147–8
Revolution at the Gates 105
superego 65
universalism 181, 207
vanguard 158–63
weakening of symbolic order 14, 95, 145
The Year of Dreaming Dangerously 2

EU authorised representative for GPSR:
Easy Access System Europe, Mustamäe tee 50,
10621 Tallinn, Estonia
gpsr.requests@easproject.com